Re-theorising the Recognition of Prior Learning

Re-theorising the Recognition of Prior Learning

Edited by

Per Andersson and Judy Harris

promoting adult learning

© 2006 National Institute of Adult Continuing Education
(England and Wales)

21 De Montfort Street
Leicester
LE1 7GE

Company registration no. 2603322
Charity registration no. 1002775

NIACE has a broad remit to promote lifelong learning opportunities for adults.
NIACE works to develop increased participation in education and training,
particularly for those who do not have easy access because of class, gender,
age, race, language and culture, learning difficulties or disabilities,
or insufficient financial resources.

You can find NIACE online at www.niace.org.uk

Cataloguing in Publication Data
A CIP record of this title is available from the British Library

Designed and typeset by Avon DataSet Ltd, Bidford-on-Avon, Warwickshire
Printed and bound in the UK by Ashford Colour Press Ltd, Gosport

ISBN: 1 86201 265 2

Contents

Foreword

The idea for this book arose in discussion amongst university-based practitioners and researchers in the recognition of prior learning (RPL). The venue was an international conference entitled 'Researching Learning outside the Academy'[1]. The editors (Judy Harris and Per Andersson) coordinated and facilitated a successful round-table discussion with the aim of identifying a research agenda for the RPL field. Judy provided a framework of five 'areas of potentially fruitful research' to kick-start the discussion: knowledge, pedagogy, learning, identity and power. The round-table session revealed a wealth of different theoretical and conceptual resources that could be brought to bear on RPL. It was agreed to use the same five areas as themes to frame a book that would be concerned with taking new approaches to theorising RPL. Contributors to the round-table discussion (and the conference more generally) were invited to develop, deepen and broaden their ideas into chapter form. A small number of complementary contributions were sourced. This book is the fruit of those labours. It owes a debt to the 2003 Centre for Research in Lifelong Learning (CRLL) conference, particularly to Professor Jim Gallacher, co-director.

The book builds on an earlier NIACE publication, *Learning from Experience: Empowerment or Incorporation*, by Wilma Fraser, which was published in 1995. Indeed, it takes up directly some of the issues Fraser raised. She questioned the radical rhetoric of RPL, arguing that practices had not impacted on 'our traditional phenomenology of knowledge and education'. Prefiguring some of the critiques in this volume, she problematised understandings of experience, raised questions about the transferability of knowledge between contexts and queried some of the emancipatory claims made in the name of RPL. The editors hope that this volume augments her sterling work.

June, 2005
Per Andersson and Judy Harris

[1] The conference was organised by the Centre for Research in Lifelong Learned [CRLL], a joint initiative between two Scottish universities – Glasgow Caledonian University and the University of Stirling. It was held at Glasgow Caledonian University, Glasgow, Scotland from 27–29 June 2003.

Information about the authors

Judy Harris is a Post-Doctoral Research Fellow in the School of Lifelong Education and International Development at the Institute of Education, University of London. Her research interests are the recognition of prior learning, work-based learning and widening participation in higher education, particularly their curricular and pedagogic implications using perspectives drawn from the sociology of education and knowledge. Her PhD thesis, *The Hidden Curriculum of the Recognition of Prior Learning: A Case Study* (Open University, 2004) was concerned with accessing adults to a South African university. She has many years' experience of policy-related research and development work, particularly in South Africa. Recent publications include her book *The Recognition of Prior Learning: Power, Pedagogy and Possibility* (2000). Judy is an associate of the Centre for Higher Education Research and Information at the Open University.

Per Andersson is a Research Fellow and Senior Lecturer in the Department of Behavioural Sciences at Linköping University, Sweden. His main research interest is educational assessment. His PhD thesis: 'To Study and be Assessed' (title translated from Swedish) is concerned with adults' and upper-secondary school students' ways of experiencing assessment. It was published and defended in 2000. Since then his research has focused on the development of RPL in Sweden. He has written a number of books and reports in Swedish and published articles in Studies in the Education of Adults (2004, with A. Fejes and S-e. Ahn) and Journal of Education Policy (2005, with A. Fejes).

Mignonne Breier is a Researcher at the Human Sciences Research Council, based in Cape Town, South Africa. Since 1994 she has specialised in qualitative research on adult literacy, RPL and curriculum issues in higher education. Currently she is focusing on professional education, and working on a case study on the profession and education of medical doctors.

Roslyn Cameron is with the School of Social Sciences at Southern Cross University, Australia. She has worked as a trainer, teacher, lecturer, RPL consultant and human resource developer across many education and training sectors as well as in a number of workplaces and cross-cultural contexts. Her research interests include access, equity, social inclusion and lifelong learning. She has a keen interest in the issues facing mature learners and workers in terms of their re-engagement with formal learning.

Paula Cleary is a Research Fellow at the Centre for Research in Lifelong Learning at Glasgow Caledonian University, UK. She has been involved in research in lifelong learning since 1999. Her current research interests focus on RPL, learning cultures in further education and the student experience in higher education.

Linda Cooper is a Senior Lecturer in Adult Education at the University of Cape Town, South Africa. She has been involved over many years in community-based and trade-union education, and has recently completed a PhD on pedagogy, learning and knowledge within the trade-union context.

Tara Fenwick is Associate Professor of Adult Education in the Department of Educational Policy Studies at the University of Alberta, Canada. Her research and teaching focus on work-related learning and education, with particular interest in knowledge politics, vulnerable workers, and identities negotiated in work.

Shibao Guo is an Assistant Professor in the Faculty of Education at the University of Calgary, Canada. Prior to that he was an Assistant Professor in the Department of Educational Policy Studies at the University of Alberta. His research interests include adult education, citizenship and immigration, multicultural and anti-racist education, and comparative and international education.

Elana Michelson is Professor of Cultural Studies and Chair of the Master of Arts in Liberal Studies at the State University of New York – Empire State College, USA. She is the co-author of *Portfolio Development and the Assessment of Prior Learning* and is a Fulbright Senior Specialist in the area of adult learning and RPL. Her theoretical work uses feminist, critical race, and lesbian and gay theory to critique conventional ideas concerning knowledge and experience and the academic practices that both sustain and are sustained by those ideas.

Ruksana Osman is Associate Professor at the University of the Witwatersrand, South Africa. She has spent six years researching and publishing in the field of RPL and adult learning in higher education in South Africa. Her present research interests are in RPL and teacher education.

Helen Peters is a Senior Lecturer at London Metropolitan University, UK, coordinating programmes for international students. She teaches on an RPL module and has worked with a range of students, including refugees and asylum seekers. She is currently researching the experience of students from different cultural and educational backgrounds who come to study in the UK and lecturers' approaches to teaching an increasingly diverse student body.

Helen Pokorny is a Learning, Teaching and Curriculum Coordinator at London Metropolitan University, UK. She has been a lecturer in higher education for 15 years and has been involved in RPL for ten years, working primarily with part-time students. Her current role includes educational and staff-development activities. Current research interests are in RPL and widening participation.

Yael Shalem is a Professor at the School of Education, University of the Witwatersrand, South Africa, where she heads the Division of Curriculum, Pedagogy and Assessment. Her teaching activities include the sociology of teaching, accountability and assessment, and the mentoring of student teachers. She has published in the fields of sociology of education, teachers' work, teacher education, sociology of pedagogy, feminist pedagogy, and quality assurance.

Carola Steinberg has been at the School of Education, University of the Witwatersrand, South Africa for seven years. She teaches on and coordinates programmes for the in-service, professional development of teachers. Before that she spent 20 years working in the field of adult basic literacy and education. Her research interests are in assessment and epistemological access for second language students.

Leesa Wheelahan is a Senior Lecturer in the School of Vocational, Technology and Arts Education at Griffith University, Australia. In 2002–2003 she led a project for the Australian Qualifications Framework Advisory Board to develop RPL principles and guidelines for all sectors of post-compulsory education and training in Australia. Her current research focus is on the role of knowledge in the curriculum.

Ruth Whittaker is a Senior Lecturer within the Academic Practice Unit at Glasgow Caledonian University, UK. She has undertaken research and development work at institutional, national and European levels in the field of RPL over many years. She is currently working as RPL Consultant to the Scottish Credit and Qualifications Framework [SCQF].

Susan Whittaker is a Research Fellow at the Centre for Research in Lifelong Learning at Glasgow Caledonian University, UK. She has been involved in research in lifelong learning for several years. Her current research interests are focused on the concept of 'learner identity'.

Michael Young is Emeritus Professor of Education in the School of Lifelong Education and International Development at the Institute of Education, University of London, UK, and Research Adviser to the City and Guilds of London Institute. His most recent books are: *The Curriculum of the Future: Strategies for Achieving Parity of Esteen in European Upper Secondary Education* (with J. Lasonen); and *Education in Retrospect: Education Policy in South Africa, 1990–2001* (with Andre Kraak).

chapter one

Introduction and overview
of chapters

Judy Harris

In this introductory chapter, RPL is defined broadly and the implications of
subtle differences in terminology and 'naming' are discussed. Consideration
is then given to the social conditions under which differing RPL practices
have developed and the range of practices that have ensued. Current
theorisations of RPL are described and critiqued and arguments made for re-
theorisations of practices. Finally, each chapter is reviewed in the light of
those re-theorisations.

What is the recognition of prior learning?

RPL is one of a range of responses to the needs of adult learners in education
and training. The key assumption is that adults have 'prior learning' which,
subject to reflection, articulation and assessment, may be worthy of
recognition and accreditation within formal education and training or
workplace contexts. Prior learning may have been acquired formally, non-
formally and/or informally; the determining factor is that it is not currently (or
fully) accredited. The outcomes of recognition can involve non-traditional
access, the award of advanced standing (or credit) within formal education
and training or serve as a basis for an individually negotiated learning programme (as in work-based learning for example).

What's in a name?

RPL is the designation used in South Africa and Australia. In the UK, the main term is the accreditation of prior (experiential) learning [APL or AP(E)L]. Practices in the USA are referred to as prior learning assessment [PLA], and in Canada as prior learning assessment and recognition [PLAR]. In Australia, distinctions are sometimes made between the recognition of *current* competence [RCC] and the recognition of *prior* learning. In France, the concept is validation (from the verb *valoir* [to be worth; to be as good as; to be equivalent to]). In Sweden, the name for practices is validering, a translation from the French (practices are referred to as the validation of 'real' [actual] competences, the validation of knowledge and competence or often simply as validation).

Different terminology emphasises different aspects of the RPL phenomenon. A common focus of most concepts, but not all, is 'prior learning', which puts the spotlight on what has been learnt before. Where the emphasis is not on 'prior' learning, it is on current competence, or simply on knowledge and competence, with no demarcation between past and present. Learning is recognised, valued, assessed or accredited – each verb carrying specific meanings, with 'recognise' and 'value' being the broadest and most general of the terms. Assessment and accreditation suggest increasing formalisation. Sometimes there is specific reference to experiential learning (as in AP[E]L), but often the experiential element of the learning under consideration is implicit. In this volume we have chosen to use the concept RPL, as the term 'recognition' can preclude or include other dimensions. However, other acronyms are used where this is convenient and/or important for a particular discussion.

Under what social conditions have RPL practices developed?

As with all educational interventions, the idea and practice of RPL have been formed and shaped by the inter-relation of historical, cultural, economic and political forces in different social contexts. Education as a whole has been influenced in profound ways by the changing socio-economic and cultural conditions of late-modernity referred to as globalisation. Attendant new forms of economic organisation have established closer relationships between the economy and education. These new relationships have been successively and successfully forged through waves of educational reforms.

Modes of knowledge production, circulation and communication have been recast. Knowledge structures have become increasingly permeable, resulting in new configurations of curricular authority, more permissive notions of curricular coherence and a widening range of curricular partnerships (Barnett, 1990; Gibbons *et al.*, 1994). Practice and theory have moved into closer proximity, especially in professional education (Eraut, 1994; Schön, 1983). Learning, assisted by technology, has become diffuse and unbounded. Dedicated learning institutions have increasingly been decentred as the main locus of learning activity. At the same time, interpretations of learning have become extended, as exemplified in 'lifelong learning' and 'life-wide learning', which include informal and non-formal learning. As learning has extended, the idea of transmission via traditional forms of pedagogy has become problematic. The focus has shifted from teachers to learners, with the latter seen increasingly as consumers of a growing range of widely available educational opportunities.

RPL has become a 'bounded' and 'named' practice under these changing conditions, which are indeed incitements to just such practices. It has become established in many parts of the world: the USA, the UK, France, Canada, South Africa and Scandinavia, for example. Although its origins are commonly traced to post-World War Two USA (Weil and McGill, 1989) when returning veterans wanted their skills recognised by universities, RPL is not a totally new phenomenon in any of the above contexts. Rather, it is the formalisation and (re)naming of pre-existing practices concerning alternative access and admissions, mature-age entry, and so on.

What's in a practice?

Driven by a mix of economic and social imperatives, RPL has been interpreted, developed, named, practised and positioned in particular ways in different countries. Put another way, the 'how' of practices has been influenced by the 'why', 'when', 'where', 'who' and 'what'. Central influences on the development and character of RPL are the values and interests driving the process. These can be:

- Provider-led: (a) higher education institutions; (b) professions; (c) further, technical, vocational education and training.
- Employer-led: (a) industry; (b) workplace.
- Trade union-led.
- Government-led.

Although the above classifications serve as a heuristic to map and understand the broad spectrum of interests at work in the field and practice of RPL, they frequently blur in practice. For example, a focus on 'competence' often links industry and further education and training, as in the UK and Australia. A government-led approach can be linked to a trade union-led approach, as in South Africa. Profession-led developments have been linked to workplace initiatives in Canada. Government-led and industry-led approaches are conjoined in qualification frameworks in the UK and Australia.

Practices developing at different times in different places have been influenced by *particular* configurations of the above 'drivers'. In the USA, the earliest approaches to RPL were provider-led (higher education), driven by an agenda of social justice, pragmatism and the need to broaden participation in formal education and training for democratic reasons (see Cameron, Chapter 6, this volume for more detail on this background). In Canada and the USA there have been substantial developments in RPL in professional contexts, driven by the same imperatives. The same driving forces are also apparent in provider-based RPL in other countries – particularly in higher education. Indeed, for many practitioners, RPL is seen as a cornerstone of the radical democratisation of 'the [education] system' – with 'system' spanning all aspects of institutional life.

RPL has been 'moved on' by national qualifications frameworks and national education and training systems, which emphasise articulation and seamlessness and which formalise informal and non-formal learning. Although such systemic devices have given weight to RPL, they have tended also to reconfigure its social meanings in the process (towards a greater economic emphasis). This has created tensions where practices have their origins in provider-led approaches and debates about whether RPL is about 'adapting to the system' or 'changing the system' (Andersson *et al.*, 2003, 2004).

Over the years a number of writers have theorised shifts in RPL practices. Butterworth (1992), writing from a UK perspective, is perhaps the best example. She conceptualises two 'ideal type' analytical models of RPL – developmental and credit-exchange – pointing to their different epistemological underpinnings and different experiences for the candidate.[1] Her developmental model is firmly predicated on experiential learning theory and practice (see below) with an espoused emphasis on social justice, inclusion and the democratisation of institutional practices. In these types of practice, RPL candidates are actively involved in evaluating their prior learning; reflection is central; and emphasis is placed on the process of learning as well as the products of learning. The creation of individual portfolios to attest to prior learning is a central feature of developmental RPL.

According to Butterworth, the emergence of the credit-exchange model coincided with the development of national vocational qualifications in the UK. In this model, learning and reflection are reargrounded in favour of a candidate providing evidence of performance and achievement. The focus shifts to credentialising.

In countries where qualification frameworks exist, the rule systems for accreditation, qualifications and curricula have been 'simplified' and standardised. However, this has by no means been a uniform process – pockets of autonomy remain. Moreover, accreditation takes different forms even within qualification frameworks, falling sometimes to individual institutions, professional bodies, industry agencies, or combinations thereof. Similarly, there is wide variation in the structuring of qualifications and the extent to which that is governed by institutional logics such as enrolment and attendance. Furthermore, the technical organisation of curricula (into outcomes) varies and is by no means the sole preserve of qualifications frameworks and/or vocational education and training: many higher education courses have long been organised in this way (especially in the USA) without the influence of national qualification frameworks. All of the above factors (and more) indicate complex backdrops for RPL practices (and practitioners).

Although this book brings together a variety of chapters drawn from experiences of RPL in the UK, South Africa, Australia, Sweden, the USA and Canada, it does not intend to be 'comparative' in the conventional sense of offering explanations of national characteristics of RPL. Rather, it is hoped that writings from different contexts, which draw attention to particular concerns, will challenge things that may be taken for granted in other contexts. More importantly, it is the principle of comparison of theoretical perspectives that guides this book. Although theoretical perspectives are undoubtedly context-related, they do have easier resonance across national boundaries and borders than do accounts of practice alone.

Current theorisations of RPL

Commonly accepted theorisation of RPL is via experiential learning theory. As Fraser (1995, p. 139) puts it: 'adults are what they have done'. Despite (or perhaps because of) the breadth of learning from experience, various attempts at definition and classification have been made. The best known is Weil and McGill's (1989) four villages. *Village one* is RPL with its focus on boosting adults' strengths, self-esteem and status through recognising their knowledge and all they have learned throughout their lives: a largely humanist, psychological and 'progressive' underpinning. *Village two* stresses processes of learning and is concerned with the development of teaching and learning methods in formal education that value and use experience. This village is concerned with the holistic development of the individual alongside contextual and institutional change. It therefore embodies humanistic and 'progressive' dimensions. *Village three* is about social change and transformation and the development of critical consciousness: a radical position. For example, some feminist perspectives on reclaiming knowledge would be located in this village. *Village four* is about personal experience as the basis for growth and the development of self-awareness: a psychotherapeutic agenda. In mapping the villages, Weil and McGill are at pains to point out that they share a common citizenship and that, as Millar (1996, p. 1) puts it, the villages have 'open borders – there is commerce among them – and there are goods and practices in common'.

Kolb's (1984) 'experiential learning cycle' guides much RPL theory and practice. This cycle has four stages. The first is 'concrete experience' or 'direct encounter'. The second is 'observation and reflection': the conscious time when individuals focus on their experience and give it meaning (usually from within existing sets of perspectives and values). The third stage is 'generalisation and abstract conceptualisation', whereby the fruits of reflection are ordered into symbolic representations. According to Fenwick (2001, p. 10), this is where the learner asks questions such as: 'What principle seems to be operating here?' The fourth stage is 'active experimentation', or the empirical testing of the ideas generated at the previous stage. It is presumed possible for a learner (or in our case an RPL candidate) to enter the cycle at any stage, although the general direction of movement remains linear and Kolb's central tenet remains constant: learning cannot happen without the cognitive and psychological process of internal, mental conceptualisation.

This learning cycle shares principles inherent in adult learning theory more broadly, particularly the theory generated by Knowles (1980), whose work also took experience as a resource for learning as its starting point. Experience, then, is one of Knowles's five principles of 'andragogy' or adult learning theory through which he argues for a learner-centred educational process, with reflection as central.

Both Knowles's and Kolb's work have roots in constructivism – a highly complex field of learning theory (see Sfard, 1998, for example). All constructivists share the tenet that 'a learner is believed to construct, through reflection, a personal understanding of relevant structures of meaning derived from his or her own action in the world' (Fenwick, 2001, p. 10). What is interesting about the constructivism of andragogy, however, is its break with notions of pedagogy, including those theorists most commonly associated with constructivism – Jean Piaget and Lev Vygotsky. Instead, Dewey's pragmatism is oft-quoted as the origin of constructivist andragogy. The Deweyan tradition emphasises the ways people learn how to construct, and deconstruct, their own experiences and meanings and to integrate theory and practice as a basis for democratic social action.

RPL practices related to current theorisations

Although the rubric of Kolb's experiential learning has been assiduously pursued in most provider-led approaches to RPL, there remain a wide range of different emphases, perspectives and concerns within and between practices. Cleary *et al.*'s (2001) study of Scotland is illustrative. They found discrete RPL processes varying in length from two weeks to nine months. There was variation in the amount of support available to candidates. They found a mix of RPL 'curricula'. In some cases, prior learning was the sole curriculum content. In others, the RPL process was framed by issues or themes. Moreover, the types of task to support movement through the stages of the experiential learning cycle were found to vary immensely.

Other differing emphases are noticeable in the wider literature (see Harris, 2004). Sometimes the processes of reflection and reflective commentary are stressed (see for example Butterworth, 1992). In other cases, individual 'stock-taking' (Storan, 1988, p. 4) or undertaking an 'inventory' of learning from experience is foregrounded (Mandell and Michelson, 1990, p. v). Other writers stress the importance of the self-assessment aspects of RPL as a basis for confidence building. Fehnel (1994, p. 26), for example, argues that, 'the recognition of prior learning has meant a very powerful affirmation of the individual, which frequently results in a new sense of self-confidence and empowerment'. For other writers and commentators, it is the social justice aspects of RPL that are most important. This is clearly evidenced in Norman Evans's large body of work. He writes about RPL as self-evidently 'natural' and 'humane', arguing that it encourages educational institutions to 'take a concerned humane view of men and women who wish to study at the formal academic level and who do not have the kind of educational record that ensures eligibility' (Evans, 1993, p. 14). Wailey and Simpson (1998, p. 4) stress the potential of RPL to drive organisational change. They offer an institution-wide conceptualisation of RPL, linking it to other functions such as academic development, career guidance, and mainstream assessment in order to enhance 'coherence' for all adult learners. Yet other writers focus on the technical and administrative aspects of recognising prior learning, such as guidelines for the award of credit (Whittaker, 1989), and the development of credit systems, outcomes and generic assessment criteria.

Why re-theorise RPL practice?

What the above, necessarily truncated, account of experiential learning theory and practice shows is that it is both a philosophy and a method. With some exceptions (for example, Michelson, 1996; Harris, 1999; Fenwick, 2001; Breier, 2003), the bulk of the RPL literature is infused with the implicit humanism, psychologism and/or shades of constructivism that characterise most adult and experiential learning theory. These embody particular conceptions of learning, knowledge, learner and educator. In this way, RPL seems to have lagged behind contemporary developments in social and educational theory. One reason for this is that RPL (and experiential learning more generally) has acquired the status of a 'social movement', one that sees itself as 'progressive' – even 'radical' – in its commitment to social justice. RPL seems to be shrouded in a discourse of righteousness where any critique of practice is taken as a critique of the principles of social justice under-pinning that practice.

Central to the RPL 'movement' is an unproblematised commitment to the 'authenticity' of learning from experience. Yet in practice it has proved difficult to draw boundaries around 'authentic' (experiential) and 'non-authentic' (presumably formal) learning, at the level of both philosophy and method. In the case of the former, Millar (1996, p. 2) argues that the commitment to authentic learning constructs the experiential learning movement as a 'quest and vision sharply contrasted with the false, mediocre or corrupt'. The quest, he claims, requires a 'negative pole' which is 'learning which is narrow, intellectual, subject-bound and has somehow come adrift from feeling or practice'. Thus, we see processes of dichotomisation at work. Fenwick (2001) argues that the methodological distinctiveness of experiential learning is also difficult to hold because the latter is equally a feature of some formal education (as in discussion, reading and structured reflection, for example).

Furthermore, although RPL is a feature of the landscape of education, training and employment at the level of policy, there is not much of it in practice. In almost all contexts, after several decades, implementation remains disappointingly low (see Merrifield *et al.*, 2000; Wheelahan, 2002; Dyson and Keating, 2003). The exception is educational institutions in the USA, most particularly those designed to cater specifically to the needs of adults. Various reasons for low implementation are advanced in the literature. For example, Dyson and Keating (2003) refer to enduring barriers at institutional, organisational, cultural and individual levels. Merrifield *et al.* (2000) suggest that RPL is time consuming and difficult.

This book starts with the hypothesis that perhaps RPL practitioners have placed too much faith in experiential learning philosophies and methodologies as the sole means to articulate, recognise, value, assess and accredit learning from experience. The premise for this book is that adult and experiential learning theory has become so internalised as *de facto* desirable in RPL that practices are often seen as unproblematic and not in need of explanation. Such a state of affairs does not allow for problematising and improving practices so as to better meet the social goals they advance. Following Millar (1996, p. 4), our view (as editors) is that there is a need 'to disturb the procedural tide of the experiential learning movement deeply, even radically'. This we do by bringing together academics and RPL practitioners who have entertained alternative theorisations of RPL drawn from broader and more contemporary social theory. We consider this to be important for three over-arching reasons:

- RPL offers a generative site in which to research changing socio-economic conditions and their effects on education.
- RPL offers a site in which to research the complexity of the issues involved in opening a path from informal, experience-based learning into formal learning situations.
- RPL links to an ever-expanding range of initiatives in widening participation in education and training, for example work-based learning. As such there is likely to be relevance beyond those practices 'named' RPL.

This collection

As mentioned in the Foreword, the starting points for the 2003 conference round-table discussion (aiming to set a research agenda for RPL) were five 'areas of potentially fruitful research': knowledge, pedagogy, learning, identity and power. A number of questions or potential lines of enquiry were presented under each area, a selection of which are presented in Figure 1. It is the editors' view that these (obviously overlapping) areas are not well-served by experiential learning theory. Some of the areas (particularly knowledge and pedagogy) are in fact silenced by experiential learning discourses.

Figure 1. Framework for the CRLL conference round-table session.

Knowledge
- What happens to knowledge in and around RPL, and how?
- In RPL practices, (how) are distinctions made between types of knowledge, especially between formal knowledge and informal/local knowledge?
- What forms of knowledge are most highly valued in RPL processes? What are silenced?
- Do adults acquire formal knowledge informally? To what extent and under what conditions?
- What knowledge structures constitute RPL candidates' prior learning?
- Under what mainstream curricula conditions can RPL be most effective?

Pedagogy
- What do RPL facilitators and candidates do in the act of 'recognition'?
- What pedagogic styles are at work?
- What happens during reflection?
- What are the most appropriate pedagogic processes to assist RPL candidates to identify and articulate their prior learning?
- Does putting together an individual portfolio prepare a candidate for a future academic learning programme?
- Can reflection and experiential learning cycle methodologies replace formal learning via acquisition?

Learning
- Is RPL about prior learning or new learning, or both?
- Is RPL an assessment process or a learning process?
- Is there some translation of knowledge going on in RPL? If there is, what learning issues are involved?
- What theories of learning underpin RPL, for example, in portfolio development and portfolio assessment?
- What other theories of learning could be brought to bear on RPL?
- Individual candidates' learning styles; how do they differ?

Identity
- What effect does RPL have on candidates' identities and self-perception?
- What happens to candidates and the way they come to know their experience?
- Individual candidates' journeys through the process; how do they differ?
- What understandings of 'self' are at work in and around RPL? For example, what understandings of self are required when candidates put together a portfolio?
- What learner identities are constructed within an RPL practice? Do different aspects of an RPL process require different identity positionings?
- How do RPL practitioners see themselves? In relation to candidates, in relation to RPL and in relation to their institutional or organisational context?

Power
- Does RPL shift traditional patterns of inclusion and exclusion in education, vocational training and working life?
- Does RPL challenge assumptions about what counts as knowledge and whose knowledge has value?
- Is RPL reproductive of existing power relations?
- Is RPL a good way to increase social inclusion?
- What is the relationship between epistemological inclusion and social inclusion?
- What discourses characterise RPL? With what power-effects?

Although individual authors use terms in slightly different ways, for the general purposes of the book, terms are used in the following ways:

- We see knowledge as a historico-social product and as representing diverse outcomes of various forms of learning.
- We view learning as the process of knowledge production and knowledge generation.
- We take pedagogy as referring to formal and informal means of teaching, transmission and induction.
- Identity is a contested term in the contemporary moment with the notion of a unified, integrated identity giving way to multiple and shifting identities and identity positionings. We are mindful of the various understandings of the term.
- Likewise, the concept of power can be seen in the traditional sociological way as hierarchical and (invariably) oppressive or as a more relational and networked phenomenon, linked to performativity, productivity and desire, for example.

The collection includes some current and influential thinking about the above themes, each chapter presenting a different style of thought and exploration. What they have in common is that they do not take for granted existing definitions and practices of RPL. Because there is a dearth of empirical, academic research in RPL, wherever possible, each chapter is grounded in empirical research. In such cases, it is possible to move from theory out to practice and from practice back to theory. Where chapters are more discursive in character, authors consider the implications of different theories for practice, and advance ideas for how practice can be developed from theoretical insights. Taken together, the chapters offer a rich resource for re-theorising RPL. They are not exhaustive however. Though the wider context for RPL is education, training and the workplace, the contributions in this collection focus particularly on provider-led RPL, and within that, mainly higher education. Although this is a limitation, there is currently a burgeoning literature on work-based learning, to which this book links in a synergistic way.

A word about the uses of the collection. We see the book as having the potential to be read for different purposes. One purpose would be to gain more insight into the theories and concepts described and applied. Another would be to focus on practice-implications via the thematic areas. A third would be to hold the chapters up as mirrors to one's own practice and see a different image as a result. Our aim is to stimulate discussion, critique, diversification and (hopefully) improvement of RPL practices. Finally, we hope that the debates in this book can be extended into broader debates around widening participation in education and training.

A review of the individual chapters

It is not easy to give a neat editorial structure to a collection of writings, each of which embodies a unique configuration of the five thematic areas. These frames may have provided useful analytical categories, but they are not empirical categories. The 'real worlds' of RPL and practitioner interest do not divide up neatly in these ways. Consequently, each contribution ranges across and even beyond the framework. In keeping with the title of the book, the chapters are arranged into theoretical clusters. There are five of these: first, a chapter that draws on assessment theory. Secondly, a set of chapters that draws on the sociology of education, particularly the work of Basil Bernstein. Thirdly, chapters that cluster loosely around poststructuralism, post-modernism and situated knowledge. Fourthly, chapters that deploy variants of activity theory in relation to RPL. Finally, a chapter that uses symbolic interactionism and social identity theory. What follows is a brief and selective outline of each chapter.

Assessment theory

In Chapter 2, Per Andersson brings assessment theory to bear on RPL. Arguing that the act of assessment is a 'black box', he shows how conceptual distinctions throw light onto the different faces and functions of RPL. Implicit in this is the premise that there is currently a certain lack of clarity around these issues.

The concepts Andersson presents highlight precisely how much of RPL practice is implicit. For example, whether assessment in RPL is operating primarily to select individuals and/or knowledge or whether it is concerned with the transformation of individuals and/or knowledge. As Andersson shows, whichever aspect is foregrounded repositions the others accordingly. He also illustrates how predictive, formative and summative assessments vary and how they embody very different social functions and put very different faces on RPL, for example, whether a practice is about assessing 'competence' or 'potential'. Similarly, both convergent and divergent approaches to assessment can be found in RPL, often leading to confusion and contestation in the field and to debates about the respective values of universal and local knowledge. Andersson discusses traditional assessment and evaluation concepts such as validity and reliability and some of the particular paradigmatic perceptions of, and alterations to, such concepts, for example, decreased emphases on reliability, changing understandings of validity, and the use of notions such as plausibility and relevance.

A kaleidoscopic array of assessment concepts, each with different philosophical and epistemological undertones, offers the reader numerous creative ways of rethinking RPL (as assessment and as practice) in relation to social function. In this way, practitioners can review their practices, and hopefully reorientate them and/or make them more internally consistent.

The sociology of education

Chapter 3 is a perspective on knowledge and curricula. Judy Harris reviews the ways in which the two concerns are dealt with in RPL, arguing that the literature is replete with unqualified assertions that RPL challenges formal definitions and ownership of knowledge. She illustrates how, although discussion of knowledge is conspicuous by its absence in the RPL literature, it cannot be silenced. Rather, it makes oblique entrances from time to time.

She argues that the most common assumption about knowledge is that *even* if there are distinctions and differences between forms of knowledge (such as formal, experiential, these can be overcome because boundaries are soft and knowledge can transfer unproblematically between contexts.

Positing this position as inadequate, Harris explores the knowledge and curricula questions further using Basil Bernstein's curriculum theory. She concludes by arguing for a more theoretical approach to RPL based on the metaphor 'knowing the borders and crossing the lines'. This involves understanding knowledge and curricula theoretically at three interrelated levels: (1) in mainstream curricula; (2) in terms of candidates' prior knowledge; and (3) in RPL 'curricula'. Implied in this is the development of a new cadre of theoretically-tooled RPL or 'widening participation' professionals. She argues that this would improve the quality of RPL practices, their theoretical rigour, effectiveness and 'epistemological accountability'.

In Chapter 4, Mignonne Breier takes up one of the 'borders' referred to above. As a complement to RPL as an assessment process prior to entry into an educational programme, she considers the recognition of prior learning *after* entry (referred to as 'rpl' in lower case). Her focus is on how informal learning or experience is 'recruited' in courses in labour law in two universities in South Africa. Both courses cater for a wide range of students: factory workers, community organisers, self-employed consultants, teachers, an attorney and one unemployed artisan in one course; and attorneys, academics, industry bargaining council staff, labour market consultants and full-time trade unionists in the other.

Transcripts of interactions between lecturers and students are interpreted in the light of three perspectives on RPL – a technical/market perspective, a critical/radical perspective and a liberal/humanist perspective. She finds that the two mainstream courses bear strong traces of critical/radical and liberal/humanist perspectives. An example of the former case would be making for alternative voices to be heard, with, for example, discussions about the experiential consequences of race and gender under apartheid and beyond. This would require a flexible curriculum. In the case of liberal/humanism, the emphasis would move towards hearing all experiences, reflecting on them and considering ways in which experiential knowledge can bridge into the formal curriculum.

She then introduces a disciplinary-specific approach. Her approach draws on Bernstein's argument about the importance in pedagogical research of examining symbolic systems (disciplines) as well as the fields within which they are positioned, suggesting that the form and structure of the discipline contributes in a fundamental way to the 'games, practices and strategies' of pedagogy. She discusses the inductive and deductive processes and principles of law and relationships between the general and the particular. A disciplinary-specific approach to 'rpl' requires adult educators to consider the nature and structure of a discipline or field of study and the relationship between formal and informal knowledge within that structure to ensure the authenticity of an RPL programme and the success within it of students with extensive practical experience but limited formal qualifications.

In Chapter 5, Yael Shalem and Carola Steinberg use a different set of Bernsteinian concepts to evaluate the social logic of RPL portfolio development as a pedagogic process. The authors' empirically-based analysis reveals ambiguous pedagogies that are both retrospective (the recognition of previously attained learning) and prospective (the assessment of readiness for a new learning environment). They argue that these two 'actions' are incompatible, claiming that the retrospective pedagogic action foregrounds 'similar to' relations and relies implicitly on social constructivist and postmodern tenets regarding the pluralism and equivalence of knowledges. This, they argue, gives rise to a humanistic (bordering on therapeutic) pedagogy, in which epistemic authority is invisible. The prospective action, on the other hand, implies a reliance on the specialised knowledge of the receiving context and a more visible pedagogic authority. The authors are of the view that RPL emphasises retrospective action and wishes away the prospective action.

In an in depth analysis of one particular RPL candidate, the authors (who were also the RPL facilitators) draw attention to their invisible pedagogic moves during the retrospective stages of the portfolio-development process. For example, the ways in which they 'classified' the prior knowledge the candidate presented. In the prospective stage, the author-facilitators imposed formal academic practices onto the candidate's account of her prior knowledge. They show how the candidate concerned continued to operate in a mixed discourse (vocational and scholastic) and was not able to 'recognise the web of beliefs' of the facilitators.

Shalem and Steinberg conclude that the pedagogy of portfolio development is mainly invisible, and that this positions RPL candidates and academic facilitators and/or assessors in different forms of 'powerlessness'. Candidates do not gain access to the rule systems of fields of knowledge – what is important, what is not, how to present ideas, and so on – and are left with a form of guess work. In their view, RPL pedagogy needs more than experiential learning methodologies – something that is capable of socialising candidates into a field of knowledge through which they will gain longer-term epistemological access and success.

Chapter 6, by Roslyn Cameron, begins by citing recent RPL research in Australia in which it is claimed that there is a gap between the promise and rhetoric of RPL practices and the reality of their contribution to greater educational and social inclusion. First she examines the limitations of current theories of participation before calling for new starting points which link micro-educational processes (of which RPL is one) to macro-level structures (social class and power relations). As a means to this end, she uses Bernstein's notion of 'pedagogic rights' and their social distribution, to illustrate: (1) some of the ways in which formal educational institutions, and their RPL practices, project values and images that alienate working-class students; (2) that knowledge is socially distributed along the same lines; and, (3) that the previous two features lead to inequitable distribution of societal material resources.

Her second line of enquiry links RPL to Bernstein's notion of the 'potential discursive gap'. This is a gap or discursive space, which is a site for alternate possibilities. She argues that such a gap exists in the relations between formal and in/non-formal knowledge. More particularly, at some stage (or at various stages) in an RPL process, a relationship of 'equivalence' has to be constructed between forms of knowledge. However, according to Cameron, the potentiality of this gap is regulated by RPL facilitators and assessors and by stringent, bureaucratic procedures – which are print-based and requiring of high levels of language skills, familiarity with formal learning systems and self-confidence. She extends a challenge to RPL practitioners to find different ways to occupy the gap by explorating different approaches and models of RPL, specifically 'process-focused' developmental/empowerment models. She also argues for the explicit embedding of RPL within curricula, instead of seeing it solely as a means of assessment. However, she lacks confidence in anything less than a political paradigm shift in favour of greater democratisation at policy and organisational levels.

Poststructuralism and situated knowledge/learning

In Chapter 7, the first chapter of this section, Elana Michelson provides a broad theoretical framework for the rest of the section. She problematises Enlightenment thinking from a perspective that draws on contemporary post-modernist, feminist, critical race scholarship and the notion of situated knowledge. Michelson shows how conventional understandings and practices of experiential learning remain trapped in such thinking. For example, assumptions of an objective reality to which the senses provide unmediated access and language an unbiased account; and a belief in a unified self, capable of occupying a commanding position. In particular, she shows how RPL methodologies, despite their 'radical' intent, mirror Enlightenment epistemology because they are grounded in commitment to the transformation of experience into knowledge through the application of reason and temporal and spatial detachment. Knowledge, thus defined, is, she argues, irretrievably bound up with social privilege and 'abstract masculinity'.

From a situated knowledge perspective, experience and knowledge occur together and co-determine each other. When the statuses of experience and reason are questioned and when universal knowledge can no longer claim to be disinterested, what remains is a mesh of situated social practices and 'standpoints'. Citing Donna Haraway, Michelson argues that all there is are 'partial, locatable, critical knowledges'.

Her viewpoints open up a range of possibilities for thinking about RPL and portfolio development. First, experience can be viewed as 'socially produced subjectivity' rather than as a neutral vehicle for knowledge production. Secondly, if all knowledge is situated, then RPL can explicitly be concerned with dialoguing across knowledges and affirming 'outside knowledge'. In these ways, Michelson claims that RPL can be repositioned to interrogate and renegotiate relationships between experience and knowledge, to grant visibility to knowledge that is divergent from academic ways of knowing and to contribute to a democratisation of epistemological authority within the academy.

In Chapter 8, Helen Peters uses Foucault's concepts of discourse, power/knowledge, biopower and technologies of power to explore why RPL practices have not succeeded in challenging academic 'hegemony' or in empowering candidates. She identifies some paradoxes in RPL discourse. For example, many practitioners see RPL as widening what counts as valid (disciplinary) knowledge, thereby undermining institutional power, whilst at the same time candidates are required (and require themselves) to 'buy into' existing institutional discourses and knowledge. Peters posits that RPL is caught in a bind, and candidates in a 'discursive struggle': practices claim to be about defying institutional technologies of power yet they actually normalise candidates. Equally paradoxically, her empirical evidence shows how candidates see their prior knowledge as different from knowledge defined by the institution, whilst RPL assessors look for something with which they are familiar.

Peters adds focus and texture to her account by using Halliday's linguistic analyses and Fairclough's critical discourse analysis to look at two practices associated with RPL. The first is the use of learning outcomes. She argues that, although outcomes purport to be transparent, equalising and democratic, their utilisation in RPL actually encourages candidates to focus on *how* they express themselves, rather than on their actual prior knowledge. They are required to appropriate and present their knowledge in modes within which they may not have operated before. As a consequence, many portfolios read like 'brochures'. Candidates interviewed by Peters experienced RPL as a process of 'squeezing' their learning into the prescribed categories of the outcomes. Conversely, the assessors in Peters's study valued the use of learning outcomes in RPL because they saved time and simplified their task.

Peters then focuses on portfolios. She tracks contrasting 'orders of discourse', arguing that candidates 'intermingle' ideational functions, for example, conveying information to an assessor and conveying their own value and belief systems and life activities. She notes how candidates slip into personal styles of writing from depersonalised learning outcomes, thereby reinserting themselves into their text. Overall, she finds that a personal discourse remains central to candidates' portfolios, suggesting little critical distancing.

Academics involved in RPL wanted portfolios to provide evidence that candidates could produce conventional academic texts. Assessors seemed to want streamlined outcomes and displayed little interest in the 'contours' of candidates' prior knowledge. Rather, they looked for a particular kind of condensed, managerial academic writing, characterised by mappings and checklists. In this way, RPL candidates were assessed in an impoverished discourse of 'doing RPL' rather than on their 'learning obtained outside educational settings' or their academic abilities. Peters concludes that a more 'emancipatory' form of RPL would be a mediatory process between forms of knowledge where assessors become more attuned to 'candidates' languages'. Her view is similar to Michelson's: RPL should contribute to according equal status to different knowledges.

In a departure from previous chapters, Chapter 9, by Shibao Guo and Per Andersson, deploys Foucault's notions of power-knowledge and a critical 'politics of difference' to focus on the transfer of credentials and prior work experience between countries. The authors begin with a review of contextual information pertaining to immigration in Canada and Sweden and examine studies pertinent to the non/recognition of foreign credentials and prior work experience. They argue that the term 'immigrant' is a social construction that has become a codified way of referring to 'people of colour who come from a different racial and cultural background, who do not speak fluent English [or Swedish], and who work in lower position jobs'.

The chapter focuses on how established norms across a range of government agencies, professional organisations, employers and educational institutions play a role in devaluing foreign credentials and work experience, thereby creating social exclusion. Guo and Andersson ask: 'Why do such inequities occur in democratic countries like Canada and Sweden, where democratic principles are upheld and where immigrants are, at least in policy, "welcome"?' In answering this question they suggest that a deficit model of difference is at work alongside commitments to cultural pluralism, and that this constitutes a form of 'democratic racism'. Secondly, they argue that knowledge has become racialised and as a result some foreign credentials are deemed to be different and inferior. Thirdly, they posit that positivism pervades the accreditation of foreign credentials. This is grounded in convergence and similarity to qualifications in the 'host' country and exacerbates attempts to value any form of difference. The authors conclude by emphasising the huge human cost of non-recognition.

In Chapter 10, Ruksana Osman draws on situated knowledge/learning and critical theory to explore candidates' and facilitators' experiences of portfolio development. She starts from the position that transformative higher education in South Africa needs epistemologies and pedagogies based on 'inclusive' theorising in which adult learners are seen as co-producers of academically valuable and creditable knowledge; knowledge acquired outside a university is acknowledged and valued, and academics are reflexive about their own social location.

Her empirical enquiry centres on portfolio development as a potential example of 'inclusive' pedagogy. She found different perspectives amongst and between candidates and facilitators. Unlike Peters, she found that candidates tended to experience their prior knowledge as connecting with academic knowledge. Overall, they were very positive about the process of portfolio development: it had an impact on their personal lives, academic lives, self-perception and self-knowledge. They also reported benefits associated with opportunities for self-critique and self-evaluation. Central to this was the importance of public declaration. (See also Whittaker *et al.*, Chapter 15, this volume.) On the negative side, candidates experienced portfolio development as time-consuming, emotionally demanding and at times confusing, especially with regard to deciding what prior knowledge to include.

Some facilitators experienced conflict in terms of their role as an RPL facilitator and as a conventional lecturer concerned with socialising students into academia. They felt uncomfortable about the interface between prior and academic knowledge in portfolios (for some, the interface sharpened rather than diminished during RPL). Prior knowledge tended to be seen through the lens of academic knowledge and was experienced as disjunctive rather than connected. Osman found other RPL facilitators who were emboldened by their role and valued candidates' theorisations of their life and work experience. She accounts for these differences by way of facilitator starting-points. Academic-facilitators starting with a view of knowledge *difference* were left 'with few moves'. They stayed in their conventional pedagogue role. Others with a more fluid sense of teaching, learning and assessment saw the potential of portfolio development as a means to contribute to a more 'emancipatory view of knowing'. For them, it proved possible to look beyond legitimised knowledge.

Osman recommends that RPL practitioners aim not for assimilation of prior knowledge into existing academic cultures, but for 'new forms of scholarship about knowing through experience and knowing through action'. These new forms could, she claims, complement academic ways of knowing and increase the reflexivity of academics about what is included and excluded in curriculum knowledge. This, in turn, could link to curriculum change and greater visibility for prior knowledge. To undergird this, she expresses a need to develop conceptual resources to theorise prior knowledge in its own terms, not only in relation to academic knowledge. The upshot would be a rebalancing of epistemological authority, allowing both candidates and academics epistemological access to each others' knowledge and a sharing of pedagogical control, thereby bringing the political goals of RPL into closer proximity with the epistemological goals of the academy.

Activity, actor-network and complexity theories
Chapter 11, by Linda Cooper, develops and deploys conceptual tools to theorise prior knowledge and informal pedagogies and processes of learning. She draws on Vygotskian and post-Vygotskian understandings of learning as a social activity, most particularly 'tools of mediation', which are the ways people act upon, and are acted upon, by culture, history and social context.

There are three types of tools: material tools, psychological tools and human beings. According to Cooper, post-Vygotskians tend to emphasise language (for example, Wertsch) or activity (for example, Engeström) as key psychological tools of mediation. In addition, Wertsch works with Bakhtin's notions of 'dialogicality' and carnival to explore the ways 'voices' come into contact. Cooper draws on all these concepts in an ethnographic case study of knowledge-generating processes in the non-formal, collective organisational context of a South African trade union.

Her research found that union 'pedagogy' is predominantly face-to-face and oral, involving code-switching between languages, 'ventriloquism', repetition, story-telling, humour and drama rooted in the 'local, working-class language-dialect of the Western Cape'. She characterises this language-dialect as 'embodied' (physical and cognitive) and 'impassioned' (intellectual and emotional). Written text, by contrast, plays an 'ambiguous role' – highly valued, but not often engaged with. She argues that these distinctive pedagogic forms have to be understood through the 'epistemology of this collective, social-action oriented site'. She analyses this epistemology by way of six features: (1) democratic values; (2) dispersal of pedagogic authority; (3) the powerful identity-construction role of union pedagogy; (4) its ideological directness; (5) the analytical and critical orientation of union pedagogy; and (6) its utopian elements.

Although union pedagogy has tools of mediation which are specific to local culture and context, the forms of knowledge drawn upon are hybrid, consisting of practical, analytical, conceptual and highly codified knowledge (from economics and law) – which articulate in complex ways (through 'weaving') with language genres such as story-telling acting as a potential bridge to more abstract forms of knowledge.

Having laid out the relationship between pedagogy, tools of mediation, epistemological goals and forms of knowledge, Cooper ends by addressing what such a configuration might mean for RPL. First, she argues that RPL candidates need to be able to draw on familiar cultural and historical resources to mediate what they know (*not* a portfolio). Secondly, in her view, RPL facilitators need to understand the candidates' knowledge terrain and to be able to 'look carefully for the cultural markers that signal more conceptual and analytic forms of knowledge that may have been experientially-acquired in informal ways' and to 'look for principled understandings and knowledge' in stories – for example, evidence of 'social analysis and social critique'. Cooper goes on to argue that RPL candidates' tools of mediation could influence and enrich academic pedagogic tools of mediation, leading to, for example, more use of dialogue and debate in mainstream curricula.

In Chapter 12, Leesa Wheelahan explores the relationship between teaching and learning and policy. To set the ball rolling, she deploys Dewey's theoretical work to review the notion of 'vocation' as a relational concept: 'A vocation is more than a set of skills. It is a sense of identity and a way of being in the world that connects different aspects of our lives'. She then explores the concept of 'graduateness' using Engeström's theory, arguing that graduateness 'is contextualised by the activity system or community of practice within which the individual is placed' and is about 'the capacity to make connections between different experiences and different ways of knowing, between theoretical and practical knowledge, codified and embodied knowledge, and explicit and tacit understandings'.

Wheelahan brings vocation and graduateness into dialogue with RPL. She locates current educational policy and reform within a neo-liberal economic paradigm and argues that as reflections of that paradigm, credentialist approaches to RPL (and to assessment more widely) should be resisted. She proceeds to map the contours of a revitalised and extended 'developmental', graduateness-oriented model of RPL that takes account of processes of learning and interconnectivities within the activity system of a vocation or community of practice.

Importantly, Wheelahan shifts the meaning of RPL from a separate, discrete activity to an *integrated* activity within *all* qualifications, thereby overcoming bifurcations between formal and experiential knowledge. She argues that it should not be possible 'to RPL' a whole qualification because people need to be able to integrate all the tools within their activity system. Rather, RPL should be concerned with that integration process, that is, a process of new, extended learning that helps candidates to use their prior knowledge to 'make connections between their different experiences and ways of knowing [...] through integrating this holistically in the context of their vocation'. Alongside this, she argues for a greater role for reflection so as to encourage holistic notions of graduateness. Reflection, she claims, can use prior learning to deepen current learning in ways that enrich the individual, the graduate qualification and the vocation.

Chapter 13 focuses on actor-network theory. This theory originates in social studies of science, in which knowledge is theorised as produced, organised and distributed through patterned networks of heterogeneous materials such as activities, artefacts, technologies and narratives of practice. The process of knowledge production takes place by 'translation', which involves changes in the networks. Actor-network theory is concerned with describing and analysing changing networks and the means by which some networks (such as certain forms of academic knowledge) become stable and powerful.

Helen Pokorny uses this theory to consider the networks and networking practices of knowledge production, organisation and ordering in RPL in UK higher education. She characterises learning outcomes as a key material in the network and illustrates how their usage renders a lot of prior knowledge invisible. A second element in the RPL network is the use of reflection, which she sees as splitting experience and knowledge and disempowering candidates by removing their experience from social context.

'Problematisation', 'interessement', 'enrolment' and 'mobilisation' are additional concepts from one particular actor-network theorist, Michel Callon. Pokorny uses these concepts to illustrate the stages through which RPL candidates' prior knowledge becomes 'punctualised' and translated into an academic network – through a series of 'tightening of grips'. First, candidates come to accept the problems and solutions offered by their RPL advisors (problematisation). Secondly, candidates accept a particular set of roles, activities and rules (interessement). Thirdly, they become more tightly engaged in a broader institutional network of regulations, actors and actants (enrolment). The final move is to mobilisation, where candidates, their learning processes and their prior knowledge are entirely channelled by the dominant network.

She concludes that actor-network theory offers an approach to overcome dilemmas associated with reflection. She argues that RPL could (and should) engage with the heterogeneity of candidate knowledge networks rather that focusing solely on convergence to academic ones. This would involve an investigation of knowledge equivalences based on detailed exploration of the internal complexity of candidates' networks. In this way, RPL could raise a more theorised challenge to the networking practices that define academic knowledge.

In the final chapter in this section, Chapter 14, Tara Fenwick introduces readers to complexity science which shares some features with actor-network theory (above), situated learning and postmodernism. Fenwick critiques RPL practices from a postmodernist, feminist philosophical perspective arguing that the pedagogic and learning processes involved are based on rationality;

the objectifying (and externalising) of knowledge, learning and experience; Cartesian bifurcations; presumed objectivity of the candidate and mentalist notions of learning. In a similar way to Michelson, she argues that identity, desires, subjectivity and location are eclipsed in RPL. Experience and knowledge become fixed in the past and separated from reflection in the present. For Fenwick, reflection as practised in RPL is erroneously portrayed as 'finding' knowledge in experience but is actually about making reinterpretations of experience based on 'socially available meanings'. The result in her view is that experience and prior knowledge get ordered and linearised by reflection.

Complexity science, she argues, offers a corrective because it avoids 'separating individual and environment, mind and body, prior and present, learning and doing'. Instead, the emphasis is on complex systems comprising *person*, *learning* and *context* – interrelated in myriad ways – unpredictable, changing, adaptive and inventive. Change at the level of person, learning or context causes reverberant changes at the other levels and new configurations of complexity that could not have been achieved independently. This change process is termed 'co-emergence'. Given that change at any level can instigate change at all others, the person is not the only agent of change. Contextual elements can be the instigators. In this way, boundaries between self and non-self are extremely permeable. Learning is central to every complex system but again is not only the property or domain of the individual. Rather, it is seen as the 'continuous creation of alternative actions and responses to changing situations, undertaken by the system's parts'. From a complexity science view, knowledge 'cannot be contained in any one element or dimension of the system, for knowledge is constantly emerging and spilling into other systems'. The best that can be achieved in terms of capturing knowledge is to gain a snapshot of the multiple, ongoing fluctuations of the complex system.

Fenwick discusses the possible implications of this theory for RPL practice. Most of her implications refer to pedagogy, and fall into three areas. First, a focus on prior knowledge as 'process' not 'product'. RPL candidates would be encouraged to see the complex system that was at work during specific times and events in their lives and the parts played by people, actions, objects, and cultural patterns. Secondly, she recommends developing pedagogic approaches within RPL that distinguish representation from learning/knowledge. By this she means that facilitators could be explicit that trying to fix anything (learning/knowledge) distorts it and the complex system of which it is/was a part. Thirdly, she raises the politics of recognition, highlighting the role of RPL assessors within their own complex systems (that is, as well as focusing on candidates' systems). Overall, Fenwick recommends more fluid engagement with prior knowledge (rather than attempts to fix it) bearing in mind that no two perspectives on a situation will be the same and that the very process of imaginative reinterpretation will impact on what is recalled. The RPL process itself becomes a complex system that could provide a theme or topic for exploration and articulation. As Fenwick puts it, the aim would be to 'help participants to make community sense of the patterns emerging within the [RPL] group's complex system, and understand their own involvement in these patterns'.

Symbolic interactionism

In Chapter 15, Ruth Whittaker, Susan Whittaker and Paula Cleary make two new departures from other chapters in the volume. First, they focus solely on identity transformation, an often-ignored but important by-product of RPL for many candidates. Secondly, they use symbolic interactionism and social identity theory (with some situated learning theory) to locate identity in social context, particularly in terms of inter-relationships. They highlight commonalities between their three theoretical sets. They all foreground social identification in social context. They all emphasise the role of 'others'. They all stress the important place of contextual norms and practices. As Whittaker *et al.* put it, all the theories 'propose the importance of what we do and with whom we interact, and the meanings attached to these in relevant social contexts'.

The authors use these conceptual resources to explore why RPL is experienced as personally transformative by so many candidates. They identify four types of identity redefinition in RPL: redefinition of what learning is; of what a learner is; of individual experience as learning experience; and, finally, a redefinition of the self as learner. They argue that the latter is a particularly important and under-valued aspect of RPL, linked to many reports of increased confidence and self-esteem.

The authors posit that the RPL process itself offers a social context with cognitive, evaluative and affective components, which stimulate and strengthen identity redefinition. Consequently, involvement in RPL allows for legitimate peripheral participation in a community of practice with key motivating factors such as anticipatory socialisation and anticipatory identification. These have future orientations and emphasise 'becoming'.

Whittaker *et al.* identify a range of significant 'others' in RPL, for example, interactions and comparisons with facilitators and fellow-candidates. They argue that an RPL process offers a range of opportunities to understand and rehearse norms and practices associated with a learner identity, such as a willingness to recognise learning from experience; participate actively in educational processes; engage with and accept help from others; accept change; be perceived as a learner; and, to engage in future learning. In drawing attention to this under-researched aspect of RPL, the authors concede that positive identity redefinition is not always the case. Candidates have to *want* to undertake and experience identity change, if not for itself, for the rewards it may bring. Furthermore, such change cannot happen when social interactions are hampered, for example, by poor communications and divergent experiences and backgrounds.

The authors end with recommendations for RPL practices. Social processes and identity transformation could be made more explicit, for example, stressing to candidates that they are taking control of their learning and using planned group work to broaden interactions. These would make RPL a site with a broader understanding of learning than in traditional sites, thereby making a contribution to both the theory and practice of lifelong learning.

Extending the theoretical discussions

Although organised theoretically, it is abundantly clear that the chapters in this volume address many aspects of our five thematic areas: knowledge, pedagogy, learning, identity and power. In some of the areas, tentative patterns of agreement begin to emerge. In others there are divergences. Most agreements and divergences are paradigm-related and a key question for RPL practitioners and theorists is the extent to which they locate their enquiries and practice within a postmodern framework.

The area of knowledge remains problematic. Are RPL practitioners to work on the basis of valid and necessary epistemological differences between forms of knowledge, or, are any such differences to be seen as modernist binaries to be contested? There is some agreement on the need to theorise candidates' knowledge in terms other than academic.

With regard to pedagogy, the portfolio is focused upon in a number of chapters but questions remain. Is portfolio development an 'inclusive' pedagogy; a conceptually muddled, contradictory and ambiguous methodology; and/or a reinscription of Enlightenment epistemology?

The chapters that focus on learning aspects of RPL cohere in their movement away from the psychologism and cognitivism of Kolb's learning cycle, and offer insightful, 'connective' and networked alternatives to some of the outmoded methodologies currently in use. In this way, they focus meaningfully on networks and systems pertaining to RPL candidates, but engage less well with corresponding higher education networks and systems.

Identity issues come through strongly in several of the chapters, particularly the call for a revitalised academic cadre of RPL practitioners, with more highly-developed understandings in all of the five thematic areas. The re-theorised links between RPL and increased candidate confidence cannot be ignored.

Broad issues of power are not resolved in these chapters. There is an enduring experiential learning type of anti-academic flavour in a number of the writings, with the academy seen as *de facto* dominant and oppressive, to be challenged by the innate democracy and authenticity of knowledge from outside. On a broader canvas, the vexed sociological agency-structure relationship remains: some writers assume too much agency for RPL and RPL practitioners; others leave individuals with little room to manoeuvre within their networks, whilst others over-determine the reproductive power of structures. Finally, and ubiquitously, the relationship between epistemological and political goals remains an open one.

In the Endword, Michael Young engages with these and other issues. He moves the agenda forward by suggesting that RPL is not only a practice that *needs re-theorising* but one which offers the possibility of *new theorising*. His closing words are both salutary and inspiring:

> Questions about knowledge, authority, qualifications and different types of learning will always be with us. Once RPL is freed from its largely rhetorical role as the great radical strategy or the great solution to inequality, it offers a unique and very concrete set of contexts for debating the fundamental educational issues that such questions give rise to and for finding new ways of approaching them.

References

Andersson, P., Sjösten, N-Å. and Ahn, S-e. (2003), *Att värdera kunskap, erfarenhet och kompetens, Perspektiv på validering*, *[*To value knowledge, experience and competence, perspectives on validation/, Stockholm: Myndigheten för skolutveckling.

Andersson, P., Fejes, A. and Ahn, S-e. (2004), 'Recognition of prior vocational learning in Sweden', *Studies in the Education of Adults*, 36(1): 57–71.

Barnett, R. (1990), *The Idea of Higher Education*, Buckingham: SRHE and Open University Press.

Boud, D., Keogh, R. and Walker, D. (1985), *Reflection: Turning Experience into Learning*, London: Kogan Page.

Breier, M. (2003), 'The recruitment and recognition of prior informal experience in the pedagogy of two university courses in labour law', PhD Thesis, University of Cape Town.

Butterworth, C. (1992), 'More than one bite at the APEL: Contrasting models of accrediting prior learning', *Journal of Further and Higher Education*, 16(3): 39–51.

Cleary, P., Whittaker, R. and Gallacher, J. (2001), *Social Inclusion through APEL: The Learners' Perspective*, National Report for Scotland, European Commission: Socrates-Grundtvig Project, Centre for Research in Lifelong Learning, Glasgow Caledonian University.

Dyson, C. and Keating, K. (2003), *The Recognition of Prior Learning: Practices in the Workplace*, Report to the International Labour Office.

Eraut, M. (1994), *Developing Professional Knowledge: A Review of Progress and Practice*, London: Falmer.

Evans, N. (1993), *AP(E)L Activities*, London: LET.

Fehnel, R. (1994), 'Pulling together: Optimising RPL', *People Dynamics*, 24 May.

Fenwick, T. (2001*), Experiential Learning: A Theoretical Critique from Five Perspectives*, Information Series, No. 385, Columbus, Ohio, ERIC Clearinghouse on Adult, Career, and Vocational Education.

Fraser, W. (1995), *Learning from Experience: Empowerment or Incorporation?* Leicester: NIACE.

Gibbons, M., Lomoges, C., Nowotny, C., Schwartzman, S., Scott, P. and Trow, M. (1994), *The New Production of Knowledge: The Dynamics of Science and Research in Contemporary Societies*, London: Sage Publications.

Harris, J. (1999), *Theories of Learning and the Recognition of Prior Learning (RPL): Implications for South African Education and Training,* Pretoria, Government of South Africa, Department of Education, National Centre for Curriculum Research and Development.

Harris, J. (2004), 'The hidden curriculum of the Recognition of Prior Learning: a case study', PhD Thesis, Open University.

Knowles, M. (1980), *The Modern Practice of Adult Education: From Pedagogy to Andragogy*, Chicago: Association Press.

Kolb, D. (1984), *Experiential Learning*, Englewood Cliffs, NJ: Prentice Hall.

Mandell, A. and Michelson, E. (1990), *Portfolio Development and Adult Learning: Purposes and Strategies*, Chicago: CAEL.

Merrifield, J., McIntyre, D. and Osaigbovo, R. (2000), *Mapping APEL: Accreditation of Prior Experiential Learning in English Higher Education*, London: DfEE.

Michelson, E. (1996), 'Beyond Galileo's telescope: Situated knowledge and the assessment of experiential learning', *Adult Education Quarterly*, 46(4): 185-96.

Millar, C. (1996), 'The experiential learning project: "If we just had a story"', Paper presented at the 5th ICEL conference, Cape Town, South Africa, July.

Schön, D. (1983), *The Reflective Practitioner*, New York: Basic Books.

Sfard, A. (1998), 'On two metaphors for learning and the dangers of choosing just one', *Educational Researcher*, 27(2): 4–12.

Storan, J. (1988), *Making Experience Count*, London: LET.

Wailey, A. and Simpson, R. (1998), 'Assessment of Prior and Experiential Learning (AP[E]L): A model for diagnosing strategic and organisational learning processes', Paper presented at the 6th ICEL conference, University of Tampere, Finland.

Weil, S. and McGill, I. (1989), *Making Sense of Experiential Learning: Diversity in Theory and Practice*, Buckingham: SRHE and OUP.

Wheelahan, L., Dennis, N., Firth, J., Miller, P., Newton, D., Pascoe, S. and Veeenker, P. (2002), *Recognition of Prior Learning: Policy and Practice in Australia*, Australian Qualification Framework Advisory Board.

Whitaker, U. (1989), *Assessing Learning: Standards, Principles and Procedures*, Chicago: CAEL.

Notes

[1] 'Candidate' is our preferred term for the people going through an RPL process. It is the term used most frequently throughout the book, although individual authors sometimes refer to 'learners' or 'students'.

chapter two

Different faces and functions of RPL:
an assessment perspective

Per Andersson

Introduction

One crucial dimension of the Recognition of Prior Learning is that the process of recognition involves some sort of assessment. This chapter focuses on RPL as the assessment of knowledge/competence. Assessment that brings the power dimension of RPL to the fore, and a discussion around this issue will contribute to a more complete picture of the different faces and functions of RPL practices. So, by applying concepts from assessment theory and practice to RPL, I hope to develop understanding of the phenomenon.

In this chapter, I discuss different perspectives of the functions and faces of RPL in terms of assessment. The first perspective is that RPL is an assessment of individuals, but at the same time an assessment of prior knowledge itself. This assessment includes processes of selection and of transformation. Assessment is also related to theories of learning and knowledge under-pinning different models of RPL. Another approach from assessment theory is to consider RPL in relation to a continuum from convergent to divergent assessment. Next, the question of the quality of RPL assessments is explored in terms of validity, reliability, plausibility and relevance. For example, a focus on different functions of assessment calls for different types of validity. Concepts such as validity and reliability are certainly not used solely for individual assessment, but also in a number of contexts of measurement and research, and ideas from these contexts help to broaden understanding. Competence and/or potential are then discussed in terms of whether assessments are about what has been and is, or about what can and will be (learnt). The discussion of RPL is also related to a general discussion of local versus universal knowledge, in the light of tensions between interest in the particularities of the individual and the potential of standardised assessment methods and commensurability. Finally, a number of the concepts used in the chapter are drawn together in a discussion about differences and possible developments in the faces and functions of RPL.

Assessment of the individual and of knowledge

In order to obtain new perspectives on the functions of RPL, I start with the work of Steinar Kvale. Kvale, a professor of educational psychology at the University of Aarhus, Denmark, has written extensively about assessment, examinations, grading and evaluation. In the model presented below, he offers a heuristic device that provides a starting point for the discussions in this chapter. Although his original model is about evaluations of educational systems and programmes, I use it here to focus on assessments/evaluations of individuals and of knowledge.

Table 2.1. Functions and focuses of educational assessment (adapted from Kvale, 1996, p. 121)

Function:	Focus:	
	Individuals	Knowledge
Selection	1	3
Transformation	2	4

What are the functions of assessments? At first glance, they have a principal function as a 'thermometer', giving information about learning. But this is only a limited perspective (the discussion that follows will broaden the perspective). At second glance, the function is the selection of individuals – for educational programmes or for positions in the labour market. Assessments can also have a transformation function – they are part of an educational process and influence learning and individual development as well as giving information. Furthermore, when the selection and transformation of individuals is placed in the foreground, the content of the assessment, the knowledge, is present in the background. If, instead, knowledge is placed in the foreground, a new perspective of the function of the assessment is acquired – it becomes a matter of selection of knowledge. Through the assessment you show what knowledge is important. Moreover, the process of defining what knowledge should be assessed might mean a transformation of knowledge, of what knowledge that counts as valid. (Kvale, 1990, 1996)

In this way, four different perspectives on assessments (or evaluations) are highlighted. Is the focus on individuals (RPL candidates, students) or knowledge (curriculum knowledge, prior learning)? Is the function selection or transformation? These perspectives will now be further elaborated in relation to RPL.

Selecting individuals

When the focus is on individual selection (1 in Table 2.1), the exchange value of knowledge is central. Assessment might lead to some sort of result in exchange for the knowledge demonstrated. It could be a grade, a test result, a certificate or some other type of documentation or credit. There are two levels of exchange value, as the assessment result probably has an exchange value in itself.

In RPL, this means that some sort of credential is often an important part and outcome of the process. It might be necessary to have the grades or the certificate to obtain admission to an educational programme or to get a job. Sometimes, more informal ways of recognising prior learning could mean that you get a job, or admission to education, directly, without making the 'detour' via the formal documentation. This actually means that the assessor has power over the individual and his or her life. The assessment is meant to be *predictive* and future-oriented – the purpose is to predict something, for example success in study. This predictive function is likely to be self-fulfilling – you are selected to what has been predicted to be your area of study/work. This is an aspect of the transforming function of RPL, which will be discussed in greater detail in the following section.

Transforming the individual

It has been shown that assessments have 'side-effects' on the process of learning, rather than functioning solely as a thermometer giving information (see for example, Kvale, 1980). These have been seen as unplanned trans-formation effects. But is this only something that happens by mistake, or is it planned? As far back as the introduction of grading by the Jesuits in 1599, these effects were described as a good alternative to threats and punishment (a description in the Jesuit text *Ratio atque institutio studiorum Societatis Jesus*, referred to by Durkheim, 1977). Assessments are actually parts of an educational process, which aims at learning and development or, in other words, transformation (2 in Table 2.1).

What does individual transformation mean in the context of RPL? In the educational system, assessment practices have mainly been related to what could/should have been learnt through formal education. The idea of RPL means that the basis of examination is broadened. It does not matter where one learns. Now it is not only possible, but seen as important and necessary, to examine all knowledge the individual has, irrespective of where that knowledge has been acquired. The results of informal and non-formal learning are examined together with the results of formal education. Any experience, anything one does, could actually lead to an assessment of learning/knowledge/competence.

This does not mean that RPL is necessarily transformative. 'Recognition of prior learning' means that the explicit purpose is *summative*; the assessment is meant to look back and sum up the learning that has already taken place. But if you have a developmental approach (Butterworth, 1992), there is a more or less explicit ambition to transform or change. The assessment becomes *formative*, which means that the purpose is to inform and change the continuing learning process. Another (trans)formative function of RPL is that it might govern the further learning often necessary before the knowledge can be used. For instance, you might need a certificate to work in a certain vocation, and if you get recognition for parts of that certificate, you are also required to learn the rest of what is demanded.

Selection of knowledge

As mentioned above, assessment practices can be seen as an assessment of the individual, but also as an assessment of knowledge (Kvale, 1990, 1996). What knowledge is valid? The selection of content for an assessment means that you define what knowledge or competence is most important within a subject/discipline or a vocation/profession (3 in Table 2.1). The content of the examination is a clear message about what knowledge it is that counts. And, consequently, you define what knowledge is not important and maybe even what is beyond the content of the specific subject area.

The construction of assessment is a process of defining valid knowledge, but the assessment process itself defines knowledge. It is here that you see what knowledge – expressed in answers and solutions – is really accepted when it comes to aspects that could not or have not been defined beforehand. The construction of criteria and assessment methods is important, but what happens in practice might be more or less different – depending on personal preferences and context as well as the fact that not everything can be foreseen and prescribed in the form of criteria.

The introduction of RPL does not only involve a shift concerning what learning process it is that 'counts' (not only formal but also non-formal and informal learning). There is also a shift when it comes to what knowledge content counts. Thus, RPL could contribute to defining a subject or vocational area through the construction of methods, criteria and so on.

Transformation of knowledge

The knowledge that is selected is not necessarily always the same. This means that there might be a transformation of what is accepted as valid knowledge (4 in Figure 1). Introducing new models of assessment, grading, certification, and so on is probably part of a transformation of what knowledge counts in a certain area.

This helps us to understand why RPL can be challenging, and even threatening, to the established system. Establishing RPL might involve transformation of what is valid knowledge. If, for example, a certain formal education or training is required to enter a specific vocation, then a lot of power might be needed to redefine the vocation in a way that is in line with the idea of RPL. For example: Is it possible that the results of informal learning could also be (part of) what is required? One probably learns different things in formal education compared to the informal work situation, but what competencies are really needed to do a good job? And what competencies do employers and trade unions define as necessary to enter the vocation? The traditional status of formal education lends it power. The state of the labour market might also influence what competencies are accepted. In a situation of unemployment and a 'surplus' of formally competent people, there is probably less demand for recognition of prior informal learning compared to a situation where there is a lack of formally competent manpower. This means that RPL practices potentially have power in relation to the limits or boundaries of knowledge.

Structural knowledge constitution – theories of learning and knowledge in RPL

The selection and transformation of knowledge has two dimensions – thematic and structural knowledge constitution (Kvale, 1996). Thematic constitution is about the content of knowledge, where selection/transformation means a 'censorship of knowledge' (Kvale, 1990). This was discussed earlier in the chapter in relation to the process of selecting and transforming knowledge. The structural dimension dealt with here is epistemological. It is about what knowledge and learning actually are. This dimension is not that obvious, but a certain type of assessment also embodies a certain theory of knowledge and learning.

Assessments draw on theories of *learning* and *knowledge* that, explicitly or implicitly, underpin practice. RPL, and other assessments, develop in a context. There might be an explicit policy in the organisation, but there might also be more or less implicit views in the context, in specific methods, or among assessors and other key persons. And through the choice of a certain RPL model one might unconsciously promote a certain view of learning and knowledge. Theories of experiential and situated learning will be used here as examples of the structural knowledge constitution of RPL, representing individual and social theories of learning respectively.

The theory of *experiential learning* and the learning cycle (Kolb, 1984) underpins much of RPL practice. The *portfolio* method is based on this theory. This is a mainly *individual* perspective. It is the individual who experiences, reflects, etc. This could be compared to the discussion by Tara Fenwick (Chapter 14, this volume), Elana Michelson (Chapter 7, this volume) and others, who promote a more developed perspective of experiential learning. Instead of the individual perspective, Michelson (1996; Chapter 7, this volume) argues for a situated knowledge perspective in experiential learning and RPL. She calls for an explicit perspective where situatedness is taken seriously, and knowledge is valued in its own terms, not only in relation to criteria from another context.[1]

However, such stances are developing theoretical perspectives, rather than reflected generally in RPL practices. It is normally individual experiences that are reflected upon and assessed (which is odd given that prior learning tends to be situated and social). The transfer from the context of experience to the context of assessment, and assessment criteria, is often taken for granted.

Theories that see learning as a *social and contextual* phenomenon, for example, *situated learning* (Lave and Wenger, 1991), do however seem to implicitly underpin some RPL practices. Situated learning is a social perspective, where the situation and the context are seen as central. You do things, learn and develop together with others in a natural setting, and the aim is to assess competence in this setting.[2] These perspectives are evident in RPL practices where some sort of *authentic* assessment is the central method.

Authentic means testing competencies in natural (for example, the workplace) or simulated (for example, the vocational training institute) settings. However, where authentic assessments are incorporated into RPL, there seems to be a trend towards *behaviourism* and credit-exchange (Butterworth, 1992). In this way, authentic assessment, although in a natural setting, becomes *atomistic* and governed by lists of competencies, describing expected behaviour in detail, rather than *holistically*. When you want to make an 'objective' assessment, in a traditional psychometric tradition, the result could easily be atomistic in this way. When more holistic assessment practices develop, the subjective dimension is emphasised. It is only the individual assessor who sees the whole picture and can interpret it in terms of competence.

Another objection to authentic assessment is the very situation of assessment. How can a situation be authentic when assessment is introduced? In one way, it could be seen as no different to ongoing assessment – you always have a boss, or a co-worker, or a customer, who (informally) assesses what you do. But even so, formal assessment is not part of the natural situation, which means that the assessment cannot be totally authentic. The 'authentic' situation is normally 'simulated'. How representative is such a situation in relation to the 'real' situation (Bowden and Marton, 1998)?

Convergent or divergent assessment

Other concepts from assessment theory that have a bearing on RPL are *convergent* and *divergent* (Torrance and Pryor, 1998).[3] A convergent assessment means assessing *if* you know/can do certain things. There are usually some criteria for what is acceptable knowledge/competence, and these control the assessment. In the context of RPL, convergent assessment has been discussed in terms of 'Procrustean RPL' (Jones and Martin, 1997; Harris, 1999).[4] In divergent assessment, the ambition is to assess *what* you know, in a more 'unprejudiced' way. It is a matter of 'exploring' the knowledge of the individual.

The concepts convergent/divergent should not be interpreted as a dualism but as the ends of a continuum. It is probably impossible to make a strictly divergent assessment. We all have some sort of implicit criteria or 'prejudice' of what it is possible to know. If the person being assessed has some other sort of knowledge/competence, we will probably not notice it, despite ambitions to the contrary. A strictly convergent assessment would take the form of a multiple-choice test – the more open questions or tasks, the more divergent the assessment.

Position on the convergent-divergent continuum also reflects a view of learning and knowledge. What is worth learning and knowing and what is it possible to learn and to know? Only what is specified in curricula and in assessment criteria? Or is learning an open-ended process where you cannot say beforehand where it will lead?

Divergence and convergence can also be discussed in relation to predictive, formative and summative functions of assessments. Divergent assessment is probably formative. It focuses on the potential of the individual, and this divergent and formative assessment could form the basis of planning future learning and studying. Convergent assessment is more likely to be summative, assessing competence in relation to certain standards. Predictive assessment is located somewhere between convergent and divergent. By means of such assessment, you try to predict if, and where, someone is likely to succeed. It is to a certain extent convergent in relation to the expected demands of the context the individual will enter. But the idea of potential is relevant here too. You cannot know exactly what knowledge or competence will be needed in the future, and with a divergent approach, success (or failure) can also be predicted in relation to different domains.

Of course, other alternatives in relation to functions are also possible. A more divergent assessment could be summative, leading for example, to a description of current competencies or a CV that gives a broad picture of competencies. Convergent assessment can be predictive and formative – if the prediction or the diagnostic assessment is made in an area with clear and unquestioned criteria, and if success can be predicted or requires further learning be identified in relation to these criteria.

The portfolio method could, for example, be more or less convergent or divergent, as well as atomistic or holistic, depending on what type of portfolio is produced. Maggie Challis (1993) discusses this in terms of the outcome-related or specific portfolio, and the self-orientated or exploratory portfolio. An outcome-related portfolio is convergent, as it is related to specific, expected outcomes of prior learning, and a self-orientated portfolio implies a divergent approach where all experiences are of initial interest.

Quality in assessment

Other concepts from assessment theory and practice relate to the quality of assessment. The concepts *validity* and *reliability* are used in this respect in educational measurement, assessments, evaluations and research. Even if validity and reliability are interpreted differently in different paradigms, the focus is still on making as good measurements and descriptions as possible, a matter that will be discussed in this part. Concepts like *plausibility* and *relevance* are also used to discuss quality in assessment.

Validity and reliability

Validity means that you assess what you intend to assess, and reliability, of course, means that the assessment is reliable and replicable. In psychometric assessment or test theory, reliability is seen as a necessary but not sufficient prerequisite of validity. High reliability is maybe not necessary to reach high validity. Feldt (1997) discusses this relation between validity and reliability, focusing on performance tests and multiple-choice tests. Even if advocates of performance test argue that such tests are more valid, there is still a view that multiple-choice tests are more reliable, and this contradicts classical test theory. But Feldt (1997, p. 377) shows that it actually is possible that 'validity [can] rise when reliability declines'.

In French, the concept of *validation* is used for RPL, and in Swedish, the concept is *validering*. This makes it even more interesting to reflect upon the validity of RPL. In RPL the intention is probably to make a fair assessment of individual competencies, based on certain individual experiences. This suggests methods of assessment adapted to individual demands with high validity. On the other hand, the need to make the assessment of competencies of different individuals comparable calls for reliable methods. Assessment results might, for example, be used when you apply for a new position or a certain education/training programme. In such cases, the comparisons between individuals, based on RPL results (and probably other assessments too), need to be as reliable as possible. This suggests more standardised assessment methods. Thus, there is a dilemma in finding methods that are individual/specific and standardised at the same time. Another aspect of reliability is that a number of independent assessments (assessing the knowledge of the same person) should give (about) the same result. This second aspect is, principally, an important criterion in RPL too, but it is not that important in practice. If the starting point is the 'eternal' lifelong learning that always takes place, then different assessments made on different occasions to some extent should give different results!

The consequence of the above discussion is a call for balance between reliability and validity and between convergence and divergence. Assessment has to be convergent, to some extent, to make fair comparisons possible, and divergent to give a fair description and assessment of the individual. This is not to say that RPL assessments are not reliable. But in a divergent and individualistic approach to assessment, there is a risk of individual qualities being overlooked if the methods are oriented to psychometric criteria of reliability, and one should be aware of this risk.

Divergent assessment could also be compared to qualitative research methods, where the call for reliability is not present in the same way as the call for validity. Reliability is, for example, not among the criteria of 'quality in qualitative research' that Staffan Larsson (1993) describes. The idea of exploring means that you can find something new, but you cannot find the same thing anew again and again. You find it once and then it is found. The next time you find something else! The next researcher finds something else too. In the same way, the 'divergent [RPL] assessor' tries to find the individual qualities in each and every person.

Four types of validity

To make claims of validity, you have to know what you intend to assess. I will discuss the meaning of four types of validity – predictive, pragmatic, content and communicative validity – all related to the different functions of assessments presented in Table 2.1.

If the focus is the selection of individuals then the main interest is *predictive validity*. It is a matter of how well the assessment can predict success in the future careers of individuals (Kvale, 1990, 1996). The predictive validity of educational assessment has been questioned. It has been shown that only a limited part of the variation in future study success can be explained by variation in grades (see for example Willingham *et al.*, 1990). Even so, it is a means of selection that is (experienced as) relatively fair – more valid than a lottery and fairer than, for example, who your parents are or how much money you have. Could we expect RPL assessments to be more predictive? If the predictive validity is relatively low, how important is it to reach high reliability in terms of comparability?

If the function of the assessment is intended to be the transformation of individuals (development, learning), then *pragmatic validity* is central. Here, validity is a question of whether the individual can use the knowledge (Kvale, 1990, 1996). If an RPL candidate gains admission to an educational programme, or to a certain vocation, then the focus will be on whether and how the individual will manage to study or do the job – compared to those who gain admission in the 'traditional' way. This raises the question of what criteria should be used to assess success – should RPL be adapted to the existing system, or should RPL be part of changing the system (Andersson *et al.*, 2003, 2004).

Pragmatic validity is also related to the formative function of RPL. Knowledge about individuals gained through assessment might be used to promote transformation. The RPL process has a role in relation to future learning. Does RPL help the development of individual potential in current and future contexts?

The function of selecting (valid) knowledge calls for yet another perspective on validity. Here, the focus would be on *content validity*. The concern is whether knowledge assessed forms a representative sample of (what is seen as) the knowledge contents of the subject/discipline/vocation/profession (Kvale, 1990, 1996). The 'traditional' psychometric approach to educational assessment is to try to make the test a representative sample of that knowledge. But then this approach is normally premised on test-takers having participated in an education programme and studied broader aspects of the subject. This may be one reason why it might be more difficult to trust an RPL assessment. RPL candidates have not taken part in a common curriculum, but have their own individual 'curriculum vitae'. This means that it is more difficult to generalise from the knowledge sample to the knowledge contents of the subject area. There is no measure for the probability of the individual having an acceptable level of knowledge in relation to the established discipline.

Another issue is that the various backgrounds of RPL candidates mean that they probably know things, learnt informally from experience, that are outside the established knowledge content but still potentially very relevant in terms of pragmatic validity. Could this 'non-traditional' knowledge be accepted? If so, it is a matter of transformation of knowledge. Could and should curriculum content be transformed? One key concept here is *communicative validity*, which is about whether the (transformed) knowledge is accepted in its context (Kvale, 1990, 1996). If a new, transformed, perspective concerning what knowledge is valid is to be established, then it has to be communicated in a way that makes it understandable and reasonable. From an illocutionary perspective (Wiliam, 2001, see below), it becomes a matter of whether the individual, post-assessment, is accepted in a community of practice with specific traditions of accepted knowledge.

Plausibility and relevance

Martyn Hammersley (1992) presents alternative criteria for quality in ethnographic research – validity and relevance. His arguments are useful for deepening understanding of validity, and quality. By validity, Hammersley means truth (conscious of the problems of reaching 'real' truth) or, rather, ensuring a reasonable level of truth. The amount of proof needed for validity depends on the plausibility/credibility of the results, the centrality of the results and the type of claim made. Relevance is related both to the context of research and to the context of practice (the context in which the research is conducted). Are the results relevant in these contexts?

Hammersley's criteria can be applied to RPL. How much, and what type, of proof is needed if the results are to be trusted? The answer to this question will probably have consequences, for example, for methods used. An example is the comparison between portfolio and authentic assessment methods discussed above. If the plausibility/credibility of the claims in a portfolio is high, then these claims might be accepted as proof of knowledge/competence. If not, there might be a need for more evidence, a need that could be satisfied by means of a competence test – an authentic assessment where it is possible to see that the candidate 'really can do it'. Willingness to accept the portfolio as proof also depends on the centrality and type of claims made. If the knowledge in question is central to the subject/vocation – part of what is considered as the most important knowledge, a higher degree of credibility will be required.

The type of claim could also vary in terms of whether it is predictive/formative assessment related to admission to an educational/training programme, or summative assessment for credit, advanced standing or even certification. Less proof could be required in RPL for admission, as the candidate will still be assessed a number of times during the educational programme itself. In RPL for credit or examination/certification, more proof will be required. The risk of passing the (final) examination without having the 'necessary' knowledge/competence is higher. Calls for authentic evidence will probably be higher in RPL for credit or examination than in RPL for admission – this is not to say that testing will not be required for admission, only that the probability could be lower.

It is here that the criterion of relevance comes into play. Evidence collected in a portfolio might be more relevant in some knowledge areas, while in others, competencies have to be shown in practice. To a high degree, this depends on the importance of product and process. If the main interest is the product, examples could be presented in a portfolio, for example, a picture of some-thing produced in a workshop. But when process is more central, the demand for authentic assessment might be higher. As a hairdresser, it is not enough to 'produce' a nice hairstyle – the process, including the relation to the customer, is also very important. Of course, the process is also important when you produce goods, it should be done in a proper way. But a document, which certifies that you have mastered the process, would be more acceptable in an area where the product is central. A corresponding document concerning the process of hairdressing has to be more credible to be accepted.

Competence and/or potential?

Concepts such as selection, transformation, formative, predictive, and so on, all point to the fact that assessments are not only, or maybe even not mainly, about what has been and is, but rather about what will be. This section deals with the relation between competence and potential, a discussion that is highly relevant for RPL as well as for other types of knowledge assessment. Assessments can be seen as competence-oriented and/or potential-oriented. Three potential-oriented perspectives on assessments will now be discussed, and 'prior' learning will be called into question in various ways.

The predictive, formative and summative functions of assessment can be related to the concepts of competence and potential and to the idea of the zone of proximal development (Vygotsky, 1978). Briefly, Vygotsky argues that you have competence – what you can do by yourself here and now – but you also have the potential to do more with others in a social context. The 'space' between your competence and your potential is your zone of proximal development. Is the focus of RPL on the competence the individual can demonstrate? Or could one (also), predictively/formatively, recognise the potential of what the individual could do in a context, together with other (more competent) people? This offers a further perspective on RPL and the assessment of competence – 'assessing competence is assessing the potential of the individual' (Pouget and Osborne, 2004, p. 59; Eraut, 1994).

Another potential-oriented perspective is presented by Dave Boud (2000). He discusses a complementary, not alternative, purpose of assessment – *sustainable* assessment. Boud argues that assessment practices should not only be an assessment of competence for the moment, but also a preparation for lifelong assessment of learning in a learning society. The consequence of this would be a greater focus on the formative aspect and the potential of the individual. This perspective of sustainability could be interesting in relation to RPL, as ongoing lifelong learning means that new 'prior learning' is always turning up, and amenable to assessment. The learning of tomorrow will be prior learning the day after tomorrow.

A third perspective with a focus on potential and transformation is whether assessments are seen as *perlocutionary* or *illocutionary* (Wiliam, 2001). Dylan Wiliam refers to John Langshaw Austin's discussion of perlocutionary and illocutionary speech acts.[5] Perlocutionary speech acts or assessments mean that you say something '*about* what has, is or will be' (Wiliam, 2001, p. 173–4). The illocutionary function, on the other hand, is 'performative', which means that the assessment performs something. It transforms the individual in a certain way – after the assessment you are something you were not before. This is best understood in terms of examinations, particularly assessments where you get a degree, a certificate or a diploma. The examination transforms you; you become an electrician, a university student, a PhD and so on. Wiliam relates this to the theory of situated learning and communities of practice. Through assessment you enter a community. An illocutionary perspective thus means that the assessment:

> . . . is better thought of not as an assessment of aptitude or achievement, or even as a predictor of future capabilities, but rather as an illocutionary speech act that *inaugurates an individual's entry into a community of practice*. (Wiliam, 2001, p. 175, emphasis in original)

These perspectives contribute further to the understanding and discussion of what are necessary, possible, and perhaps, inevitable functions of RPL.

Local and universal horizons of meaning

This discussion of validity and reliability and of divergent and convergent assessment methods can be viewed as a reflection of the postmodern foregrounding of the importance of local narratives in relation to universal metanarratives: 'With the collapse of universal metanarratives as foundations of valid knowledge, local narratives come into prominence. Particular, heterogeneous, and changing language games replace a global horizon of meaning' (Kvale, 1996, p. 134). But the new metanarrative seems to be that of the economy. One aspect of globalisation is a call for commensurability, for example, when it comes to the evaluation of knowledge (Kvale, 1996).

Knowledge is measured, and countries are compared, as well as schools and individuals.

In the context of RPL, I will discuss this dilemma at the individual level. We can focus on reliable and commensurable assessments of knowledge, or we can try to make a divergent assessment of the individual (competence). Will the main assessment method be standardised testing, or 'humanistic-anarchistic exams' (Kvale, 1990, pp. 131–3)? Maybe there should not be a main method but, rather, different methods, from different points on this continuum. We can also ask why we have this individualistic approach to RPL. The focus on the individual could be seen as a manifestation of Western values rather than a universal 'truth', considered in the light of conceptions such as situated learning (Michelson, 1997; Pouget and Osborne, 2004).

The focus on assessments, measurement, commensurability and so on could also be understood in relation to the concept and discussion of 'govern-mentality' (Foucault, 2003). Different governmentalities mean different ideas about how the subject, and consequently the population, should act and how we are governed according to these ideas. The dominating governmentality today, for example, in relation to adult learning, is the idea of responsible and self-governing individuals (Fejes, 2005), who transform themselves as a result of indirect governing.

RPL could be seen as part of this development, analysed by Michel Foucault, where the subject is governed through different types of examination. Knowledge about the subject is created through tests, grading and examinations, and this knowledge is then used in the process of governing. In this way, power and knowledge are closely related to each other, which is illustrated in the concept 'power-knowledge' (Foucault, 1980). This becomes a matter of governing and transforming individuals by means of assessment, which can be understood as techniques of surveillance:

> Disciplinary power, the power in modern social formations, functions through the practice of surveillance. Subjects are constructed in their individuality and subjectivity by a process of itemisation and atomisation as they become subject to the categorisations generated to 'understand' and 'learn' more about them and their actions. These categories are embodied in dossiers, files and records of various kinds. As the need to regulate increases, so does the need to know more about

> individuals. Hence the knowledge generated and the categories
> needed to classify this knowledge increases. Surveillance
> becomes ever more pervasive and intrusive yet without
> appearing to be oppressive. (Edwards and Usher, 1994)

Thus, the basis of governing the subject (through RPL) is the generation of knowledge about the subjects learning broadened to include any learning from any situation in life. The focus on responsibility and self-governing might mean that even informal learning is governed in a certain way. It is not unlikely that people want to learn things that can become useful assets. Why not choose activities where you learn things, why not look at educational programmes on the television, or join an association where, for example, qualified leader training is part of the package? In this way, the potential of RPL could govern and extend existing governmentality.

Conclusion

This chapter has raised a number of questions concerning RPL as an assessment of knowledge and competence. The functions of assessing individuals and knowledge, respectively, imply different and complementary faces of RPL, such as selection and transformation; these different functions have been summarised in Table 2.1 and discussed extensively. A number of other concepts have also been emphasised in the discussion, concepts that help us talk about, discuss and develop different applications of RPL. Most of these concepts are summarised in Table 2.2, which shows a pattern that is not a dichotomy but a tentative ordering of the discussion, showing two different faces. This pattern can be used by RPL practitioners as a template to evaluate the faces and functions of their own practices, and by researchers as a starting point for new analyses.

RPL is a phenomenon that can be both adapted to or change the system (for example, the educational system, and/or the working life system). When the practice of RPL is adapted to the system, it is also likely to be convergent, more closed and conforming to existing criteria of what should be known, assessing whether someone knows these things. On the other hand, an RPL practice with the potential and maybe even ambition to change the system will probably be more open and divergent, trying to explore what a candidate 'really' knows.

The structural constitution of knowledge, where we take varying

Table 2.2 Faces of RPL – A number of aspects, and possible differences in focus

Aspects of RPL	Difference in focus	
Relation to the system	RPL adapted to the system	RPL changing the system
Close/openness	Convergence	Divergence
Foundation of trust	Reliability	Validity
Focus of measurement	Commensurability	Particularity
Horizon of meaning	Universal/global	Local
Constitution of knowledge	Atomism	Holism
Orientation	Competence	Potential
Functions	Selection	Transformation
	Summative, predictive	Formative

epistemological positions by employing different RPL applications, means that different views of knowledge could be embodied in different assessment methods. When you want reliability and commensurability, you might apply methods that imply an atomistic constitution of knowledge, expressed in limited modules and closed criteria, multiple-choice tests, and so on. A focus on validity and particularity implies a need for holism. You would probably want to make a fair assessment and description of the individual and her competence, while respecting the specific context of origin.

An assessment with summative and predictive functions is probably, but not necessarily, adapted to an existing system. It is likely that the summative function is related to some sort of convergent criteria of the competence needed in order to get a grade or a certificate. A selection through prediction of success is based on whether you are likely to succeed in a certain, existing system. But it is also possible to develop more divergent and specific assessments with summative or predictive functions. A formative assessment to some extent has to include openness to the potential of individuals as well as to changes in the system. If you are not willing to change the way you teach and/or organise learning, based on the results of the formative assessment, then it actually does not have this transformative function.

It is always necessary to develop trust in assessment methods, and two main foundations of trust are reliability and validity. Convergent assessment also means that reliability is a necessary prerequisite – validity is necessary too, but limited by reliability. Divergent assessment, however, places a focus on validity, and high reliability is not necessary in the same way. Convergence and reliability are also necessary when you are interested in commensurability, something that is of high interest in (Western) society today. But if you are more interested in the individual and his/her particular experience and competence, then you would prefer divergent methods with high validity. This means that the different faces have more or less different horizons of meaning – the universal/global horizon or the local horizon. Questioning of the relation between validity and reliability has become more prevalent as universal narratives are questioned and local narratives are foregrounded. Maybe there will be a change in views of learning and knowledge, where the specific individual competence and potential, situated in a social context, is made more visible. But an increased focus on commensurability and convergent, comparable assessment is also possible. What role will RPL play in such developments? And will RPL be a sustainable assessment whilst at the same time contributing to the self-governing process?

References

Andersson, P., Sjösten, N-Å. and Ahn, S-e. (2003), *Att värdera kunskap, erfarenhet och kompetens, Perspektiv på validering*, /To Value Knowledge, Experience and Competence, Perspectives on Validation/, Stockholm: Myndigheten för skolutveckling.

Andersson, P., Fejes, A. and Ahn, S-e. (2004), 'Recognition of prior vocational learning in Sweden', *Studies in the Education of Adults*, 36(1): 57–71.

Boud, D. (2000), 'Sustainable assessment: rethinking assessment for the learning society', *Studies in Continuing Education*, 22(2): 151–67.

Bowden, J. and Marton, F. (1998), *The University of Learning*, London: Kogan Page.

Butterworth, C. (1992), 'More than one bite at the APEL: contrasting models of accrediting prior learning', *Journal of Further and Higher Education*, 16(3): 39–51.

Challis, M. (1993), *Introducing APEL*, London: Routledge.

Durkheim, E. (1977), *The Evolution of Educational Thought. Lectures on the Formation and Development of Secondary Education in France*, London: Routledge & Kegan Paul (the original, 'L'evolution Pédagogique en France', published in 1938).

Edwards, R. and Usher, R. (1994), 'Disciplining the subject: the power of competence', *Studies in the Education of Adults,* 26 (1): 1–14.

Eraut, M. (1994), *Developing Professional Knowledge and Competence*, London: The Falmer Press.

Fejes, A. (2005), 'New wine in old skins: changing patterns in the governing of the adult learner in Sweden', *International Journal of Lifelong Education,* 24 (1): 71–86.

Feldt, L.S. (1997), 'Can validity rise when reliability declines?', *Applied Measurement in Education*, 10(4): 377–87.

Foucault, M. (1980), *Power/Knowledge: Selected Interviews and other Writings 1972–1977*, New York: Pantheon.

Foucault, M. (2003), 'Governmentality' in Rabinow, P. and Rose, N. (eds) *The Essential Foucault: Selections from the Essential Works of Foucault 1954-1984* (pp. 229–45), New York: The New Press.

Guilford, J.P. (1967), *The Nature of Human Intelligence*, New York: McGraw-Hill.

Hammersley, M. (1992), *What's Wrong with Ethnography? Methodological Explorations*, London and New York: Routledge.

Harris, J. (1999), 'Ways of seeing the recognition of prior learning (RPL), what contribution can such practices make to social inclusion?', *Studies in the Education of Adults*, 31(20): 24–39.

Jones, M. and Martin, J. (1997), 'A new paradigm for recognition of prior learning (RPL)' in Fleet, W. (ed.) *Issues in Recognition of Prior Learning: A Collection of Papers*, Melbourne: Victoria RPL Network.

Kolb, D.A. (1984), *Experiential Learning: Experiences as the Source of Learning and Development*, Englewood Cliffs, N.J.: Prentice-Hall.

Kvale, S. (1980), *Spillet om karakterer i gymnasiet, Elevinterviews om bivirkninger af adgangsbegrænsning,*/The grading game in upper secondary school, pupil interviews about side-effects of restricted admission/, København: Munksgaard.

Kvale, S. (1990), 'Evaluation and decentralisation of knowledge' in Granheim, M., Kogan, M. and Lundgren, U.P. (eds) *Evaluation as Policymaking: Introducing Evaluation into a National Decentralised Educational System* (pp. 119–40), London: Jessica Kingsley Publishers.

Kvale, S. (1996), 'Evaluation as construction of knowledge' in Hayhoe, P. and Pan, J. (eds) *East-West Dialogue in Knowledge and Higher Education* (pp. 117–40), Armonk, New York and London, England: M.E. Sharpe.

Larsson, S. (1993), 'Om kvalitet i kvalitativa studier',/On quality in qualitative studies/, *Nordisk Pedagogik*, 13(4): 194–211.

Lave, J. and Wenger, E. (1991), *Situated Learning: Legitimate Peripheral Participation*, Cambridge: Cambridge University Press.

Michelson, E. (1996), 'Beyond Galileo's telescope: situated knowledge and the assessment of experiential learning', *Adult Education Quarterly*, 46(4): 185–96.

Michelson, E. (1997), 'The politics of memory: the recognition of experiential learning' in Walters, S. (ed.) *Globalization, Adult Education and Training. Impacts and Issues* (pp. 141–53), London and New York: Zed Books.

Pouget, M. and Osborne, M. (2004), 'Accreditation or *validation* of prior experiential learning: knowledge and *savoirs* in France – a different perspective?', *Studies in Continuing Education*, 26(1): 45–65.

Torrance, H. and Pryor, J. (1998), *Investigating formative assessment*, Buckingham: Open University Press.

Vygotsky, L.S. (1978), *Mind in Society: The Development of Higher Psychological Processes*, Cambridge, Massachusetts: Harvard University Press.

Wiliam, D. (2001), 'An overview of the relationship between assessment and the curriculum' in Scott, D. (ed.) *Curriculum and Assessment* (pp. 165-81), Westport, Conneticut: Ablex Publishing.

Willingham, W.W., Lewis, C., Morgan, R. and Ramist, L. (1990), *Predicting College Grades: An Analysis of Institutional Trends over Two Decades*

Notes

[1] This discussion about experiential learning will not be further elaborated in this chapter, as it is discussed in a number of other chapters in this volume.

[2] There are a number of slightly different theories about learning as a social phenomenon. Neither these nor perspectives of experiential learning will be dealt with in detail here, as this is a chapter about assessment, not about learning theories. The main point is hopefully made through the examples used.

[3] The concepts divergent and convergent have been used previously by Guilford (1967) and Kolb (1984) in a way that is parallel to this, but to describe different types of knowledge.

[4] 'According to Procrustes, a ruler in Greek mythology, everyone could fit into his bed regardless of their size and shape. If anyone was too short, he placed them on the rack and stretched them. If they were too long, he would chop of their feet' (Jones and Martin, 1997, p. 16).

[5] In Austin, J.L. (1962), *How to Do Things with Words*, Oxford and New York: Oxford University Press.

chapter three

Questions of knowledge and curriculum in the recognition of prior learning

Judy Harris

Introduction

This chapter tackles the issues of knowledge and curriculum in the theory and practice of RPL. It begins with a review of the ways these issues are (or are not) dealt with in the RPL literature. The review utilises concepts such as knowledge 'transfer', knowledge 'matching', knowledge 'equivalence' and 'hard' and 'soft' boundaries to analyse different approaches within practices. The main line of argument is that the experiential learning discourses that are so dominant in RPL embody a stance that is anti-formal knowledge and that this leads to silences, paradoxes and contradictions around knowledge and curriculum in RPL theory and practice.

In the second part of the chapter, conceptual resources from the sociology of knowledge/education are presented and evaluated with regard to their usefulness for enhancing understandings of knowledge (and curricula) in and around RPL. Basil Bernstein is a curriculum theorist concerned with analysis of the internal workings of education practices in relation to the production, reproduction and transformation of culture through consciousness. An exposition of his concepts is accompanied by illustrations of their empirical usage.

The chapter concludes that, although there are provisos in using Bernstein's concepts, they do provide a powerful language for theorising knowledge and curricula in RPL, thereby contributing to making RPL practices more epistemologically accountable. Moreover, they challenge some conventional thinking in the RPL field, for example, the taken-for-granted efficacy of weakening knowledge boundaries in the pursuit of 'progressivism'. Finally, an overarching approach to theorising knowledge and curricula in RPL is proposed, using the metaphor 'knowing the borders and crossing the lines'. This metaphor broadens the remit of RPL to relate to theoretical enquiry at three interrelated levels: (1) within mainstream higher education curricula; (2) in terms of the nature of the knowledge(s) that candidates bring to RPL; (3) within RPL 'curricula'. It is argued that RPL practitioners need to understand (and operate at) all of these levels if their practices are to become more nuanced and more genuinely socially and epistemologically inclusive. Such understandings would help establish RPL as an arena of contemporary academic concern combining a clear theoretical rationale, the development of practices and the realisation of political and policy objectives.

Knowledge and curricula in the RPL literature

Knowledge issues

The literature is replete with assertions that RPL practices challenge formal definitions and ownership of knowledge. Yet, paradoxically, experiential learning and RPL theorists and practitioners are extremely cautious about entering the knowledge domain and seldom discuss disciplinary or formal knowledge. Although discussion of knowledge is conspicuous by its absence, it cannot be silenced, making oblique and implicit entrances into the literature from time to time, as the following sections outline.

Knowledge boundaries and knowledge transfer

One implicit position on knowledge is that there are *no differences* between various forms – such as between Heron's notions of experiential (practical and personal) knowledge and formal propositional knowledge (Burnard, 1988).[1] Butterworth (1992, p. 40) for example, asserts that RPL candidates 'have already acquired some of the skills, knowledge and understanding which a qualifying institution offers on a specific course'. A further, often implicit, position on knowledge in RPL is a 'soft boundary' approach, whereby any distinctions that might exist between forms of knowledge are consciously or unconsciously taken to be readily amenable to 'transfer' between contexts.[2] The basic argument is one of *similarity and continuity* between forms of knowledge. Mandell and Michelson (1990, p. 147) argue that there is a 'natural transition between previous experiential learning and new academic modes of thought', and between 'academic and nonacademic cultures of knowledge' (Michelson, 1998a, p. 42).

Other positions on knowledge are evident in the literature. Mandell and Michelson (1990, p. viii) argue that RPL is a site where different 'cultures of knowledge' meet, each with a different historically accorded authority (dominant or subjugated). Michelson (1998) positions RPL as a vehicle for recognising and therefore equalising epistemologically unequal cultures of authority, based on *difference*. Writing from a labour educator perspective, Spencer *et al.* (2000, p. 3) argue in a similar way that knowledges can be different on account of history, struggle and ideology. However, they do not recommend recognising this in the formal context via RPL:

> Most experiential learning is specific, related to a particular
> situation or problem adults are faced with, and does not easily
> translate into the kind of learning associated with academic
> courses. [. . . E]xperiential learning is not inferior to formal
> learning, it is different; there are times when it closely
> resembles academic learning but there are many occasions
> when it does not (Spencer *et al.*, 2000, p. 3).

Some of the RPL literature from South Africa takes a 'hard boundary' approach to knowledge. Breier (1997) argues that learning in an informal context will produce *different knowledge* from that in a formal context. Osman *et al.* (2000, p. 12) write about an RPL pilot which had as one of its research questions an assumption of knowledge difference, but relationship, in: 'How do experiential and academic learning articulate with each other?' Ralphs and Motala (2000) view both soft and hard boundary proponents from a critical distance. With regard to the former, they argue that there is little clarity in higher education as to what constitutes academic knowledge, and that propositional knowledge can relate both to academic learning and to particular fields of practice and experience. From a hard boundary perspective, they present an alternative argument, that it cannot be assumed that propositional knowledge is achieved through experiential learning, and that perhaps '[l]ife experience does not necessarily develop cognitive skills except under specific conditions' (Ralphs and Motala 2000, p. 5).

In my own work (Harris, 2000) I draw attention to relationships between different forms of knowledge context by context, arguing that in some educational sites academic knowledge and experiential knowledge may be closer than in others. This is similar to Fraser (1995) who argues that RPL is based on an unproblematised notion of learning transfer without questioning what and whose knowledge is likely to transfer in the most efficacious ways.

Knowledge 'matching'

The concept of 'matching' throws more light (obliquely) onto the knowledge issue. As RPL has become more credential-oriented, greater attention has been paid to this phenomenon. Candidates link their prior knowledge to external requirements emanating from standards, curricula outcomes, or from more embedded understandings.

There is a continuum of views about what matching means. Most of the literature suggests understandings of matching as 'equivalence' (of prior experiential knowledge and external requirements) in ways that imply identicality or similarity. Luedekke (1997, p. 217), in a final report on a three-year research project in Canada (exploring the viability of RPL), sees prior learning as needing to be 'consistent' with the institution's offerings. For Starr-Glass (2002, p. 3) the process of what he calls finding 'varying degrees of similarity' is a form of 'concurrent validity' which 'tends to make the practice of APL an exercise in mapping the familiar'.

At the other end of the 'matching' continuum are approaches that advocate that prior learning be assessed for its difference from external requirements. Here, equivalence would be seen as 'of equivalent value', not necessarily the same. These approaches tend to be aspirational rather than actual. Brennan and Williams (1998, p. 34) raise a challenge to define more creative 'boundaries or thresholds to mark the limits of acceptable diversity' in terms of the assessment of prior experiential knowledge. Michelson (1997, p. 43) is critical of the fact that prior experiential knowledge has to 'have some relationship to a branch of enquiry that exists somewhere in the academy'.

Table 3.1 Knowledge in the RPL literature

Position on knowledge	Position on knowledge boundaries
Same knowledge	Soft
Similar knowledge	Soft
Different knowledge	Hard
Different, subjugated and preferable knowledge	Change the boundary

Arguing from a feminist, situated knowledge and postmodernist perspective, she makes the case for all knowledge to be seen as a social product and as partial. This, she argues, extends an invitation to RPL to recognise divergent yet complementary knowledge from 'epistemologically unsanctioned lives' (Michelson, 1996, p. 649; see also Chapter 7, this volume). The above positions on knowledge are summarised in Table 3.1.

Curriculum issues

The literature suggests that RPL is much more common, and indeed successful, at a postgraduate, post-experience level (Cleary *et al.*, 2001; Lahiff, 1998; Butterworth *et al.*, 1993).[3] Various reasons for this are advanced.

One reason is that the curricular focus on specialist knowledge and skills at this level is close to the contextualised nature of learning from experience. A second and related reason is that postgraduate professional programmes foreground practice as the focus of theoretical work. Colyer and Hill (1998, p. 162–3), for example, describe mainstream courses in health care as giving 'equal weight to increasing and refining the theoretical and value base of practice, the experience of practice in diverse settings and the opportunity to develop higher level cognitive skills of evaluation and reflective judgment'.

A third, related, reason is that postgraduate professional programmes are frequently designed using the principles of 'reflective practitioner' (Schön, 1993) and 'reflection-in-action'. An example is the argument put forward by Butterworth *et al.* (1993, p. 2) for choosing to design an RPL process around a particular diploma, because course materials 'offer the model of the reflective practitioner and suggest self-review and analysis of learning outcomes as strategies to achieve this'.

At undergraduate level, the literature suggests much more caution about RPL (Trowler, 1996; Peters, 2000). This is further borne out by Cleary *et al.* (2001, p. 21): 'to date, there appears to have been difficulties in accommodating experiential learning into more formal and traditional types of learning, particularly at levels other than postgraduate study'. However, there is little exploration as to why this might be. If reasons are advanced, they usually centre on the recalcitrance of 'traditional' academics, rather than on the structure and organisation of knowledge.

Some of the RPL literature attempts to engage RPL practitioners in mainstream curriculum change. Most commonly, this change is conceptualised in technical and programmatic terms, such as the development of learning outcomes. For example, Evans (1987, p. 24) argues for 'looking at a syllabus, and turning it on its head. Instead of describing the ground to be covered in a course, it means thinking about a course in terms of asking what a student can do at the end of the course, given that that ground has been covered'.

Such a position does not go far enough for many proponents of RPL. Some of the South African RPL literature picks up most pointedly on relationships between curriculum, knowledge and power. According to Ralphs and Motala (2000, p. 4), it has been possible to ask particular kinds of questions in post-apartheid South Africa because, 'as a society in transition we have not collectively decided on what knowledge is important, how to determine the social and individual value of such knowledge, how such knowledge is to be assessed, who will be responsible for making such value judgments and other similar questions.' In a similar vein, Breier (1997) makes the point that the development of national unit standards in South Africa will have little effect on social inclusiveness and the success of RPL unless they embody the types of knowledge that characterise informal learning processes and non-dominant discourses and knowledges.

At the level of individual curricula, Michelson (1996, p. 648–9) argues that RPL practitioners could concern themselves with substantive change. She articulates the need for RPL practitioners to, 'institutionalize the refusal to privilege academic knowledge as less partial and less materially situated than that derived from other workplaces and social locations'.

A close reading of the RPL literature reveals that the relationship between RPL and mainstream curricula is a complex one, involving paradoxes and contradictions. I have argued (Harris, 2000) that RPL should not tie itself uncritically to practices that increase the utilitarianism and instrumentalism of education, at the expense of a broader critical or 'radical democratic' underpinning. In struggling to promote curricula that are more inclusive for adults generally and RPL candidates specifically, proponents of RPL seem to find themselves uncritically endorsing a weakening of the boundaries around formal knowledge. Taylor (1996, p. 293) suggests that RPL enthusiasts should consider (alongside the drive for flexibility and access) that at the current time, universities need to 'safeguard their independence, their disinterested research ethic, their role as independent commentators/critics, and their status as the guardians of high quality learning'. For him, this means that RPL processes need to be devised that do not undermine the 'continuing independence' of institutions or 'their professional integrity'. Moreover, many who claim a role for RPL in challenging the nature of curricula (and the forms of knowledge inscribed in them) seem to do so from a basis of aspiration. There is little empirical evidence to suggest that RPL has achieved its goals in this regard, except in institutional contexts that were already committed and oriented to the needs of adults.

Conclusions

The knowledge issue as debated (or not) in the RPL literature seems riddled with silences, paradoxes and contradictions. On the one hand, advocates of RPL claim that there are no differences between academic knowledge and experiential knowledge. On the other hand, the literature is replete with references to similarity and continuity between different forms of knowledge. The central assumption is that *even if* there are distinctions and differences between forms of knowledge these can be readily overcome because boundaries are soft and knowledge can and should transfer unproblematically between contexts (despite evidence that such boundary crossing is notoriously difficult within higher education). The paradox is that if there is no distinction to be made between prior experiential knowledge and formal knowledge, then transfer is not necessary, as the latter implies change and movement. However, if there *are* distinctions between forms of knowledge, then transfer (as change and movement) *is* an appropriate term. But then, if prior knowledge has to undergo change in order to be recognised, perhaps RPL is a less appropriate term?

In some quarters, there are very real concerns about conflating different forms of knowledge.[4] Rather than being self-evidently 'progressive', it is argued that the dismissal of differences between knowledges is harmful for learners and for knowledge production. Anzaldua (cited in Muller, 2000, p. 71) discusses the social cost of dispensing with knowledge differences. For her, the knowledge playing-field is *not* a level one, and those who declare that it is, run the risk that people will 'stub their toe especially severely on the reefs of social hierarchy which are not displaced but merely removed from view'. In terms of knowledge production, Young (2003, p. 11) argues that disciplinary knowledge has 'paradigmatic status as the basis for future knowledge'. As such there is a 'pedagogical [. . .] and epistemological price to pay for dispensing with such boundaries' (*ibid*, p. 3).

The curriculum issue in RPL is equally confused, with few theoretical tools to explore curricular possibilities. Again, the literature is more about rhetorical claims than reality. Shalem and Steinberg (Chapter 5, this volume) argue that many writers in the South African context (including myself, in their view) advocate curriculum change on the basis of a particular reading of 'conditions of possibility'. These they claim are derived from theoretical perspectives such as social constructionism and postmodernism rather than from actual conditions 'on the ground' in the institution. The posited conditions, they argue, do not exist. What is clear is that experiential learning theory has not provided RPL with a theory of knowledge or a curriculum language.

Conceptual resources to engage with knowledge and curricular issues

In this section I present and evaluate aspects of Bernstein's curriculum theory. His is a conventional sociological project following a cumulative path over four decades.[5] He built a single, increasingly elaborated conceptual framework offering resources for an analysis that can connect 'issues of face-to-face social construction of knowledge with issues of institutional location and structure, it must connect issues of discourse with a broader sociological analysis of the state, economy and social change' (Singh and Luke in Bernstein, 1996, p. xii). Bernstein's overriding concern was to analyse the internal workings of education practices in relation to the production, reproduction and transformation of culture through consciousness. The concepts reviewed below are those most pertinent to the knowledge and curricula questions in RPL.

Classification
Classification is a structuralist concept adapted from Durkheim.[6] It refers to the organisation of knowledge into curricula – more specifically, to the boundaries between knowledge and subjects (mathematics, sociology, physics, and so on). It is about the space between categories of knowledge; a space which stems the flow of discourse. Bernstein argues that this space or silence is preserved by power. Classification and associated stratifications and distributions of knowledge determine who gets access to what forms of knowledge. Where classification is strong, things are kept apart. This means that curriculum subjects are highly differentiated. In strong classifications the knowledge structure tends to be cumulative and based on increasingly abstract principles. Along with this is a specific and demarcated sense of identity – the physicist, for example. Weaker classifications are associated with 'progressive' education and with the blurring of boundaries between disciplinary knowledge bases.

When the strength of classification changes, power and control also change, and resistance frequently ensues:

> . . . changes in organisational practices, changes in discursive
> practices, changes in transmission practices, changes in psychic
> defences, changes in the concepts of the teacher, changes in
> concepts of the pupils, changes in the concepts of knowledge
> itself, and changes in the forms of expected pedagogic
> consciousness (Bernstein 1996, p. 29–30).

With regard to RPL, the concepts of strong and weak classification facilitate an analysis of mainstream curricular contexts and their particular modes of organisation and attendant power relations, including how accessible and responsive they are likely to be to initiatives such as RPL. It becomes clear why effecting curricular change in mainstream subject areas that are strongly classified meets greater resistance than change in more weakly classified areas.

Collection and integrated curriculum codes

A collection curriculum code is where contents are *closed* from each other, that is, strongly classified. It is the traditional, academic curriculum associated with disciplinary knowledge. In the integrated code, contents stand in *open* relationship to each other. The nature of the open relationship is such that the contents do not splinter into separate entities but are held together by a 'relational idea', '[i]ntegration, as it is used here, refers minimally to the *subordination* of previously insulated subjects *or* courses to some *relational* idea, which blurs the boundaries between the subjects' (Bernstein, 1971, p. 53).

In the *collection code* there are tight controls on the production of new knowledge and on what new knowledge enters the curriculum. Collection code can also drive the structuring of institutions, presenting as clearly demarcated and segmented subject tracks for teachers and an oligarchic management structure. Junior staff tend to operate and interact mainly vertically within their subject or departmental hierarchy. This consolidates strong subject loyalties. Because of the specificity of identities, there tend to 'be weak relations between staff with respect to pedagogic discourse' (Bernstein, 1996, p. 25). On the other hand, strong internal boundaries permit the co-existence of diverse ideological affiliations.

The *integrated code* makes sense in terms of what it is not: it is not collection code. The 'relational idea' is the mechanism for weakening traditional classificatory boundaries around subjects. The latter lose their significance as their content/knowledge is selectively restructured. As mentioned, this involves a shift 'from content closure to content openness'. In contrast to strong classifications (with a pedagogic movement to abstract principles), the pedagogic process in integrated code curricula starts with attention to the deep structure of the subject. Bernstein suggests that this leads to early 'exploration of *general* principles and the concepts through which these principles are obtained'. This entails an increased emphasis on 'how knowledge is created' in the intellectual domain (ways of knowing) rather than on the longer-term process of acquiring the states of knowledge themselves (Bernstein, 1996, p. 60–1).

The structuring of institutions becomes more visible (and vulnerable) in this curriculum code. Boundaries between inside and outside tend to be more permeable because communications flowing into the institution are less tightly controlled. Internally, these forms of knowledge organisation require greater horizontal communication – committees, working parties, curriculum groups and so on, often with learner involvement. Staff from different specialisms need to cooperate and communicate within shared tasks. Differences need to be integrated and networked rather than be a source of specialisation and separateness. It is claimed that the integrated code is more demanding of educators' time and ability and places both teacher and learner in different positions of accountability and discipline.

In terms of RPL, these concepts provide further resources for analysis of mainstream curricula by adding more vocabulary to classification. It becomes possible to link curriculum organisation and change with institutional modes of organisation, identities and authority structures. The concepts also offer resources with which to identify and theorise broad changes in education in the contemporary moment. Although the ways in which knowledge is organised in the integrated code make it *potentially* more suitable in contexts where the focus is on widening participation and RPL, cautionary issues are also raised, for example, that curriculum change needs to be undertaken in a judicious way, so as to balance the benefits of widening participation against drawbacks associated with the wholesale economisation of education. There is a danger of conflating different social projects. Moreover, it needs to be borne in mind that the integrated curriculum code is far more ambiguous in its knowledge structures and social relationships than the collection code.

Horizontal and vertical discourses and associated knowledge structures

Horizontal and vertical discourses are late additions to Bernstein's theoretical framework. They elaborate the sacred/profane dyad. A *horizontal discourse* is typified (analytically) as local, everyday, usually oral, segmentally organised, tacit, multi-layered, context-specific and context-dependent knowledge.[7] It is common-sense knowledge in so much as everyone (potentially) has access to it and in so far as it has a common history 'arising out of common problems of living and dying' (Bernstein, 1999, p. 159). Horizontal discourses are therefore culture- or context-embedded (within families, peer groups, communities or workplaces, for example – and so, often highly affective). They require the specificities of the particular context (practices and relationships, for example) in order to be activated and realised. Where such specificities are absent, or cannot be 'unproblematically read', the 'competence/literacy' associated with the discourse may not be able to be demonstrated (Bernstein, 1996, p. 179). Although the competences/literacies are localised, they are not inflexible and there are variations in 'correct' strategies.

Horizontal discourses are acquired tacitly in equally context-specific and segmented ways, through local activities such as exemplar modelling. Bernstein argues that in horizontal discourses knowledge circulates beyond its immediate context through individual 'repertoires' and group 'reservoirs'. In circumstances where there is free-flowing contact, both can be increased, and exchanges between the two can take place. Conversely, the isolation of individuals and/or groups will restrict the flow of discourse and limit exchange and development. There is a mutually reinforcing relationship between social relations and horizontal discourse: Bernstein sees social relationships as generating the discourse but also, the discourse strengthening social relations and encouraging 'forms of social solidarity' (Bernstein, 1999, p. 160). It is hardly surprising, therefore, that horizontal discourse becomes a resource for popular social movements concerned to empower those who experience themselves as silenced and excluded by vertical discourses. As such, the validation of horizontal discourse links to the aims and objectives of some experiential learning and RPL practices.

Vertical discourses originate from and develop within formal institutions. The oft-cited definition is as follows:

> A vertical discourse takes the form of a coherent, explicit,
> systematically principled structure, hierarchically organised, *or*
> it takes the form of a series of specialised languages with
> specialised modes of interrogation and specialised criteria for
> the production of texts. (Bernstein, 1996, p. 171)

This is the antithesis of the analytical construct of horizontal discourse. Importantly, there is no localisation and no segmentation – instead, specialised symbolic assemblages of knowledge are integrated at the level of meaning rather than in terms of relationships between segments. These assemblages are created through 'recontextualisation' rather than through segmentation. Recontextualisation involves the movement of discourses from a context of production to a context of transmission. Vertical discourses are therefore created and circulated to different groups and individuals by *formal* pedagogic means (mainly). They do have a social context, but not the embedded one of horizontal discourse. They circulate through explicit recontextualisation and ongoing evaluation. The two analytical discourses are summarised in Table 3.2.

Table 3.2 Vertical and horizontal discourse (adapted from Bernstein, 1999)

	Vertical discourse	Horizontal discourse
Practice	Official/institutional	Local
Distributive principle	Recontextualisation	Segmentation
Social relation	Individual	Communal

Associated knowledge structures

Bernstein makes a very important set of distinctions within vertical discourse – by way of two knowledge structures. The most vertical and the easiest to understand is the *hierarchical knowledge structure*. The natural sciences are the best example of this. Usually characterised by the collection curriculum code, the development of knowledge in this structure is cumulative – towards 'more and more general propositions which integrate knowledge at lower levels and across an expanding range of apparently different phenomena' (Bernstein, 1996, p. 173). Knowledge bases develop through opposition between theories with (usually post-positivist) attempts to refute new knowledge/theories and 'to incorporate them into more general propositions' (Bernstein, 1999, p. 163).

The second knowledge structure within vertical discourse is the *horizontal knowledge structure*. Such structures are usually motivated by the integrated code (or a weak collection code). They are most frequently found in the knowledge structures of the social and human sciences. According to

Bernstein, they do not give rise to hierarchical and cumulative structures, but 'instead, to a series of specialised languages, each with its own specialised modes of interrogation and specialised criteria':

> . . . a series of expanding non-translatable, specialised languages
> with non-comparable principles of description based on
> different, often opposed, assumptions. [. . .] Horizontal
> knowledge structures develop by *addition* of another specialised
> language. (Bernstein, 1996, p. 173)

What counts as knowledge 'development', then, is the addition of another language, often characterised by a new 'speaker' or theorist. A new language offers:

> . . . the possibility of a fresh perspective, a new set of questions,
> a new set of theories, and an apparently new problematic, and
> most importantly, a new set of speakers [. . .] used to challenge
> the hegemony and legitimacy of more senior speakers.
> (Bernstein, 1999, p. 163)

These two knowledge structures are summarised in Table 3.3. A central difference between hierarchical and horizontal structures is the degree of hierarchical, integrative and cumulative principles. Yet, horizontal knowledge structures can also vary according to *grammar*. Strong grammars are 'based on explicit, formally articulated concepts, relations and procedures, as in economics and linguistics' (*ibid*, 1999, p. 174). These are capable of generating '. . . "relatively" precise empirical descriptions and/or of generating formal modelling of empirical relations'. In weak grammars, 'concepts, relations and procedures are much less formally articulated as in sociology and social anthropology' (Bernstein, 1996, p. 174). Whilst hierarchical knowledge structures invariably have very strong grammars, horizontal knowledge structures can have strong(ish) or weak grammars.[8]

Whilst horizontal knowledge structures appear to be more porous to initiatives such as widening participation and RPL, according to Bernstein they create problems for learners. In hierarchical knowledge structures, exceptionally strong *grammars* mean that learners can 'recognise' the language of the subject (physics, for example) and can also 'realise' the language more easily (that is, produce appropriate texts). Moreover, the knowledge structure tends not to change – the explanatory and descriptive powers simply extend.[9] Conversely, in horizontal knowledge structures like the social

Table 3.3 Knowledge structures within vertical discourse

Hierarchical knowledge structures	Horizontal knowledge structures
Collection curriculum code	Integrated curriculum code (or weak collection code)
Cumulative, integrative movement to general propositions	Addition of specialised languages
Strong grammars for explanatory power	Strong(ish) or weak grammar – more perspectival

sciences, learning can be difficult, the grammar is weak and learners often find it difficult to recognise and realise appropriate discourse. In these conditions, it is likely that theorists' names will be useful resources for signalling an appropriate language. As a result, according to Bernstein (1999, p. 164), 'managing names and languages together with their criticisms becomes both the manner of transmission and acquisition'.

Another feature of horizontal knowledge structures that renders them potentially tricky for non-traditional learners is that pedagogy involves 'recontextualisation via perspective'. This means that the teacher chooses a style and a lens to teach through, which are often tacit and invisible to the learner. Bernstein cites the example of sociology:

> At the level of the acquirer [the learner], this invisible perspective [. . .] is expected to become how the acquirer reads, evaluates and creates texts. A 'gaze' has to be acquired, i.e. a particular mode of recognizing and realizing what counts as an 'authentic' sociological reality. (ibid, p. 164–5)

The learner's job is to acquire the teacher's gaze. Once acquired, it becomes equally 'invisibly active' but enables the learner to 'look at (recognise) and regard, and evaluate (realise) the phenomena of legitimate concern' (ibid, 1999, p.171–2, footnote 8). It is the tacit nature of this process that has the potential to create problems for non-traditional students who have not been 'schooled' in the discipline.

However, in terms of curricular accessibility for such students, horizontal knowledge structures *do* share some features with horizontal discourse that hierarchical knowledge structures do not. They share serial and segmental structuring. Furthermore, both have *'potentially* volatile contents' (Bernstein, 1996, p. 178), meaning that their boundaries are relatively porous to additions and omissions. They also share tacit modes of acquisition. Horizontal discourse can also be said to share the 'gaze' as a way of acquiring particular cultural realities. Some useful and interesting examples of these overlaps are given. For example, Bernstein (1996) argues that some horizontal knowledge structures appropriate (recontextualise) resources from horizontal discourse:

> In History we have seen the development of oral history, in
> English the incorporation of popular media and narrative, in
> Sociology the rise of ethnography, in Feminist Studies (and to
> some extent in Black Studies) experiential/confessional
> narratives have been given the status of methodology, whilst
> Cultural Studies, virtually a postmodern collection code, takes
> as its data (but not exclusively so) the fashions, foibles and
> spectacles drawn from HD [horizontal discourse]. The internal
> structure of HKS [horizontal knowledge structures] creates the
> potential for such recontextualising . . .

These shared features and overlaps can be seen as favourable to initiatives such as RPL. However, the danger, according to Bernstein, is that because of some very fundamental incompatibilities, recontextualisation does not necessarily lead to more effective learning and progress: '[a] segmental competence, or segmental literacy, acquired through horizontal discourse, may not be activated in its official recontextualising as part of a vertical discourse, for space, time, disposition, social relation and relevance have all changed' (Bernstein, 1999, p. 169). What Bernstein is suggesting is that, despite similarities, there are discontinuities in some areas. When segments of horizontal discourse become subject to the rules of the formal context, learners (or RPL candidates) do not necessarily know why or how this has happened, and are no better off as a result (they do not understand the recontextualisation process). Furthermore, in the process of delocation and relocation, the social basis of horizontal discourse (including its power relations) is removed. This reduces the latter's efficacy as an active force against domination.

I have tried to show some of the implications of horizontal and vertical discourse for RPL. Importantly, these concepts provide resources for more nuanced analysis of mainstream curricula suggesting that RPL will be different under horizontal and hierarchical knowledge structures. This is because there are likely to be more similarities between horizontal knowledge structures and horizontal discourse.[10] Although horizontal discourses provide 'hooks' into vertical discourse, certain things need to change to enable successful incorporation of the former into the latter. The process is further complexified because horizontal knowledge structures are more invisible and tacit than hierarchical knowledge structures. This suggests that in the context of horizontal knowledge structures RPL might involve explicit recontextualising and theorising of horizontal discourses, prefiguring, therefore, particular kinds of formal teaching. These ideas will be developed in forthcoming parts of the chapter.

Using the concepts in empirical research

I used all of the above concepts to support an analysis of the process of designing and implementing an RPL pilot in a university department in South Africa: a process that I had been involved in myself as a facilitator (Harris, 2004). The RPL pilot aimed to access a cohort of experienced adult educators without degrees, to a two-year, part-time postgraduate advanced diploma for educators of adults. The concepts enabled me to draw conclusions about knowledge and curricula – at each of three interrelated levels.

Within mainstream higher education curricula

On the basis of analysis, I argued (Harris, 2004) that the diploma in question could be seen as a horizontal knowledge structure with a relatively strong grammar and relatively strong classification of knowledge.[11] In a context of intense political change, the diploma's social project at that time was the reconstruction of the role of adult educator through building a cadre of critically transformative intellectuals. The course was grounded in the importance of social location, theory, critique and critical rationality in order to understand and explain various forms of constraint and from there to understand the complex terms and conditions of agency that in turn translate into theoretically and analytically informed educator practice. As a horizontal knowledge structure, it drew on the specialised languages that make up the knowledge structure of education as a curriculum subject – the sociology of education, the philosophy of education, curriculum theory, cultural theory, discourse theory and so on. It was a relatively cognitive and inductive professionalising course.

The course opened by way of two formal modules – lecture- and reading-based. The first was called 'Social Theory' and the second 'Discourses of Learning'. These modules provided the main specialising languages – the general theory of the course. I argued (Harris, 2004) that the character of the diploma, its specialised languages and its strong(ish) grammar rendered it more strongly classified overall than is usual in such programmes. In its formal parts, it was structured so as not to let too much outside knowledge over its boundaries. As discussed, horizontal knowledge structures are usually associated with the integrated curricula code. On the strength of analysis, I claimed that although this was indeed the case, the diploma and the department as a whole (in terms of its internal organisation and so on) were motivated by the collection code, as far as was possible. An example of a collection code characteristic in the diploma pedagogy was a reluctance to teach the deep structure of the subject, relaying on more tacit processes of longer-term acquisition. As such, the course was relatively hard to access, epistemologically. There seemed to be different and competing social projects at work – the social project of the diploma and the social project of widening participation through RPL.

Within RPL curricula

The discrete RPL 'curriculum' or programme that was developed in order to access students to the diploma was essentially a horizontal knowledge structure with a weak grammar modelled on our *a priori* understandings of the diploma curriculum.[12] Materials for RPL were recontextualised for their potential to speak, in some way, to the diploma curriculum. On analysis (Harris, 2004), each of the texts or materials used carried messages, and modelled or brokered implicit and 'ideal-type' candidate positions.

Two recontextualising principles, of which (as facilitators) we were not fully aware, were increasingly at work during the design and implementation of the RPL process. I characterised this as a form of academic drift. First, *practitioner knowledge was to be delimited and distanced* – valued, but only up to a point. Secondly, *a range of academic practices and standpoints were important*: it was these that would count. In the end, and unbeknownst to us as facilitators, the 'gaze' of RPL required candidates to be critically reflective on themselves, and their practice, in a very particular and complex way: the way of the diploma (Harris, 2004).

Areas of prior knowledge that fell outside of this 'gaze' did not count, indeed were often not seen. I argued that all of the RPL activities 'invited' candidates to reflect/model the 'gaze' back to us. That was what counted as 'success'.

Indeed, this was confirmed by the formal assessment of portfolios in the university department. The pedagogic discourse of the diploma became the evaluative discourse of RPL.

In terms of the nature of the knowledge(s) that candidates bring to RPL

I analysed (Harris, 2004) contiguities, congruences, continuities, distances, divergences and ruptures between prior experiential knowledge and the RPL curricular 'gaze' in order to explore what prior knowledge patterns correlated with 'success' (or otherwise) in this context.

Life-work-education background had prepared particular individuals in different ways for taking up the role of RPL candidate. Successful candidates had acquired the horizontal knowledge structure of the diploma (as exemplified in the RPL curriculum) by dint of four 'prior affordances' (concept adapted from Billett, 2001): proximity to vertical discourse, being 'schooled' in reflective practice, a clear pedagogic identity as an educator, and a well-developed learner identity. For example, the candidates surveyed had had varying degrees of proximity to vertical discourse and this did not always derive from formal schooling but from the 'pedagogisation' of everyday life through political struggle or from exposure to texts and literacy with a history of critique based on textual deconstruction. For the most successful candidates in this pilot, reflection was highly naturalised, especially intro-spective and personal styles of reflection. The most efficacious affordances regarding pedagogic identity as an educator were gleaned from non-formal educator practice at a grass-roots, community-focused level, particularly if that involved a range of roles such as policy development and critique, research, evaluation and curriculum development. Prior learner identities characterised by early experiences of apprenticeship chimed with the RPL gaze. Conversely, candidates with knowledge bases such as business admini-stration and management, those with a predominantly oral background, and those without a textual, introspective experience of reflection were disadvantaged by this particular RPL process.

In summary, Bernstein's conceptual framework led me to claim that the RPL case in question had a hidden curriculum which rewarded particular ways of thinking and acting. It confirmed prior experiential knowledge that was similar to that valued in the context and in so doing brought the former under the rule of the latter. Much of this academic drift was unconscious. It also brought to the fore the issue of competing 'progressive' projects – the social project of the diploma course and the social project of RPL.

The usefulness of Bernstein's conceptual resources

In appraising Bernstein's oeuvre, account needs to be taken of the critiques of his positioning and ideas. Many of these apply to his earlier rather than later work. The locus of critique seems to be his structuralism. This has consequences at several levels and in several ways. First is a tendency towards reproductionism and determinism and a perceived lack of agency. Bernstein's response to these criticisms is that it is necessary to understand reproductive tendencies (constraints) in order to envisage alternatives. Atkinson (1985) makes the case that Bernstein offers conceptual tools with which to diagnose the complexity of social relations (including their reproductive tendencies and discrepancies) as a basis for intervention and change, not more reproduction.

Dualisms, binaries and dyads come in for criticism as instantiations of Descartes' modernist distinctions. Such criticisms revolve largely around perceptions of implicit hierarchies and preferences in Bernstein's dyads, and his lack of attention to relationships between polarities. For example, commentators have associated horizontal discourses with a disparaging view of informal knowledges. This was certainly not Durkheim's original perspective. Others argue (and I would agree) that these views represent an erroneous reading and deployment of Bernstein's work: the dyads are not empirical categories but analytical ones, developed precisely to facilitate the analysis of inter-relationships which they are criticised for impeding. Atkinson (1985, p. 31) maintains that, 'the categories are not intended to represent self-contained entities, nor is the model a static one. It is apparent, indeed, that the analysis is intended to capture a process of transformation and change'.

A persistent set of criticisms relates to Bernstein's early work and accusations of working-class deficit. The result, according to Davies (1995, p. 41), is that the idea of deficit became powerfully lodged in the lexicon of a wide range of educationists, often at the level of catchphrase or cliché. In some instances, Bernstein's work has been seen as a justification for the inevitability of deficit. Bernstein argues that his position could not have been further from that, in that his concern was to provide an explanation for unequal performance not a defence of it. My own view is that Bernstein presents his work in ways that make these kinds of misreadings possible.

Finally, Bernstein's 'hard boundary' view of knowledge is not popular in some quarters. Bernstein is critical of a so-called 'progressive' weakening of knowledge boundaries that relies on a parallel denigration of strongly classified knowledge. His concern is with the social arrangements and practices that keep things apart (rather than the forces that bring them together) which 'in turn create[s] categories of the included and the excluded' (Bernstein and Solomon, 1999, p. 273).

Set against these provisos are the advantages of this framework. It offers a generative conceptual and analytical language far beyond that afforded by experiential learning theory. It also foregrounds powerfully the ways in which RPL is about much more than physical access: the embracing of knowledge and curriculum as central to RPL engages a wider set of concerns to do with organisational structures, principles of social organisation, social relations, professional identities, power, control and consciousness. For these reasons I would argue that Bernstein's work is worthy of attention in debates around theorising RPL.

Knowing the borders and crossing the lines

On the strength of the above-mentioned research (Harris, 2004), I proposed an approach to RPL that links Bernstein's concepts to the hard and soft boundary metaphor: one that 'knows the border and crosses the line' (Anzaldua, cited in Muller, 2000, p. 71). I rephrased this 'know the *borders* and cross the *lines*', to emphasise that there are multiple borders. I see 'knowing the borders' in terms of both hard *and* soft boundary theories, thereby avoiding 'boundary wars'. My position is that some knowledge boundaries are harder/softer than others and some RPL candidates' prior experiential knowledge is more or less vertical than others. The metaphor can be inserted into Table 3.1 to form Table 3.4.[13]

Table 3.4 Knowing the borders and crossing the lines

Position on knowledge	Position on knowledge boundaries
'Know the borders'	*Soft or hard depending on prior experiential knowledge and receiving curriculum conditions*
Same knowledge	Soft
Similar knowledge	Soft
Different	Hard
Different, subjugated and preferable knowledge	Change the boundary

The final step in this chapter is to relate 'knowing the borders' to the above-mentioned three levels of analysis to generate some pertinent lines of enquiry for RPL. The levels have been re-ordered to take account of the prospective character of future analysis.

Within mainstream higher education curricula

Designers and implementers of RPL could develop the means to become theoretically aware of the gaze/discourse of mainstream curricular contexts within which RPL candidates have to operate if they are to be successful in the longer term. Different curricular logics could be described and explained. Findings at the level of individual programmes could be aggregated into broader categories, such as differences between undergraduate and postgraduate programmes in particular cognate areas.

If RPL is to be conceptualised as a two-way bridge between existing main-stream curricula and non-traditional students, it is likely that the former will need to move in the direction of integrated code, although this is not without problems as discussed earlier in the chapter. A key question seems to be: Under what mainstream curricular conditions would RPL (and individual RPL candidates) succeed best? A corollary question is: Is there an epistemological price to be paid for the political project of widening participation? How are both imperatives to be balanced?

In terms of the nature of the knowledge(s) that candidates bring to RPL

Analysis of congruences and divergences between prior experiential knowledge (for example, various types of practitioner role and practice, sites of practice, knowledge bases) and curricula 'gazes', provides a basis for understanding patterns of prior knowledge that correlate with 'success' (or otherwise) in specific contexts. This could strengthen what Starr-Glass (2002) calls the 'predictive validity' of RPL, by focusing on potential and 'a much broader correlation between the ways in which knowledge is acquired, processed and utilised by those who prove, in the long term, to be successful or well-adapted in academic or vocational terms' (Starr-Glass, 2002, p. 223). What is implied here is the need for retrospective research on 'successful' RPL candidates in order to build an evidence base.

Within RPL curricula

On the basis of analysis at the above two levels, curricula and programmes for RPL should come into focus. Where candidates' prior knowledge is close to the curricular conditions of the receiving context, then such candidates will perhaps only need opportunities to practise, confirm, and develop confidence. This could involve working with recontextualised mainstream curriculum texts. Where there is a distance between candidates' prior knowledge and the receiving curricular 'gaze' then candidates will need more formal induction.

Conclusion

The ability to identify, describe and analyse at each of the above levels seems important to the development of a theoretical understanding of RPL (and widening participation more generally). Such an understanding could help identify spaces for change within mainstream curricula; focused and explicit interventions for particular candidates (rather then the many one-size-fits-all models currently in use); and more conscious, alternative and contextually appropriate curricular logics and possibilities for RPL programmes. It could perhaps locate RPL as a site for diagnostic and explanatory research, and for the 'reflexive monitoring of the process of epistemological exclusion and admission' (Millar, 1996). This would help establish RPL as an arena of contemporary academic concern combining a clear theoretical rationale, the development of practices and the realisation of political and policy objectives.

References

Atkinson, P. (1985), *Language, Structure and Reproduction: An Introduction to the Sociology of Basil Bernstein*, London: Methuen.

Bensusan, D. (ed.) (1997), *Whither the University*, Cape Town: Juta.

Bernstein, B. (1971), 'On the classification and framing of educational knowledge' in Young, M. (ed.) *Knowledge and Control: New Directions for the Sociology of Education*, London: Collier Macmillan.

Bernstein, B. (1996), *Pedagogy, Symbolic Control and Identity: Theory, Research, Critique*, London: Taylor and Francis.

Bernstein, B. (1999), 'Vertical and horizontal discourse: An essay', *British Journal of Sociology of Education*, 20(2): 157–73.

Bernstein, B. and Solomon, J. (1999), 'Pedagogy, identity and the construction of a theory of symbolic control: Basil Bernstein questioned by Joseph Solomon', *British Journal of Sociology of Education*, 20(2): 265–79.

Billett, S. (2001), 'Coparticipation at work: Affordance and engagement' in Fenwick, T. (ed.) *Sociocultural perspectives on learning through work*, New Directions in Adult and Continuing Education Vol. 92, San Francisco: Jossey Bass/Wiley.

Breier, M. (1997), 'Whose learning? Whose knowledge? Recognition of prior learning and the National Qualifications Framework' in Bensusan, D. (ed.) (1997), *Whither the University*, Cape Town: Juta.

Brennan, L. and Williams, S. (1998), 'Awards and rewards: APEL in the context of post-graduate and post-experience programmes' in Crocker, D. *et al.* (eds) (1998), *APEL Beyond Graduateness*, Norwich: SEEC.

Burnard, P. (1988), 'Experiential learning: some theoretical considerations', *International Journal of Lifelong Education*, 7(2): 127–33.

Butterworth, C. (1992), 'More than one bite at the APEL: contrasting models of accrediting prior learning', *Journal of Further and Higher Education*, 16(3): 39–51.

Butterworth, C., Edwards, R. and Raggat, P. (1993), 'Making experience count: accrediting your prior learning – an evaluation of the APL project in the School of Education', Internal document, Open University.

Cleary, P., Whittaker, R., Gallacher, J., Merrill, B., Jokinen, L. and Carette, M. (2002), *Social Inclusion through APEL: The Learners' Perspective*, Comparative Report, European Commission: Socrates-Grundtvig Project, Centre for Research in Lifelong Learning, Glasgow Caledonian University.

Colyer, H. and Hill, Y. (1998), 'Use of APEL in a post-registration health and social care M.Sc. programme' in Crocker *et al.* (eds.), *APEL Beyond Graduateness*, Norwich: SEEC.

Crocker, D., Ellis, D., Hill, Y., Storan, J. and Turner, I. (eds) (1998), *APEL Beyond Graduateness*, Norwich: SEEC.

Davies, B. (1995), 'Bernstein, Durkheim, and the British Sociology of Education' in Sadovnik, A. (ed.), *Knowledge and Pedagogy: The Sociology of Basil Bernstein*, Norwood, NJ: Ablex Publishing Corporation.

Evans, N. (1987), *Assessing Experiential Learning: A Review of Progress and Practice*, London: Longman for FEU publications.

Fraser, W. (1995), 'Making experience count . . . towards what?' in Mayo, M. and Thompson, J. (eds) *Adult Learning, Critical Intelligence and Social Change*, Leicester: NIACE.

Harris, J. (2000), *Recognition of Prior Learning: Power, Pedagogy and Possibility*, Pretoria: HSRC.

Harris, J. (2004), 'The hidden curriculum of the Recognition of Prior Learning: a case study', PhD Thesis, Open University.

Lahiff, A. (1998), 'APEL for post-compulsory education and training (PCET) practitioners' in Crocker *et al.*, *APEL Beyond Graduateness*, Norwich: SEEC.

Lueddeke, G. (1997), 'The accreditation of prior experiential learning in higher education: a discourse on rationales and assumptions', *Higher Education Quarterly*, 51(3): 210–24.

Mandell, A. and Michelson, E. (1990), *Portfolio Development and Adult Learning: Purposes and Strategies*, Chicago: CAEL.

Mayo, M. and Thompson, J. (eds) (1995), *Adult Learning, Critical Intellegence and Social Change,* Leicester: NIACE.

Michelson, E. (1996), '"Auctoritee" and "experience": Feminist epistemology and the assessment of experiential learning', *Feminist Studies*, 22(3): 627–55.

Michelson, E. (1997), 'Multicultural approaches to portfolio development' in Rose, A. and Leahy, M. (eds), *Assessing Adult Learning in Diverse Settings: Current Issues and Approaches*, New Directions for Adult and Continuing Education.

Michelson, E. (1998), 'Re-membering: the return of the body to experiential learning', *Studies in Continuing Education*, 20(2): 217–31.

Millar, C. (1996), 'The experiential learning project: "if we just had a story"', Paper presented at the 5th ICEL conference, Cape Town, South Africa, July.

Muller, J. (2000), *Reclaiming Knowledge: Social Theory, Curriculum and Education Policy*, London: Routledge Falmer.

Osman, R., Shalem, Y., Castle, J. and Attwood, G. (2000), 'The recognition of prior learning: early lessons, challenges and promise', Paper presented at the Joint Education Trust conference, Midrand, South Africa.

Peters, H. (2000), *Report on Research into the Recognition of Prior Learning at the University of Cape Town*, University of Cape Town, June.

Ralphs, A. and Motala, E. (2000), 'Towards an RPL strategy for 2000–2005: a work in progress', Working document, Johannesburg: Joint Education Trust.

Rose, A. and Leahy, M. (eds) (1997), *Assessing Adult Learning in Diverse Settings: Current Issues and Approaches*, New Directions for Adult and Continuing Education, San Francisco: Jossey-Bass.

Sadovnik, A. (ed.) (1995), *Knowledge and Pedagogy: The Sociology of Basil Bernstein*, Norwood, New Jersey: Ablex Publishing Corporation.

Schön, D. (1993), *The Reflective Practitioner*, New York: Basic Books.

Singh, P. and Luke, A. (1996), 'Series editor's preface' in Bernstein, B., *Pedagogy, Symbolic Control and Identity: Theory, Research, Critique*, London: Taylor and Francis.

Spencer, B., Briton, D. and Gereluk, W. (2000), 'Crediting adult learning', Unpublished paper, Athabasca University, Canada.

Starr-Glass, P (2002), 'Metaphor and totem: exploring and evaluating prior experiential learning', *Assessment and Evaluation in Higher Education*, 27(3): 222–31.

Taylor, T. (1996), 'Learning from experience: Recognition of Prior Learning (RPL) and professional development for teachers', *Asia-Pacific Journal of Teacher Education*, 24(3): 281–93.

Trowler, P. (1996), 'Angels in marble? Accrediting prior experiential learning in higher education', *Studies in Higher Education*, 21(1): 17–30.

Young, M. (ed.) (1971), *Knowledge and Control: New Directions for the Sociology of Education*, London: Collier Macmillan.

Young, M. (2003), 'Durkheim, Vygotsky and the curriculum of the future', *London Review of Education*, 1(2): 100–17.

Notes

[1] I use the term (prior experiential) knowledge rather than (prior) learning or (prior) experience. I reserve the term 'learning' for processes and activities that generate knowledge.

[2] See Muller (2000) and Young (2003) for writings about hard and soft knowledge boundaries.

[3] This is certainly the case in the UK.

[4] The origins of these concerns undoubtedly lie in Durkheim's analyses of the medieval Trivium and Quadrivium and the 'sacred' and 'profane' and his efforts to reconcile individualism and solidarity in modern societies. The profane refers to practical and immediate responses to everyday exigencies, without which living would be impossible. The sacred is more collective, religious, shared and social, enabling people to make connections between unrelated events and to transcend the specificities of everyday life. For Durkheim, what were important were the *structural differences* between forms of knowledge, not any sense of superiority of one over another. It is interesting to note the difference between French readings of Durkheim's work and Ango-Saxon ones. In the former, Durkheim is seen as a forerunner of French structuralism, whereas in the latter he is viewed as functionalist and conservative.

[5] He is a controversial figure for reasons that will be discussed later in the chapter.

[6] Bernstein was inspired by Durkheim. He introduces power and a social basis to Durkheim's concepts of sacred and profane knowledge and deploys them as the basis for an analysis of types of curriculum knowledge, arguing that the former provided the historical basis for disciplinary knowledge.

[7] '[W]ithout integrations of meanings or co-ordinating principles' (Bernstein, 1999, p. 160).

[8] Strength and weakness must be seen as relative within horizontal knowledge structures.

[9] Except in times of paradigm shift.

[10] This is not to suggest that RPL candidates' knowledge is horizontal discourse. As my research has shown (Harris, 2004), the contrary is frequently the case and the relationships between the two are complex. Bernstein holds that vertical discourse can be acquired informally through particular mentorship relationships, for example. However, some prior experiential knowledge will inevitably be horizontal.

[11] Relative to similar courses in other institutions.

[12] The use of the term RPL 'curriculum' would be anathema in many RPL contexts. Here it signified the fact that there was a programme, textual materials, activities, and so on. Because of the nature of the diploma curriculum, I argued that this particular RPL curriculum recontextualised fewer resources from horizontal discourse than is the case in most RPL processes.

[13] This figure only shows 'knowing the borders'. 'Crossing the lines' is more of a pedagogic concern, not dealt with in this chapter.

chapter four

A disciplinary-specific approach to the recognition of prior informal experience in adult pedagogy: 'rpl' as opposed to 'RPL'[1]

Mignonne Breier

Scenario A

The setting is a large university lecture hall. It is early evening and a class of about 38 adults are listening to a lecture on the law that revolutionised worker-employer relations after South Africa's transition to democratic rule in 1994 – the Labour Relations Act [LRA] of 1995. The lecture is part of an 11-week part-time programme offered by the Law Faculty of a university which I shall call University A and the focus tonight is on the dispute resolution body established in terms of the LRA, called the Centre for Conciliation, Mediation and Arbitration [CCMA], and its powers in relation to conciliation. Lecturer A is a labour lawyer and part-time commissioner in the CCMA. Among the class are factory workers, community organisers, self-employed consultants, teachers, an attorney, two full-time students and one unemployed artisan. All but 14 have trade union affiliations: two are full-time unionists, three are shop stewards, five are members of executive committees. It is a certificate course, which means it is not credit-bearing within the university, and has virtually open admission criteria. The convenors of Course A are committed to providing educational opportunities for adults with experience of labour law but limited formal qualifications, and have admitted students with less than matric (the school-leaving certificate after 12 years' schooling), even students with less than Grade 10 (10 years' schooling), if they have practical experience of labour law. Matric is usually the minimum requirement for study at a university in South Africa. The rest of the students have a vast range of formal educational qualifications – from matric to a master's degree in law from Oxford University in the UK.

The class tonight is marked by repeated interruptions by the students. Lecturer A is stating general laws and procedures relating to conciliation and the students have many queries from their own experience. One student, a woman in her late thirties who was previously a shop steward and is now a full-time social science student at University A, tries to tell of her own experience of a CCMA case which contradicts one of the general rules which the lecturers has provided. Lecturer A encourages her to tell her personal narrative but her responses are hesitant and he is impatient. He exhorts her to adhere to the general rule, says that he personally has had occasion to act in accordance with the general rule and there have been other cases like his. For her purposes, he concludes, she should merely 'apply the general rule'.

Lecturer A:	Only disputes that have been referred, only disputes that came into operation after the 11th of November 1996 can be dealt with by the CCMA. All disputes that arose prior to the 11th November 1996 need to be dealt with in terms of the old provisions.
Student A:	It depends why you are dealing with this.
Lecture A:	Okay, you tell me why, give me an example.
Student A:	An incident that happened prior to the 11th November.
Lecturer A:	Like what? Dismissal?
Student A:	Unfair labour practice that occurred prior to that and then the institution has the recognition agreement.
Lecturer A:	Yes.
Student A:	Right. They [inaudible words] procedure within certain time frame, right, according to the recognition agreement, with the result time has

lapsed, okay, right, the case is still pending, there is still a case hanging, now, after 11th November 1996, the case landed up at the CCMA but it happened prior to the 11th November. Those circumstances couldn't.

Lecturer A: Well, it's very difficult to talk about the specifics of that in the absence of the specific circumstances. The general rule is, let's just say there might be very, very, very particular circumstances, the general rule, and again I would like to suggest for your purposes – apply the general rule. The general rule is that any dispute that arose before the 11th November 1996 can't be dealt with in terms of the dispute resolution procedures in the Act. There might be very extreme and particular circumstances, but I've had occasion to dismiss a dispute because it arose prior to the 11th November 1996 and there're [stutter] a whole host of disputes that were dealt with on that basis, and by and large they are unfair labour practice disputes because now there is no chance of you getting an unfair dismissal dispute condoned, to have it heard now when it arose before the 11th of November.

Scenario B

The setting is a large lecture hall at another university on the other side of town. Lecturer B, another labour lawyer who is also a part-time commissioner at the CCMA, is talking about grounds for dismissal. The course is a post-graduate diploma in Labour Law and the 64 students include attorneys, academics, staff of the CCMA and of industry bargaining councils, government officials, labour relations consultants, full-time students who have recently completed law degrees and full-time trade unionists. The minimum requirement for admission to a course at this level is usually a degree, but the course convenors, like those of Course A, recognise that there are many adults with extensive experience of labour law, but limited formal qualifications, who might benefit from a course like this. For this reason they have admitted 10 students with matric only. Among them are five trade unionists.

In the exchange below, Student B, an attorney, wants to know whether one can dismiss a worker on grounds of incompatibility, which is not specified in the Act. Lecturer B states that there are only three grounds for dismissal. They do not include incompatibility but this does not mean that the courts do not allow dismissals on these grounds. They just 'fudge' the issue, he says, and he explains further how the courts 'get around these things':

Student B: [first name of lecturer] just because you can't put something in a category, that doesn't exclude you from dismissing someone for incompatibility? Because you can't, because it doesn't fit a category, does it mean it doesn't exist as a ground?

Lecturer B: Do you mean incompatibility? Because it is not listed in the Act?

Student B: Ja, does it mean you can't dismiss him?[2]

Lecturer B: My understanding is that you can only dismiss on three grounds: it's misconduct, incapacity, operational (requirements).

Student B: [Inaudible].

Lecturer B: That's what I am saying. We all understand an employer must at the end of the day be able to dismiss where the workplace has been undermined because of people who can't co-exist and you have gone to the lengths of trying to make it work and it hasn't. And that's what I am saying. What the courts will do is they will fit it back into one of those categories or they will just fudge it and call it incompatibility and not raise the issue. The courts are very good at doing at that. They just don't raise the issue, they say incompatibility, they don't point out, oh hell you know, we have had a look at the act, there's no(thing) here, they just say incompatibility. And everybody is too sensible to challenge it because they know at the end of the day it's a wise decision even if it is not technically

in line with what the Act says. So that is how
courts get around these things.

Commonalities and differences

The exchanges above were tape-recorded in the course of an extended study
of the recruitment (Ensor, 1999) and recognition of prior informal experience
in adult pedagogy (Breier, 2003). The study included observation and audio-
recording of the lectures in Courses A and B, analysis of lecture transcripts,
course notes, student assignments, exam questions, exam scripts and all
marks achieved, as well as semi- and unstructured interviews with selected
students and lecturers. Drawing on Bernstein (1996) and various proponents
of systemic network analysis (Halliday, 1973; Bliss, Monk and Ogborn, 1983;
Brown and Dowling, 1998), a 'language' for the description of the relationship between formal and informal knowledge in pedagogy was developed. It
is described in detail in Breier (2004) and will not be dealt with in this
chapter. What is of concern here is the significance of the study for the recognition of prior work or life experience, and learning from that experience, in
adult pedagogy *post-entry*. I call this 'rpl' (lower case) as opposed to 'RPL'
(in capital letters), which conventionally refers to the recognition of prior
learning in *pre-entry* assessment processes.

The commonalities and differences between the two transcript extracts point
to important issues for 'rpl':

- In Scenario A the lecturer is emphasising the general rule, while
  also admitting there are exceptions. In Scenario B the lecturer is
  repeating the general rule, but emphasising the way in which it
  is dealt with informally.

- In Scenario A the student is referring to a case in which she was
  personally involved but is drawing on this experience in
  impersonal terms – 'there is a case . . .'. Later in the session,
  when she refers to the case again, she uses the pronoun 'we' to
  indicate her own involvement. In fact she was the complainant
  and therefore the central figure. In Scenario B the student is
  asking his question in impersonal legal terms.

- In Scenario A the lecturer recruits his own personal experience
  – 'I have had occasion to dismiss a dispute' – and this supports

the general rule. In Scenario B the lecturer does not recruit his own experience, although elsewhere in the course he does do so.

- In Scenario A the lecturer interrupts the student and does not affirm her contribution. In Scenario B the lecturer does not obviously affirm the student but his response is in sympathy with the student's suggestions.

- The student in Scenario A is a woman who was classified under apartheid as 'coloured', with a working-class background. Student B is a white male attorney. Both lecturers are white men and, as stated earlier, labour lawyers.

How could one interpret these interactions?

The literature on RPL would seem an obvious starting point for an interpretation of these interactions, for the complexity of recognising informal experience in an academic environment is given particular attention here, even if it is usually considered in relation to pre-entry assessment processes rather than post-entry pedagogy. It has become common to distinguish between three broad perspectives on RPL which I have categorised as the technical/market, liberal/humanist and critical/radical perspectives (Thaver, Naidoo and Breier, 2002; Breier, 2003). My categorisation follows Harris (1997, 1999) in particular, but also Boud (1989), Weil and McGill (1989), Butterworth (1992) and Luckett (1999). Osman (2003) has since also presented a three-part classification.

The technical/market perspective
The technical/market perspective accompanies a human capital view of education which prioritises knowledge, skills and values that will be of benefit to the economy, sees students as 'consumers' or 'clients' whose passage through higher and, most often, further education is increasingly facilitated by means of modularisation and credit frameworks.

This perspective is associated with technical and some professional training and with generic skills instruction. RPL within this tradition includes the accreditation of learning from informal experience provided it can be matched against pre-defined learning outcomes. This is usually done through challenge tests, examinations, demonstrations and the production of 'evidence' and sometimes through 'outcomes-orientated portfolios' (Harris, 2000) that seek credit against specific learning outcomes. South African education policy conceptualises RPL within this perspective, through its emphasis on formal learning outcomes, specific as well as generic. This is despite the rhetoric of the policy which promotes RPL as a major vehicle of redress for those educationally disadvantaged by apartheid, rather than one of many features of an adult-friendly, student-centred learning environment, as in other countries.

Neither course had been shaped within the technical/market tradition. Course A was one of several run by a project which was set up at University A in 1993, with financial support from overseas funders, to offer training, research and resources services to trade unions, NGOs and departments in the new democratic government. It had a social transformatory rather than market ideology although, as the funders tried to encourage self-sustainability and began to withdraw funding, the project was becoming increasingly reliant on courses like these to finance their activities. Lecturers on Course B told me that the university saw that course, with its high fees and large classes, as an income generator for the institution, but they themselves were committed to the social and redress relevance of the course which they felt offered adults with extensive experience an opportunity to gain a formal qualification. This did not mean that they saw a direct link between the experience of the student and the knowledge and skills imparted in the course, and certainly there was no accreditation for this purpose. In both courses, RPL was strictly for access only. Course B did, however, offer the generic skills training which is valued in the market place and in the practice of law as a profession. This took the form, primarily, of teaching students how to access information about legislation and case law.

The courses bore stronger traces of the critical/radical and liberal/humanist perspectives and it is on these that I will concentrate.

The critical/radical perspective
According to Harris (1999), this perspective is associated with social movements such as trade union or feminist groups and critical, emancipatory discourses that view education as a means to transform the individual and society. Learning from work and life experience is seen to result in forms of knowledge that are ignored by official pedagogic processes (worker knowledge, indigenous knowledge, women's knowledge, and so on). In its radical form, learning from informal experience is seen as the basis for group consciousness-raising, community action and social change (Weil and McGill, 1989). Here Marx's concept of 'false consciousness' (Marx, 1977)

and Freire's concept of 'conscientization' are major influences (Freire, 1970, 1973, 1985). Within these traditions, RPL is seen as a strategy for social redress, a means whereby subjugated or marginalised groups or forms of knowledge can gain access to the academy and challenge the authority of hegemonic discourses.

Some versions of this perspective draw on social constructionist and standpoint theories, which problematise notions of knowledge, experience and subjectivity. There are many knowledges, it is argued, and all are socially constructed and of equal value, if not currency. 'Reason' is situated and culturally and politically influenced, rather than 'universal' and there are many valuable ways of knowing which do not depend solely on reason. Experience should not be seen (as in the work of liberal/humanists who will be discussed later) as 'coherent, consistent and a site for rational intellectual excavation' (Fraser, 1995, p. 19) nor separated from its history or social and ideological conditions (Brah and Hoy, 1989). Furthermore, subjectivity is not unified and autonomous as in the liberal/humanist position but seen as shifting, multiple and situated, shaped and distorted by everyday power relations (Usher, 1992).

The association of informal knowledge with the dominated (typically black and female) and formal knowledge with the dominant (typically white and male) is a theme that threads through the work of Michelson (1996a, 1996b, 1997, 1998, 1999) in particular. An American academic, she has visited South Africa frequently to assist in the conceptualisation and implementation of RPL and her work has had an important local influence. Her writings, from the 'standpoint' of 'traditionally marginalized voices', seek to challenge 'the foundations of academic power' and invite a 'sharing of epistemological authority' (Michelson, 1996a).

Michelson (1996a, p. 189) argues that in current RPL procedures, 'only experience can be exceptional', knowledge has to be presented as similar to that of others and 'recognizable in terms set by universalised academic norms'. She suggests 'a different conceptual underpinning for [RPL]' that sees knowledge as situated and grants visibility in the academic environment to 'outsider knowledge that is valuable for its divergence from academic ways of knowing, not only its similarity' and 'rewrites the relationship between experiential learning and 'academic authority' (Michelson, 1996a, p. 185).

Harris, whose extensive research and writings on RPL in South Africa have positioned her as another key figure in the field both locally and internationally, conceptualises a 'Trojan-horse model of RPL' which she describes as 'aspirational' and 'in the making'. She suggests it could become 'part of an inquiry into the social construction of knowledge and curricula'. In this model there would be bold attempts to 'value prior learning in and of itself rather than solely in terms of its degree of fit with existing standards or curricula or with the cognitive capacities deemed necessary to succeed in traditional terms' (Harris, 1999, p. 136).

The critical/radical perspective invites one to view the scenarios in terms of themes of marginalisation, voice and power and their relationship to different forms of knowledge. In this view it is significant that the student in Scenario A is a 'coloured' woman, a single parent, from a working-class background, trying to acquire a degree at a relatively late stage of life, whose experience of the CCMA was as a complainant and worker. The lecturer on the other hand is white and male and, as a CCMA commissioner, occupies a powerful position within the hierarchy of labour law practice. So too is lecturer B but in his scenario there is a greater balance of power. Student B is also a white male and a lawyer, even if a newcomer to the field of labour law.

The student in Scenario A represents a voice marginalised from the discourses of power in her work, in her domestic life and in terms of the law. In the trade union movement, however, she is a person of status and in her social science studies she has been given opportunities (unusually in an academic context) to describe personal experiences, with successful results She is also familiar with the narratives of redress ('from sweeper to engineer') associated with the RPL vision of the National Qualifications Framework. She has come to this course to have her experiences 'credentialled'. However, her experiences are vastly different to those of her lecturer and in this context she needs to present them as similar to his or at least recognisable to him in order to have them heard. She does so hesitantly and inarticulately and without recourse to the legal language which student B invokes in Scenario B. Lecturer A invites student A to give an example but when it turns out to be complex and difficult for her to recount and for him to understand, he interrupts her and exhorts her to adhere to the general rule. In contrast, Student B presents a question rather than a comment and presents it in legal terms. His intervention is heard and affirmed. This could be seen as a clear example of the inequality of power relations between (white) lecturer and (black and female) student and of the requirements of the academy that knowledge should be presented on its terms alone.

An interpretation along critical/radical lines might well plead for recognition of alternative voices, such as Student A's and at the very least an 'opening up' of discussions about the experiential consequences of race and gender under apartheid and beyond. This would demand a curriculum that was flexible, even negotiable, or a new curriculum entirely. The challenge would be to bring this about without disadvantaging those who urgently need a qualification, whatever its curriculum might entail, in order to obtain employment.

The liberal/humanist perspective

The liberal/humanist tradition emphasises that the prior experience of learners, and particularly adult learners, should be valued and used as a resource for further learning; and that learning should be active, meaningful and relevant to real life agendas (Weil and McGill, 1989). A great deal has been written, within this tradition, about adult learning and appropriate pedagogical practices. Kolb's (1984) theorisation of the process of experiential learning as involving four stages within a 'learning cycle' – concrete experience, reflective observation, abstract conceptualisation and active experimentation – underlies numerous texts on experiential learning, RPL and adult education (for example, Boud *et al.*, 1985; Fraser, 1995; Harris *et al.*, 1994; Jarvis, 1995).

Knowles (1980, pp. 9–12) emphasises the value of adults' experience describing it as the 'richest source of learning' in an adult education setting which, if ignored or devalued, will be perceived by adult learners as rejection of themselves as persons because they derive their self-identity from their experiences. Later, Knowles came to acknowledge that experience also has negative effects – bias, habits, prejudices – which need to be examined (Knowles, 1990). This theme is taken up by Brookfield (1998) who argues there is no basis for assuming that a learner's experience always constitutes a rich resource that educators can build on. In fact the converse is often the case and adult experiences can be distorted, self-fulfilling, unexamined and constraining. In addition, not all adults have the same capacity to learn from experience.

The liberal/humanist perspective has influenced portfolio-development practices in RPL, in particular, encouraging applicants to reflect on their life histories for self-developmental as well as academic purposes.

Looking through the lens of liberal humanist theory, it is not surprising that Student A felt resentment after the class and said that the lecturer was 'biased' and 'out of touch with real experience'. Her experience was not heard, let alone used as a resource. There was no opportunity for 'critical reflection' which might have led her to see the complexity of her personal experience and its relationship to the general rule. In a lengthy interview some time after the class, Student A told me that her case had in fact not been dealt with by the CCMA, as she suggested in class. It had only been put on the roll and allowed a brief hearing. The commissioner, after considering the issue concerning the dates and telling her and her representative that he was not allowed to hear such a case, told the parties to pursue the recognition agreement which existed between them. In terms of this agreement they were required to settle a dispute by mediation or arbitration. And so, in the end, the dispute was heard and resolved by an independent arbitrator and her case was not in fact in contradiction of the general rule which the lecturer was emphasising. Student A said Lecturer A should have given her a 'hearing' but conceded 'there was no time'.

A liberal/humanist perspective would exhort lecturers to provide opportunities for their students to recount their experiences, reflect on them and then consider the ways in which their learning supports or differs from that of the formal knowledge. The aim would be to support the student to gain 'epistemological access' (Morrow, 1992), not to overhaul the curriculum. The challenge would be to do this in a limited period of time, within the context of a non-negotiable curriculum, in a manner that does justice to the student's experience.

A disciplinary-specific perspective

I would like to suggest a fourth way of looking at these scenarios. In doing so, I do not seek to negate the significance of the perspectives described above but rather to suggest that all lack a dimension which is crucial to the understanding of the kind of issues raised in Scenario A and which might throw light on poor performance in courses like this by adults with extensive practical experience but limited exposure to academic discourses. This approach requires one to consider the nature and structure of the discipline or field of education concerned, the relationship between formal and informal knowledge within that discipline or field and the extent to which the pedagogic discourse mirrors that relationship. In this regard, it becomes an example of Harris's (Chapter 3, this volume) notion of 'knowing the borders and crossing the lines' (drawing on Anzaldua in Muller, 2000).

In delineating this approach I draw on the work of Basil Bernstein, who has argued the importance in pedagogical research of examining symbolic systems (disciplines) as well as the fields within which they are positioned, suggesting that the form and structure of the discipline could contribute in a fundamental way to 'games, practices and strategies' (Bernstein, 1996, p. 170). I will first discuss three broad approaches to legal education in general before considering two sets of underlying principles which are of particular relevance to the 'games, practices and strategies' which I observed in Courses A and B. The first concerns the inductive and deductive processes and principles of law, the second the relationship in law between the general and the particular.

Approaches to law and legal education

Particular emphases and interpretations have resulted in three broad approaches to legal education:

- The 'formalist' approach emphasises legal rules, principles, objectivity and rationality, and sees legal reasoning as an exact form of inquiry. This approach, which has to date been the dominant approach to legal education in South Africa, has been described as 'acontextual' because it 'relies in large part on concealment and constraint of the larger context within which the rules and principles operate' (Fedler and Olckers, 2001, p. 61).

- The 'realist' approach emphasises the personal, subjective factors that influence judgments, legal events and the messiness of law in practice. A common theme is that 'a judge's biography (including what was on the menu for lunch) will affect how he or she decides a case' (Fedler and Olckers, 2001, p. 13).

- The 'social context' approach to law, informed by feminist legal theory and critical race theory, emphasises that the law affects people differently depending on their circumstances and is therefore 'relative depending on context' (Fedler and Olckers, 2001, p. 69). Legal practitioners are also exhorted to get to know themselves and their biases and prejudices and the phallo- and Euro-centrism of law in South Africa is emphasised.

Basic principles in law

The inductive and deductive principles of the practice of law form the first set of basic principles that need to be taken account of in any analysis of legal pedagogy. The practice of law is essentially a deductive process – the application of rules, principles and concepts, as well as the generalities derived from the outcomes of multiple cases – to particular, real-life experience. It is recognised, particularly by those who follow a realist approach, that this is not a clear-cut process. The law can take various forms in practice as it is interpreted and applied by individual judicial officers who are not 'ideological virgins', as the prominent South African judge, Edwin Cameron, has put it (Fedler and Olckers, 2001, p. ix). It is for this reason that the reading of case law is a very important part of the work of a lawyer or legal academic, even the most 'black letter' formalist. The development of legal rules, on the other hand, is largely an inductive process. Laws change with economic and social circumstances as well as changing views of justice. Law, as a discipline or field of education, is integrally bound to the practice of law and to a greater or lesser extent, depending on its focus, reflects that structure. This means among other things that it has a number of divisions each reflecting an area of application and that each division shares common deductive and inductive principles.

The second set of basic principles that are relevant to an analysis of legal pedagogy, concerns the inherent tension in law between the general and the particular. Laws state what rational human beings ought to do or not to do, and it is generally accepted that laws should be reasonable, equitable and general in the sense of widely applicable. (This does not mean that laws have not been developed, as in the South African apartheid era, for example, that meet none of these criteria.) Contradictorily, the generality of the law ensures that the 'general case' is always illusory. As Dostoevsky ([1866] 1963, p. 306) put it in his novel 'Crime and Punishment':

> . . . the general case, the case for which all legal forms and rules
> are intended, for which they are calculated and laid down in
> books, does not exist at all, for the reason that every case, every
> crime, for instance, as soon as it actually occurs, at once
> becomes a thoroughly special case and sometimes a case unlike
> any that's gone before.

The generality of law also ensures that even 'just' laws are not always felt to be equitable by those to whom they are applied. Bourdieu (1990, p. 184) has noted that a judgement which is 'most formally in conformity with the formal rules of law may be in formal contradiction with the evaluations of the sense of equity'. Social context theorists emphasise the contextual factors which influence this 'sense of equity'. In this vein, Elana Michelson has reminded me of Anatole France's wonderful comment about the majestic equality of

French law which forbade the rich as well as the poor to sleep under bridges, to beg in the streets and to steal bread (France, 1894).

A disciplinary-specific analysis

An analysis of Scenarios A and B in terms of the disciplinary-specific approach would remind one firstly that the *inductive principle* relating to the development of laws is particularly pertinent in the field of labour law. Many aspects of the post-1994 labour legislation are the result of pressures by workers and trade unions for change, as du Toit, Woolfrey, Murphy, Godfrey, Bosch and Christie (1998, p. 17) have pointed out. With this in mind, it is not surprising that many of the unionists on Courses A and B found it difficult to submit themselves to pedagogical hierarchy, nor that students like Student A quoted above had expectations that their experience would be credentialed. (She said in an interview that she enrolled for the course 'to get my experience on paper').

The analysis would also show that the lecturer in Course A was adopting a formalist approach while Lecturer B was adopting a realist approach. In accordance with the deductive principle of law, both approaches require a *'generalizing gaze'* which views the particular in the light of the general. Here, drawing on Bernstein (1999, p. 172), I am using the term 'gaze' to refer to the perspective of the expert (in this case, the lecturer) transmitted tacitly to non-experts (students) which enables them to recognise what is relevant to the discipline and how to construct a legitimate text.

This gaze was in conflict with the orientation of students with very limited formal education, as well as those who had expectations that their personal experience would be of great value and would be 'recognised' (as Student A did). They tended to see the general in the light of the particular rather than the reverse, focusing on the particularity of their experience in relation to the general rule and often found a mismatch. They had a localising rather than generalising gaze.

These students were particularly frustrated by the lecturers' recruitment of their (the lecturers') own personal experience. This experience was associated with the lecturers' dominant position in the legal hierarchy and (particularly if they were white males) in society in general. Furthermore, this experience was used to support rather than contradict the general rule, as the students' experience did. These students needed a particular orientation to pedagogy involving suspension of judgments on the power relations of the pedagogic hierarchy, if only temporarily, in order to concentrate on the rule which the lecturer was trying to convey.

Such a situation is made more complex by discourses of RPL that create the expectation that prior informal experience can usefully be recruited by the student in any educational context and will be recognised to the extent that it can count for access or credit. Course A had several students with this kind of expectation, ranging from a factory worker with less than 10 years schooling to Student A, a third-year university student who had been praised in her social science studies for descriptions of her personal experiences. Their expectations in this context blinded them to the 'symbolic labour' (Breier, 2003, p. 235) associated with any formal learning. I am referring here not only to the pedagogic effort required to master the content and literacies of a formal programme, but also to the extent to which students are prepared to be implicated in the imposition of 'symbolic violence' (Bourdieu and Passeron, 1990) upon themselves. The extent of this labour varies from student to student depending on the extent to which his/her natural mode of participation differs from that which is expected. In this context this labour is necessary in order to acquire a generalising gaze.

A disciplinary-specific analysis in the context of professional education also exhorts the lecturer to investigate the *relationship between formal and informal* in the field of practice and compare this with the way in which it is depicted in the field of education in general, and in the pedagogic discourse of a specific programme in particular. In this light, it would be noted that there was far greater congruence between practice and discipline in Course B than there was in Course A. Although both courses required the student to view individual cases, they differed in the manner in which they tried to reflect those cases and legal practice more broadly. While Course B made no attempt to hide the messiness of the law in practice and students were referred to actual reported cases to see the manifold ways in which it was interpreted and applied, Course A tried to simplify the law into a set of rules and procedures. The world of legal practice was presented in the form of hypothetical examples or examples from the lecturer's personal experience, carefully tailored to support the general rule. Were it not for the interjections of students like Student A, the discourse would have borne little relation to the complexity of real life.

Better pedagogical practice

Liberal/humanist and critical/radical approaches invite a reconsideration of the curriculum and pedagogy of a course to accommodate students' experience and level the balance of power between lecturer and student for self-developmental and/or social-transformatory purposes. They are consistent with realist and social context approaches to the law. In contrast, a disciplinary-specific approach to analysis of pedagogic issues is concerned with the authenticity of a programme in relation to the discipline and field of practice. In this context, it asks to what extent the curriculum and pedagogy reflect the logic of the field of practice and of education (in this case labour law), in particular the relationship between formal and informal knowledge. Where there is incongruity, the kind of conflict depicted in Scenario A can be expected.

Good practice in terms of the disciplinary-specific approach would require the lecturer in any course to explain to students the relationship between their experience and the logic of the discipline or field of study, and the extent to which the course and its assessment processes differed from that logic. This was attempted obliquely in Course B where students were shown how to access legal information in a manner consistent with the practice of law, and necessary for the completion of their assignments. In Course A there was no such induction even though the examination mode of assessment, requiring repetition of the content of rules, and their application to hypothetical cases, was a substantial departure from legal practice. There was also no explication of the literacies of the course even though many of the students had limited schooling or had not studied in a formal context for decades. It is not surprising that students admitted on the basis of their experience did not do well in Course A (only two out of 11 passed) while in Course B they achieved a higher pass rate than students with higher formal qualifications.

Educationists who have considered the role of the everyday in school mathematics have suggested that the informal should be used to provide an entrée to the formal (Dowling, 1993, 1995; Ensor, 1999; Taylor, 1999) and that students should be taught to know the border between informal and formal and how to cross the line (Muller, with Taylor, 2000). Harris (2000, pp. 100–101) drawing on the work of Michelson and Gibbons *et al.* (1994) has suggested that curricula should start with applied knowledge and then move towards 'more propositional, Mode 1' knowledge (the reverse of the usual trend in higher education from theory to application).

My research showed that in the field of labour law education, borders between formal and informal, applied and propositional knowledge are not clear. Scenario B illustrates the complex interweaving of formal and informal in the courses I observed. In labour law the applied knowledge *is* Mode 1 (Gibbons *et al*, 1994) and cannot be separated for either analytical or pedagogical purposes. There is also the assumption in the above admonitions that lecturers will be able to gain sufficient knowledge of the experience of the student, indeed of informal knowledge more generally, in order to show the connections between the rule and the everyday and scaffold induction into the esoteric domain. This is not easy within the confines of a fixed curriculum with fixed periods for lectures. Anecdotes like Student A's are difficult to relate to unless both communicants have had the same or similar experiences (Muller, 2000, also makes this point) or the experience is described in vivid and comprehensive visual terms. Lecturers need a great deal of time and patience or a great deal of experience 'on the ground' to 'recognise' and 'hear' the accounts presented by their students. The question could also be raised as to whose experience counts. Courses like A and B attract a vast range of students. Whose experience should form the basis of the scaffolding? The unionists? The lawyers? The human resource managers? The full-time students? The academic content of a course – the rules, principles, concepts and their application in case law – provides a necessary common denominator. The crucial issue is the way in which particular cases are reflected in the pedagogic discourse. Do the representations reflect the logic of the field of practice? In this case, to what extent do they mirror the relationship between formal and informal knowledge in the practice of labour law?

References

Bernstein, B. (1996), *Pedagogy, Symbolic Control and Identity*, London: Taylor and Francis.

Bernstein, B. (1999), 'Vertical and horizontal discourse: an essay', *British Journal of Sociology of Education*, 20(2): 157–73.

Bliss, J., Monk, M. and Ogborn, J. (1983), *Qualitiative Data Analysis for Educational Research: A Guide to Use of Systemic Networks*, London: Croom Helm.

Boud, D., Keogh, R. and Walker, D. (1985), *Reflection: Turning Experience into Learning*, London: Kogan Page.

Boud, D. (1989), 'Some competing traditions in experiential learning' in Weil, S. and McGill, I. (eds) *Making Sense of Experiential Learning*, London: Society for Research in Higher Education and Open University Press.

Bourdieu, P. (1990), *The Logic of Practice*, Cambridge: Polity Press.

Bourdieu, P. and Passeron, J. (1990), *Reproduction in Education, Society and Culture*, London: Sage Publications.

Brah, A. and Hoy, J. (1989), 'Experiential learning: a new orthodoxy?' in Weil, S. and McGill, I. (eds) *Making Sense of Experiential Learning*, London: Society for Research in Higher Education and Open University Press.

Breier, M. (2003), 'The recruitment and recognition of prior informal experience in the pedagogy of two university courses in Labour Law', PhD thesis, University of Cape Town.

Breier, M (2004), 'A network analysis of formal and informal knowledge in adult pedagogy', *Journal of Education*, 33: 5–26.

Brown, A. and Dowling, P. (1998), *Doing Research, Reading Research: A Mode of Interrogation for Education*, London and Washington: Falmer Press.

Brookfield, S. (1998), 'Against naieve romanticism: from celebration to the critical analysis of experience', *Studies in Continuing Education*, 20(2): 127–42.

Butterworth, C. (1992), 'More than one bite at the APEL: Contrasting models of accrediting prior learning', *Journal of Further and Higher Education*, 16(3): 39–51.

Du Toit, D., Woolfrey, D., Murphy, J., Godfrey, S., Bosch, D. and Christie, S. (1998), *The Labour Relations Act of 1995: A Comprehensive Guide*, Second Edition, Cape Town: Butterworths.

Dostoevsky, F. [1866] (1963), *Crime and Punishment*, London: Everyman.

Ensor, P (1999), 'A study of the recontextualising of pedagogic practices from a South African pre-service mathematics teacher education course by seven beginning secondary mathematics teachers', PhD Thesis, University of London, published on microfilm in *Collected Original Resources in Education*, 24(3).

Fedler, J. and Olckers, I. (2001), *Ideological Virgins and Other Myths*, Cape Town: Justice College and University of Cape Town.

France, A. [1894] (1942), *Le Lys Rouge*, Paris: Calman-Levy.

Fraser, W. (1995), *Learning from Experience: Empowerment or Incorporation?*, Leicester: NIACE.

Freire, P. (1970), *Pedagogy of the Oppressed*, New York: Seabury Press.

Freire, P. (1973), *Education for Critical Consciousness*, New York: Seabury Press.

Freire, P. (1985), *The Politics of Education: Culture, Power and Liberation*, Massachusetts: Bergin and Garvey.

Gibbons, M., Limoges, C., Nowotny, H., Schwartzman, S., Scott, P. and Trow, M. (1994), *The New Production of Knowledge*, London: Sage Publications.

Harris, J., Saddington, T., and McMillan, J. (1994), 'Recognition of Prior Learning: International models of assessment', Report prepared for the National Training Board, South Africa.

Harris, J. (1997), 'The Recognition of Prior Learning (RPL) in South Africa: Drifts and shifts in international practices: understanding the changing discursive terrain',

Unpublished paper prepared for the Research and Development Programme in the Recognition of Prior Learning in Higher Education, Human Sciences Research Council, University of Cape Town and Peninsula Technikon.

Harris, J. (1999), 'Ways of seeing the Recognition of Prior Learning: What contribution can such practices make to social inclusion?', *Studies in the Education of Adults*, 31(2): 124–39.

Harris, J. (2000), *RPL: Power, Pedagogy and Possibility*, Pretoria: Human Sciences Research Council.

Jarvis, P. (1995), *Adult and Continuing Education: Theory and Practice*, London: Croom Helm and New York: Nichols Publishing Company.

Knowles, M. (1980), *The Modern Practice of Adult Education*, Chicago: Association Press.

Knowles, M. (1990), *The Adult Learner: A Neglected Species*, Houston: Gulf Publishing Co.

Kolb, D. (1984), *Experiential Learning*, New Jersey: Prentice-Hall.

Luckett, K. (1999), 'Ways of recognising the prior learning of rural development workers', *South African Journal of Higher Education*, 13(2): 68–81.

Marx, K. (1977), *Selected Writings*, McLellan, D. (ed.), Oxford: Oxford University Press.

Muller, J. (2000), 'Intimations of boundlessness' in Muller, J. *Reclaiming Knowledge*, pp. 75–93, London: Routledge.

Muller, J. with Taylor, N. (2000), 'Schooling and everyday life' in Muller, J. *Reclaiming Knowledge*, pp. 56–74, London: Routledge.

Michelson, E. (1996a), 'Beyond Galileo's telescope: situated knowledge and the assessment of experiential learning', *Adult Education Quarterly*, 46(4): 185–96.

Michelson, E. (1996b), 'Taxonomies of sameness: the recognition of prior learning as anthropology', Paper delivered at the International Consortium on Experiential Learning Conference, University of Cape Town, Cape Town, South Africa, July 1996.

Michelson, E. (1997), 'The politics of memory: the recognition of experiential learning' in Walters, S. (ed.) *Globalization, Adult Education and Training: Impacts and Issues*, pp. 141–53, London: Zed Books.

Michelson, E. (1998), *Expanding the Logic of Portfolio-assisted Assessment: Lessons from South Africa*, Saratoga Springs, NY: National Center for Adult Learning.

Michelson, E. (1999) 'Social transformation and the Recognition of Prior Learning: Lessons for and from South Africa', *South African Journal of Higher Education*, 13(2): 99–102.

Morrow, W. (1992), 'A picture holds us captive' in Pendlebury, S., Hudson, L., Shalem, Y. and Bensusan, D. (eds) *Kenton-on-Broederstroom 1992: Conference Proceedings*, Johannesburg: Education Department, University of the Witwatersrand.

Osman, R. (2003), 'Equity, justice and RPL? A glance from three perspectives', paper presented at the conference of the South African Association for Research and Development in Higher Education, Bellville, South Africa, 25–27 June 2003.

Rogers, C. (1969), *Freedom to Learn*, Ohio: Charles E Merrill Publishing Company.

Usher, R. (1992), 'Experience in adult education: a post-modern critique', *Journal of Philosophy of Education*, 26(2): 201–13.

Weil, S. and McGill, I. (eds) (1989), *Making Sense of Experiential Learning*, London: Society for Research in Higher Education and Open University Press.

Note

[1] The original version of this chapter was published in *Studies in Continuing Education* (2005), 27(1): 51–65. Revised and reprinted with permission of the journal. Journal's website: http://www.tandf.co.uk

[2] Ja means yes.

chapter five

Portfolio-based assessment of prior learning: a cat and mouse chase after invisible criteria[1]

Yael Shalem and Carola Steinberg

Introduction

Institutions of higher education in South Africa are being encouraged to find ways to recognise the informal learning of historically disadvantaged adult learners. Recognition of learning acquired outside higher education institutions is politically and socially important in a country where people have been deliberately deprived of opportunities for formal learning. In line with new policy (South African Qualifications Authority [SAQA], 1997) formal university credit may be granted to candidates who can show equivalence of competence gained through work and life experience. This process of assessment, or Recognition of Prior Learning, permits candidates to proceed from work experience to a qualification route (Department of Education, 1998, p. 33).

In view of the social and cultural processes that have been shown to have an effect on assessment, educational research has begun to foreground the importance of learning environments in which a communicative climate promotes open and fairer processes of assessment (Broadfoot, 1998). In order to facilitate RPL assessment, portfolio-based experiential learning programmes are being advocated. These programmes are expected to give RPL candidates an opportunity to revisit what they know and to articulate it within an academic mode of knowing (Osman *et al.*, 2000). Portfolios have been singled out as a mode of assessment in which learners can both show a rich picture of their development over time and engage reflexively with what they have learnt (Gipps, 1999, p. 377). Implicit in this is the assumption that continuous informal dialogue between teacher and students enhances students' understanding of, and respect for, the knowledge base of what they do and so empowers their social identity (Borthwick, 1995; Shulman, 1998; Wolf, 1998).

Much current research and policy on RPL is premised on the notion that 'experiential learning' (Kolb, 1984; Boud *et al.*, 1985) that is, learning from experience, can be made equivalent to a disciplined academic way of learning (Usher and Edwards, 1994; Lather, 1992; Michelson, 1996a, 1996b; Beckett and Hager, 2000). Among researchers of RPL there is a general agreement that through the right kind of assistance from the facilitator or assessor, portfolio-development programmes can empower candidates to 'find' knowledge in what they already do and to understand it in a new (academic) way (Mandell and Michelson, 1990; Stuart, 1996, Peters, 2000). A 'portfolio' is considered a flexible tool of assessment (Harris, 2000, p. 122), a mode of assessment that can 'tap learning derived from many sources' (Michelson in Harris, 2000, p. 121), a tool for reflexive engagement, or a means for an interface between previously acquired competencies and academic knowledge.[2]

This chapter critically evaluates the capacity of the assessment processes involved in such portfolio-based RPL programmes to transmit clear sets of criteria for what an RPL candidate is required to demonstrate. The chapter uses data collected during a research project which investigated the promotion of RPL in the School of Education at the University of the Witwatersrand, Johannesburg, South Africa.[3] We examine the social relations of assessment that developed between the facilitator/assessors[4] (who were located in an academic field of practice) and the candidates for RPL (who attempted to demonstrate the knowledge they had gained from experience). Drawing on Bernstein's (1990) distinction between two pedagogical types, 'visible' and 'invisible', we analyse the instructional logic of the pedagogy used to recognise the nature of the prior learning that students brought. We employ this distinction to explain the specific social logic that underpins the pedagogy of portfolio-based assessment of experiential learning, focusing primarily on the distribution of power in the pedagogical relationship, its assumptions with regard to knowledge specialisation and thus its implications for a learner's acquisition of knowledge. We then go on to examine some of our pedagogical experiences during the RPL portfolio-development programme, highlighting the ways in which some of the demands of prior learning assessment constrained our ability to specify the criteria for the learning we set out to recognise.

The central claim of this chapter is that since the pedagogical interface between the experiential knowledge of RPL candidates and the academic knowledge of portfolio-development programmes is structured by hybrid forms of pedagogy that are predominantly 'invisible', both the candidates and the facilitator/assessors are positioned in different forms of powerlessness: the candidates are positioned in an intense state of perplexity, not knowing which idea matters more or how to access the ways in which ideas are selected and combined, whereas the facilitator/assessors, who are more clearly located in a field of knowledge that is structured by certain criteria of specialisation, are dominated by the personalised forms of communication typical of portfolio development, and cannot find any systematic way to transmit criteria to the candidates.

The dilemma of the RPL assessors' authority

In their recognition of prior learning, assessors have to diagnose two very different aspects of a candidate's competence: the candidate's capacity to demonstrate competence already acquired and the candidate's readiness to join a qualification or to learn at an appropriate level in a particular learning programme. Thus the process of recognising prior learning involves the simultaneous enactment of two very different forms of action – one being *retrospective* and the other being *prospective*. The recognition of previously attained learning is a *retrospective action*, in that it aims to establish the presence of a candidate's accomplishment, acquired in a specific area of specialisation at work. Providing access to education is a *prospective action*,[5] in that it prepares candidates for the future demands of the academic learning programme they wish to enrol for. In the case of portfolio-development programmes assessing experiential learning, both of these actions form necessary parts. The dilemma is that each draws on very different conceptual resources and embodies very different power relations between the assessor and the candidate. The *retrospective* action arises out of political and ethical imperatives. In order to understand what the candidate is bringing, the assessor needs to background the authority of well-researched knowledge and rational argument, thus making the pedagogical authority of the facilitator/ assessor 'invisible' (Bernstein, 1990). The *prospective* action positions the assessor in their field of specialisation and requires that academic recognition is granted by the authorities of a specific knowledge field, in accordance with the regulatory and constitutive logic of that field. In the *prospective* action, the pedagogical authority of the assessor is thus more 'visible' (Bernstein, 1990).

The most common practice of Recognition of Prior Learning is some form of assessment of the competence tacitly embedded in a specific performance. As part of the retrospective action, candidates may, for example, be asked to write an extended essay on 'labour relations and collective bargaining'; do a clinical performance assessment in 'Nursing Care'; write a short biographical essay with a focus on the experience of teaching young children; or present a written portfolio which includes life history, an essay and work-place evidence of effective school management (Joint Education Trust, 2000).

Reading off candidate's competence from such performances involves a projection of similarity between what the candidate writes and what the assessor knows. The retrospective action of assessing competence gives primacy to 'similar to' relations (Bernstein, 1996, p. 64). It uses pedagogical strategies to assist candidates to recognise and express similarity relations. Strategies include training candidates to use certain words and expressions to describe their experience; taxonomies for breaking down experience; terminology for generic skills; and even supplying candidates with a sort of 'identity kit' 'which comes complete with the appropriate instructions on how to act, talk and write so as to take on a particular role that others will recognise' (Peters, 2000, pp. 7–9).

Epistemologically, the retrospective action relies on the postmodernist critique of rationalism (see, for example, Harding, 1991). At the heart of this critique is the view that 'different knowledge is available from different "standpoints", that is from social and historical locations' and that assessors need to relinquish the image of 'the rational consciousness constructing knowledge in detached and splendid isolation' (Michelson, 1996a, p. 192), so that they will be able to see that all knowledge (academic and experiential) is invariably partial (see also Hager, 1998; Harris, 1999). This opposition to rationalism is typically articulated through questioning the epistemological authority of the field of academic practice:

> What has become clear is that RPL cannot be separated from
> broader epistemological, political and ethical issues. Questions
> such as: Whose knowledge is important? Who benefits from
> RPL, and who is disadvantaged and how? Who acts as
> gatekeepers and on whose authority? Whose standards and
> outcomes are used, and how are they arrived at? How are
> assessment methods arrived at, and what kind of inputs do adult
> learners have into the use of those methods and the assessment
> process itself? point to the fact that constructions of knowledge,

> what is worth knowing, and (then) how knowledge is assessed, reflect particular power relations in society. (Ralphs and Buchler, 1998, p. 12)

> In the process of accreditation of workplace experience the pedagogy of experiential learning can indeed be liberating, empowering and free of 'discipline(s)', [. . . be] part of the process of creating 'active subjects' (Usher and Solomon, 1999, p. 162).

This conceptual stance burdens the *retrospective* action: it foregrounds pluralism of knowledge and assessment, social interests and power, while it backgrounds disciplinary knowledge, criteria for assessing what counts as knowledge and the reliability of assessment methods.

Yet the instructional logic of the pedagogy employed in portfolio-development programmes also includes the *prospective* action of reading a candidate's readiness for new learning through an assessment of her performance during the programme. This suggests that when assessing performance, the assessors must in particular consider those criteria that they believe are necessary for performance of the tasks or skills associated with the knowledge practice to which the candidate seeks access. Specialisation presumes that assessors draw on a field of knowledge, as in 'regional fields' (Bernstein, 1996) like sociology of education or language and literacy. It recognises that there are certain debates and a preferred perspective, which specialise the knowledge area that the candidate claims to know about. It also recognises that, as academic practitioners, the assessors are bound by the social logic that regulates their field of practice. The *prospective* action recognises that different forms of knowledge have serious consequences for how they are acquired (Breier, 1998); that different pedagogical paths enable or constrain 'epistemological access' (Morrow, 1993); that some instructional methods and technologies of delivery are more appropriate for enhancing learning than others (Muller, 1998); and that the logic of a field of practice regulates the ways an academic recognises another practice or assesses the value of specific elements within it (Shalem, 2001).

Taken together, the weak emphasis on disciplinary knowledge in the retrospective action and the reliance on specialised knowledge in the prospective action, places the assessors in a contradictory position, with profound implications for portfolio-based assessment of prior learning. The retrospective action motivates RPL assessors to try and 'find'[6] competence even if it is tacit and does not resemble traditional paradigms of university knowledge (Ralphs and Motala 2000, p. 7). Hence the attacks on 'the language of the textbook' (Mezirow, 1990) and a preference for life history and biographical approaches (Stuart, 1996; Harris, 2000). Candidates should not be bound to satisfying predetermined specific criteria. In fact, in the retrospective action, criteria bind the assessors only. When assessing, they are expected to focus on what is present in the candidate's knowledge – to downplay propositional knowledge, to equalise the relationship between theory and learning from experience, to offer a great deal of support to candidates so that they 'learn the rules of the game and how to apply it to their own personal situations' (Peters, 2000, p. 4) and to look for broad equivalence rather than direct equivalence between candidates' display of learning and academic knowledge (Harris, 2000).

In their role of preparing candidates for future study, on the other hand, the assessors have to be much more careful not to give a false message about simple equivalence between experiential learning and formal conceptual-isations. Potentially, the prospective action could be used to develop a more explicit set of criteria and practices for recognition in that it is based on the specialisation of a particular knowledge field. The problem, however, is that in a portfolio-development programme the prospective action is marginalised. It becomes heavily dominated by a personalised mode of communication that is over-determined by the need to affirm presences through continuous informal commentary and assistance in the articulation of meanings. Although the assessors know which concepts in their field of knowledge they are drawing on when they give feedback, the context of personal communication makes it inappropriate to make visible the specialised set of criteria they are using. This increases the risk of mis-recognition – it dictates a level of engagement that denies that ideas have a specialised structure and that their acquisition requires a certain instructional sequence and order. To illustrate this dilemma, we turn now to an example drawn from our pedagogical experience in running a portfolio-based RPL programme.

Enabling inter-subjectivity: From me (my story) to mine and your story (the case of Lindiwe)

In this section of the chapter we illustrate the analysis of the two actions involved in the assessment of prior learning by using a short case study from our programme. Initiated by the Joint Education Trust (JET), our portfolio-development programme attempted to bring the knowledge-base of practice and of academia into dialogue. We recruited students by advertising for educators who wanted to enter a postgraduate Bachelor of Education (BEd Honours) programme, but who did not have the appropriate qualifications and who were willing to try the RPL route. We accepted six candidates, most of them school principals/heads or teachers with 15–25 years of teaching experience. Once recruited, the candidates attended a one-semester portfolio-development programme, at the end of which they could apply for access to the BEd Honours programme or for advanced standing within it. The RPL programme engaged with two topics, school culture and accountability, selected from the field of sociology of education and relevant to the practices of all the candidates. Much of the academic activity in the programme took place around the feedback given to the candidates in writing their personal portfolios. Initially, we had planned to read about ten articles during the programme. We changed in response to a claim made in RPL workshops at JET that a focus on texts overshadows the candidates' experience, and also because of the extended time that candidates needed so as to understand the academic texts. We read two articles during the six-month programme.

Our reflection here is based on a range of data: videotapes of seminars, copies of candidates' assignments, portfolio drafts and our formative feedback (recorded) to the candidates. We examined the classroom discussions and the ways in which one of the candidates in particular, Lindiwe, responded to our formative feedback, analysing the development manifested in her assignments and portfolio drafts. Lindiwe is a 49-year-old woman, a primary school teacher, whose 22 years of teaching experience included five years as the principal of her school. In the analysis of the constitutive aspects of the communication between Lindiwe and ourselves, we try to avoid 'otherising' ways of engagement by either side. Our analysis works with what Wenger calls 'fundamental duality' (1998, p. 65), a conceptual position which advocates a pedagogy that unveils the presuppositions hidden by the knowledge practices of each side. We do not believe that furthering the ethical project of RPL is served by the simple antagonism that is created in the current debate and which fetishises notions like 'domination of the academy' (Michelson, 1996a, 1998) and 'inequalities of cultural capital' (Stuart, 1996; Harris, 2000).

We found the role of the facilitators/assessors in the *retrospective* action to be mainly therapeutic, praising and identifying certain expressions and statements made by Lindiwe. From the perspective of the *prospective* action, however, segments of Lindiwe's personal discourse needed to be joined together through the structuring operations of the specialised language of school management, which she was not aware of, but nevertheless made claim to. Our role as assessors was to select a conceptual unifier to drive the construction of her narrative, deciding what can fit together, and in which order and form. Let's look at this process more closely by following some of the steps we took in our work with Lindiwe.

Lindiwe began articulating her experience in the mode of a private conversation. She described the difficulties encountered in obtaining her post of principal, how she was 'robbed', because, although the interview panel chose her as an applicant, the job was initially given to a male Head of Department (HOD) at the school. She lodged a complaint, made public the documentation of the interview panel and eventually got the job. She described the HOD as a 'power hungry man' and mentioned the conflicts she had had with him since that time. She backed up her judgement with anecdotes like 'when he was acting vice-principal, he called himself "the principal"!' The telling of this story was brokered through questions, asked by ourselves and other students. When Lindiwe was asked a question, she responded by filling in some details and apologising in certain places for not giving the relevant details in their right order. Her main focus was on articulating the chain of events that together portrayed 'the defence' for her harsh judgement of her colleague. Lindiwe told her story with minimum interruptions from us or from the other students. She told it without any particular requirements (criteria) on how to convey the evidence on which her story drew.

From our perspective as assessors in the retrospective action, listening to 'a story from experience' had to be done with some kind of duality between the opposite codes of 'interruption' and 'flow'. We had to negotiate (of course implicitly) our epistemic authority. We had to keep a tenuous balance between, on the one hand, accepting that Lindiwe's description of her experience was trustworthy and, on the other, querying elements in the story which did not make logical sense or requesting additional information that would contribute to the prospective action. This continued to form a very fragile pedagogical relationship throughout the six months that we worked with Lindiwe on her portfolio. Through the initial conversation with her it became clear that she was facing difficulties that were important to her as principal in a specific field of practice (teaching and school management) and in a specific historical context (a complex process of transition from apartheid to democracy, characterised by teachers' demoralisation and the breakdown of authority relations in many state schools). In this conversation, Lindiwe stated her goal as a school manager quite explicitly: 'I should be able to make my teachers do everything without me pushing them from behind.' We heard this in a dual mode: from the vantage point of the *retrospective* action, we accepted Lindiwe's 'democratic goal' as a segment of her story, while from the *prospective* action mode we recognised it as an approach to school management that could be developed and understood in more nuanced ways.

The *retrospective* action continued in Lindiwe's first presentation of the topic for her portfolio. Lindiwe created a mind map of concepts, a web of ideas which she presented as the main components of professionalism (Figure 5.1).

Figure 5.1 The main components of professionalism, according to Lindiwe

She used these components together with concrete examples to convey her message that 'teachers do not care'. During her presentation, Lindiwe went through each category one by one. She did not present them in any particular order, she did not analyse their position in a view of professionalism. Rather, she used them to repeat her message. Her use of this message over-determined the voice of each category. For example, whether she talked about empathy or relevance, her conclusion was that teachers lacked these qualities because they did not care. Lindiwe also did not differentiate between time and context. She lumped together teachers from the last decade and today, presenting the government-teacher relationship as a continuum, while ignoring the specific state of emergency that existed in South Africa during the struggle against apartheid in the mid-1980s, when her story started. She did not specify any reasons for why teachers resorted to actions that she categorised as 'lack of care'. Nevertheless, we read the selection of the mind map as a positioning device, offered as a 'boundary object' (Wenger, 1998, p. 106) that conveyed to us that Lindiwe recognised 'preferred' ways of knowing in an academic context. We began the process of feedback by negotiating a possible symmetry between our invisible criteria of specialisation and her symbolically constructed presence of competence.

In our assessment of Lindiwe's prior learning, we used epistemological means to *classify* the components of her message (the different facets of professionalism) and the extent to which she was aware of the relationship between them. The classification was invisible – we chose how to classify on the basis of our specialisation. What Lindiwe heard, though, were questions that we (and other students in the group) posed to her. Here is an example of how our invisible act of classification worked:

> Lindiwe: I know that from 1985 onwards, teachers and students
> mobilised and went on strike, salaries deducted only from
> MATU (not TUATA) teachers.[7] In 1989 teachers dumped
> preparation files at Church Square, SADTU formed in 1990,
> leading to strikes, no order in schools and pupils idled about,
> state of emergency, children taught under surveillance of the
> police.

We knew the relationships between these propositions through our knowledge of their historical context. For example, we knew that each of the teachers' unions mentioned by Lindiwe held a different ideological affiliation; and we understood these affiliations in their context: the political contests which took place at the time in an attempt to win teachers' collaboration with the anti-apartheid social forces. But with limited time and authority for *prospective* actions, we struggled to reposition her fragmented understanding of teachers' struggles during the 1980s. We would have needed time allocated in a formal learning programme to show her the impact of these historical events on teachers' professional identity today. The removal of this kind of specialised background within the RPL portfolio process constrained our educational authority, as we did not have control over the conceptual path Lindiwe was taking.

Lindiwe's first three written drafts were dominated by personal stories. The first draft focused on her conflict with the colleague and was dominated by anecdotes like 'an HOD is undermining me'; 'I was accused of financial mismanagement'; 'young teachers refuse to sign register'; 'exams not collected from the office'; 'Group of junior phase teachers work hard' etc. The second was dominated by 'self promotion anecdotes' that echoed an RPL text, given to the candidates, on how to get a college credit. It seems that Lindiwe translated our requests for more discrimination into more anecdotal information. We felt as if we were drowning in the sheer volume of her anecdotes. Her tone was adversarial, positing an unbridgeable gap between 'these bad teachers' and 'the ideal teachers'. At that point, we embarked on the *prospective* action: we focussed Lindiwe's attention on the language, the logical connectedness and the significance of specific segments which we selected and foregrounded in our discussions with her. We imposed a conceptual frame drawn from a loose reference that she had made in one of her earlier assignments.[8] We drew on the concepts – 'social order', 'rituals' and 'continuity' – that Lindiwe had used to locate her claim that the culture of learning and teaching was breaking down in her school (and in other schools too) and that teachers did not care. We 'hooked onto' these concepts in order to bind the information into a frame that could show how over time (1978–2000) and in relation to specific historical turns (state oppression, teachers' struggle, liberation, policy transition and school reform) the 'authority relations' between government and teachers changed, and how this affected her, first as a teacher and later as a principal.

The new frame enabled us to work with Lindiwe on the relationship between 'order', 'discipline', 'respect' and 'participation'. This enabled her to put together discipline, regulation and autonomy, a relationship that seemed odd to her in view of common sense formulations that tend to position regulation and autonomy as opposites. Slowly, Lindiwe moved away from a very prescriptive engagement with ideas. In her eighth draft, she began writing with some measure of descriptive elaboration. She began to re-place her view of professionalism, which had been tied to her personal conflicts with colleagues at school, by looking at the context of these conflicts, in terms of political change, national curriculum change and her own change of role in becoming a principal. In her last draft she wrote:

> The seminars had contributed more on my side. I used to take
> matters personal [sic] and capitalised on that. For example my
> first writings were composed of issues concerning conflict
> between the HOD and myself. Gradually I grew intellectually, I
> had to focus on my management style of leadership.
> Accordingly [. . .] my school is gradually progressing well
> towards a democratic change.

Nevertheless, the invisibility of the frame continued to throw obstacles in our path – neither Lindiwe nor any of the candidates could recognise the web of beliefs from which these concepts were drawn. This gave rise to a jigsaw puzzle between Lindiwe and ourselves. In her writings, Lindiwe drew on glimpses of our specialised language to explain the relationship between discipline, regulation and autonomy. She used sociological descriptors taken from the two articles we read, together with discredited conceptions of education promoted during the apartheid era and mixed them with learner-centred conceptions of teaching which are popular in South Africa today. In her last draft Lindiwe wrote (emphasis ours):

> From Bernstein I know there are school's rituals, i.e.
> instrumental and expressive, which are very important in
> *moulding the child to proper adulthood.* The child has to be
> taught as a whole, i.e. holistically. He has to acquire knowledge,
> skills and acceptable values and norms. The child as a client has
> to be treated as an individual according to his or her capabilities
> as *children are unique.*

Here the descriptive language of Bernstein, ('instrumental' and 'expressive' 'rituals') is used to justify a basic slogan of Fundamental Pedagogics,[9] ('moulding the child to proper adulthood') and explained by using the language of Curriculum 2005,[10] ('knowledge, skills and values', 'treated as an individual') without any sense of differentiation or possible conflict between these concepts.

RPL and invisible pedagogy

The pedagogy of RPL is situated in a specific, very complex relationship between two distinct fields of knowledge production. The central pedagogical aim of RPL is to enable access and transition from one discursive field to another. Enabling access and transition involves attuning candidates to the differentiation between the experience and knowledge they are drawing on and the concepts and language of the academic specialisation to which they are bringing their knowledge. It requires a convergence between two histories of learning, each forming its own respective discourse – a 'vocational dis-course' (knowledge *from* experience) and a 'scholastic discourse' (knowledge *separated from* experience). In selecting a portfolio topic, for example, the RPL candidate offered her 'learning *in* the practice' as an object of evaluation for 'knowledge *from* experience' to assessors who worked in a field in which the dominant *modus operandi* is formalisation (Bourdieu, 1998). This relation positions the topic as potential 'subject matter'. The candidate's moment of selecting a topic is thus a dual moment of recognition for the assessor: it enables recognition of learning *in* practice but it also positions this learning in a particular field of knowledge, thus requiring an assessment of the level of performance in relation to the criteria of that field.

Both the vocational and the scholastic discourses use terms, concepts and representational forms, that is, 'reifications' (Wenger, 1998); both foreground particular foci and tools of conceptual organisation; and in their interface both background, that is, leave implicit, conceptual resources as well as rationales that inform particular modes of engagement. The degree to which each discourse makes its construction explicit is not defined *a priori* but depends on which enterprise the discourse is interfacing with. An RPL portfolio-based assessment programme for access sets up an enterprise of reading, writing and speaking which dictates, in an *invisible* way, which statements and express-ions of ideas will count as abstractions to be used in order to direct, open or close what can be said, when and how. It does this in an invisible way since it signals a low degree of specialisation; it appears to say: 'all knowledges are equivalent'. Although in the process of translation from one discourse to another the assessor brings a *prospective* gaze or makes judgements according to certain criteria that matter in her area of specialisation, these criteria remain invisible to the candidate because the area of specialisation is not taught. It continues to operate only as the background knowledge of the assessor, from which the candidate is separated. The following list summarises some of the ways in which invisible pedagogy constrains the candidate during the process of translation from vocational to scholastic knowledge:

1. When the relationships between fields of knowledge (for example, sociology, management and curriculum) are not classified, it is very difficult for candidates to access how ideas are combined and which idea matters more. This gives candidates a semblance of full participation, as it appears that ideas do not have special membership.

2. When the relationship between fields of knowledge is not classified and articulated, particularly when a programme draws on a range of knowledge areas and their respective disciplines, RPL candidates find it very difficult to position themselves pedagogically. They often do not know what is appropriate to say and when; they often struggle to demarcate their issues from the specific message of the text. Their participation (by way of

concrete examples or looking for the relevance to their own situation) has to be positioned continuously.

3. When the demarcation between the scholastic mode of production of knowledge and the everyday vocational mode of production of knowledge is denied, candidates might realise quickly that assessors want them to stop recycling stories (concrete examples) and frame them in a generalised form, but they do not know how to do this. Because the assessor does not control the order, the pacing and the content of the knowledge brought to the portfolio, and because the assessor can only pace and order her teaching in response to the development of the writing, the instructional order continues to be segmented. This makes it difficult for candidates to access the form in which to present their ideas in the portfolio and its effectiveness (or lack of effectiveness) for knowledge production. Furthermore, from the perspective of the assessor, reading chunks of life history can be overwhelming and is often met with very fragmented segmental feedback. Therapeutically, the assessor cannot ignore the stories but, performatively, she can only really respect their significance if they form part of a bigger whole. Hence, the assessor often reifies an anecdotal style with an overall structuring action.

4. When the speciality of each field is denied and yet the assessor works with specialised criteria, albeit in an invisible way, candidates have to continuously guess, as in a cat and a mouse chase, about the significance of the feedback they get, for example, why they have been asked to engage with a specific idea in a specific way. This is one of the most difficult aspects of invisible pedagogy, as any pedagogical attempt to read across the two fields (to 'broker'; Wenger, 1998, p. 108) is inhibited by the loose structure of the pedagogy of the programme itself. Messages about structure and order of ideas in a candidate's portfolio can only be given retrospectively, in response to the ideas and emphases the candidate selected. This results in multiple submissions of drafts, each sorting out some problems and revealing others that were hidden before.

5. When the candidate does not have a base from which to evaluate what knowledge was selected into the RPL programme (why certain meanings are in the foreground and others are in the

background), the form of the discussion, the order of the
programme and the assessment of their participation remain
invisible and thus real epistemological access is fenced.

The degree of invisibility produced by the mix between what appears as non-specialisation of knowledge and specialisation of criteria prevents candidates from knowing the bases of their assessor's authority. This is, according to Bourdieu, a case of symbolic violence.[11] At the heart of the argument of symbolic violence are the power relations that develop between social agents. Power relations are accentuated or weakened by the degree to which agents can recognise 'the speciality of the context that they are in' (Bernstein, 1996, p. 31), or the degree to which criteria are made visible. According to Bernstein, who acknowledges Bourdieu's notion of symbolic violence, it is the context and the criteria that shape how learners recognise the key rules of the practice:

> The markings of the categories, from the point of view of the
> acquiring subject, provide a set of demarcation criteria for
> recognising the categories in the variety of their representations.
> The sets of demarcation criteria provide a basis for the subject
> to infer recognition rules. The *recognition rules* regulate what
> goes with what: what meanings may legitimately be put
> together, what referential relations are privileged/privileging.
> (Bernstein, 1990, p. 29)

The main point here is that the social space of academic discourse gives primacy to order and progression of knowledge, which are regulated by conceptual tools like classification, integration and scaffolding. What is not obvious is how the power to use these tools is distributed pedagogically. When that pedagogy is predominantly invisible, the candidates *and* the facilitator/assessor are continuously negotiating the timing, the order and the legitimacy of what is being said. An extensive degree of invisibility enhances the captivity of *both* in the discursive background from which they each speak, read or write.

Conclusion

One of the main problems with current research on RPL is that advocacy positions (Michelson, 1996a, 1997, 1999; Johnston and Usher, 1997; Edwards and Usher 1999) tend to lean toward one pole only (the *retrospective* action of assessment) and in this way deprive the recognition of experiential learning of its real academic complexity. Through our examination of the double action of the assessment of prior learning we show that the conceptual difference between the two actions and their co-existence cannot be wished away, and that this has complex ramifications for what can be achieved. From a pedagogical perspective, our analysis critically evaluates the capacity of the assessment processes involved in a portfolio-based experiential learning programme to transmit clear sets of criteria of what an RPL candidate is required to demonstrate.

Our central aim has been to describe the pedagogical complexity hidden in the experiential learning approach advocated for RPL. This complexity arises from the two very different aims which facilitators/assessors are expected to attain simultaneously: recognition of prior learning and socialisation into a field of knowledge. We do not doubt the insights that candidates gain when reflecting on their experience. However, we question the value of a pedagogy that foregrounds knowledge equivalence and personalised modes of communication and so obscures the criteria of specialisation necessary for access and success.

References

Beckett, D. and Hager, P. (2000), 'Making judgement as the basis for workplace learning: Towards an epistemology of practice', *International Journal of Lifelong Practice*, 19(4): 300–11.

Bernstein, B. (1990), *The Structuring of Pedagogic Practice*, London: Routledge.

Bernstein, B. (1996), *Pedagogy Symbolic Control and Identity Theory, Research, Critique*, London: Taylor & Francis.

Borthwick, A. (1995), 'Body of evidence. With portfolios, students really show their stuff', *Vocational Education Journal*, 70(3): 24–6.

Boud, D., Keogh, R. and Walker, D. (eds) (1985), *Reflection: Turning Experience into Learning*, London: Kogan Page.

Bourdieu, P. and Wacquant, L. (1992), *An Invitation to Reflexive Sociology*, Cambridge: Polity Press.

Broadfoot, P. (1998), 'Records of achievements and the learning society: a tale of two discourses', *Assessment in Education: Principles, Policy and Practice*, 5(3): 447–77.

Breier, M. (1998), 'The role of the generic skill in lifelong learning: panacea or pipe-dream?', *Journal of Education*, 23: 73–97.

Department of Education (1998), *Education white paper 4: preparing for the twenty-

first century through education, training and work, Pretoria: Department of Education.

Edwards, R. and Usher, R. (1999), 'Disciplining the subject: the power of competence', *Studies in the Education of Adults*, 26(1):1–14.

Evans, N. (1999), 'Experiential learning; find it, assess it, credit it. What's the problem?', Paper presented in the SAARDHE Conference, June/July 1999, Peninsula Technikon.

Gipps, G. (1999), 'Socio-cultural aspects of assessment', *Review of Research in Education*, 24: 355–92.

Harding, S. (1991), *Whose Science? Whose Knowledge?*, Ithaca NY: Cornell University Press.

Hager, P. (1998), 'Recognition of informal learning: challenges and issues', *Journal of Vocational Education and Learning*, 50(4): 521–35.

Harris, J. (1999), 'Ways of seeing the Recognition of Prior Learning (RPL): what contribution can such practices make to social transformation', *Studies in the Education of Adults*, 31(2): 124–39.

Harris, J. (2000), *RPL: Power, Pedagogy and Possibility*, Pretoria: HSRC.

JET (2000), 'RPL challenges higher education and workplace practice', 3–5 October Joint Education Trust, Johannesburg, mimeo.

Johnston, R. and Usher, R. (1997), 'Re-theorising experience: adult learning in contemporary social practices', *Studies in the Education of Adults*, 29(2): 137–53.

Kolb, D. (1984), *Experiential Learning*, Englewood Cliffs, NJ: Prentice-Hall.

Lather, P. (1992), *Getting Smart: Feminist Research and Pedagogy with/in the Postmodern*, New York: Routledge.

Mandell, A. and Michelson, E. (1990), *Portfolio Development and Adult Learning: Purposes and Strategies*, Chicago: Council for Adult and Experiential Learning.

Mezirow, J. and Associates (1990), *Fostering Critical Reflection in Adulthood*, San Francisco: Jossey-Bass.

Michelson, E. (1996a), 'Beyond Galileo's telescope: situated knowledge and assessment of experiential learning', *Adult Education Quarterly*, 46(4): 185–96.

Michelson, E. (1996b), 'International case study on prior learning assessment, Empire State College, State University of New York', Case Study Evaluation commissioned by the Research and Development Programme in the Recognition of Prior Learning, Cape Town, HSRC, UCT and Peninsula Technikon.

Michelson, E. (1997), 'Multicultural approaches to portfolio-development' in Rose, A. and Leahy, M. (eds) *Assessing Adult Learning in Diverse Settings: Current Issues and Approaches,* San Francisco: Jossey-Bass.

Michelson, E. (1998), 'Re-membering: the return of the body to experiential learning', *Studies in Continuing Education*, 20(2): 217–33.

Michelson, E. (1999), 'Carnival, paranoia and experiential learning', *Studies in the Education of Adults*, 31(2): 140–54.

Morrow, W. (1993), 'Entitlement and achievement in education' in Criticos, C. *et al.* (eds) *Education: Reshaping the Boundaries.* Proceedings of the twentieth Kenton Conference held at Scottburgh, Natal, Durban, School of Education.

Muller, J. (1998), 'The well-tempered learner: self regulation, pedagogical models and teacher education policy', *Comparative Education*, 34(2): 177–93.

Osman, R., Shalem, Y., Steinberg, C., Castle, J. and Attwood, G. (2000), 'Promise and problems in RPL: the JCE and WITS projects in teacher and adult education', Paper presented in the JET conference on RPL, Johannesburg, 3–5 October 2000.

Peters, H. (2000), 'Language strategies for RPL and experiential learning', Paper presented in the JET conference on RPL, Johannesburg, 3–5 October 2000.

Ralphs, A. and Buchler, M. (1998), 'The NQF and the recognition of prior learning', *JET Bulletin*, No. 8 July 1998.

Ralphs, A.and Motala, E. (2000), 'Towards an RPL strategy for 2000-2005: A work in progress', Paper presented in the JET conference on RPL, Johannesburg, 3–5 October 2000.

Shalem, Y. (2001), 'Recognition of prior learning in and through "the field" of academic practice', *Perspective In Education*, 19(1): 53–75.

Shulman, L. (1998), 'Teacher portfolios: a theoretical activity' in Lyons, N. (ed.) *With Portfolio in Hand: validating the new teacher professionalism*, New York: Teacher College Press.

South African Qualifications Authority (1997), 'Draft regulations governing the activities of national standards bodies', *Government Gazette*, No. 17970.

Stuart, M. (1996), 'Discursive terrain of power – the academy, credits, assessment and recognition of prior learning', *Case Study Evaluation*, commissioned by the Research and Development Programme in the Recognition of Prior Learning, Cape Town, HSRC, UCT and Peninsula Technikon.

Usher, R. and Edwards, R. (1994), *Postmodernism and Education*, London: Routledge.

Usher, R. and Solomon, N. (1999), 'Experiential learning and the shaping of subjectivity in the workplace', *Studies in the Education of Adults*, 31(2): 155–63.

Wenger, E. (1998), *Communities of Practice: Learning, Meaning, and Identity*, Cambridge: Cambridge University Press.

Wolf, D. (1998), 'Portfolio assessment: sampling student work', *Educational Leadership*, 46(7): 35–9.

Notes

[1] A longer version of this chapter was published in *Pedagogy, Culture and Society*, 10(3): 425–48, 2002. It was called 'Invisible criteria in a portfolio-based assessment of prior learning: A cat and mouse chase'. Revised and reprinted with permission of the journal.

² Portfolio-development programmes are usually offered to candidates of RPL before entering a formal programme and are used to provide either access to, or advanced standing in, a formal programme of study.

³ The research project arose out of a joint venture between the School of Education and the Joint Education Trust [JET], a research institute and donor agency for educational innovation in South Africa.

⁴ Although the final portfolios were sent to an external assessor for a decision, the facilitators of the portfolio development prgrammme functioned throughout as assessors, because of the formative nature of the feedback they provided. In the rest of the chapter, we mainly use the term 'assessors' because this chapter focuses on the dilemmas of assessment, but it needs to be understood that this refers to a combination of the roles of facilitators and formative assessors.

⁵ We would like to thank Lynne Slonimsky for coining these terms for us.

⁶ Note the title of a paper by one of the 'founders' of RPL – 'Experiential learning; find it, assess it, credit it. What's the problem?' See Evans (1999).

⁷ MATU was a local, progressive, anti-apartheid teachers' union, while TUATA was a more government-friendly teachers' association. SADTU (South African Democratic Teachers Union), founded later as an amalgamation of several local teachers' unions, was a very powerful force in the struggle against apartheid and still represents the majority of teachers today.

⁸ This was a reference to Bernstein's argument that rituals in education serve to maintain social order and continuity, in chapter 2 of *Class, Codes and Control, Volume 3*. We read the paper in the first half of the programme.

⁹ Fundamental Pedagogics was the theoretical underpinning for the Christian National Education promoted by the apartheid government. It emphasised order and obedience and the unquestioned acceptance of the written word.

¹⁰ Curriculum 2005 is the new national educational policy, which is derived from constructivist understandings and emphasises critical thinking, learner-centredness, social justice and the development of skills and values in an outcomes-based education system.

¹¹ Bourdieu argues that 'symbolic power as the power to constitute the given by stating it, to act upon the world by acting upon the representation of the world, does not reside in "symbolic systems" in the form of an "illocutionary force". It is defined in and by a definite relation that creates belief in the legitimacy of the words and of the person who utters, and it operates only inasmuch as those who undergo it recognise those who wield it' (Bourdieu and Waquant 1992, p. 148). (See also Andersson, Chapter 2, this volume, concerning the 'illocutionary' aspect of assessments.)

<u>chapter six</u>

RPL and the disengaged learner: the need for new starting points

Roslyn Cameron

Introduction

This chapter explores aspects of Recognition of Prior Learning practice that relate directly to the inability of RPL to act as a mechanism for social inclusion for disengaged learners. Disengaged learners is a term which encompasses those groups that have little or no engagement with formal post-compulsory education and training. The chapter begins by establishing the background of RPL in Australia followed by a brief description of the research and literature emanating from its introduction and practice. Empirical evidence supporting the claim that RPL has not acted as a mechanism for social inclusion will then be presented. Next, the complex nature of non-participation in formal learning settings is addressed. Theories, models and approaches of non-participation will be critiqued prior to a theoretically-based analysis of RPL and the disengaged learner. Bernstein's (2000) analysis of pedagogy, symbolic control and identity provides a basis for linking micro-processes of education to macro-forms of social class and power relations (Sadovnik, 2001). Of particular interest will be Bernstein's exploration of the distribution of *pedagogic rights* and the notion of the *potential discursive gap*.

RPL: The Australian context

The training reform agenda of the Federal Labour government of Australia in the early 1990s provided the impetus for a national framework of qualifications along with competency-based training and assessment. RPL was introduced as one of ten principles of this framework and subsequently became part of the charter establishing the Australian Qualifications Framework [AQF] in 1995. The Australian Qualifications Framework Advisory Board [AQFAB] commissioned a report in 2003 into the policy and practice of RPL across the four sectors of post-compulsory education and training: higher education; vocational education and training; adult and community education; and secondary schools. The Australian National Training Authority [ANTA] commissioned a second report, the purpose of which was to identify and analyse what drives and creates barriers to effective implementation of RPL in the vocational education and training sector.

The promise of social inclusion: Has RPL delivered?

The AQFAB and ANTA commissioned reports focus on policy frameworks and implementation issues, as does much of the Australian literature on RPL in general (Wilson and Lilly, 1996; Smith and Keating, 1997; Bateman and Knight, 2002; Doddrell, 2002; Brophy, 2004). During the initial stages of its introduction many Australian researchers focused upon the potential benefits of RPL. It has been 15 years since RPL was first established and research is now more focused on whether these benefits have come to fruition (Mattner, 1997; Pithers, 1999; Smith, 1999; Bowman, *et al.*, 2003; Wheelahan, *et al.*, 2003). The general consensus is that RPL has failed to fulfil its promised potential of encouraging traditionally under-represented and disadvantaged groups to access formal education and training. To paraphrase a common theme within the literature, there is a gap between the promise and rhetoric of RPL and the actual reality.

The two commissioned reports provide empirical evidence to support this. Both conclude that the up-take of RPL was relatively low: the national aggregate figure was 4 per cent for 2001 with equity groups (definition to follow) having relatively lower rates of RPL up-take. The ANTA report found that the major determinant of RPL was AQF level and the second major determinant was age. In other words, the higher the AQF level the more RPL activity was recorded and in terms of age most RPL applicants were in the 20–39 year age group.

The AQFAB report summarises the characteristics of RPL applicants across the sectors as:

Overall, RPL was more likely to be received by older students, and by students who were studying part-time. Students who were working full-time were more likely to receive RPL. Unemployed students received the least RPL and credit transfer. Students who were not in the labour force did not achieve the same level of RPL as did students who were working part-time [. . .] Broadly speaking those who are mid-career, established in the workforce, older, work full-time, and in associate-professional, professional or managerial occupations benefit most from RPL. (Wheelahan, *et al.*, 2003, p. 20)

The AQFAB report concludes that the main beneficiaries of RPL are those with experience of previous success in post-compulsory education and training. It is students with significant accumulated educational capital who are familiar with formal learning systems and associated discourses who are more likely to utilise the RPL process.

These findings have been supported by international research. Cleary *et al.* (2002) researched the Accreditation of Prior Experiential Learning [APEL] in five countries; England; Finland; France; Scotland; and Spain. They concluded that the extent of activity was very limited with APEL processes being very resource intensive and bureaucratic. They found that a significant proportion of APEL applicants already had academic qualifications and the majority of APEL learners were in their twenties and thirties. In practice APEL was not linked to social inclusion with the exception of targeted APEL for marginalised groups, although this type of activity was in itself limited.

Understandings of disengagement and non-participation

Literature, policy and commentary concerned with equity, social inclusion, access and participation in formal education and training refer to non-participants by way of a variety of descriptors: non traditional students; mature-age returners; underrepresented groups; equity group members; those alienated and marginalised from formal learning systems; second chance learners; the disenfranchised; the disaffected; those experiencing multiple or compound disadvantage; those with little or no post-compulsory education and training; and the socially excluded. This range of descriptors reflects the problems involved in trying to explain such a complex and widespread phenomenon.

The Australian context – the rethinking and regrouping of equity groups

Australia has used an equity group approach. Equity groups refer to six population sub-groups, which are targeted in education and training policies:

- women;
- Aboriginal and Torres Strait Islanders;
- people from non-English speaking backgrounds;
- people with a disability;
- people living in rural and remote areas;
- people from low socio-economic backgrounds.

The majority of research into access and participation in post-compulsory education and training focuses on equity group members who are already participating in formal education and training. Research is usually concerned with participation rates, retention, support services and outcomes. Other research tends to focus on creating or establishing learning pathways between education and training sectors, with a strong emphasis on young people who are about to complete their compulsory education.

Recent research in the vocational education and training sector has identified new and emerging equity groups and sub-groups. Dumbrell *et al.* (2003) identified three additional equity groups: early school leavers; the long-term unemployed (especially those in seven geographically identified areas and mature aged); and prisoners and juvenile offenders. John (2004) identified unemployed students and those under 19 years as additional equity groupings. This has complemented research analysing the nature of multiple and compound disadvantage. Golding and Volkoff (1998) call attention to the limitations of single-group approaches to equity targeting due to their inability to accommodate the diversity within groups and the cumulative effects of disadvantage. The authors have developed a model for accommodating diversity which not only takes into account the complex nature of disadvantage but also points to those groups of people identified as equity groups not targeted and considered in equity policies and provision:

> We need to acknowledge that there are a huge number of
> people, both male and female, who are not being targeted at all
> by current equity efforts, because they are less obvious and
> don't even make it into the picture as stakeholders. While equity
> research is most often focused on existing learners there are
> clear barriers which prevent many people from reaching first

base. We need to accommodate these people and their needs.
(Golding and Volkoff, 1998, p. 3)

Together this research offers valuable insights into the complex nature of disadvantage, which in turn provides new starting points and frameworks for developing more effective strategies and approaches to achieving social inclusion. Models and approaches to RPL, which take into account the needs of those who are disengaged from learning, need to be explored. In Cameron and Miller (2004a) we advocate the need to expand and broaden perspectives in relation to RPL, access and pathways with the view to encouraging innovative practice in promoting lifelong learning. We recommended innovations around 'developmental' models of RPL.

Due to the limitations of this chapter a detailed synopsis of the literature concerning models of RPL is not possible. Major contributions to the literature have come from Britain, Australia and South Africa. The key contributors have been Butterworth (1992); Butler (1993); Trowler (1996); Jones and Martin (1997); and Harris (1999). Table 6.1 below outlines characteristics and features from the literature and summarises these under the two poles of the continuum of RPL models: the credential and the developmental/empowerment models. The dominant model of RPL in Australia is the credentialing or credit-exchange model. The figure does not allow for the four models outlined by Harris (1999). These deserve a separate and more considered response, which cannot be undertaken within the confines of this chapter.

The main innovation of the developmental/empowerment model was to take a community-based approach and a holistic approach to learners and learning:

> We need to broaden our vision of recognition possibilities to
> encompass features of the developmental model. Approaches
> and models that are not limited by a direct relationship to
> assessment or credit exchange but focused on the learner and
> the learning process. Approaches situated in the spaces and
> places, which the larger community identifies with and which
> are framed by the wider objectives of lifelong learning for all.
> (Cameron and Miller, 2004a, p. 5)

Research conducted on Australian mature-aged jobseekers and their use/non-use of RPL came to similar conclusions:

Table 6.1 Models of RPL – two poles of a continuum (adapted from Cameron and Miller, 2004a)

	Credential Model	Developmental/ Empowerment Model
Ideology	Market-orientated vocationalism.	Person-orientated humanism.
Epistemology	Behaviourist – knowledge and skill acquisition as objectively measurable, aggregative.	Knowledge and understanding seen as constructed by the individual and integrated into their cognitive structures.
Discourse	Human Capital theory. Discourse of efficiency, accreditation, competence, access, transparency, equality of opportunity and mobility.	Humanism. Discourse of individual development and empowerment through confidence building, self improvement and self actualisation.
Features	Based on frameworks of vocational qualifications and job-role notion of competence	Learning process in its own right – with intrinsic value.
	Knowledge and competence seen as products. Onus is on the applicant to provide 'proof'. Driven by competences in standards. 'Equivalence'	Reflective process acts as a transformative social mechanism. Self-direction basis for enhancing self knowledge. Tutor role central – assisting learners to make links between different learning contexts in dialogue.
	The claimant exchanges proof of past achievements for course credits.	Claimant can receive credit plus significant personal and professional development.
Focus	Outcome. Commodity exchange.	Process. Learner centred. Equity principles embedded.

> Relevancy of the current credentialing model of RPL practised
> in Australia is a major issue for mature-age job seekers in terms
> of recognition of prior learning. It is also the starting point
> whereby alternate approaches to RPL can be contemplated. This
> research has pointed to the need to adopt approaches and
> models of RPL, which are relevant to the current needs of
> mature-age job seekers. It is argued here that the answer to
> these problematic issues lies in approaches to RPL, which draw
> from developmental models of RPL. (Cameron, 2004, p. 95–6)

The research identified three levels of recognition: self-recognition; informal recognition; and formal recognition. It concluded that for mature-aged jobseekers the key issues were related to the self and self-recognition. That is in building self-confidence and self-esteem, and processes of reflection to encourage the identifying and revaluing of skills and knowledge. This coupled with techniques to assist them to present and express their skills and knowledge at an informal level through resumes, interview techniques and job search related activities for example (Cameron, 2004, p. 96).

The limitations of theories of non-participation

There have been large amounts of research and a vast number of studies conducted across many countries in the last 40 years in the area of non-participation. McGivney (1993), in her review of the literature on non-participation, refers to three main characteristics of non-participants. They tend to be older adults (rates of non-participation are particularly high for retired men). They are characterised by minimum compulsory educational attainment and by indicators of low socio-economic status. McGivney develops non-participant typologies from the literature, which have similarities to the designated equity groups in Australian policy initiatives discussed above. Tobias (1998, p. 21) argues that irrespective of location and educational setting, adults from certain sections of the community tend to participate minimally in any form of educational activity. He cites specific groups such as working-class people in low paid or subsistence jobs; those who have been unemployed for extended periods; those with little formal schooling; older adults; women with dependent children from working-class backgrounds; ethnic minorities and others whose cultural traditions have been subordinated or suppressed.

McGivney (1993) posits that reasons for non-participation are multi-dimensional and complex and that many of the theories which have been developed to explain the phenomenon have focused on the interaction of the deterrents first categorised by Cross (1981) as *situational, institutional* and *dispositional*. McGivney (1993, p. 24) puts forward an interaction of external (environmental and situational) and internal (dispositional) factors as seeming to typify the theories which have been developed to explain non-participation. Nonetheless, she concludes that it is the sheer size, diversity and complexity of non-participation, which contributes to the fact that no one theory can explain it.

Furthermore, there have been relatively few attempts to enter the world of disengaged learners and to explore their subjective experience. As mentioned, there are vast amounts of research and studies in the area of non-participation, primarily large survey-based quantitative studies. Quantitative studies far outweigh the relatively small number of qualitative studies. Both Tobias (1998) and Harrison (1993) refer to the lack of interpretive and qualitative research in the area of non-participation. Tobias not only concludes that there is very little qualitative research but also very little sociologically-informed research, that is, research which investigates historical and biographical processes which structure post-compulsory education and training patterns, experiences, interests and views of working-class populations. Tobias lists several studies, which have taken this approach before describing his own.

Harrison refers to the work undertaken by Weil (1986) and Moss (1988) as examples of interpretive and qualitative research. Other notable research, which has taken an interpretative and qualitative approach, is that of Gorard *et al.* (1999), Golding and Volkoff (1999) and Gallacher *et al.* (2000). The latter research refers to the growing consensus that the traditional focus on typologies may oversimplify a very complex picture and that their own study has begun to unravel the complexities of the social processes and wider structural influences underlying participation and non-participation (Gallacher *et al.*, p. 22).

RPL as a form of access: what basis does it have in theory?

Theories of participation and the research generated by them have shaped governmental policy and institutional practice regarding responses to non-participation. These responses can be categorised as approaches, models and strategies for widening participation and access. As a form of access provision, RPL has been shaped by those particular theories, research and policies. Moreover, responses to any perceived failure of an access mechanism are also shaped by these theories, research and policies. In Australia, the responses to the failure of RPL to fulfil a social justice imperative have generally focused on identifying barriers, usually in the form of institutional and dispositional barriers.

I would argue these responses are superficial (in that they focus on problems associated with RPL processes at a procedural level) and narrow in scope (they remain confined by the limitations imposed on RPL practice from being perceived as a form of assessment).

In Cameron and Miller (2004c), we critiqued the dominant credentialing model of RPL (see table 5.1) at three levels. First, in terms of the assumptions inherent in the model – assumptions relating to RPL applicants' levels of literacy, familiarity with systems of formal learning and ability to translate life and work experience into formal, codified knowledge. Secondly, in terms of a 'hierarchy of values' which operates around different sites of knowledge, which confers greater value on knowledge acquired formally than that acquired in informal or non-formal settings. Lastly, in terms of the lack of relevancy of the model to a large number of people, especially those in transition and in economically vulnerable positions (Cameron and Miller, 2004c, p. 5).

Harrison's (1993) discussion of the central issues of access contends that the starting point for developing effective access approaches must be an analysis of why the large majority of non-participants are from socially, economically and educationally disadvantaged backgrounds. Then, and only then, can effective theories and models be built to enable those adults to become engaged in learning opportunities, which benefit them, their communities and society in general, Harrison (1993, p. 6) goes on to argue that a 'feature of the access debate has been its tendency towards an atheoretical, even knee-jerk response to the facts of non-participation'. Bolting access courses to the front of existing provision is convenient because it:

> . . . allows the responsibility for representative take-up to be
> located with the Access course providers, or better still, with the
> individual learner. Since little fault can be found with the
> existing structure of opportunities, the fault must lie with
> the individual who is unable to perceive what a good thing
> education really is. Low up-take is not problematised in terms
> of the nature of the education being offered, its relevance to the
> individual, the assumptions behind it. (Harrison, 1993, p. 7)

Although Harrison is referring to Access courses, his statements echo RPL provision. In Australia the responses to the low up-take of RPL have been generally limited and narrow due to the lack of theoretical input into the research and debate surrounding current practice.

The starting point for the next section of this chapter is the dearth of sociologically-informed qualitative research and theoretical frames which link micro-processes of education with macro-structures. What is needed is more in-depth analyses of RPL and related processes which investigate relations of power, the value systems which surround different forms of knowledge and the role of identity. There is a need to question the assumptions and power relations surrounding RPL and what constitutes legitimate, valuable and relevant knowledge. Such explorations could provide greater insights and an in-depth foundation from which to better inform practice. The starting point, then, needs to be theoretical frameworks, which attempt to link micro-educational processes to the macro-sociological levels of social structure, class and power relations. The chapter will now turn to the meta-theory developed by Basil Bernstein, a prominent theorist in the sociology of education, to explore RPL and the disengaged learner. Bernstein's *pedagogic rights* and the distributive principles of these rights are discussed in relation to schooling, however they are also relevant to post-compulsory education and training.

Bernstein's Pedagogy, Symbolic Control and Identity, RPL and the disengaged learner

The book *Pedagogy, Symbolic Control and Identity* (2000) is an attempt to 'link microprocesses (language, transmission, and pedagagy) to macroforms – to how cultural and educational codes and the content and process of education are related to social class and power relations' (Sadovnik, 2001, p. 5). The work centres on the key concepts of educational codes, pedagogic discourse and practice and their relationship to symbolic control and identity. Initially, the discussion here will examine Bernstein's treatment of the relationship between education and democracy through *pedagogic rights* and how the distribution of these rights contributes to disengagement from formal learning. The discussion will then move to the concept of the *potential discursive gap*.

Democracy and pedagogic rights

Bernstein (2000) saw education as having a crucial role in the knowledge base of society, groups and individuals and as such playing a substantial role in the reproduction and distribution of injustices – the 'inequalities in the orientation towards, and distribution and transmission of pedagogic knowledge' (2000, p. xix). He developed a model of pedagogic rights to measure rights and their (frequently unequal) distribution. They are the rights of individual *enhancement, inclusion* and *participation*. He describes these in terms of the conditions they produce and the levels at which they operate.

The first right, individual *enhancement*, is the right to the means for critical understanding and envisioning of new possibilities. It is linked to the condition of confidence, which operates at an individual level. The second right, *inclusion*, runs across social, intellectual, cultural and personal dimensions. It does not entail being absorbed. Rather, it implies a right to be separate and autonomous, although operating at a predominantly social level. The third right, *participation,* includes participation in discourse, discussion, practice and outcomes – the right to participate in the procedures that construct, maintain and change social order. This right is concerned with civic practice and operates at a political level. Table 6.2 below is a diagrammatical representation of these pedagogic rights, their conditions and levels.

Table 6.2 Pedagogic rights, conditions and levels (Bernstein, 2000, p. xxi)

Rights	Conditions	Levels
Enhancement	Confidence	Individual
Inclusion	Communitas	Social
Participation	Civic discourse	Political

The distributive principles of pedagogic rights

Bernstein uses this model to measure the distribution of these rights to students within a school. The rights are assigned through distributive principles, which operate at the level of images, knowledge, resources, access and acquisition. Bernstein suggests that:

> . . . there is likely to be an unequal distribution of images,
> knowledges, possibilities and resources which will affect the
> rights of participation, inclusion and individual enhancement of

groups of students. It is highly likely that the students who do not receive these rights in the school come from social groups who do not receive these rights in society. (Bernstein, 2000, p. xxii)

Distribution of images

Bernstein aptly uses the metaphor of a mirror to describe how a school projects a certain image based upon its ideology. These images are projections of a hierarchy of values, which he contends are ultimately class values. The issue is which class values are excluded and which are included in these projected images? It is also about the acoustics of the school. 'Whose voice is heard? Who is hailed by this voice? For whom is it familiar?' (Bernstein, 2000, p. xxi).

As part of Weil's (1986) qualitative research on non-traditional learners in traditional higher education institutions in England, learners' experiences of initial schooling were examined. Weil found that feelings of 'alienation', 'fragmentation' and 'conflict' were present as was a view that 'learning' and 'initial schooling' had not been compatible. Non-traditional learners associated learning with life experience, not the classroom, which Weil found was strongly linked to social class. Such a finding makes the use of appropriate models of RPL for access for disengaged learners even more compelling. The following account of one learner's experience of initial schooling highlights Bernstein's mirror metaphor:

> . . . The teachers were like aliens from another planet. They had different accents, different ways. No idea about working-class behaviours and attitudes. Their lives were so removed from ours. It was like being taught by people from another planet [. . .] I never regarded school as a learning place. Learning took place on the street, or at home, in life. (White working-class woman) (Weil, 1986, p. 224)

Australian research focusing on the senior secondary school experiences of a group of access students who had made a successful transition to university found examples of exclusive school practices which marginalised the working-class students, even when the school was described as state-run, 'disadvantaged' and servicing a working-class area. The research also found a common feeling of alienation from peers, low self-esteem and dissociation from school (Bland, 2004, p. 5).

One of the main barriers to RPL identified in the Australian research is the lack of awareness of RPL by potential applicants/learners. Is this due to a reluctance of institutions of formal learning to actively promote RPL in general? Or could it be partly explained by the fact that RPL is only promoted through existing networks? If RPL is promoted within existing course information, for example, then those groups who are disengaged from formal learning systems are the least likely to find out about it. I would argue that the manner (mediums) in which formal learning (and RPL) is promoted and to whom (symbolised by visual images within promotional material), contributes greatly to this 'mirror' metaphor and significantly influences 'who is being hailed' by these images and acoustics. RPL is one of many institutional practices, which combine to present certain values and images, and as such it values certain ideologies and associated knowledges over others.

Distribution of knowledge
Bernstein contends that in schooling knowledge is differentially distributed to different social groups. Different knowledges have different values assigned to them and therefore different levels of power and potential. This is reflected in the subjects chosen by certain groups which reflect gender, socio-economic status and ethnicity and which affect future occupational segregation. For example the under-representation of women in certain knowledge fields (sciences and engineering), the orientation of working-class males to the trades and the lack of student diversity in high-status professional education such as medicine.

Different categories of knowledge are differentially distributed by institutions of formal learning. The same principle applies *between* institutions in terms of the perceived status of different types of institutions within and between sectors of post-compulsory education and training. Learning choices made by low socio-economic and marginalised groups of students within their secondary schooling greatly influence their future employment, engagement with continuing learning, economic status and social positioning.

Ball *et al.* (2002, p. 70) echo the above in their investigation of choice of, and in, higher education [HE]. Their research points to the fact that debates about increasing participation in higher education which focus on barriers only tell part of the story: 'The distribution of classes and minority groups within HE and across HE institutions has to be understood as the outcome of several stages of decision-making in which choices and constraints or barriers interweave. Many students, especially working-class students, never get to a position where they can contemplate HE'. The researchers argue that:

> . . . choices are infused with class and ethnic meanings and that choice-making plays a crucial role in the reproduction of divisions and hierarchies in HE, but also that the very idea of choice assumes a kind of formal equality that obscures 'the effects of real inequality'. HE choices are embedded in different kinds of biographies and institutional habituses, and different 'opportunity structures'. (Ball *et al.*, 2002, p. 51)

This research, like Bernstein's theoretical framework, has linked the micro-processes surrounding participation and choice in higher education with macro-issues of class and ethnicity. It explores and analyses the effects of what Bernstein refers to as the distributive principles of pedagogic rights, specifically at the level of knowledge distribution.

Distribution of resources, access and acquisition

The distribution of material resources generally follows the distributive patterns of the distribution of images and knowledge in an inverse relation. As a consequence, the images and knowledge that have greater value are allocated greater material resources. This in turn affects the access and acquisition of school knowledge.

The potential discursive gap

The *potential discursive gap* is created within one of the three rules of the pedagogic device that provides the intrinsic grammar of pedagogic discourse. The interrelated rules are the distributive rules, the recontextualising rules and the evaluative rules. The potential discursive gap features within the distributive rules which distinguish between two classes of knowledge: the thinkable and unthinkable classes. Table 6.3 below identifies the characteristics of these two classes of knowledge.

Table 6.3 Two classes of knowledge (Bernstein, 2000, pp. 28–9)

Unthinkable	Thinkable
Esoteric	Mundane
Knowledge of the other	The otherness of knowledge
Controlled by:	Controlled by:
Higher agencies of education	Primary and secondary schools

The potential discursive gap occurs as a result of Bernstein's macro-level analyses of the two worlds of the material, everyday mundane and thinkable and the immaterial, transcendental and unthinkable. These worlds, in 'simple' societies, were controlled by religious systems and cosmologies. In medieval times, the gap between the two worlds was regulated by the first institutionalisations of knowledge. In modern societies, Bernstein contends that these classes of knowledge continue to be controlled and managed by education systems. The unthinkable is controlled by the higher agencies of education while the thinkable is managed by primary and secondary schools (Bernstein, 2000, p. 29).

A potential discursive gap is created when meanings are not consumed by the context and/or wholly embedded in a context. When meanings have an indirect relation to a specific material base, because of that indirectness, there is a gap. This is not considered to be a dislocation of meaning; it is a gap. This gap or space can become a site for alternative possibilities. Any distribution of power will attempt to regulate the realisation of this potential and will always regulate it in its own interests. 'The control over access to the site is accomplished by a selection of agents who have been previously and legitimately pedagogised [. . .] the very pedagogic process reveals the possibility of the gap and shapes the form of its realisation' (Bernstein, 2000, p. 31).

The potential discursive gap and RPL

This concept will be removed from the level of macro-analysis in which it appears in Bernstein's theoretical framework and reapplied to the micro-level of educational practice surrounding RPL, particularly the relationship between sets of knowledges (knowledges acquired formally and non- or informally). Aspects of the creation of the potential discursive gap remain. As outlined above, these include the conditions for its creation (order of meanings and the form of their abstraction), how the classes of knowledge are controlled and how the potential discursive gap is regulated. A gap is created when an indirect relationship between classes of knowledge is created.

Davison's (1996) discussion of 'equivalence' and RPL refers to RPL as a site that assigns meaning. He argues that 'more often than not "equivalence" between uncredentialled learning and any identified academic requirements has to be *constructed*. RPL is often a site for meaning *assigning*.' (Davison, 1996, p. 13, emphasis mine). When the notion of a potential discursive gap is applied to these classes of knowledge RPL can be seen to inhabit this site. A set of questions follow:

- If RPL inhabits this potential discursive gap then who is regulating the site?
- Who are the agents who have been legitimately pedagogised to control access to the site? What are the possibilities and potential of this site?
- What are the alternative realisations of the relation between the formal and informal? What are the benefits and dangers?

It is to these questions, which strike to the heart of the potentiality of RPL, that attention is now turned.

Regulation of the site

The legitimately pedagogised regulators of this discursive gap are the teachers, trainers and academic staff responsible for the design, implementation and practice of RPL within their respective institutions of formal learning. Concerns about maintaining academic standards and quality assurance issues emanating from some of these pedagogised regulators have formed the basis of much resistance to the implementation and practice of RPL. Usher (1989) argues that the fear of a diluting of academic standards is one of the major barriers to further progress in widening access. He describes these academic standards as part of a paradigmatic network, which is currently being challenged by oppositional cultures, which are increasingly less marginalised. Such a challenge comes in the form of RPL:

> . . . there is a gradual recognition of an alternative situatedness which is more than rhetorical. The most obvious indicator is the 'discovery' of personal knowledge and experiential learning. Of course, these are things which many practising educators have always recognized. The difference now is the recognition beyond this marginalised group. The notion that personal knowledge might be 'worthwhile' is obviously a major challenge to the dominant knowledge paradigm. When it is allied to the further claim that this knowledge ought to be 'accredited' and can be an alternative to formal qualifications, we are potentially in the realms of a shift to an alternative set of practices rather than marginal adjustments (Usher, 1989, p. 76).

This challenge to the paradigmatic network increasingly originates from groups of the legitimately pedagogised and creates what Bernstein (2000, p. 31) refers to as the paradox, which 'reveals the possibility of the gap'.

Researchers and educators interested in theories and practices which explore the links between knowledge generated from formal and informal/non-formal learning are playing a role in revealing this possibility in one of the forms of its realisation: RPL. However, RPL practice can also be part of the regulation of the site. As mentioned in the section *The promise of social inclusion: Has RPL delivered?*, RPL research in Australia has referred to a gap between the promise of RPL and the actual reality. The possibility of the gap has been revealed but the full potential of the gap is regulated through stringent and highly bureaucratic procedures and approaches within RPL which contain within them assumptions about RPL applicants' levels of literacy, familiarity with systems of formal learning and their abilities to translate knowledge acquired informally into formal, codified knowledge. Regulation of the site also occurs through a 'hierarchy of values' attached to different sets of knowledge and relations of power which are exercised in the RPL process.

To take this discussion further, the majority of RPL processes in Australia are cumbersome, bureaucratic, lengthy, predominantly print-based and place great demands and expectations upon applicants. Mattner (1997) described RPL processes as restricting access due to exhaustive print-based criteria which applicants are required to complete and compile on their own, just to reach the first stage. He also noted the need to have sufficient English language skills, self-confidence and a culturally sensitive process. Usher (1989) refers to the formidable sequence of hurdles in the four stages of assessing experiential learning and describes RPL as ensnared in procedures which have become a 'restrictive and suffocating strait jacket' instead of a mechanism for access (Usher, 1989, p. 79).

It could be argued that other possibilities exist that exploit the potential discursive gap in RPL. These include the incorporation of work-based learning into higher education curricula and the growing attention given to participatory learning theories such as those that originate from sociocultural theory or activity theory. Theories that use situated cognition or situated learning and the notion of communities of practice could also be seen as possibilities of the site.

The potential discursive gap can be seen to reveal its potential and its possibilities and the ways in which these possibilities and the forms of their realisation are highly influenced by the regulators of the site. The bureaucratic 'strait jacket' nature of RPL procedures along with underlying assumptions about RPL applicants, the problematic notion of translation and the hierarchy of values attached to different forms of knowledge all contribute to the fact that the full potential of RPL as a discursive gap is yet to be realised.

The possibilities, potential and benefits of the site: alternate realisations

The possibilities, potential and benefits of this site combine to form a large part of what was envisaged as the socially-inclusive purposes and promise of RPL. As a consequence, alternative realisations of the site, which would fulfil these socially inclusive aims, are yet to eventuate. They would require a major paradigm shift as advocated by Usher (1989) and Alheit (1999). In Alheit's (1999) elaboration of a critical approach to a learning society he refers to the political core of the learning society debate as being the:

> . . . realisation that informal learning in modern societies can unfold its quality only if the intermediary locations for learning (companies, organizations and educational institutions) change in parallel, if genuinely new learning environments and new learning publics come into being. A generally accepted informalisation of learning cannot be achieved without democratisation (Alheit, 1999, p. 78).

In later work focusing on the tension between two perspectives of lifelong learning. Alheit and Dausien (2002) argue for paradigm shift at three levels if the phenomenon of lifelong learning is to be realised. These levels include the macro-level (policy), the meso-level (organisational) and the micro-level (individual). It is the meso-level paradigm shift that is of most interest here. They argue for a paradigm shift among educationalists:

> . . . at the institutional meso-level, in respect of a new 'self-reflexivity' of organizations that should conceive of themselves as 'environments' and 'agencies' of complex learning and knowledge resources, and no longer as administrators and conveyors of codified, dominant knowledge (Field, 2000, in Alheit and Dausien, 2002, p. 18)[1]

A paradigm shift at both the macro- and meso-levels is required within institutions before the practice of RPL at the micro-level can begin to encompass features which fully take advantage of the possibilities of the *potential discursive gap*.

Conclusion

Starting from the disjuncture between rhetoric and reality, this chapter has explored RPL as a form of access for disengaged learners through an analysis of the influence of traditional theories of participation and non-participation. These theories and related research have shaped the institutional practices of access and RPL and have tended to focus on barriers or deterrents. I have argued that the perceived failure of RPL to act as a mechanism for social inclusion in Australia and the responses to this failure have been superficially focused on procedural issues and are narrow in scope due to a limiting perception that RPL is just another form of assessment. New starting points of analysis are needed which utilise theoretical frameworks linking these micro-educational processes to macro-sociological levels of social structure, class and power relations. Aspects of Bernstein's theory of pedagogy, symbolic control and identity were explored in relation to RPL in an attempt at one such starting point. Particular attention was given to the model of pedagogic rights as a theoretical frame for gaining greater insight into the phenomenon of disengagement. The concept of the potential discursive gap was then applied to formal and informal/non-formal sets of knowledge as a means to theorise the discursive location of RPL. Because the potential discursive gap can become a site for alternate possibilities it will be (and is) regulated by those in positions of power wishing to control the site in their own interests. The discussion explored the ways in which the site of RPL is regulated and how the paradox of this control on access to the site, through legitimately pedagogised agents, ultimately reveals the sites' possibilities and potential. It is the control on access to the site by these selected agents, which has restricted RPL practice and shaped its realisation. As a consequence, RPL practice is characterised by several features, which have greatly limited its potential as a mechanism of social inclusion. These include highly bureaucratic procedures, assumptions underpinning RPL practice in terms of RPL applicants' abilities and familiarity with formal learning systems, and, a hierarchy of values surrounding differently derived forms of knowledge.

The use of different models and approaches to RPL could assist the site to become less regulated. Developmental/empowerment models of RPL would provide more relevant and supportive opportunities for RPL applicants with little or no post-compulsory education and training. This would also allow for the identity change of RPL assessors from regulators of the site to facilitators of a process, which would take greater advantage of the potential of the site and the possible forms of its realisation. Explicitly embedding RPL within all courses/curricula instead of viewing it as a form of access or assessment would further open up the possibilities of the site. The site has the potential for faciliating a paradigm shift – one that acknowledges the interconnectedness and complex interplay between informal, non-formal and formal learning and knowledge bases. The site also has the potential to allow groups of disengaged learners the structural opportunity to have their learning and associated knowledges valued and legitimated, thereby assisting in the realisation of Bernstein's pedagogic rights of enhancement, inclusion and participation.

References

Alheit, P. (1999), 'On a contradictory way to the 'learning society': a critical approach', *Studies in the Education of Adults,* 31(1): 66–82.

Alheit, P. and Dausien, B. (2002), '"The double face" of lifelong learning: two analytical perspectives on a "silent revolution"', *Studies in the Education of Adults,* 34(1): 3–22.

Ball, S., Davies, J., David, M. and Reay, D. (2002), '"Classification" and "judgement": social class and the "cognitive structures" of choice of higher education', *British Journal of Sociology of Education,* 23(1): 51–72.

Bateman, A. and Knight, B. (2002), *Giving credit. A review of RPL and credit transfer in vocational education and training sector, 1995 to 2000,* NCVER, Adelaide, Australia.

Bernstein, B. (1971), 'On the classification and framing of educational knowledge' in Young, M. (ed.) *Knowledge and Control: New Directions for the Sociology of Education,* London: Collier-Macmillan.

Bernstein, B. (2000), *Pedagogy, Symbolic Control and Identity: Theory, Research, Critique,* Lanham, MD: Rowan & Littlefield Publishers Inc.

Bland, D. (2004), 'From old to new learning identities: charting the change for non-traditional adult students in higher education', paper presented at *Social Change in the 21st Century,* October 2004, Centre for Social Change, Brisbane, QUT, Australia.

Bowman, K., Clayton, B., Bateman, A., Knight, B., Thomson, P., Hargreaves, J., Blom, K., and Enders, M. (2003), *Recognition of Prior Learning in the Vocational Education and Training Sector,* Adelaide: NCVER.

Butler, L. (1993), 'The assessment of prior learning: relating experience, competence and knowledge' in Calder, J. (ed.) *Disaffection and Diversity Overcoming Barriers for Adult Learners,* pp. 159–69, London: The Falmer Press.

Butterworth, C. (1992), 'More than one bite at the APEL', *Journal of Further and Higher Education,* 16(3): 39–51.

Brophy, G. (2004), 'Ensuring good practice through good policy in recognition', paper presented at the *13th National VET Research Conference*, July 2004, Tweed Heads, NCVER.

Bryant, I. (1994), 'Hijacking experience and delivering competence: some profess-ional contradictions' in Armstrong, P., Bright, B. & Zukas, M. (eds) *Reflecting on Changing Practices, Contexts and Identities,* Conference Proceeding, papers from the 24th Annual Conference SCUTREA.

Cameron, R. (2004), *RPL and Mature Age Jobseekers,* Canberra: Adult Learning Australia.

Cameron, R. and Miller, P. (2004a), 'Recipes for recognition and lifelong learning: community based approaches to fostering learning transitions', paper presented at *Making Connections: Transition to University,* 26–28 September, Carseldine Brisbane, QUT.

Cameron, R. and Miller, P. (2004b), 'RPL: why has it failed to act as a mechanism for social change?', paper presented at *Social change in the 21st Century*, October 2004, Centre for Social Change, Brisbane, QUT, Australia.

Cameron, R. and Miller, P. (2004c), 'A transitional model of recognition', paper presented at *12th Annual International Conference on Post-Compulsory Education and Training,* 6–8 December, Gold Coast, Centre for Learning and Research, Griffith University, Australia.

Cleary, P., Whittaker, R., Gallacher, J., Merrill, B., Jokinen, L. and Carette, M. (2002), *Social Inclusion through APEL: The Learners' Perspective,* European Commission: Socrates-Grundtvig Project, Glasgow: Glasgow Caledonian University.

Cretchley, G. and Castle, J. (2001), 'OBE, RPL and adult education: good bedfellows in higher education in South Africa?', *International Journal of Lifelong Education,* 20(6): 487–501.

Cross, K.P. (1981), *Adults as Learners*, San Francisco: Jossey Bass.

Davison, T. (1996), '"Equivalence" and the recognition of prior learning (RPL)', *Australian Vocational Education Review,* 3: 11–18.

Doddrell, E. (2002), *The Evolution of RPL in Australia: From its Origins to Future Possibilities*, Thesis, Murdoch University, Melbourne, Australia.

Dumbrell, T., de Montfort, R. and Finnegan, W. (2003), 'Equity in VET. An overview of the data for designated equity groups' in *Equity in Vocational Education and Training: Research Readings,* Adelaide: NCVER.

Edwards, R. and Ribbens, J. (1998), 'Living on the edges: public knowledge, private lives, personal experience' in Ribbens, J. and Edwards, R. (eds) *Feminist Dilemmas in Qualitative Research: Public Knowledge and Private Lives*, Sage: London.

Falk, I. and Balatti, J. (2003), 'Role of identity in VET learning' in *Conference Proceedings of the 11th Annual International Conference on Post-compulsory Education and Training*, Gold Coast, Australia, Centre for Learning Research, faculty of Education, Griffith University, Australia.

Gallacher, J., Crossan, B., Leahy, J., Merrill, B. and Field, J. (2000), *Education for*

All? Further Education, Social Inclusion and Widening Access, Glasgow: Centre for Research in Lifelong Learning.

Golding, B. and Volkoff, V. (1998), 'Measuring disadvantage through outcomes: some issues', *Gender Matters,* Spring: 3–4.

Golding, B. and Volkoff, V. (1999), *Creating Outcomes: Individuals and Groups on the VET Journey: Report of a Major Longitudinal Study of Student Experiences over the course of their Vocational Education and Training in Australia*, Volumes 1 and 2, Australia: The VET journey, Centre for the Study of Higher Education, Australian National Training Authority [ANTA].

Gorard, S., Rees, G., Fevre, R., and Furlong, J. (1997), 'Learning trajectories: predicting patterns of adult education and training' in Armstrong, P., Miller, N. and Zukas, M. (eds) *Crossing Borders Breaking Boundaries,* 27th Annual SCUTREA Conference Proceedings (pp. 187–94), Birbeck College, University of London.

Harris, J. (1999), 'Ways of seeing the recognition of prior learning (RPL): what contribution can such practices make to social inclusion?', *Studies in the Education of Adults,* 31(2): 124–39.

Harrison, R. (1993), 'Disaffection and access' in Calder, J. (ed.) *Disaffection and Diversity. Overcoming Barriers for Adult Learners,* London: The Falmers Press.

Humm, M. (1990), 'Subjects in English: autobiography, women and education' in Thompson, A. and Wilcox, H. (eds) *Teaching Women; Feminism and English Studies*, Manchester: Manchester University Press.

Jarvis, P. (2000), '"Imprisoned in the global classroom" – revisited: toward an ethical analysis of lifelong learning' in Appelton, K., Macpherson, K. and Orr, D. (eds) Papers from the inaugural international Lifelong Learning Conference, Yeppoon, Queensland, Australia, July.

John, D. (2003), 'Quantifying the impact of equity overlap in VET' in *Equity in Vocational Education and Training: Research Readings,* Adelaide: NCVER.

Jones, M., and Martin, J. (1997), 'A new paradigm for recognition of prior learning (RPL) in Fleet, W. (ed.) *Issues in Recognition of Prior Learning; A Collection of Papers,* Australia: Victorian RPL Network.

Jones, L. and Moore, R. (1993), 'Education, competence and the control of expertise', *British Journal of the Sociology of Education,* 14(4): 385–97.

Mattner, S. (1997), 'RPL: Between policy and practice', *Australian Vocational Education Review,* 4(1): 16–23.

McGivney, V. (1993), 'Participation and non-participation: a review of the literature' in Edwards, R., Sieminsli, S. and Zeldin, D. (eds) *Adult Learners, Education and Training,* London: Routledge in association with Open University.

McGivney, V. (1999), *Informal Learning in the Community. A Trigger for Change and Development*, Leicester: NIACE.

Moss, W. (1988), *Breaking the Barriers. Eight Cases of Women returning to Learning in North London*, London: ALPHA.

Paczuska, A. (1999), ' Never mind the outcomes, what about the experience: lifelong learning, autobiography and skills for progression to higher education' in Oliver, P. (ed.) *Lifelong and Continuing Education,* pp. 143-58, Aldershot: Ashgate.

Pithers, R. (1999), 'Recognition of prior learning: Promises and emerging reality', *Australian Vocational Education Review,* 6(1): 10–16.

Sadovnik, A. (2001), 'Basil Bernstein (1924-2000)', *Prospects: The Quarterly Review of Comparative Education,* XXXI(4): 687–703.

Smith, E. and Keating, J. (1997), *Making Sense of Training Reform and Competency Based Training,* Wentworth Falls: Social Science Press.

Smith, V. (1999), 'Recognition of prior learning: rhetoric versus reality', *Australian Journal of Career Development,* 8: 8–10.

Tobias, R. (1998), 'Who needs education and training? The learning experiences & perspectives of adults from working class backgrounds', *Studies in the Education of Adults,* 30(2): 120–41.

Trowler, P. (1996), 'Angels in marble? Accrediting prior experiential learning in higher education', *Studies in Higher Education,* 21(1): 17–30.

Usher, R. (1989), 'Qualifications, paradigms and experiential learning in higher education' in Fulton, O. (ed.) *Access and institutional change,* Buckingham: Open University Press.

Weil, S.W. (1986), 'Non-traditional learners within traditional higher education institutions: discovery and disappointment', *Studies in Higher Education,* 2(3): 219–35.

Wheelahan, L., Dennis, N., Firth, J., Miller, P., Newton, D., Pascoe, S., and support from Brightman, R. (2003), *A Report on Recognition of Prior Learning (RPL) Policy and Practice in Australia in 2002, including National Principles and Operational Guidelines for RPL in Post-Compulsory Education and Training. Final Report February 2003,* commissioned by the Australian Qualifications Framework Advisory Board, Australia.

Wilson, J. and Lily, M. (1996), *Recognition of Prior Learning,* Adelaide: NCVER.

Notes

[1] The authors are making several points; this is one of them. For each point they list a source. Field (2000) is the source for this point.

chapter seven

Beyond Galileo's telescope: situated knowledge and the recognition or prior learning[1]

Elana Michelson

By the aid of the telescope anyone may behold this in a manner which so directly appeals to the senses that all the disputes which have tormented philosophers through so many ages are explored at once by the irrefragable evidence of our eyes.

(Galileo Galilei)

Introduction

RPL, known in the United States as Prior Learning Assessment, emerged out of the student-centred educational movements of the late 1960s and early 1970s. It is the product of a time in which the presence of large numbers of non-traditional university students was both cause and effect of structural innovations, including programmes for individualised and distance education and what in American English was known as 'universities without walls'. In many ways, RPL reflected the spirit of that time and place: it was rooted in a particularly American ideal of educational fair play and social mobility, encouraged more permeable borders between the academy and the community, and affirmed the liberal humanist faith in the meaning of experience for human agency (Michelson and Mandell, 2004).

Yet that spirit, deeply felt as it was, was based on assumptions about experience and knowledge that went largely unexamined. It seemed self-evident that broad-minded approaches to education would include a respect for the ability of people to learn in a variety of places and styles and that the willingness of colleges and universities to recognise such learning was a mark of openness and flexibility. It seemed equally obvious that RPL itself was an important progressive innovation. Resting on such values as creativity, autonomy, and 'good old American know-how', RPL was consistent with the meritocratic belief in educational access as the key to both personal transformation and social equity.

In recent decades, RPL has been introduced in many other countries across the world. Emerging at differing historical moments in, for example, Canada, Great Britain, Ireland, France, the Netherlands, Australia, New Zealand, and South Africa, RPL has taken on the political and philosophical marks of its disparate new settings. Thus in Britain, RPL emerged in conjunction with the changing class base of higher education and the country's evolution into a multicultural society. In South Africa it was introduced by the African National Congress and the black trade union federation as a way to overcome the wage and education gap left by Apartheid. In New Zealand, it was importantly connected to issues of aboriginal education, as is also the case in Canada.[2]

In spite of its reworking through international practice, the undertheorisation of RPL practice continues to be the norm. The few standard models for how adults learn experientially have substituted, until very recently, for a sustained engagement with the philosophical underpinnings of RPL. For all its celebration of experience, RPL remains trapped within a model of transcendental rationality and individual cognition that is shared by white academic cultures across the globe and that are, indeed, taken for granted within Western cultures. That this model of cognition is often taken as self-evident – and therefore pre-theoretical – is the effect of philosophical foundations whose intellectual history and cultural specificity have been erased. In the face of its internationalisation and in spite of greater attention to the relationship between race, gender, nationality and educational opportunity, RPL practice has remained largely closed to the challenge of feminist, post-colonialist and critical race theorists who see the knower as historically and socially particular and view the glorification of transcendental knowledge as itself an epistemological power move.

In this chapter, I want to revisit the epistemological foundations within which RPL is typically practised. In doing so, I will pay specific attention to the portfolio-assisted evaluation of university-equivalent knowledge. I will do so for several reasons. First, portfolio essays are normative; in producing them, students are typically required to replicate both the logic and disciplinary organisation of academic subject matter. Because they are required to make knowledge claims consistent with the norms of the academy, students must closely examine those norms and at least appear to internalise them. They must familiarise themselves with the contours of the disciplines and sufficiently grasp academic discourse to argue for themselves in its terms. Secondly, because it explicitly casts autobiographical questions as epistemological ones, and vice versa, portfolio-mediated RPL cannot help but enact, not only a theory of knowledge, but a theory of the self. The relationship of self to others, the assumptions concerning reason and the distinction between universal and partial knowledge are aspects of a particular version of selfhood that allows or disallows the articulation of particular kinds of knowledges.

Portfolios thus provide an explicit meeting point for philosophical premises, institutional policies, and social relations of power and offer a uniquely fruitful site for exploring how practices of experiential learning both enact and contest hierarchies of epistemological authority. In this chapter, I will examine the ways in which conventional understandings of experiential learning remain trapped in the very Enlightenment epistemologies they purport to challenge. I will then explore how the alternative epistemologies being offered by theories of situated knowledge might both invigorate RPL practice and allow RPL to challenge the power relationships within which knowledge is legitimated and recognised.

Galileo's telescope and Enlightenment theories of knowledge

The term 'experiential learning' is used consistently in the discourse of adult education, and I have used it thus far for purposes of ease and familiarity. In the following discussion of philosophical premises, I will use the term 'knowledge' instead of 'learning' to connote a socially constructed understanding of the world rather than an internalised, developmental process and to focus on the ways in which theories of 'experiential learning' are theories of knowledge, not cognition: in other words, epistemologies.

Experience, reason, and knowledge: the universal knower
Western epistemology traditionally concerns itself with the relationships among experience, reason and knowledge. As developed most extensively in

the course of the Enlightenment, those relationships can be expressed as follows: experience is transformed into knowledge through the right exercise of reason, and proper procedures exist that enable this transformation to occur. Key to this formulation is the assumption that both experience and language are transparent, that is, that the senses provide unmediated access to reality and that the language we use to describe that reality merely names what is there for all to see.

The claim by Galileo that forms the epigraph to this chapter represents an important tension in the Enlightenment view of knowledge. On the one hand, the appeal to 'irrefragable evidence' announces a profound democratisation of knowledge. Freed from the arbitrary dictates of institutional and political power, knowledge can be generated by anyone because its ultimate source is experience and because the procedures for its formulation – instrumentation, measurement, and reason – are available to all. The individual conscious mind, not the received wisdom of the ages, is now both the origin of, and the validating mechanism for, knowledge; this tenet, often referred to as 'epistemological individualism', holds that human beings gain knowledge of the world as autonomous, contemplative beings, not as members of active and historically evolving communities (Jaggar and Bordo, 1989, p. 3).

At the same time, and in spite of epistemological individualism, the assumption that experience is transparent and that reason is universal means that knowledge can be more than merely subjective. We can hold some truths to be self-evident – the formulation is originally Locke's – because both the raw materials of reality and the organising framework of reason are available to anyone. The same move that ostensibly democratises knowledge, therefore, universalises the human knower: the same knowledge is available to all because, no matter where we are situated, everyone will see the same thing. The ideal knower is interchangeable with all others; able to rise above the human contingencies of emotion, historicity and social position, the rational, knowledge-making self is disembodied and depersonalised (Flax, 1990).

Feminist philosophers have named this view of knowledge 'abstract masculinity' (Hartsock, 1983). As Susan Bordo makes clear, abstract masculinity does not adhere in anatomical maleness: it names 'not a biological category' but, rather, a 'cognitive style, an epistemological stance. Its key term is detachment: from the emotional life, from the particularities of time and place, from personal quirks, prejudices and interests, and most centrally, from the object [of knowledge] itself' (Bordo, 1986, p. 451). The term identifies a number of related epistemological positions: the scripting of the male as the universally human, the belief in an 'objective' knowledge that erases its own historical contingency and the claim for dispassionate and disinterested truths. Sandra Harding's analysis in *Whose Science? Whose Knowledge?* (1991) sees claims for 'disinterested' and 'objective' knowledge as doubly materially located: first, in the concrete life experiences of economically-privileged white males and, secondly, in the use of those claims as historically-situated power moves.[3]

Thus, Enlightenment epistemologies posit a distinctive relationship between experience and knowledge and the process through which one becomes the other: to be seen as valid, knowledge must be purged of its origins in particularised experience, abstracted from the place of its making, and dehistoricised. What we have here, in effect, is a narrative of detachment that is at once temporal and spatial. While knowledge is grounded in experience, its construction requires that knowledge gradually be abstracted from experience; 'intuition' (perception) is a first-order activity through which human beings access the world, while what Descartes called 'deduction' and Locke 'demonstration' are second-order activities in which direct sensory inputs are sorted and acted upon by the mind.

Universal knowledge and the (un)marked body

There is another quality contained in the Enlightenment view of knowledge that will be important to the discussion that follows, namely, the relationship between claims to universal knowledge and social privilege. As feminist and post-colonialist scholars have pointed out, the claim that the reliable knower is interchangeable with all others serves to erase the social distinctions that have historically delimited epistemological authority. The supposedly 'objective' mind is the product of the 'unmarked' body, a body that is not seen as socially particularised because its specificities – maleness, whiteness, health, affluence, and so on – have been normalised as universally human but are more accurately seen as the specificities of social privilege. The series of dualisms that structure epistemological authority in Western cultures – mind/body, rational/emotional, objective/ subjective, abstract/concrete – associate the 'marked' body, in turn, with the denigrated second term of those dualisms, conjoining epistemological to social marginalisation and limiting Galileo's supposed 'anyone' to quite specific social categories.

Thus, the new procedures through which Enlightenment science generated knowledge coded the authorised knower as a very particular human being. According to the paradigmatic seventeenth-century figure Sir Robert Boyle, for example, only Protestant gentlemen of independent means could attest to the truth of an observation. Individuals who were by definition dependent, such as servants and women, could not be credible witnesses, while merchants were too self-interested and Catholics too crafty to be relied on to tell the truth (Shapin, 1994). In the intervening centuries, maleness, whiteness, Europeanness and economic prosperity have continued to be associated with the privileged first term of the dualisms. Women, native peoples and workers, among others, have in turn been associated with the despised second term of the dualisms and characterised as irrational, emotional, and partisan.

Indeed, on various fronts and across a number of centuries, an extraordinary amount of attention has been placed on excluding different categories of people from the ranks of 'experiential learners', distinguishing between those who can and cannot make meaning from their own experience, and then denying people economic and political rights based on their supposed inability to interpret their own experience. With the emergence of democratic government, for example, the denial of political rights – the withholding of the franchise from women and workers and the appropriation of the non-European world – was justified on the grounds that such people could not learn from experience. Women's greater emotionality precluded a reasoned understanding of the world and would play havoc with the deliberations of public life (Gatens, 1988). Members of the working classes were children in need of instruction, not adults who could learn from their mistakes (Vicinus, 1974). Africans could not make inferences based on experience and observation and thus were incapable of governing themselves (Masolo, 1994; Mudimbe, 1988). Arabs were too backward to understand their own best interests or else too degenerate and lazy to try (Said, 1978). Seen in this regard, the human sciences can be understood as a series of social practices for managing the unruly experience of the Other: colonialist anthropology for the natives; sociology and scientific management for the working class; and medicine and psychiatry for the three closely-related categories of women, homosexuals and lunatics.

The epistemology of experiential learning

That knowledge is rooted in experience was an organising principle of adult learning for much of the twentieth century. Inspired by John Dewey's insistence on 'the organic connection between education and personal experience' (Dewey, 1938/1963, p. 25), theories of adult learning challenged rigid, subject-centred pedagogies and did much to reground knowledge in contextualised and diverse life experience. These theories have importantly recognised organisations of knowledge that are at odds with academic disciplines and insisted that students differ markedly in both demographics and learning styles.

The Enlightenment sources of experiential learning theory

Ultimately, however, mainstream theories of adult learning replicate rather than challenge the Enlightenment view of knowledge. According to David Kolb (1984), for example, knowledge is created through a continuous four-step process: concrete experience serves as the basis for observation and reflection, which are then used in the formation of abstract concepts and generalisations; these, in turn, can be tested through active experimentation as new situations arise. Restated in slightly different terms, unmediated experience provides the Lockean raw material from which knowledge can be constructed. That material is then acted upon by the mind via observation (the controlled application of the senses) and reflection (the self-conscious application of reason). Out of this sensate and mental activity, the individual abstracts testable and verifiable knowledge from experience.

Kolb, it would seem, does not intend to replicate the universalised Enlightenment individual. He explicitly argues that adults construct knowledge differently depending on background experiences, learning styles and, in some cases, gender, class and culture. Yet the 'learning cycle' described above, which is the model for much portfolio development and is by far the most influential part of his work, replicates Enlightenment epistemology quite closely. The sides of his diagram are the methods of science – observation, experimentation, and reason – through which, according to Galileo and Locke, the mind transforms experience into knowledge. Top and bottom, in turn, replicate the Cartesian dichotomy between immediately available data and ideas constructed within the mind. Reality is seen as 'simply there, grasped through a mode of knowing here called apprehension' (Dewey, 1938/1963, quoted in *ibid.* p. 43); comprehension is a second-order activity, the product of applied rationality. The knowledge thus abstracted is the product of an individual mind; at the same time it takes the form of universalised concepts that are at significant spatial and temporal remove from the original experience.

I have used Kolb as an example because he is at once representative and influential, but the key elements of Enlightenment epistemology – knowledge as a transformation of experience, reason as the sanctioned path to knowledge, and the universal knower – underpin treatments of adult learning that are otherwise quite disparate. Drawing heavily on both Dewey and humanistic psychology, Malcolm Knowles (1973/1990), for example, focuses on the examination of experience, the importance of rational self-knowledge and the relationship of reason to both autonomy and community. In Knowles' case, those principles are placed within an unreserved ideology of epistemological individualism,[4] leaving him with a self-actualising 'adult learner' who is at once highly individualistic and curiously devoid of human specificities. Approaches to adult learning inspired by Jürgen Habermas evidence similar patterns. While Jack Mezirow (1991), for example, questions the ideal of the autonomous knower and contends that all knowledge is constructed within power-laden social processes, he still maintains, citing Habermas, that we arrive at our best knowledge through the exercise of reason and that, freed from bigotry through dialogue and self-reflection, all knowers can arrive at congruent truths. A similar echo of Enlightenment epistemology also characterises many of the unspoken assumptions behind the works of Paulo Freire and his followers.[5] While the life experience of the poor *is* the subject matter of the Freirean curriculum, the perspectives of the poor on their own experience are seen as partial and subjective, while the educator's role is 'the organised, systematised, and developed "re-presentation" of that experience' (Freire, 1974, p. 82). The parallel dualities that join rationality to social status, ironically, reemerge in Freire's citing of Mao: the educator's goal is to 'teach the masses *clearly* what we have received from them *confusedly*' (Freire, 1974, note 7, emphasis mine).

Enlightenment epistemology and RPL

When we turn from theories of experiential learning to the practice of RPL, we find many of these same elements, with the distinction between *experience* and *learning* re-inscribing the dualisms discussed above. For all the celebration of the diversity of experience, learning must be presented as being similar to that of others and recognisable in terms set by universalised academic norms. In writing portfolios, students are required to replicate the steps of universal rationality, transcending the singularities of their experience and situation and placing their knowledge within universalised categories.

Instructions concerning the construction of portfolios vary from institution to institution, but the policies of most institutions closely parallel that of my own: 'Empire State College does not award credit for *experience*. Credit is granted to degree-seeking students for verifiable college-level *learning*, either knowledge or skills, acquired through life or work experience, not for the experience itself' (Empire State College, 2004, emphasis mine). This distinction between experience and knowledge is widely considered a fundamental principle of good RPL practice.[6] To be sure, the distinction is maintained for a number of important reasons: it institutionalises the refusal to grant credit for time spent passively and inattentively in a particular environment (hours spent asleep in a theatre, for example), and it encourages an awareness of knowledge as active and human-made. Still, the narrative mode thus imposed on students produces a specific algorithm in which the abstraction of knowledge from experience is cast as a chronological event. Experience always happens first; knowledge is the later product of experience acted upon by reason. The process of constructing a portfolio requires students to re-enact that same chronology, first revisiting and describing the original experiences, then reflecting on and identifying the knowledge thus produced.

This temporal distancing is matched, moreover, by expectations of spatial distance. To be accredited, knowledge much be detached from the site of its production and be 'transferable', to use the standard word, both to other sites of action and to the academic environment. Because knowledge will be assessed, not for its immediate relevance but for its similarity to academic ways of knowing, the university replaces the original site of production as the place from which knowledge is valued and meaning assigned.[7] Thus, for all its radical implications about the sites from which academically valid knowledge can be generated, RPL replicates the irony at the heart of Enlightenment theories of knowledge: while the experiential origins of knowledge are acknowledged and, indeed, extolled, knowledge is credited only to the degree that experience has been transcended, so that both the site of its production and the particularities of the self have been excised.

Experience and the critique of Enlightenment epistemology

In recent years, post-modernist, feminist and critical race theorists have interrogated the Enlightenment self as the autonomous agent of knowledge, problematised the transparency of experience and language and questioned the disinterestedness of claims to rationality.[8] In so doing, they have reopened the question of how experience relates to knowledge, examined how each of them acquires visibility and value and offered a democratisation of knowledge far different from that of Galileo's telescope. This has profound implications for academic approaches to knowledge that privilege detached and universalised reason, as well as specific ramifications for RPL.

Experiential learning as situated knowledge

First, contemporary theory argues that experience is not transparent. Far from giving us unmediated access to reality, experience itself is mediated by a host of social and discursive formulations that tell us what the world is like and who we are within it. Rather than being the Lockean raw material that is subsequently given order and meaning by the mind, experience enters our consciousness already organised by ideology, language and material history. This means, in turn, that experience and knowledge are neither chronologically nor logically distinct. They are more helpfully seen as mutually determined, with knowledge shaping experience as much as the reverse. This is not to say that the examination of experience cannot produce new knowledge, but it does mean that experience itself is, at least in part, knowledge-driven. There is no escaping what theorists call the hermeneutic circle; because experience cannot be known in the first place outside of material structures, social relationships and socially available meanings, the knowledge through which we organise meaning cannot be separated from experience.[9]

That our experience is shaped by discourse and sociality does not mean, however, that everyone's experience is the same. To the contrary, precisely because culture and history run through us, we experience the world differently as men or women, as members of nations, classes and races, and as products of specific material structures, languages and ideologies. This defines us as knowers who are very different from the interchangeable, universal knowers of the Enlightenment; we know the world as particular, socially-located beings, not as autonomous but abstract entities (Haraway, 1991).

'Situated' knowledge is the term often used for this alternative epistemology. As Donna Haraway uses the term, it names an epistemology that insists on 'the particularity and embodiment of all vision' (Haraway, 1991, p. 189) and the 'limited location' (*ibid.*, p. 190) from which any of us can view the world. According to Haraway, the alternative to abstract masculinity is not relativism but rather 'webbed accounts' of the world in which 'partiality and not universality is the condition of being heard to make rational knowledge claims' (*ibid.*, p. 195). It is only through the acknowledgement that our vision is inevitably partial that we can be accountable for how – and what – we come to know. What we need and, indeed, all we can offer are 'partial, locatable, critical knowledges sustaining the possibility of webs of connections called solidarity in politics and shared conversations in epistemology' (*ibid.*, p. 191).

The insistence that *all* knowledge is situated knowledge uncovers the power move behind the claims of the unmarked body to knowledge that transcends its own social location. It names such claims, rather, as concrete social acts that both rely on 'the body, the hand, the material work, the working world' (Smith, 1987, p. 77) and at the same time render those practices invisible. Feminist theorists in particular have revisited the criteria through which different forms of knowledge are differentially seen and valued, not only holding that knowledge-production is a social process whose legitimation is connected to political power but arguing, further, that traditionally denigrated forms of knowledge – those created through 'women's work' and manual labour, for example – can correct the distortions of knowledge produced through pretensions to disinterested and disengaged reasoning (Harding, 1991).

Experiential learning and the interrogation of reason

One aspect of this redefinition of the knower is a challenge to the Enlightenment emphasis on dispassionate, abstract reason as the sole reliable faculty through which knowledge can be made. As a number of feminist and critical race theorists argue, the Western concept of reason is not culturally neutral, but is the product of a specific intellectual history. Its privileging at the expense of other dimensions has distinct implications for the kinds of knowledge that are sanctioned and the ways human beings are unequally valued based on the kinds of knowledge they create. First, the valorisation of reason has historically conjointed with the concomitant denigration of other avenues to knowledge such as emotion, the body, and manual labour. Those sources of knowledge, in turn, have traditionally been associated with social groups, such as women and Africans, who have not been granted epistemological authority (Collins, 1991; Lorde, 1989; Minnich, 1990; Grosz, 1993). Secondly, the privileging of Reason – and the capital R is important here – serves to erase the multiple forms of systematic thought through which human beings understand the world. Human beings evaluate information and solve problems in multiple ways, many of which show sustained and careful habits of mind that can surely be called rational. Reason understood narrowly, however, as a detached and rule-bound process for arriving at universal knowledge within the individual mind, belies alternative dialogic, social and active modalities of thought. Rather than rising above the interestedness of power struggles and desires, the myth of abstract, transcendental Reason itself 'is used to maintain power differentials in a world in which reason is identified with dominant groups and emotion with subjugated ones' (Jaggar, 1989, p. 157).[10]

An interesting case in point has recently surfaced in the South African literature on RPL. Mignonne Breier (2001, 2003, Chapter 4, this volume) has studied the ways in which prior learning was and was not legitimated in two university-based labour law courses to which adults had gained entry on the basis of their experience. While no formal RPL mechanism took place, Breier closely analysed the degree to which experiential learning was granted epistemological recognition within the courses and charted the analytical and rhetorical strategies used by lecturers and learners.

The adult learners participating in both these courses included predominantly white professionals and predominantly black trade union activists. Breier found that, while the professionals, like the course lecturers, argued from general rules and used strategies that appealed to law in the abstract, the shop stewards appealed to the particular, using specific incidents and cases to argue against the validity of the general rule. The unionists were less likely to 'play the [academic] game' (Breier, 2003, p. 264), a game which, Breier argues, required them to understand the abstract rules of classification that mediated the use of personal experience and to think and speak in hypothetical terms. Lacking an understanding of the game, they were often seen to be missing the point of the lectures, failing to grapple successfully with abstract modes of thought and thus either participating inappropriately or retreating into silence during class.

As Breier argues, the data are evidence of the need to teach the expected forms of thought and communication to non-traditional learners first entering the academy and to develop curricula in which the relationship of formal to informal structures of knowledge and general to specific statements at least roughly resembles that of the field of practice. But the data can be interpreted in other ways. A particularly conservative reading would point to the dangers of RPL, to the lack of 'equivalence' between experiential and academic learning and/or the inadvisability of admitting non-traditional learners into conventional academic study.

In line with the theoretical framings of this chapter, it is also possible to interpret the data as evidence of the social locatedness of knowledge and the power-ladenness of claims for abstract and 'objective' modes of thought. Interpreted in this manner, the shop stewards' insistence on the gap between the general law and the specific application was not evidence of a failure of abstract thought or an inability to grasp the rules of the academic game. Rather, it hints at forms of academic gamesmanship at work in the classroom under the radar and out of the awareness of the lecturers. As a number of trade unionists recounted to Breier, they had joined the class, not to earn academic credentials for themselves, but to gain knowledge that they could take back to their union. Discerning in the lecturers a pro-management bent and a preference for the white professional students, they saw no advantage in arguing. Instead, they chose to hang back, as Breier describes it, having 'resolved beforehand to accept the ideological orientation of the course, and not get involved in debates about it, but rather get as much information as they could' (Breier, 2003, p. 213). Similarly, while at least one shop steward viewed the lecturers' case studies as 'fakes' (Breier, 2001, p. 7) and seemed unable to think hypothetically, others quickly learned to use the hypothetical voice to their own advantage, specifically to manipulate the lecturers into providing free legal council. There is, in other words, more than one form of the academic game.

Perhaps even more to the point, this reading of the data suggests that there is no such thing as an objective or abstract understanding of the law, only a variety of equally located positions in which claims to abstraction and objectivity function both to further, and to mask, power moves. Seen in that regard, what the trade unionists were evidencing was not a failure of abstract thought but rather an oppositional and hard-earned epistemological politics. The relationship between the law as written in the abstract and as experienced in practice had different implications for various groups and individuals in the classroom, with the law appearing more generalisable from some social locations than others. According to one professor who taught on the course, 'your legal academic bases him or herself on the study of hundreds of cases. What happens in your one workplace or ten workplaces [. . .] is almost irrelevant' (Breier, 2001, p. 6). One unionist, however, who was not able to adjust to the expectations of the course, pointed to the irrelevance of the general and the importance of what she called the 'small, nitty gritty things' of practice. 'If I should go according to rules and regulation guidelines [. . .] then I'd lose all my cases' (*ibid.*, p. 8). Breier points out that even a careful pedagogy that 'explain[s] to students the relationship between their experience and the logic of the discipline' still raises the question of the situatedness of knowledge. 'Whose experience', she asks, 'should form the basis of the scaffolding? The unionists? The lawyers? The human resource managers? The full-time students?' (Breier, 2005, p. 63). While Breier suggests that a viable curriculum and pedagogy must provide 'a necessary common denominator' (*ibid.*), it is clear that any such commonality remains a contested terrain.

If experience is not transparent, if reason is not epistemologically and politically neutral, and if there is no universal, interchangeable knower, then the notion of objective and transcendental knowledge cannot be sustained. Once we relinquish the image of the rational consciousness constructing knowledge in detached and splendid isolation, what is left is a mesh of social practices through which human activity is delineated and given meaning and which are sometimes shared and sometimes contested among people and social groups. We thus arrive at an epistemology that holds knowledge to be at once a social product and invariably partial; different knowledge is available from different 'standpoints', that is, from social and historical locations. Knowledge is local, interested, relational; it is created by active human groups in the process of sustaining the human world. It is always socially and historically situated, that is, always embedded within the matrix of social relationships and social activity.

Situated knowledge and the assessment of experiential learning

There is, then, nothing disinterested or innocent about the process through which knowledge is given value. Its valuing takes place through concrete social practices in which specific knowledge – and, therefore, specific knowers – are publicly and institutionally valued and in which questions of epistemological authority explicitly confront questions of power inequality. RPL within educational institutions relies on the power of the academy to determine what kind of knowledge 'counts' and translates epistemological legitimacy into currencies – credits, degrees, professional credentials – that lead to social status and material rewards. RPL is an important innovation; in addition to being of considerable practical help to adult learners, it can also be a means for revisiting the social relationships within which knowledge is legitimated and for expanding the fund of human understanding by giving space to outsider knowledges. But it does not invariably do either of those things.

An early example of RPL in France is instructive in this regard. In the late 1980s, Amina Barkatoolah (1989) analysed programmes to grant the professional status of engineer to workers who had gained their technical skills experientially. In France, as elsewhere, the title of engineer is traditionally achieved through earning a degree. However, a special system administered by the Ministry of Education allowed experienced technical workers to be awarded an *Ingenieurs Diplomes d'Etat* (National Diploma in Engineering) on the basis of work-based knowledge articulated in portfolios.

In important respects, the programme was consistent with RPL's association with equity and opportunity. Without certification, these technical workers had little employment mobility and were not being remunerated appropriately. At the same time, the terms of the assessment undermined any facile notions of RPL as an instrument of social justice in the following ways. While awarded by a governmental body and relying on both academic and professional evaluators, certification was based on criteria that reflected the power and interests of powerful social groups, specifically the desire of management for adaptable and acquiescent employees. The RPL process included the investigation of personality traits through psychological tests and handwriting analysis, thus joining the evaluation of knowledge to a power-laden and far-from-disinterested appraisal of disposition and behaviour (Barkatoolah, 1989). One of the French terms for RPL, *reconnaissance des acquis* (assessment of prior learning) underscores this point when read in English, suggesting Taylorism, the unidirectional gaze and the surveillance of workers by management. Galileo's telescope meets Bentham's panopticon.

To a more or less explicit degree, all RPL practices are similarly embedded in matrices of power. University-based RPL is defended on the grounds that it does *not* challenge academic claims to epistemological authority: it posits academic knowledge as the norm around which judgments of inclusion and exclusion can be made; it extends the academy's traditional gate-keeping function; and it calibrates the legitimacy of students' knowledge according to samenesses and correspondences. RPL's complicity with institutional and social power, in fact, has been grounds for its rejection by some experiential educators (Weil and McGill, 1989). These educators contrast RPL negatively with such practices as Freirean pedagogy and feminist consciousness-raising, in which the examination of experience encourages insurgent perspectives. And there is concern, even among proponents of RPL, that RPL replaces collectivist explorations of experiential learning that have been powerful in struggles for social change (Cooper, 1998).

I would argue, however, that RPL can become an important venue for revisiting the relationship between authorised and devalued forms of knowledge *precisely because it formalises it*. It is therefore a node for negotiating epistemological visibility and for re-examining the notion of authoritative community. By relocating RPL within an epistemology of situated knowledge, we can reconfigure it as a dialogue across alternative modalities of knowledge. If *all* knowledge, including academic knowledge, is partial, then RPL can become an invitation to attend to traditionally marginalised voices, treat alternative experiences of the world as grounds for contesting the primacy of any and acknowledge the value of both confluence and divergence in disparate knowledge claims. Rather than endorsing academic rights to unidirectional judgment, RPL can foster a reciprocal interrogation of the premises and power relationships within which the academy functions: definitions of experience and knowledge; the privileging of abstract masculinity; the institutional power of the academy itself.

First, a reconceptualised RPL might broaden the opportunity for students and faculty alike to interrogate their experience, treating it not as unmediated sensory data, but as the socially-produced subjectivity through which we locate ourselves in the world. The dialogue thus initiated would allow us to inquire what knowledge is born of personal and social history, within bodies marked by class, race and gender, out of feelings of anger and love. The knowledge thus generated cannot be understood solely as the product of detachment and reason. Such knowledge is felt, embodied, sensed; it remains rooted in experience. It is partial in both senses of the word: partisan and incomplete.

Secondly, if all knowledge is situated knowledge, then similarity to academic knowledge cannot be the sole criterion for assessment; there will be times at which a path of inquiry with compelling explanatory power will lead to knowledge that is not congruent with academic forms of truth. This, of course, raises a number of questions: what makes a fact or an idea compelling? Compelling to whom? The point for the moment is that RPL can provide the opportunity to recognise knowledge that is not 'academic' because it is not available from positions of epistemological and social privilege. It can become a site for articulating and affirming what feminist and critical race theorists call 'outsider knowledge', that is, knowledge that is visible from and produced within experience of life in marginalised social categories. This is not a question of epistemological relativism[11] or, as it is too often argued, a softening of academic 'standards'. On the contrary, by seeing the lives of women, people of colour and workers as sites from which knowledge is produced, we can correct inaccuracies and broaden the range of knowledge via 'knowledge claims that are different from and in some respects preferable to knowledge claims grounded in the lives of men in the dominant groups' (Harding, 1991, p. 47). Thus, the presence within the academy of this alternative approach to RPL gestures towards a re-membering of the subject and object of knowledge and begins to reconfigure the politics of epistemology.

Ultimately, of course, a reconceptualised RPL also challenges the foundations of academic power, specifically its monopoly over professional credentialing and the awarding of degrees. By substituting dialogue and mutual recognition for what was unidirectional judgment, we destabilise the basis on which validation is given and invite a sharing of epistemological authority.

Conclusion

I am not suggesting that, by itself, RPL can alter the power relationships within which universities operate. The gate-keeping function of the academy is maintained by both honourable scholarship and entrenched social privilege, and many people have a stake in both. RPL policies alone will not reformulate the relationships among cultures of knowing or the social hierarchies they justify; challenges to systems of legitimation must often come from outside those systems and be based in broad political struggles for resources and legitimacy. But at the very least, RPL is a way of making the criteria of judgment visible and, therefore, potentially negotiable: for whose knowledge gets to 'count'; for who may judge whom, and on what basis; for the procedures whereby knowledge is rewarded; and whose interests those procedures serve.

The insistence that knowledge is situated has become an important venue for contesting the authority of univocal interpretive communities, rivalling Galileo's telescope in its epistemological insurgency. Reinscribed within a theory of situated knowledge, RPL can become a venue for examining how each of us moves back and forth between our own particular stories and the social production that is knowledge and for challenging oppressive taxonomies of knowledge and the power relationships they enact. It can grant visibility to knowledge that is valuable for its divergence from academic ways of knowing, not only its similarity, and affirm knowledge produced outside epistemologically-sanctioned locations, through dialogue within (and, when we are lucky, between) historically-situated communities.

References

Alcoff, L. and Potter, E. (eds) (1993), *Feminist Epistemologies*, New York: Routledge.
Barkatoolah, A. (1989), 'Some critical issues related to assessment and accreditation of adults' prior experiential learning' in Weil, S.W. and McGill, I. (eds) *Making Sense of Experiential Learning: Diversity in Theory and Practice*, Milton Keynes: Society into Research in Higher Education and Open University Press.
Bhabha, H. (1994), *The Location of Culture*, New York: Routledge.

Bordo, S. (1986), 'The Cartesian masculinization of thought', *Signs*, 11: 439–56.

Brah, A. and Hoy, J. (1989), 'Experiential learning: a new orthodoxy?' in Weil, S.W. and McGill, I. (eds) *Making Sense of Experiential Learning: Diversity in Theory and Practice*, Milton Keynes: Society into Research in Higher Education and Open University Press.

Breier, M. (2001), 'How to bridge the "great divide": the dilemma for the policy and practice of "recognition of prior learning" (RPL) in South Africa', *Perspectives in Education*, 19(4): 89–107.

Breier, M. (2003), *The Recruitment and Recognition of Prior Informal Experience in the Pedagogy of Two University Courses in Labour Law*, Unpublished doctoral dissertation, Cape Town: University of Cape Town.

Breier, M. (2005), 'A disciplinary-specific approach to the recognition of prior informal experience in adult pedagogy: "rpl" as opposed to "RPL"', *Studies in Continuing Education*, 27(1): 51–65.

Brookfield, S. (1987), *Developing Critical Thinkers*, San Francisco: Jossey-Bass.

Collins, P.H. (1991), *Black Feminist Thought: Knowledge, Consciousness, and the Politics of Empowerment*, New York: Routledge, Chapman, and Hall.

Cooper, L. (1998), 'From "rolling mass action" to "RPL"', *Studies in Continuing Education*, 20(2): 143–57.

Dewey, J. (1938/1963), *Experience and Education*, New York: Collier.

Empire State College (2004), Advanced Standing through Prior Learning Assessment, Satatoga Springs, NY: Empire State College. Available online at http://www.esc.edu/esconline/across_esc/asssessment.

Evans, N. (ed.) (2000), *Experiential Learning Around the World*, Philadelphia, PA: Jessica Kingsley.

Fenwick, T. (2000), 'Expanding conceptions of experiential learning: a review of the five contemporary perspectives of cognition', *Adult Education Quarterly*, 50(4): 243–72.

Flax, J. (1990), Postmodernism and gender relations in feminist theory' in Nicholson, L. (ed.) *Feminism/postmodernism*, New York: Routledge.

Foucault, M. (1990), The Order of Things: An Archeology of the Human Sciences, London: Routledge.

Freire, P. (1974), *The Pedagogy of the Oppressed*, New York: Seabury.

Gatens, M. (1988), 'Towards a feminist philosophy of the body' in Caine, B., Grosz, E.A. and DeLepervanche, M.M. (eds) *Crossing boundaries: Feminisms and the critique of knowledges*, Boston: Allen & Unwin.

Grosz, E. (1993), 'Bodies and knowledges: feminism and the crisis of reason' in Alcoff, L. and Potter, E. (eds) *Feminist Epistemologies*, New York: Routledge.

Haraway, D. (1991), 'Situated knowledges' in *Simians, Cyborgs, and Women: The Reinvention of Nature*, New York: Routledge.

Harding, S. (1991), *Whose Science? Whose Knowledge? Thinking from Women's Lives*, Ithaca, NY: Cornell University Press.

Hartsock, N. (1983), *Money, Sex, and Power: Toward a Feminist Historical Materialism*, New York: Longman.

Hart, M. (1991), 'Liberation through consciousness raising' in Mezirow, J. and Associates, *Fostering Critical Reflection in Adulthood: A Guide to Transformative and Emancipatory Learning*, San Francisco: Jossey-Bass.

Hill, D. (2004), 'The wholeness of life: a native North American approach to portfolio-development at First Nations Technical Institute' in Michelson, E. and Mandell, A. *Portfolio Development and the Assessment of Prior Learning: Perspectives, Models, and Practices*, Sterling, VA: Stylus.

Jaggar, A. (1989), 'Love and knowledge: emotion in feminist epistemology' in Jaggar, A. and Bordo, S. (eds) *Gender/Body/Knowledge: Feminist Reconstructions of Being and Knowing*, New Brunswick, NJ: Rutgers University Press.

Jaggar, A. and Bordo, S. (1989), 'Introduction' in *Gender/Body/Knowledge: Feminist Reconstructions of Being and Knowing*, New Brunswick, NJ: Rutgers University Press.

Keddie, N. (1980), 'Adult education: An ideology of individualism' in Thompson, J. (ed.) *Adult Education for a Change*, London: Hutchinson.

Knowles, M. (1990 [1973]), *The Adult Learner: A Neglected Species*, Houston: Gulf.

Kolb, D. (1984), *Experiential Learning*, Englewood Cliffs, NJ: Prentice Hall.

Lorde, A. (1989), 'The uses of the erotic' in Plaskow, J. and Christ, C.P. (eds) *Weaving the Vision: New Patterns in Feminist Spirituality*, New York: Harper Collins.

McKelvie, C. and Peters, H. (1993), *APL: Equal Opportunities for All?*, London: Routledge.

Mezirow, J. (1991), *Transformative dimensions of adult learning*, San Francisco: Jossey-Bass.

Michelson, E. (1996a), '"Auctoritee" and "experience": feminist epistemology and the assessment of experiential learning', *Feminist Studies*, 22(3): 627–55.

Michelson, E. (1996b), 'Usual suspects: experience, reflection, and the (en)gendering of knowledge', *International Journal of Lifelong Education*, 15: 438–54.

Michelson, E. (1998), 'Re-membering: The return of the body to experiential learning', *Studies in Continuing Education*, 20(2): 217–33.

Michelson, E. (2004), 'On trust, desire, and the sacred: a response to Johann Muller's Reclaiming Knowledge', *Journal of Education*, 32: 7–30.

Michelson, E. and Mandell, A. (2004), *Portfolio Development and the Assessment of Prior Learning: Perspectives, Models, and Practices*, Sterling, VA: Stylus.

Minnich, E. (1990), *Transforming Knowledge*, Philadelphia: Temple University Press.

Mudimbe, V.Y. (1988), *The Invention of Africa: Gnossis, Philosophy, and the Order of Knowledge*, Bloomington, IN: Indiana University Press.

Muller, J. (2000), *Reclaiming Knowledge: Social Theory, Curriculum and Education Policy*, London: Routledge/Falmer.

Narayan, U. and Harding, S. (2000), *Decentering the Center: Philosophy for a Multicultural, Postcolonial, and Feminist World*, Bloomington, IN: Indiana University Press.

Odora Hoppers, C. (ed.) (2002), *Indigenous Knowledge and the Integration of Knowledge Systems: Toward a Philosophy of Articulation*, Claremont, SA: New Africa Books.

Peters, H., Pokorny, H. and Johnson, L. (2004), 'Cracking the code: the assessment of prior experiential learning at London Metropolitan University' in Michelson, E. and Mandell, A. *Portfolio Development and the Assessment of Prior Learning: Perspectives, Models, and Practices*, Sterling, VA: Stylus.

Ryan, A.B. (2001), *Feminist Ways of Knowing: Towards Theorising the Person for Radical Adult Education*, Leicester: NIACE.

Said, E. (1978), *Orientalism*, New York: Pantheon.

Shapin, S. (1994), *A Social History of Truth: Civility and Science in Seventeenth Century England*, Chicago: University of Chicago Press.

Smith, D. (1987), *The Everyday World as Problematic: A Feminist Sociology*, Boston: University of Massachusetts Press.

Tennant, M. (1986), 'An evaluation of Knowles' theory of adult learning', *International Journal of Lifelong Education*, 5(1): 113–22.

Vicinus, M. (1974), *The Industrial Muse*, London: Croom Helm.

Weil, S.W. and McGill, I. (1989), 'A framework for making sense of experiential learning' in Weil, S.W. and McGill, I. (eds) *Making Sense of Experiential Learning: Diversity in Theory and Practice*, Milton Keynes: Society into Research in Higher Education and Open University Press.

Weiler, K. (1991), 'Freire and a feminist pedagogy of difference', *Harvard Education Review*, 61: 449–74.

Whitaker, U. (1989), *Assessing Learning: Standards, Principles, and Procedures*, Chicago: Council for Adult and Experiential Learning.

Notes

[1] This chapter was originally published in a different form in 1996 in *Adult Education Quarterly*, 46(4): 185–96. Revised and reprinted with permission of the journal.

[2] For a helpful survey of RPL developments internationally, see Evans (2000). For a discussion of RPL among immigrant groups in Britain, see Kelvey and Peters (1993) and Peters *et al.* (2004). For a discussion of aboriginal approaches to RPL in Canada, see Hill (2004).

[3] I have explored theories of experiential learning and RPL from the feminist perspective at greater length elsewhere. See Michelson (1996a, 1996b, and 1998).

[4] For a critique of the individualism in Knowles' work, see Tennant (1986). For a broader critique of the individualist bias of much adult learning theory, see Keddie (1980).

[5] For an extensive critique of these issues in the works of Freire, see Weiler (1990).

[6] The guidelines for quality assurance promoted by the Council for Adult and Experiential Learning (CAEL) and articulated in Whitaker (1989) names this as the first principle of good practice.

[7] The requirement that all accreditable knowledge closely resemble academic forms of learning is at the heart of both arguments for and the critiques of RPL. Proponents argue that this quality not only insures that academic rigour is maintained but that portfolio-development thus provides an opportunity for students to orient themselves to the particular tonalities and organisations of knowledge in the academy. The construction of a portfolio 'constitutes a schooling in academic discourse' (Peters *et al.*, 2004, p. 166). This same process, which Peters *et al.* refer to as 'cracking the code', has also been criticised as fraught with implicit or explicit criteria that students do not understand, so that the process becomes what Shalem and Steinberg (Chapter 5, this volume) call a 'cat and mouse chase'.

[8] The critique of Enlightenment epistemology has spawned a vast literature. For helpful introductions to a variety of views, see Foucault (2001[1970]), Haraway (1991); Alcoff and Potter (1993); Bhabha (1994); Shapin (1994); Narayan and Harding (2000); Odora-Hoppers (2002).

[9] Discussions of adult education often stress the ways in which unexamined assumptions can distort our experience of the world. Brookfield (1987); Knowles (1973/1990); and Mezirow (1991) for example, all discuss the ways in which critical self-reflection can free us from distorting influences of culturally transmitted beliefs. The position I am taking here, one shared by Brah and Hoy (1989), Hart (1990), Ryan (2001) and other theorists of adult learning, differs in insisting that we always experience within power relationships, material history and culturally imposed structures of meaning. For a helpful survey of newer approaches to experiential learning, see Fenwick (2000).

[10] For a feminist and critical race critique of the power-ladenness of claims concerning reason, see Minnich (1990). For a more detailed discussion of this point within adult education theory, see Michelson (1996b).

[11] The attempt to critique too-narrow positivist epistemologies and introduce a broader range of criteria for legitimating knowledge is often subject to the charge of relativism, with relativism understood as the belief that all accounts of the world are equally valid and that there are no criteria or procedures for adjudicating between competing knowledge claims. Proponents of situated knowledge have clearly distinguished their position from relativism. Donna Haraway, for example,

maintains that relativism, like abstract masculinity, is a 'way of being nowhere while claiming to be everywhere equally' and that this purported equality of interpretation 'is a denial of responsibility and critical enquiry'. Relativity, she continues, 'is the perfect mirror twin' of universalised knowledge claims in that 'both deny the stakes in location, embodiment, and partial perspective; both make it impossible to see well' (1991, p. 191). For an example of this charge levelled against the pedagogy of experiential learning, see Muller (2000). For a counter to this argument, see Michelson (2004).

<u>chapter eight</u>

Using critical discourse analysis to illuminate power and knowledge in RPL

Helen Peters

Introduction

RPL is usually defined as a means of crossing borders and breaking down barriers between everyday lives and formal education, with implications for the nature of higher education teaching and study, who comes to university and what happens when they get there. It is generally represented as an emancipatory strategy to facilitate access to higher education for those who have not followed a traditional educational route. Practices aim to open universities to a different type of student, to challenge the academy to look at different forms of knowledge and to promote different assessment strategies. In the UK, pioneering developmental work was undertaken by Norman Evans from 1979 onwards. In 1986, he founded the Learning from Experience Trust 'to put into action at higher education level the brief that it gave itself [. . .] to work on the borders between formal education and the world of work and life' (Evans, 2000, p. 70). This brief followed the ideas of Kolb (1984, p. 38) who described experiential learning as 'the process that links education, work and personal development', and Weil and McGill (1989, p. 3) who divided experiential learning into four 'villages' with one, the 'APEL village', being 'concerned with assessing and accrediting learning from life and work experience as the basis for creating new routes into higher education'.

Achievement of these aims in universities in the UK has not been unproblematic. Awarding credit for types of learning and knowledge which have not been categorised and defined by academic institutions can be seen as striking at the very core of most higher education, by undermining the parameters of bodies of knowledge which have been established through research and for teaching purposes, and suggesting that other forms of knowledge are equally worthy of academic recognition.

This chapter is concerned primarily with power and knowledge in and around RPL. To address these issues in a broad way, I introduce and utilise concepts from Foucault and Chouliaraki and Fairclough. The second part of the chapter is empirical and aims to problematise discursive aspects of RPL. Here, I use Chouliaraki and Fairclough's critical discourse analysis and ask whether 'the discursive dimensions of [the RPL] practice [. . .] meet the communicative needs of the participants' (Chouliaraki and Fairclough, 1999, p. 33). My empirical research involves close examination of a small corpus of texts including university documents, student writing and interviews with students and assessors. These data were collected during the progress of a cohort of students through an RPL process over one academic year in one particular university context in the UK. I interviewed six lecturers, from four different academic departments, who had experience of assessing RPL candidates. I collected and analysed the work of 12 students and interviewed four of them on their experience of portfolio preparation. I examine in detail texts consisting of learning outcomes, interviews and portfolios, analysing how two RPL candidates, in particular, struggled to express their knowledge in the required ways.

I end by drawing some conclusions about how RPL is actualised currently in the university under investigation, and discuss the implications this may have for RPL participants and for the future of RPL as an academic activity.

Foucauldian concepts

A number of Foucauldian concepts have the potential to illuminate fundamental issues associated with power and knowledge in the implementation of RPL. 'Discourse' is defined as the productive means by which relations of power are established, consolidated and implemented. Academic disciplines have their own discourses which embody particular understandings and forms of knowledge. However, for Foucault, 'discipline' is a complex term, with two main meanings. One meaning is an area of academic study (as outlined above) and a second is a strict regime. Through discipline exercised upon a person, power is exercised and knowledge constituted – knowledge which is then subject to evaluation and judgment. According to Foucault, academics who work within their 'discipline' have learnt the rules and submitted to them in order to be recognised as contributors to their specialist body of knowledge. Their power lies in their expertise, their accepted position in their discipline and their ability to evaluate and judge the work of others. This evaluation usually takes place through examinations and related assessments, which Foucault (1977, p. 184) describes as 'technologies of power' combining 'the deployment of force and the establishment of truth'. For Foucault (*ibid*, p. 185), 'the superimposition of the power relations and the knowledge relations assumes in the examination all its visible brilliance'. As an example of this he describes (1973, p. 66) how medical teaching evolved from the recognition of individuals as doctors on 'proof of capacity' and competence, irrespective of whether or not they had studied (in the formal sense), to the requirement for all doctors to qualify through attending recognised medical schools and passing examinations. Thus, the power to determine who can be considered 'qualified' has become established and is wielded in educational institutions around the world. Yet, Foucault asserts that individuals do not simply submit to such power but simultaneously exercise it: '[t]hey are not only its inert or consenting target: they are also the elements of its articulation [. . .] The individual which power has constituted is at the same time its vehicle' (1980, p. 98). This exemplifies Foucault's concept of 'biopower', in which power/knowledge is conceived as an agent of transformation as well as discipline.

Foucault (*ibid.*, p. 81) argues that there have been changes in attitudes to knowledge, evident in an increased valuing of life over theory and of local over universal. He describes this as 'an insurrection of subjugated knowledges' – hitherto unrecognised historical contents and 'a whole set of knowledges that have been disqualified as inadequate to their task or insufficiently elaborated: naïve knowledges, located low down on the hierarchy, beneath the required level of cognition or scientificity' (*ibid.*, p. 84). For Foucault, the struggle for recognition of different forms of knowledge is not one which is 'opposed to the contents, methods or concepts of a science, but to the effects of the centralising powers which are linked to the institution and functioning of an organised scientific discourse within a society such as ours' (*ibid.*). He stresses the importance of struggling against the power-effects of scientific discourses which determine what constitutes valid knowledge.

What do these concepts suggest about RPL?

RPL aims to accord recognition to knowledge which is unlikely to fall neatly within the pre-determined categories of recognised disciplines. It therefore challenges institutionalised traditions for the recognition of valid knowledge and learning. For Foucault, the power of the examination transforms a student into a 'case', classified according to a disciplinary norm. RPL, on the other hand, is premised on a view that learning should be recognised on its own terms, based on recognition of the uniqueness of individuals and the contextualised nature of their learning. There is an implicit assumption in the discourse of RPL that, when successful, candidates may contribute to challenges to the knowledge represented by the disciplines. In this way, aspects of RPL link to the notion of 'subjugated knowledge'. These issues place RPL in a paradoxical situation. Candidates are asking for recognition for their individualised learning gained outside formal education, thereby challenging the status quo, but at the same time they are claiming a place within the educational hierarchy and consequently according value and credibility to that hierarchy. In this way, RPL candidates are required to 'buy into' the discourses of the disciplines and of RPL itself if they are to achieve their own personal aims. The process is thus discursively complex. There are strands of both challenge and containment. Formal disciplinary knowledge and its power-effects on individuals seem to be simultaneously challenged and maintained.

Chouliaraki and Fairclough's concepts

Chouliaraki and Fairclough (1999, p. 24) recognise the validity of Foucault's 'biopower' as an invisible, self-regulating force which potentially subordinates all those involved in a social practice. Although Foucault perceives all forms of power as entailing resistance and sees discourse as incorporating both the productive effects of social practice and negative aspects of power structures, this does not go far enough for Chouliaraki and Fairclough. They criticise Foucault for the 'absence of an orientation to practice and to struggle' (ibid., p. 90). Consequently, they retain a conceptualisation of power as relations of domination: 'capitalist relations between social classes but also patriarchal gender relations as well as racial and colonial relations which are diffused across the diverse practices of a society'. They also retain a greater sense of individual and collective agency, in terms of the capacity to change existing discourses or to build new discursive relations and identities.

Fairclough (2001, p. 16) defines discourse as 'language as social practice', lying somewhere between language and social structure. He views discourse as 'always provisional and indeterminate, contested and moreover, at issue in social relationships'. Writing about dominant educational discourses in the UK, he argues (1999, p. 80) that teachers and learners are positioned by a discourse that emphasises the 'vocationally-oriented transmission of given knowledge and skills'. Within this model he suggests that the definition of 'what counts as knowledge or skill (and therefore what does not), for whom, why and with what beneficial or problematic consequences' is problematic (*ibid.*) because his view of educational institutions is that they should be spaces for greater argument and for the opening up of new knowledges.

For Fairclough, people's lives are increasingly shaped by discourses which determine how the world is, their place in it, what they do and how they see themselves. Moreover, ethnic and cultural diversity have led to correspondingly different languages, dialects and communicative styles. What is important is for individuals to work out who they are and how they relate to others in society. He argues for greater awareness of the ways different discourses work within social practices in order to bring about social and personal change: '[i]t is on the basis of [. . .] understandings of how discourse works within social practices that people can come to question and look beyond existing discourses, or existing relations of dominance and marginalisation between discourses' (*ibid.*, p. 74).

The relationship of these concepts to RPL
RPL can be seen as located at the apex of a three-sided conflict: the struggle for recognition of hitherto unvalued knowledge or knowledges, the struggle to broaden and open up traditional disciplines, and the fight against the dumbing down of knowledge through vocationalism.

The concepts discussed above suggest that, as a social practice concerned with change and democratisation, RPL needs to be explicit about different discourses, supporting candidates in identifying, using and challenging them. This is a central issue when candidates define their learning from experience and represent it for recognition by the formal educational establishment. Do they conform to existing representations or challenge them? Are they aware of the power dynamics inherent in what they are doing?

In Fairclough's conceptual framework, an RPL process would make these social practices and discourses visible, including the structural power relations embedded in them. The interactive practice of representation of self and knowledge in RPL would be turned into a much more critical act. RPL could be seen as the conscious and deliberate construction of a particular identity, including discussion of inherent dangers. For example, if candidates are buying into an academic discourse, this will inevitably involve a certain reformulation of self and identity. Making this more explicit could help overcome at least two of the risks inherent in RPL processes. First, that candidates submit their learning (and their lives) for scrutiny by academics with no particular expertise or allegiance to understanding what is being represented. There are obvious power issues here. Secondly, a particular discursive self tends to be manufactured for the purpose of gaining RPL credit. The struggle faced by candidates seeking to claim RPL is against a dominant and conventional concept of 'the student' as an individual who comes to an educational establishment to learn, and who is conceived by the establishment as a 'non-knower' rather than a 'knower', someone to be initiated into the discipline rather than bringing their own contribution to the sum of knowledge. In order to overcome this, RPL candidates tend to have to appropriate the discourse of the academy in order to present a credible case to those from whom recognition is sought. They need to convince assessors that the nature of the knowledge they are presenting is on a par with disciplinary knowledge as determined by those who contribute to the creation and maintenance of the discipline.

Various means of assessment verify the knowledge students acquire on traditional academic courses. RPL candidates subvert these procedures by undergoing assessment without having followed a course. Systems and strategies have been set up within higher education institutions to accommodate assessment of prior learning in a way that matches conventional assessment methods for knowledge acquired through study, and therefore reassures academics that standards are being maintained. Assessment via RPL requires candidates to develop an awareness of the assessment methods and criteria, and the discourse in which these are expressed – things that students being assessed conventionally are already familiar with. In this way, RPL has been colonised by a traditional university assessment discourse which exerts a high degree of control over what is accepted as valid knowledge. So, although RPL can be seen as pushing back boundaries by accepting aspects of individuals' identities and knowledge as valid in an academic context, it is often the case that new delimiting boundaries are created at the same time. Chouliaraki and Fairclough's ideas suggest that these processes could be made more explicit, or challenged, in the social practices of RPL. As Michelson (1996) has argued, RPL cannot be a neutral device. It will either contribute to the maintenance of traditional academic conventions or be a means of bringing other discourses into the academy.

Using critical discourse analysis

If RPL is a discursive struggle, is critical discourse analysis a useful tool in that struggle? In this section I add empirical analysis to the above by looking in detail at some texts produced in an RPL process in one university. Fairclough (1992, p. 231) defines critical discourse analysis as ways of looking at social practices through the properties of texts, and in particular looking at changes of practice. He describes analysis as involving a progression 'from interpretation of the discourse practice (processes of text production and consumption), to description of the text, to interpretation of both of these in the light of the social practice in which the discourse is embedded'. Analysis includes the nature of the participants and the intended readers/hearers, the purposes for which texts are created and the ideologies that inform the practices within which the texts are located.

I also draw on Halliday's (1994) systemic functional linguistics [SFL] in which he argues that it is not possible to discuss the meaning that a speaker/ writer is trying to convey without examining the linguistic forms (words and grammatical structures) through which it is conveyed. He deploys several concepts to establish the context of an instance of language use: 'field' meaning the social action in which language is embedded; 'tenor' to denote the relationship between participants; and 'mode' to refer to the forms of com-munication selected. These three concepts correspond to the ideational, interpersonal and textual functions of messages, which are realised through the lexicogrammatic systems of transitivity, mood and theme. Transitivity describes how choices relating to verbs (particularly between the active and passive voice) are used to represent events in different ways and to convey the ideational message or content of the text. Mood (or modality) refers to how the creator of a text expresses greater or lesser degrees of certainty in inter-personal communication. Theme focuses on how the elements of a sentence are positioned to alter the focus of the sentence and link it to others in a text.

Learning outcomes

Learning outcomes are a lynch pin of the type of RPL practised in the university where my research was carried out. They form part of what I call

the 'genre of RPL' – using Chouliaraki and Fairclough's (1999, p. 63) definition of genre as 'the sort of language (and other semiosis) tied to a particular
social activity', and as 'a specifically discursive structuring or ordering of a
social practice, a regulative device through which relations of power are
realised as forms of control' (ibid., p. 144). For many RPL practitioners,
learning outcomes are the standard against which learning from experience is
measured. For example, Betts and Smith (1998, p. 89) argue that the process
of mapping experience against the content of modules 'can only be
accomplished successfully if learning outcomes have been explicitly
identified in the module design'. They continue, '[t]he crucial issue as far as
we are concerned is that the student must identify explicitly the learning
outcomes against which mapping is to take place and the university must
agree that these are appropriate and at the right level'. This sounds like a
highly convergent assessment process (see Andersson, Chapter 2 in this
volume), although Betts and Smith do mention that some institutions allow
students to propose personal learning outcomes which do not match existing
validated modules. Learning outcomes are taken to be de facto synonymous
with a student-centred philosophy of learning because 'learning outcomes are
sufficiently transparent for the student to be able to put the case and prove that
the outcomes have been met' (ibid., p. 90).

The above statements become problematic when looked at from the perspective of critical discourse analysis. Learning outcomes form part of a discourse
which has been developed as a means of tabulating knowledge taught in the
institution and as a means of controlling the recognition of knowledge from
outside. The words 'sufficiently transparent' imply familiarity with the concept of outcomes, the learning they represent and the context in which they
are embedded. Betts and Smith's statement assumes that 'the student' is able
to make a judgement as to what quantity and type of evidence will match the
learning outcomes. In so doing, the expectation is that students (or RPL
candidates) understand the view an assessor in an academic institution will
take. Hussey and Smith (2002, p. 225) associate learning outcomes with
modern management techniques and the commodification of learning, as a
means of translating 'knowledge how' into 'knowledge that', which militates
against the recognition of learning through participation. They argue that the
clarity and explicitness of learning outcomes are dependent on their being
interpreted against 'a prior understanding of what is required'. This raises an
important consideration for RPL: candidates are expected to be able to
operate in (and have their knowledge assessed in) a discourse within which
they may never have operated before.

The grammatical structure of learning outcomes

A striking aspect of learning outcomes is the very specific language they employ in delineating segments of knowledge or learning. They take the form of what Halliday (1994) calls 'little texts' (other examples are newspaper headlines or instructions). The context requires these texts to be shortened and highly condensed, although as Halliday points out, they may in fact remain long, as in lecture notes for example. Their distinct grammar entails the omission of elements normally present – the nature of the text determining what is left out. Most learning outcomes consist of an introductory sentence such as 'The student will be able to:' or 'I have the ability to:' followed by a variety of forms of 'little text'. However with increased usage, the introductory sentence is sometimes omitted altogether. The effect of representing 'skills and knowledge' in this format is to depersonalise and systematise the content and abstract it from context.

Box 8.1 is a generic set of learning outcomes used in the university concerned to facilitate the assessment of students' prior or current work experience.

Box 8.1 Set of learning outcomes

- Demonstrate s/he has operated effectively both independently and with others.

- Communicate appropriately with colleagues and superiors.

- Show s/he took a rational and organised approach, applying previously known or new techniques and/or methodologies, to the tasks set.

- Describe and evaluate the structure, major activities and responsibilities of the organisation.

- Evaluate critically his/her performance abilities.

No introduction or explanation is included, and in Halliday's terms the theme of each outcome is the verb. As in many learning outcomes the subject and modal element of the verb are omitted, so that the focus of the text is on the activity rather than the person. A number of assumptions are made about the workplace: that several people work there, that communication takes place between them and that a hierarchy operates (reference to 'colleagues' and 'superiors'). 'Work' is constructed to exclude such forms as self-employment, consultancy or creative activity, which may take place alone. The tenor is the voice of authority instructing a person without authority. It is comparable to some of the documentation that employees have to fill in as part of 'performance appraisal'.

The emphasis is on the value of reflection and the ability to express the products of reflection rather than on the actual practical knowledge of a workplace and/or the ability to function within it. The structure of the text and the division into separate learning outcomes is evidence of the requirement for a particular formulation to lend the content meaning. The assumption is that the content would not carry appropriate meaning if formulated differently, for example, as a narrative or a description. Fairclough (1999) argues that the practice of establishing ways of describing things, which then becomes *the* accepted way (and other ways unacceptable), is a means of imposing particular social practices. There is, thus, a new code that students need to apply to their real-life experiences in order to connect the latter with higher education and in-so-doing re-categorise what they know about themselves and their lives. This may well be a difficult process for the uninitiated to undertake.

RPL candidates' experiences of learning outcomes

All the candidates interviewed, except one, listed the learning outcomes they were claiming RPL credit for separately from the rest of their portfolio text. They each used different strategies to draw up their learning outcomes. One used the learning outcomes of an existing course module and attempted to match her experience to these for one of her claims, then designed her own outcomes for another claim. Another candidate drew on the learning outcomes of a module she had already studied to create her own learning outcomes to claim for another. Two candidates developed their learning outcomes without reference to those of existing modules. All struggled to express their learning from experience within the framework of the discourse of learning outcomes. I will cite the experience of two RPL candidates, Lynette and Susan, and analyse their comments on the process.

Before deciding to undertake a submission for RPL, Lynette and Susan both perceived themselves as 'experienced', but not in a way they thought relevant to their university studies. Lynette said, '[m]y work had mainly consisted of work within the community, so therefore I didn't think academically it would have been valuable'. Susan reported, 'I did think I had knowledge that was valuable and my experiences I thought were very valuable but I didn't actually think it would be able to be used in university'.

Lynette and Susan both position themselves as having to conform to 'criteria' or 'structure' in order to be successful:

> Me: In terms of the writing, how did you decide to do that?
> Susan: I looked at examples of peoples' work.
> Me: Other peoples' claims for RPL?
> Susan: Yes that's right. I mean you look at successful ones and how they presented them and you kind of then structure it in a way that you know is going to be a winner, if you like.

And:

> Me: What gives you the idea, where do you get that from?
> Lynette: From my learning here, reading through the materials, that's when I got the idea that this isn't just about writing about 'oh look this was my experience'. It has to fit into somewhere and I think when you do your learning outcomes that's where you realise that you are working to criteria . . . It's their structure, they work within their structure and I have to respect that and try and fit my experiences into that structure.

In the context of RPL, activities take place that involve candidates using language in particular ways. Susan and Lynette demonstrate awareness of this and imply that the task of conforming to the genre is not an easy one, even though they both wrote their own learning outcomes rather than trying to match their experience to existing ones:

> Me: So did you find that the learning outcomes inhibited you or were they helpful?
> Lynette: I think they inhibited me and I think before I hand in my work I may have to change them.

The impression is given of learning from experience being tailored to fit the requirements of the RPL genre, which effectively shapes the learning and the candidates', and subsequently the assessors', understanding of it. This is borne out by some of the metaphors the candidates used to describe the writing process (emphasis mine):

> Lynette: You come with all your experiences and you've got to *unsift and funnel* it through into that form of academia . . . I'm having to learn a new language. I'm having to come out of my

normal natural self [. . .] and *repackage myself* in order to pass through that process.

Susan: I suppose with academic language you are sort of forced into a little box in a way.

The metaphors 'unsift and funnel', 'repackage' and 'forced into a little box' have a physical resonance, of material being moulded or reshaped. Lynette also used 'a runaway horse' to describe her account of her learning from experience. They present a picture of a discourse which they experience as constraining and hard to conform to, resulting in examples of conflicting orders of discourse in some of the texts of their portfolios, to which I now turn.

Portfolios

Susan wrote a portfolio describing how she used knowledge gained in theology studies at a bible college to set up and run study groups. She chose to write her RPL submission in essay form with learning outcomes clearly described but incorporated into paragraphs describing the context in which they had taken place (rather than listed separately). In her introduction she says:

> I will demonstrate that I can reflect and theorise on aspects of theology through listening to lecturers, studying books, evaluating and investigating for myself and then that I have been able to apply these theories in a practical way by organizing, teaching and provoking discussions on the subject . . . in essence putting an element of Kolb's cyclical theory into practice in that he believes that learning happens when there is a connection between thinking and doing.

Her language exemplifies the RPL genre through the vocabulary used: 'demonstrate', 'reflect', 'theorise', 'evaluating', 'investigating' 'organising', as well as the low modality 'can', 'have been able to' and the reference to Kolb. In subsequent sections of her submission, however, Susan combines this with the expression of her deeply felt religious beliefs:

> Many thought Jesus would lead a rebellion against the Romans to conquer by force but this was never his plan. His plan for

> defeating his enemy was to surrender his life. In a small
> discussion group situation I was able to teach about 'free will',
> how we have opportunities to choose our own destinies rather
> than to drift through life making no decisions about our futures,
> that we have choices, and with this opportunity, that differs
> from that of the animal kingdom who live only by their
> instincts, we instead can be resolute about our purpose in life.
> This inspired the group to reflect upon where their lives were
> going, each being challenged to change, diversify and draw
> their own conclusions.

In the first two sentences of the above quotation, Susan makes clear her personal status as a believer, not just a student of theology. She does this with statements that use modality to express certitude ('this was never his plan'). The third sentence switches to the RPL genre with 'I was able to', but continues in a voice of religious conviction, although the paragraph ends with another sentence in RPL genre, describing an activity and its consequences, rather than expressing a belief. The intermingling of two ideational functions is evident: that of conveying information to the assessor about her abilities; and that of conveying the religious truths that have motivated the activities she describes. In her final paragraph the RPL genre dominates again with the reference to learning outcomes, the focus on herself with the use of personal themes ('me', 'my being', 'I') and vocabulary similar to the first quotation above:

> Clear learning outcomes for me have been my being stimulated
> to investigate without bias (if that is possible), to formulate and
> construct ideas, to correlate this information, making it
> understandable to small groups, to teach and provoke them to
> investigate and discuss and to formulate their own ideas. I have
> been able to motivate and clearly communicate to those
> assisting me in the discussions, working as a team.

Susan's religious beliefs are interwoven with her description of her knowledge and abilities creating the hybridity which Chouliaraki and Fairclough (1999, p. 13) describe as 'inherent in all social uses of language' but which tends to be discouraged in academic texts.

Lynette was more familiar with the academic environment than Susan since she had already been involved in part-time work at the university, teaching Creative Writing to groups of young people, refugees and asylum-seekers as part of widening participation initiatives. She chose to draw on this experience in her portfolio, which, like Susan's, illustrates conflict and hybridity resulting from her efforts to conform to the RPL genre and at the same time express her personal involvement in the activities she describes. She presented her learning outcomes as follows in Box 8.2.

Box 8.2 An RPL candidate's learning outcomes

My experience in facilitating Creative Writing workshops . . . has meant that I am able to:

1. Enable people to express themselves through creative writing.

2. Plan a course of creative writing sessions for different groups e.g. young adults, asylum seekers.

3. Introduce the group to different forms of writing.

4. Conduct and lead creative writing sessions that meet the needs of a specific group.

5. Monitor and evaluate a course and its delivery.

The portfolio paragraphs which elaborate on Lynette's learning outcomes tend to start in the more formal RPL genre and to become progressively more personal and engaged:

As a facilitator it is my responsibility to encourage participants to write by first explaining that there are no right or wrong ways in this creative writing workshop, unlike academic writing at school or university, but to just let the pen flow and free-write. I let them know that they will not be judged by anybody. In relation to my work with the young people, I found they needed a little bit more encouragement to put them at their ease.

The above quotation starts with reference to her role as 'facilitator' rather than to herself as an individual, whereas subsequent sentences focus on her personal involvement in particular instances, as in 'I let them know' and 'I found they needed'. In contrast, other paragraphs focus on the writing process and participants other than herself ('they' as opposed to 'we') reading more like a brochure or informative document, although in every case she appears as an individual at some stage:

> In dramatic writing work participants are encouraged to write a
> dramatic account of their lives as a witness to injustice. They
> are then asked to look at it in the form of a dramatic script with
> characters playing the role. After sharing and discussing all our
> work we will then choose between us one piece of work and
> start to look at how we can craft it into a script for radio. I have
> to emphasise that radio is the theatre of the mind, a theatre of
> sound, so that whatever is read needs descriptions.

The progression in the above quotation is interesting. Starting with the participants as theme and the passive verb forms – 'are encouraged' and 'are asked' – it moves to the collective ('our work' and 'we') where she includes herself with the participants, ending with an acknowledgement of her responsibility and central role with 'I' and the high modal 'have to'. The text reflects an image of the activity as she experiences it and a view of herself as involved in a formal process of 'conducting' and 'leading' a group, but also involved at a very personal level. The voice in the quotation below is more personal and informal than at the start of the previous quotation, contributing to the impression of a hybrid text:

> Being there for them is essential when it comes to my role of a
> facilitator as like the lady who read in her language, one could
> sense and then see that it was painful for her but with support
> and encouragement she managed to break through her barrier
> and overcome her fears of expressing herself.

Susan's religious convictions and Lynette's personal involvement in the workshops she runs are central to their portfolios, with considerations of the requirements of the RPL claim framing them. Elements of the RPL genre are identifiable in each case but the difficulties in adapting to this while expressing personal and individual perceptions are apparent in the switching of voices exemplified by differences in transitivity, mood and theme. Both students signalled their perception of this conflict in their comments on the process earlier in this chapter. Interviews with academics also revealed conflicting feelings about the assessment of submissions for RPL.

Academics' reactions to learning outcomes and portfolios

Overall, assessors expressed an openness of attitude towards RPL, suggesting that the concept has impinged on the consciousness of the academy and that the principle that knowledge can be acquired in different but equally valid ways is established. All of the RPL assessors interviewed emphasised the importance of 'learning outcomes'. It was evident that these have become part of the discourse of the institution, part of the literature on RPL and presented to students as a useful tool for describing learning from experience. All assessors wanted to see RPL candidates' learning related to clear learning outcomes and in most cases they wanted to see these, in turn, related to specific module descriptions. This is despite the advice given in the staff guidance booklet for RPL, which specifies that the latter is not necessary and in many cases it 'will be inappropriate to follow the standard assessment set out for the module in the case of the assessment of learning derived from experience'. Assessors used the terminology of learning outcomes discourse: 'transferable skills', 'competencies', 'capabilities'. 'We're very big nowadays on learning outcomes and capabilities', said one. They also used phrases such as 'written appropriately', 'to comply with certain academic requirements' and wanted to see 'examples of good practice in essay writing'. One assessor expected students to demonstrate that they 'can write, read, edit, take charge of a text'. Overall, the expectation was that RPL candidates would have skills related to the production of academic texts and be able to apply these in their RPL portfolios.

Speed and simplicity of assessment were also required. One assessor wanted a contents page or a proforma 'so that you can very quickly flip through . . . and see what they've done' and 'say tick, tick, tick'. Another talked about 'looking at the learning outcomes and sort of mentally ticking them off', adding 'you make the assessor's job very easy if you produce a check list and show you have already been through that and checked it'. A further assessor said an RPL candidate should 'write a very brief synopsis about [the] syllabus and how she meets the learning outcomes . . . this makes the accreditation process simpler'. In a similar vein, another said 'I particularly liked the way she has mapped her experience against the learning outcomes'. What assessors did not like was 'too much detail', 'repetition' and writing that was 'verbose'. This suggests that lecturers assessing prior learning expect a different kind of text from that which they expect traditional students to produce as part of their taught modules. The required RPL texts are charac- terised by some features of academic form but also the features of a check list, resulting in a fundamentally hybrid form. Traditional students studying modules and writing coursework are demonstrating learning outcomes, yet are not expected to make this explicit in the way that RPL candidates are required to. The importance of candidates getting this right was emphasised by assessors, not just because the characteristics of a portfolio make the work of the assessor easier or more arduous, but also because, as one said, 'I think one has to accept the effort which has gone into producing this portfolio as an example of some form of skill base', implying that this in itself contributes to the award of credit. Where an assessor felt that a particular candidate 'failed' to demonstrate competence in the RPL genre through having 'mistargetted his application' and showed a 'lack of attention to detail in choosing modules', this counted against the candidate irrespective of the fact that he had 'considerable previous knowledge applicable to the course'. RPL portfolios thus characterise candidates in assessors' eyes in terms of both prior knowledge and a particular kind of writing skill.

Assessors' perception of the need to integrate the assessment and award of RPL credit into the rigidly-defined practices devised for the assessment of taught modules, specifically the use of learning outcomes, thus seems to make the process arduous for students and conflict with their desire to capture the nature of their knowledge and identities in a meaningful way in their submissions.

Conclusions

In the institution under consideration (and others where the learning outcomes approach to RPL is used), a set of procedures has been set in place, constituted by means of an academic discourse, which enables RPL to become an integral part of the assessment process across the university. This serves to reassure academics, and assessors evidently perceive learning outcomes as an important and practical means of identifying knowledge and enabling it to be accredited. However, candidates see them as part of the 'funnel' or 'box' through which they have to 'squeeze' their account of their learning. For lecturers, learning outcomes form part of a system for checking and ticking off information that simplifies their task. For students they are an 'inhibiting' requirement with which they have to comply.

Although assessors are sympathetic to the idea of RPL, they also perceive it as an inconvenience, with candidates having the responsibility to make the task of assessment easy for them, rather than RPL being an area for discussion and negotiation. One academic (with a designated responsibility for RPL in his department) said in a meeting: 'Lecturers are not against RPL, it's just that students don't know how to present claims'. RPL has thus become something *candidates need to learn to do*, rather than something that acknowledges who they are and what they already know. One result of this is that RPL becomes an assessment of candidates' ability to produce documentation of their experience, which meets criteria set by assessors, in other words an assessment of their ability to operate within the RPL genre and academic discourse.

The discourses of modularisation and learning outcomes that have developed in higher education in the UK, and which are currently viewed by many as the appropriate vehicle for the implementation of RPL, do little to empower those starting from a position outside the academic community, and everything to maintain control within it. In the years since RPL was first introduced in universities in the UK it has become more and more bound up in documentation for the purposes of quality control, for example, handbooks of guidelines and criteria for RPL practitioners. However, the number of candidates coming forward has remained static or decreased in most institutions.

For RPL to empower those seeking it, knowledge gained outside formal education must be recognised by educators as of potentially equal status to that gained inside. This entails accepting knowledge content as equivalent even when it is expressed in a form that is different from the form academic knowledge normally takes and created by a discourse that is different from academic discourse. This is a difficult concept to introduce to academics. Writers such as Michel Feutrie and David Starr-Glass have explored the possibilities of more emancipatory forms of RPL, which, rather than being set up as a hurdle to overcome, could function as a mediatory procedure. This would promote understanding between academics, professionals and practitioners and between mature students and the lecturers who teach them. Starr-Glass (2002, p. 228) considers that in the practice of RPL: 'We should learn the candidate's language . . . They must not be forced to use a way of communicating that is alien and restrictive to them' because '[t]he evaluation of prior experience is an exploration of the candidate's territory, and an exploration that must engage both the candidate and the invited evaluator'. Conventional academic assessments generally look for signs of something familiar, since the representation of learning is being matched against pre-set criteria. Assessors and facilitators of RPL need to be trained to value the unfamiliar – learning that has come from sources never imagined, represented in unfamiliar ways. Opening up the assessment process could help to move it 'from a one way evaluation to a reciprocal, almost contractual, process of identification' (Feutrie, 2000, p. 208).

My critical discourse analysis has shown that the practice of RPL may be failing in some ways to meet the communicative needs of those engaged in it. It has demonstrated that discourse as defined by Foucault (1980) is at the heart of the process and that acquisition of academic discourse and an RPL genre may take disproportionate importance in relation to the knowledge and expertise of the candidate. On the other hand, the task of awarding credit for knowledge presented in forms which do not conform to those established within academic institutions requires a shift in perspective that many academics might be reluctant to take. As Stierer (2000, p. 193) says: 'Institutions of higher education use language to sustain and legitimate an epistemological hegemony – that is an ideology which positions students of any type as relatively powerless'. The practice of RPL was conceived as a means of empowering students and challenging this hegemony, however the latter has to date proved largely resistant to the challenge.

References

Betts, M. and Smith, R. (1998), *Developing the Credit-based Modular Curriculum in Higher Education*, London: Falmer.

Chouliaraki, L. and Fairclough, N. (1999), *Discourse in Late Modernity*, Edinburgh: Edinburgh University Press.

Evans, N. (2000), *Experiential Learning Around the World: Employability and the Global Economy*, London: Jessica Kingsley.

Fairclough, N. (1992), *Discourse and Social Change*, Cambridge: Polity Press.

Fairclough, N. (1999), 'Global capitalism and critical awareness of language', *Language Awareness*, 8(2): 71–83.

Fairclough, N. (2001), *Language and Power*, Harlow: Longman.

Feutrie, M. (2000), 'France: the story of La Validation des Acquis (Recognition of Experiential Learning)' in Evans, N. (ed.) *Experiential Learning Around the World: Employability and the Global Economy*, London: Jessica Kingsley.

Foucault, M. (1973), *The Birth of the Clinic*, London: Tavistock Publications.

Foucault, M. (1977), *Discipline and Punish, The Birth of the Prison*, Harmondsworth: Penguin.

Foucault, M. (1980), *Power/Knowledge Selected Interviews and Other Writings*, C. Gordon (ed.), London: Harvester Wheatsheaf.

Halliday, M.A.K. (1994), *An Introduction to Functional Grammar*, London: Arnold.

Hussey, T. and Smith, P. (2002), 'The trouble with learning outcomes', *Active Learning in Higher Education*, 3(3): 220–33.

Kolb, D. (1984), *Experiential Learning*, Englewood Cliffs, NJ: Prentice Hall.

Michelson, E. (1996), 'International case study on prior learning assessment, Empire

State College, State University of New York', Case Study Evaluation commissioned by the Research and Development Programme in the Recognition of Prior Learning, Cape Town, HSRC, UCT and Peninsula Technikon.

Starr-Glass, D. (2002), 'Metaphor and totem: exploring and evaluating prior experiential learning', *Assessment and Evaluation in Higher Education*, 27(3): 222–31.

Stierer, B. (2000), 'Schoolteachers as students: academic literacy and the construction of professional knowledge within Master's courses in education' in Lea, M.R. and Stierer, B. (eds) *Student Writing in Higher Education*, Buckingham: SRHE and Open University Press.

Weil, S.W. and McGill, I. (1989), 'A framework for making sense of experiential learning' in Weil, S.W. and McGill, I. (eds) *Making Sense of Experiential Learning*, Buckingham: SRHE and Open University Press.

chapter nine

The politics of difference: non/recognition of the foreign credentials and prior work experience of immigrant professionals in Canada and Sweden

Shibao Guo and Per Andersson

A central aspect of RPL is that it is often a matter of transfer. Learning from one context is to be recognised in another context. Someone with knowledge from informal or non-formal learning in everyday or work life may want this to be recognised in the formal educational system, or in a new work place. It may also be the case that someone with formal education or training from one country wants recognition for this in a new country. Immigrant professionals may have formal credentials and prior work experience from their country of origin and seek recognition elsewhere. Yet, knowledge, experience and formal credentials are not necessarily accepted when transferred to a new context. This chapter addresses this issue as an example of how the situatedness of experience, learning and credentials is a problematic issue in RPL. If there are calls for equivalency, this makes it even more difficult to secure recognition of experience and credentials in the new context.

We use the situation in two countries – Canada and Sweden – as illustrative examples. These countries have both similarities and differences, making it possible to deepen the analysis, as well as to advance broader aspects of the theme. The chapter draws on perspectives from critical theory and post-modernism. It examines the relationship between knowledge and power, as expressed in this problematic transfer of credentials and experience. We argue that the main problems are the epistemological misperceptions of difference and knowledge, and the ontological foundations of positivism and liberal universalism that dominate current recognition practices.

Introducing the problem of non-recognition

Today, Canada and Sweden are immigrant countries. Immigration has played an important role in transforming both countries into ethno-culturally diverse and economically prosperous nations. The 2001 Census of Canada (Statistics Canada, 2003a) reveals that as of 15 May 2001, 18.4 per cent (or 5.4 million) of Canada's total population of 30 million were born outside the country, and that 13.4 per cent identified themselves as visible minorities. According to the Ethnic Diversity Survey (Statistics Canada, 2003b), almost one-quarter (23 per cent) of Canada's total population of 22.4 million people aged 15 years and older were identified as first-generation Canadians who were born outside Canada. The latter number indicates that a large proportion of the new immigrants are adults.

Sweden has a total population of 9 million people. In 2003, 12 per cent were born outside the country. Among those aged 16 years and older, 13.7 per cent were born outside Sweden. This means that a higher proportion of new immigrants in Sweden are adults, but the difference is not as large as in Canada (Integrationsverket, 2005). A main difference between the two countries is that Sweden does not have a long history of immigration. The 12 per cent born abroad today marks growth when compared to 1 per cent in 1940 and 7 per cent in 1970 (Ekberg and Rooth, 2000). The development of immigration has, among other things, resulted in a growing interest in the recognition of foreign vocational competence (Andersson et al., 2004).

When immigrants come, they bring their language, culture, values, educational background and work experience to the new society. Generally, Canada and Sweden have been extolled as open and tolerant societies. Their commitment to diversity and social justice has been admired by many nations in the world. On the other hand, both countries have been criticised for failing to move beyond 'tolerance' to fully embrace differences as valid and valuable expressions of human experience. With respect to the latter, one of the most outstanding issues pertains to the non-recognition of immigrants' foreign credentials and work experience. A number of studies have revealed that many highly-educated immigrant professionals experience deskilling or decredentialising of their prior learning and work experience.

This chapter examines the politics of difference as manifested in the non-recognition of the credentials and prior work experience of immigrant professionals in both countries. It is organised into four parts. It begins with a review of contextual information pertaining to immigration in the two countries. The second section examines studies pertinent to non-recognition of foreign credentials and prior work experience in Canada and Sweden. Thirdly, the chapter analyses current debates on differences and knowledge, in particular, those relating to how these factors are perceived and treated by mainstream Canadian and Swedish societies in the process of foreign credential recognition. Finally, we conclude that assessment and recognition of prior learning is a political act. While certain forms of knowledge are legitimised as valid, the learning and work experiences of foreign-trained professionals are often treated as suspicious or inferior.

Contextual information

Immigration past and present in Canada and Sweden

Immigration has always played a central role in the nation building of receiving countries. The economic and demographic interests of the receiving nation are usually the driving forces behind immigration. For example, in the nineteenth century massive immigration was used as a strategy to populate and develop western Canada. Worker-class immigrants played an important role in the development of the Swedish economy after the Second World War and until the beginning of the 1970s. In addition, immigration has also served as a means of social and ideological control. In deciding which groups are the most desirable and admissible, the state sets the parameters for the social, cultural and symbolic boundaries of the nation, as manifested in historically racist Canadian immigration policies. From the Confederation of Canada in 1867 to the 1960s, the selection of immigrants to Canada was based on racial background, with British and western Europeans being deemed the most 'desirable' citizens, while Asians and Africans were considered 'unassimilable' and therefore 'undesirable'. After the Second World War, Canadian immigration policy continued to be highly restrictive despite external and internal pressures for an open-door policy (Knowles, 1997). Sweden has had an open-door policy as regards Nordic neighbour countries (Finland, Norway, Denmark, Iceland) and has been a member of the European Union since the mid-1990s. A policy of allowing worker-class immigrants has been transformed to a restrictive policy towards migrants themselves, with a relatively open policy concerning refugees since the mid-1970s.

Immigrants come to Canada and Sweden under four major categories: the skilled worker class, the business class, the family class, and refugees. The admission of skilled workers is based on education, occupation, language skills, and work experience. The second category includes experienced business people who are expected to invest or establish businesses in the hosting societies. For example, Canada has three classes of business immigrants: investors, entrepreneurs and self-employed people, each with separate eligibility criteria. Skilled workers and business immigrants are also referred to as economic immigrants. Family-class immigration reunites close family members of an adult resident or citizen of the hosting country, such as child, parents, spouse or common-law partner. Refugee protection is usually offered to those who fear returning to their country of nationality or habitual residence because of war, fear of persecution, torture or cruel and unusual treatment or punishment.

In the mid-1960s, Canada was experiencing 'the greatest postwar boom' in its history (Whitaker, 1991, p. 18). Skilled labour was required to help build this expansionary economy, but Europe, as the traditional source of immigrants, was not able to meet these needs due to the labour demands of its own economic recovery. Thus the Canadian government turned its recruitment efforts to traditionally restricted areas – developing countries. In 1967 a 'point system' was introduced by the Liberal government, which based the selection of immigrants on their 'education, skills and resources' rather than their racial and religious backgrounds (*ibid.*, p. 19). According to Whitaker, this new system represented 'an historic watershed,' and 'did establish at the level of formal principle that Canadian immigration policy is "colour blind"' (*ibid.*).

Whitaker points out that the 'point system' was generally successful in reversing the pattern of immigration to Canada away from Europe and towards Asia and other developing countries. By the mid-1970s, there were more immigrants arriving from the developing than the developed world. The largest number came from Asia, followed by the Caribbean, Latin America, and Africa. Between 1968 and 1992, 35.7 per cent of 3.7 million immigrants admitted came from Asia; and 58 per cent of 1.8 million immigrants who arrived in Canada between 1991 and 2001 were also from the same region (Li, 2003; Statistics Canada, 2003a).

Immigrant selection practices since the mid-1990s have given more weight to education and skills, favouring economic immigrants over family-class immigrants and refugees. As Li (2003) notes, this new shift was based on the assumption that economic immigrants brought more human capital than family-class immigrants and refugees and therefore were more valuable and desirable. According to Li, economic-class immigrants made up more than half of all immigrants admitted throughout the late 1990s. Among them, a considerable number are highly educated professionals, particularly scientists and engineers. In the year 2000, of the total 227,209 immigrants and refugees admitted, 23 per cent (52,000 individuals) were admitted as skilled workers (Couton, 2002). Despite Canada's preference for highly skilled immigrants, and despite the fact that these professionals bring significant human capital resources to the Canadian labour force, a number of studies have shown that many experience barriers to having their foreign credentials and work experience recognised after they arrive in Canada (Basran and Zong, 1998; Henry *et al.*, 2000; Krahn *et al.*, 2000; Li, 2001; Mojab, 1999; Reitz, 2001).

Swedish history is different, characterised mainly by emigration. Beginning in the seventeenth century and with a peak in the late nineteenth and early twentieth centuries, Swedish emigration patterns are similar to those of other western European countries. During the period 1851-1930, almost 1.2 million Swedes left for America. 97 per cent of them went to the USA, and 1.6 per cent went to Canada. The number of Swedish immigrants in Canada is actually higher, as people went on from the USA to Canada (NE, 1991). Drawn from a total Swedish population of about 6 million in 1930, this out-migration was enormous. Even taking account of the refugees who came during the Second World War, until at least the middle of the twentieth century Sweden was a rather mono-cultural country. Since the 1930s there have been more immigrants than emigrants, but the numbers of the former were low during the 1930s and 1940s.

In the middle of the twentieth century, Sweden was a step ahead of many other European countries in terms of economic development. Sweden was not involved in the Second World War and thus nothing was destroyed. Economic development grew significantly but there was a lack of qualified labour. There was discussion of a 'reserve of talent' or a 'reserve of ability' (Härnquist, 2003) and how this reserve could be educated and made use of. Still, there was an immediate need for competent workers, and as a result of this need many skilled worker-class immigrants came to Sweden at the end of the 1940s and into the 1950s.

These immigrants came mainly from the Nordic countries and southern Europe (Italy, Greece and so on). In addition, a number of refugees came from Eastern European countries, for example, Hungarians fleeing the 1956 uprising. In the 1960s there were still a high number of worker-class immigrants, mainly from the Nordic countries and from Yugoslavia, and refugees from Eastern Europe and Greece (Gustafsson *et al.*, 2004). The difference in the 1960s was that the immigrants had lower qualifications as they were required for less-qualified positions in industry (Bevelander, 2000). Lower labour demand led to more restricted immigration policy and the number of immigrants from outside the Nordic countries declined (Gustafsson *et al.*, 2004). Since the 1970s there has been a change in the Swedish immigration. The number of worker-class immigrants has been reduced, and the number of refugees and family-class immigrants has increased significantly. Refugees mainly came from Chile in the 1970s, the Middle East in the 1980s, and the former Yugoslavia and the Middle East in the 1990s (Gustafsson *et al.*, 2004). The shifts in immigrants' origins are shown in the following figures: in 1970 more than 90 per cent of those born abroad came from Europe (60 per cent from the Nordic countries). By the end of the 1990s, 30 per cent were born in the Nordic countries; 35 per cent in other European countries; and 35 per cent in countries outside of Europe (Ekberg and Rooth, 2000).

The social construction of 'immigrant'

At the centre of this analysis are immigrants themselves. It is important to review what this term means. According to Li (2003), the notion of 'immigrant' is socially constructed. He argues that it is often associated with people of non-white origin. In the context of Canada, early settlers came mainly from Europe. Only since the 'immigrant point system' was introduced in 1967 has Canada attracted an increasing number of immigrants from developing countries, notably Asia and Africa. Descendants of early European settlers, now long-established Canadians, do not think of themselves as immigrants. As Li puts it, the term 'immigrant' becomes a codified word for people of colour who come from a different racial and cultural background, who do not speak fluent English, and who work in lower position jobs. Li maintains that the social construction of 'immigrant' uses skin colour as the basis for social marking. These individuals' real and alleged differences are claimed to be incompatible with the cultural and social fabric of 'traditional' Canada, and they are therefore deemed undesirable. Immigrants are also often blamed for creating urban social problems and racial and cultural tensions in the receiving society. The social construction of immigrant places uneven expectations on immigrants to conform over time to the norms, values, and traditions of the receiving society.

In Sweden, 'immigrant' is used as a broad concept including worker-class immigrants, family-class immigrants, and often also refugees. The main signifier in the social construction of an 'immigrant' is language – whether or not fluent Swedish is spoken (Broomé *et al.*, 1996). Swedish is a very 'small language' compared to Canada's official languages of English and French, i.e. the Swedish-speaking area is limited to Sweden and localised parts of Finland. Finns constitute a large proportion of the worker-class immigrants in Sweden, but Finland-Swedish is still a dialect that differs significantly from mainstream Swedish. This makes it difficult and time-consuming for most immigrants to join Swedish contexts, where language competence, that is, Swedish, is an important prerequisite (unless the society embraces multilingualism!). As in Canada, there is also a process of 'othering the other', a socially constructed division between 'we' and 'the others', but in this case 'culture' and language are used as the main 'explanations' of difference (Osman, 1999).

The assessment of foreign credentials: Mapping the process

Foreign credentials can be defined as any formal education higher than a high-school diploma, including professional or technical qualifications and any degrees, diplomas or certificates received outside Canada (or Sweden) (Statistics Canada, 2003c). Canada's immigrant selection system awards points to applicants with advanced educational qualifications. Prior to arriving in Canada, immigrants do not normally receive any reliable information about the recognition of foreign credentials. Upon arrival, they need to navigate through a complex and possibly lengthy, costly and frustrating process on their own. There is no central or national place where they can go to have their credentials evaluated. Depending on the purpose of the evaluation, immigrants may need to approach one or all of the following organisations: 1) provincial and territorial credential assessment services; 2) regulatory or professional bodies; 3) educational institutions; and 4) employers. The outcomes of the evaluation may serve one of the following purposes: general employment; studying in Canada; and professional certification or licensing in Canada.

Five provincial and territorial agencies provide credential assessment services to immigrants. These agencies are the International Qualifications Assessment Service (Alberta); International Credential Evaluation Service (British Columbia); Academic Credentials Assessment Service (Manitoba); World Education Services (Ontario), and the Education Credential Evaluation (Quebec). These five agencies have formed the Alliance of Credential Evaluation Services of Canada [ACESC] to facilitate the dissemination and exchange of information regarding international education. Small licensing bodies may need help from these organisations to determine the equivalency of foreign credentials. However, large professional associations (for example,

the College of Physicians and Surgeons) usually conduct their own assessments to determine whether applicants need further training or tests in order
to re-enter their professions in Canada. While professional and regulatory
bodies determine the professional standing of the qualification, the assessment of foreign credentials for the purpose of academic study resides firmly
in the hands of education providers (such as universities and colleges).

In Sweden, there is a system for the recognition of foreign examinations,
which are assessed in terms of their equivalence to Swedish counterparts
(HSV, 2005). The National Agency for Higher Education evaluates higher
education programmes leading to the recognition of a qualification for at least
two years. This evaluation does not mean that a Swedish qualification is
awarded, but it is intended to provide guidance for employers. It can also be
used in an application for Swedish higher education, which is necessary in
order to secure a Swedish qualification. A right to the recognition of 'real
competence' in relation to admission requirements has been introduced, and
RPL for credit in higher education is also possible (and developing).

This system for recognition in Sweden is not open to all professions. When it
comes to 'regulated professions' where authorisation, certification and so on
are required – physicians, attorneys-at-law and accountants for example –
foreign qualifications are subject to the review of the responsible bodies. For
example, the qualifications of physicians and other professions in the health
care sector are assessed by the National Board of Health and Welfare. There
are also various systems for language tests, language courses and
complementary training.

Given the diversity of assessment and licensing bodies, no generalisations can
be made regarding national criteria for evaluating foreign qualifications.
Reviewing the requirements of a number of such bodies in Canada, processes
usually deploy the following criteria: level and type of learning; duration of
study programme; status of issuing institutions; the education system of the
country concerned; and the authenticity, currency, relevance, trustworthiness
and transferability of the credential. In evaluations made by the Swedish
National Agency for Higher Education, attested or certified copies of
certificates and so on are required as part of the application and criteria are
applied. The most important are the length of the programme; the level at
which subjects have been studied; theses or papers required; and the
objectives of the programme.

Document verification offers no guarantee of license to those found to have equivalent education. Some accreditation processes require foreign-trained professionals (for example, in medicine) to take a certification examination in combination with language testing and/or to undertake a period of internship or practicum in the licensing country. Although successful immigrant professionals will obtain a certificate or license to practice their profession, they then need to find an employer who is willing to offer them a job. Moreover, assessments of the same credentials by different institutions are often inconsistent.

Mata (1999) maintains that immigrant professionals may encounter a number of barriers in the process of having their foreign credentials recognised. First, they get poor information on accreditation procedures. Secondly there is no national body responsible for the evaluation of foreign credentials. Thirdly, there is no agreed-upon national standard. Educational and professional standards vary by province. In Sweden there are a number of national bodies with responsibly for different professions and the standards vary, especially between regulated professions.

Foreign credentials and prior work experience: deskilling and discounting

Wanner (2001) claims that non-recognition of foreign credentials and prior work experience is the 'central immigration issue of the new century not only in Canada, but in all postindustrial societies receiving immigrants' (*ibid.*, p. 417). In a study of 404 Indo- and Chinese-Canadian immigrant professionals in Vancouver, Basran and Zong (1998) report that only 18.8 per cent of their respondents worked as professionals (doctors, engineers, school/ university teachers, and other professions) after immigrating to Canada. The authors determined that the most important factor for lack of admission to professional occupations, and resulting downward social mobility, was the non-recognition or devaluation of foreign credentials. Basran and Zong further point out that immigrant professionals are usually caught in a 'double bind.' In the first place, non-recognition of foreign credentials prevents them from accessing professional jobs in Canada and acquiring Canadian work experience, which subsequently makes it difficult for them to become qualified for other professional jobs.

Highly-educated refugees also encounter similar barriers. In a study of 525 refugees, Krahn, Derwing, Mulder and Wilkinson (2000) demonstrate how those with high educational and occupational qualifications experienced downward occupational mobility after arriving in Canada. In comparison with Canadian-born individuals, refugee professionals are more likely to experience unemployment and under-employment (such as part-time and temporary employment). A lack of recognition of prior learning and work experience was identified as the top contributing factor to this downward mobility. Other factors included a shortage of Canadian references and work experience, English language difficulties and employer discrimination. Krahn *et al.* emphasise that in the process of recognising foreign credentials, professional associations often function as labour market shelters. By retaining strict control over the adjudication of foreign credentials, these associations restrict competition for well-paying professional jobs.

The situation for immigrant women is even worse. Gannage (1999) and Ng (1996) argue that the classification of 'immigrant women' has served to commodify them in employers' eyes, and in the labour force more generally, thereby reinforcing their class position as providers of cheap, docile labour to the state under exploitive conditions that are often permeated by racism and sexism. In her research with immigrant women, Mojab (1999) finds that skilled women faced deskilling in Canada. She maintains that developed capitalism simultaneously creates and destroys jobs, and requires both the skilling and deskilling of the labour force. Highly skilled immigrant women are usually seen as potential source of manual labour. They face unemployment or are pressured into non-skilled jobs. Mojab argues that access to the job market is not determined by education alone, but is constrained by other factors such as gender, national origin, race and ethnicity. Finally, she points out that systemic racism and ethnicism affects immigrants differently. Women from developed countries (such as the USA, Australia, Britain or New Zealand) are treated differently from those originating in developing countries. Only those with financial resources at their disposal can afford the 'Canadianisation' of their experience.

In Sweden, the proportion of the population aged 25-64 with higher education is about the same for those born outside (18.7 per cent in 2003) as for those born in the country (18.4 per cent) (Integrationsverket, 2004, p. 240). An analysis of the 26–45 age cohort of non-European immigrant professionals (with at least three years' higher education) arriving in Sweden between 1991 and 1997, shows the same problem of non-recognition as in Canada (Berggren and Omarsson, 2001). 65 per cent in this group have a job, compared to 90 per cent of those born in Sweden (the rest are unemployed, studying or in labour market programmes). It is also less likely that working immigrants have a job that corresponds to their formal qualifications. 39 per cent of those born outside western Europe have a qualified job (that is, corresponding to their formal qualification), compared to 85 per cent of those born in Sweden. Notably, even among those with a formal qualification from Swedish institutes of higher education, only 64 per cent of those born outside western Europe have a qualified job. About one-third of those from Africa and Asia can expect to get a qualified job, half of those from Latin America and eastern Europe, and two-thirds of those from North America (*ibid.*). Thus, there is a problem with the recognition of foreign credentials, but the problem varies depending on one's origin. Even with a Swedish education a citizen is much less likely to have a qualified job if s/he was not born in Sweden.

As mentioned, Sweden has a formal system for recognition of foreign academic credentials. If the qualification is recognised as equivalent to a Swedish qualification, an individual is more likely to secure a qualified job. The difference between qualifications recognised as equivalent or non-equivalent is most significant in the health care sector, where a number of professions are regulated, and require formal authorisation or certification. Here 80 per cent of those with an equivalent qualification have a qualified job, compared with only 20 per cent of those with non-equivalent qualifications. In the technical/scientific area, the corresponding figures are 56 per cent and 36 per cent. Further, many working immigrants are employed within the area of their qualification, but at a lower level. This means that employers have employees with relevant qualifications, who are not being fully used or remunerated. Thus there is considerable existing competence that could be recognised and utilised (Berggren and Omarsson, 2001).

A comparison of employment rates among all Swedish immigrants aged 16-64 (including refugees) and a corresponding group of native Swedes shows significant differences depending on immigrants' national origins. In 1969, the employment rate of immigrants from Finland and Yugoslavia was 120 per cent of that for natives and the corresponding rate for immigrants from Germany was 103 per cent. A comparison with the figures from 1999 show another picture: the rate for Finland was 93 per cent; for Germany 89 per cent; and for the former Yugoslavia 71 per cent (Gustafsson *et al.*, 2004). Thus, the situation has worsened for worker-class immigrants, as illustrated by the decreasing employment rate for immigrants from Finland and Germany. An increasing number of refugees has contributed to a significantly lower employment rate in the (former) Yugoslavian group, compared to the Finnish and German groups. Finally, other immigrants who have come as refugees have problems getting a job – the average employment rate in 1999 among people from Africa and Asia was 62 per cent of that for natives (Gustavsson *et al.*, 2004).

The aforementioned research findings have been validated by government sources of data. Differences emerge in comparing unemployment between native-born and foreign-born populations in Sweden and Canada. The average unemployment in 2003 among 15-64 year old Swedish-born citizens was 4.8 per cent (5.2 per cent for men and 4.4 per cent for women), compared to 11.1 per cent for immigrants (12.7 per cent for men and 9.5 per cent for women). The corresponding figures for Canada (but data referring to 2002) were 6.0 per cent for Canadian-born citizens (6.2 per cent for men and 5.8 per cent for women) and 8.0 per cent for immigrants (7.3 per cent for men and 8.8 per cent for women) (OECD, 2005, p. 88–90). Thus, the employment gap between native-born and foreign-born populations in Sweden is greater than in Canada. This could be because of the higher proportion of refugees in Sweden and of labour migrants/worker-class immigrants in Canada.

The Longitudinal Survey of Immigrants to Canada [LSIC] (Statistics Canada, 2003c) is a comprehensive survey conducted by Statistics Canada and Citizenship and Immigration Canada that aims to study the process by which new immigrants adapt to Canadian society. Findings from the first wave of interviews with 12,000 immigrants aged 15 and over, who arrived in Canada between October 2000 and September 2001, reveal that finding employment was the area with most reported difficulties. Among those who were employed at the time of the survey, 60 per cent were not working in the same occupational field as before arriving in the country. This number seems to be lower than that reported in other studies, but is still significant. The survey also reveals that many immigrant professionals experience major shifts from prior occupations in natural and applied sciences and management (for men) and business, finance and administration (for women) to occupations in sales, services, processing and manufacturing. Lack of Canadian experience and lack of transferability of foreign credentials were reported as the most critical hurdles to employment. A low level of skill in either official language was another important contributing factor to this occupation shift. One important finding was the connection between place of birth and the possibility of finding a job within the same field as prior to arriving in Canada. The survey reports that while 60 per cent of newcomers did not find jobs in the same occupational field, more than 60 per cent of immigrants who were born in the United States (63 per cent), Australia (68 per cent), and New Zealand (68 per cent) were successful in finding employment in the same occupational field. These figures suggest that while foreign credentials and work experience can be transferred beyond national borders; those benefits are enjoyed by immigrants from only a small number of countries.

How does the non-recognition of foreign credentials and prior work experience affect immigrants? Reitz (2001) points out the significant impact on earnings. Using 1996 Canadian census micro-data, Reitz assessed the annual immigrant earnings deficit caused by skill under-utilisation to be $2.4 billion (Canadian). According to Reitz, immigrants receive a much smaller earnings premium for their education – on average half that of native-born Canadians. He also maintains that immigrant men and women receive about one-half to two-thirds as much benefit from work experience as do native-born workers of the same gender. Another important finding is that there are wide variations in earnings among immigrants from different origins. In general, immigrant men from origin groups outside Europe earn anywhere between 15 and 25 per cent less than most of the European origin groups. However, origin-group earnings differences for immigrant women are much less than for men. Reitz further notes that if foreign education explains part of the origin-group earnings differentials, it means that Canadian employers treat schooling in certain countries of origin, mostly Asia, Africa, the Caribbean and Latin America, differently than schooling in other (mostly European) countries. This finding confirms Mansour's (1996, p. 2) observation that 'the issue is particularly acute for immigrants with qualifications from anywhere other than Europe or North America'.

In Sweden the average earnings of immigrants are lower than for those of Swedish birth, which reflects both the lower employment rate and the often part-time nature of the work. In 1999, the average earnings of men born outside Sweden were 61 per cent of those born in the country and the corresponding figure for women was 69 per cent. As in Canada, there are also large differences depending on country of origin. Immigrants from the Nordic countries, western Europe and North America (mainly worker-class immigrants) have slightly lower earnings, and immigrants from countries outside Europe (mainly refugees) have much lower earnings. Eastern and southern Europe are somewhere in between, but there are also differences depending on when different groups came to Sweden. For example, in 1999, men from Finland earned 82 per cent of the earnings of Swedish-born men, and women from Finland 101 per cent of native women. The corresponding figures for people from the USA was 96 per cent for men and 80 per cent for women; for Hungary 71 and 87 per cent; for Chile 55 and 68 per cent; for Bosnia 43 and 44 per cent; for Iraq 21 and 16 per cent; and for Somalia 16 and 17 per cent (Gustafsson *et al.*, 2004). This shows clearly the differences between countries of origin, arrival times and reasons for migration in terms of position in the labour market. In addition, the fact that immigrants who have studied mainly in Sweden earn about the same as natives (and more than those who have studied abroad) (le Grande *et al.*, 2004) could signify that a main problem is the (non) recognition of foreign credentials and work experience.

The politics of difference and recognition: epistemological and ontological misconceptions

The above discussion demonstrates that many organisations in Canadian and Swedish societies, including government agencies, professional associations, employers and educational institutions, play a role in the valuing (or not) of foreign credentials and prior work experience. As a consequence, immigrant individuals and families, along with their receiving societies as a whole, suffer severe impacts. Explanations are advanced that focus on the supply and/or demand of competence. The supply discussion highlights the question of whether immigrants' professional competence is the 'right' competence, or whether something is deficient in this source of 'human capital'. An interest in the development of the labour market puts the focus on the demand side. Bevelander (2000) (and others) have shown that structural changes in the labour market in a developed country generate demands for new skills and competencies. For example, manual labour employment is gradually disappearing as a result of technological advances, efficiency improvements and companies moving their manufacturing plants to low-wages countries. On the increase are demands for teamwork and interpersonal skills, information and communication technology skills and (native) language proficiency. This shift has made it more difficult for professional immigrants in the labour market, as many lack the native language fluency, cultural capital and 'soft' skills that are increasingly in demand. In other instances, they are assumed to not have these skills, which leads to an increasing 'statistical' discrimination by employers (Bevelander, 2000).

While some studies have suggested causes for the under-valuing of foreign credentials, many have failed to question the root cause. In our view, given the impact of under-valuation on individual identities (Gottskalksdottir, 2000), understanding the problem in terms of the economy is not enough. Many critical questions remain. We need to find out why such inequities occur in democratic societies like Canada and Sweden, where democratic principles are upheld and where immigrants are, at least in policy, 'welcome'. Furthermore, as this issue has been identified in numerous studies over a number of years, we must ask why the situation has not improved. Thus a key question is: what prevents us from moving forward? Drawing on perspectives from critical theory and postmodernism, we offer the following observations in an attempt to provide more in-depth answers to this question. The first two considerations pertain to epistemological misconceptions of difference and knowledge; the second two relate to the ontological foundations of the assessment and recognition of foreign credentials.

Epistemological misconceptions of difference and knowledge

First, non-recognition of foreign credentials and prior work experience can be attributed to a deficit model of difference. One of the articulations of multicultural societies like Canada and Sweden is a commitment to cultural pluralism. However, a number of commentators (Cummins, 2003; Dei, 1996; Fleras and Elliott, 2002; Ghosh and Abdi, 2004; Moodley, 1995) argue that pluralism is only endorsed in superficial ways. The tendency is to prefer 'pretend pluralism,' which means to 'tolerate rather than embrace differences' (Fleras and Elliott, 2002, p. 2). In practice, differences are exoticised and trivialised. Minor differences may be gently affirmed in depoliticised and decontextualised forms such as food, dance and festivities. Substantive differences, however, tend to challenge hegemony and resist co-option. As a result, these are perceived by many as deficient, deviant, pathological or otherwise divisive. We would argue that one of the hurdles preventing the full recognition of immigrants' educational qualifications and professional experience is the prevailing attitude toward difference. In fact, negative attitudes and behaviours toward immigrants co-exist with commitments to democratic principles such as justice, equality and fairness. Henry *et al.* (2000) refer to the co-existence of these two conflicting ideologies as 'democratic racism'. According to these authors, democratic racism prevents governments from changing the existing social, economic and political order, and from supporting policies and practices that might ameliorate the low status of people of colour, because such policies would be perceived as in conflict with, and a threat to, liberal democracy.

Secondly, knowledge is used as power to keep out the 'undesirable'. Critical theorists and postmodern scholars (Cunningham, 2000; Foucault, 1980; McLaren, 2003) maintain that: knowledge is power; knowledge is socially constructed, culturally mediated and historically situated; and knowledge is never neutral or objective. The nature of knowledge as it pertains to social relations prompts us to ask the following questions: What counts as legitimate knowledge? How and why does knowledge get constructed in the way it does? Whose knowledge is considered valuable? Whose knowledge is silenced? Is knowledge racialised? Studies have clearly shown that, while immigrants from developing countries encounter difficulties with their foreign credentials and work experience, those from developed countries (in

Canada, countries such as the USA, Australia, Britain or New Zealand; in Sweden the Nordic countries, Germany or the USA) have relatively success-ful experiences. It can therefore be speculated that knowledge *has* been racialised. As Li (2003) rightly points out, the term 'immigrant' becomes a codified word for people of colour who come from a different racial and cultural background, and who do not speak the language of the receiving country fluently.

The knowledge possessed by immigrants is deemed inferior because their real and alleged differences are claimed to be incompatible with the 'traditional' cultural and social fabric. It seems clear that power relations are embedded in social relations of difference (Dei, 1996, p. 63). In Canada, this hierarchy of knowledge and power is rooted in an ethnocentric past, where immigrants from Europe and the USA were viewed as the most desirable and those from developing countries as undesirable. Sweden has a rather monocultural history and most immigrants until the middle of the 1970s were worker-class immigrants. Labour migration has, to a large extent, been followed by the arrival of refugees. This helps us understand the problems refugee immigrants meet in Sweden – their credentials and prior work experiences are not asked for in the Swedish labour market. Canada's commitment to the point immigration policy, and Sweden's present policy of admitting refugees and asylum seekers, do not permit the countries to recruit immigrants on the basis of racial and national origins. We argue that in lieu of stated policies, the devaluation and denigration of immigrants' knowledge and experience becomes the new head tax to keep out 'undesirables'. It seems as if this has been used as a new strategy to maintain the subordination of immigrants and to reinforce the extant power relations in Canada and Sweden.

Ontological foundations: positivism and liberal universalism

Thirdly, the assessment and recognition of foreign credentials in Canada and Sweden is characterised by positivism. Positivists believe that an objective world exists 'out there', external to the individual (Boshier, 1994), and that if something exists, it can be measured (Young and Arrigo, 1999). Studies cited here have shown that this objectivist ontology has been the driving force behind the current practice of assessment and recognition of foreign credentials (see also Michelson, Chapter 7, this volume). Existing schemes of recognition search for an absolute truth regarding knowledge and experience. They adopt a set of 'value-free' criteria, which discount the social, political, historical and cultural contexts within which such knowledge has been produced. They claim that 'neutral' assessment and measurement occurs under the auspices of professional standards, quality and excellence without any question of whose standards are in place, and whose interests they serve. Although immigrants are allowed into the country, professional standards deny them access to employment in their professions. Krahn *et al.* (2000) argue that the real purpose of such standards is to restrict competition and to sustain the interests of the dominant groups. Criteria-based, convergent assessments make it more difficult to accept differences and equivalencies in competence, as compared to a more divergent system (see Andersson, Chapter 2, this volume).

Fourth, in assessing foreign credentials, positivism is juxtaposed with liberal universalism, which exacerbates the complexity of the recognition process. As Young (1995) notes, liberal universalism posits that universality transcends particularity and difference; universality promotes assimilation while a politics of difference makes space for multiple voices and perspectives. In applying a one-size-fits-all criterion to measure immigrants' credentials and experience, liberal universalism fails to address the following questions: Who establishes criteria? Whose interests are represented and served by these standards? What constitutes valid prior learning? What should we do with knowledge that is valid but different? What forms of knowledge become Canadian or Swedish 'equivalent'? Sometimes the rejection of immigrants' qualifications may be simply seen by practitioners as an effort to reduce risks, but these risks may be wrongly perceived as a result of ignorance about the credential in question (Reitz, 2001). It seems clear that by refusing to recognise immigrants' qualifications and experience as legitimate knowledge, liberal universalism privileges a regime of truth that perpetuates oppression and disadvantage.

Conclusion

We conclude that RPL is a political act. Our findings reveal that many immigrant professionals in Canada and Sweden have experienced devaluation and denigration of their prior learning and work experience after arriving in their new country. As a result, many of them have experienced significant, demoralising and disempowering downward social mobility. In the process of assessment and recognition of prior learning for immigrant professionals, there is obviously a missing 'R'. Lack of recognition can be attributed to a number of causes. First and foremost, there are epistemological misperceptions of difference and knowledge. A deficit model of difference can lead to a belief that differences are deficiency, that the knowledge of immigrant professionals, particularly those from developing countries, is incompatible and inferior, hence invalid. It appears safe to claim that knowledge has been racialised and materialised on the basis of ethnic and national origins. Furthermore, ontological commitment to positivism and liberal universalism exacerbates the complexity of this process. This study demonstrates that by applying a one-size-fits-all criterion to measure immigrants' credentials and experience, liberal universalism denies immigrants opportunities to be successful in a new society. It also reveals that professional standards and excellence have been used as a cloak to restrict competition and legitimise existing power relations. The juxtaposition of misconceptions of difference and knowledge with positivism and liberal universalism forms a new head tax to exclude the 'undesirable,' and to perpetuate oppression in Canada, Sweden and undoubtedly in other countries as well.

It is evident that current approaches to RPL for immigrant professionals are serious barriers rather than facilitators of this process. This study urges the development and adoption of more inclusive frameworks which fully embrace all human knowledge and experience, no matter which ethnic and cultural backgrounds they emerge from. Failing that, immigrants will continue to be alienated and barred from exercising the full range of their skills, citizenship and potential in their receiving societies.

References

Andersson, P., Fejes, A. and Ahn S-e. (2004), 'Recognition of prior vocational learning in Sweden', *Studies in the Education of Adults*, 36(1): 57–71.

Basran, G. and Zong, L. (1998), 'Devaluation of foreign credentials as perceived by visible minority professional immigrants', *Canadian Ethnic Studies*, 30(3): 6–18.

Berggren, K. and Omarsson, A. (2001), *Rätt man på fel plats – en studie av arbetsmarknaden för utlandsfödda akademiker som invandrat under 1990-talet*, /The right man in the wrong place – a study of the labour market for academics born abroad who immigrated during the 1990s/, Stockholm, Arbetsmarknadsstyrelsen, Ura 2001:5.

Bevelander, P. (2000), *Immigrant Employment Integration and Structural Change in Sweden 1970–1995*, Lund Studies in Economic History 15, Södertälje: Almqvist & Wiksell International.

Boshier, R.W. (1994), 'Initiating research' in Garrison, R. (ed.) *Research Perspectives in Adult Education* (pp. 73–116), Malabar: Krieger.

Broomé, P., Bäcklund, A-K., Lundh, C. and Ohlsson, R. (1996), *Varför sitter 'brassen' på bänken? Eller Varför har invandrarna så svårt att få jobb?*, /Why is it so difficult for immigrants to get a job?/, Stockholm: SNS Förlag.

Couton, P. (2002), 'Highly skilled immigrants: Recent trends and issues', *Canadian Journal of Policy Research*, 3(2): 114-23.

Cummins, J. (2003), 'Challenging the construction of difference as deficit: Where are identity, intellect, imagination, and power in the new regime of truth?' in Trifonas, P. (ed.) *Pedagogies of Difference: Rethinking Education for Social Change* (pp. 41–60), New York: Routledge Falmer.

Cunningham, P. (2000), 'The sociology of adult education' in Wilson, A. and Hayes, E. (eds) *Handbook of Adult and Continuing Education* (pp. 573–91), San Francisco: Jossey-Bass.

Dei, G.J.S. (1996), *Anti-Racism Education: Theory and Practice*, Halifax: Fernwood Publishing.

Deshler, D. and Grudens-Schuck, N. (2000), 'The politics of knowledge construction' in Wilson, A. and Hayes, E. (eds), *Handbook of Adult and Continuing Education* (pp. 592–611), San Francisco: Jossey-Bass.

Ekberg, J. and Rooth, D-O. (2000), *Arbetsmarknadspolitik för invandrare*, /Labour market politics for immigrants/, Rapport till Riksdagens Revisorer, Växjö: Växjö University, School of Management and Economics.

Fleras, A. and Elliott, J. (2002), *Engaging Diversity: Multiculturalism in Canada*, Toronto: Nelson Thomson Learning.

Foucault, M. (1980), *Power/Knowledge: Selected Interviews and Other Writings*, 1972-1977, New York: Pantheon Books.

Gannage, C. (1999), 'The health and safety concerns of immigrant women workers in the Toronto sportswear industry', *International Journal of Health Services*, 29(2): 409–29.

Ghosh, R. and Abdi, A.A. (2004), *Education and the Politics of Difference: Canadian Perspectives*, Toronto: Canadian Scholars' Press.

Gottskalksdottir, B. (2000), *Arbetet som en port till samhället. Invandrarakademikernas integration och identitet*, /Work as a gateway to society. Immigrant academics' integration and identity/, Licentiate's Dissertations in Sociology 2000:2, Lund: Sociologiska institutionen, Lunds universitet.

Gustafsson, B., Hammarstedt, M. and Zheng, J. (2004), 'Invandrares arbetsmarknadssituation – översikt och nya siffror', /Immigrants' labour market situation – overview and new figures/ in SOU 2004:21, *Egenförsörjning eller bidragsförsörjning? Invandrarna, arbetsmarknaden och välfärdsstaten, Rapport från Integrationspolitiska maktutredningen* (pp. 15–55), Stockholm: Justitiedepartementet.

Härnquist, K. (2003), 'Educational reserves revisited', *Scandinavian Journal of Educational Research*, 47(5): 483–94.

Henry, F., Tator, C., Mattis, W. and Rees, T. (2000), *The Colour of Democracy*, Toronto: Harcourt Brace & Company.

HSV (2005), http://www.hsv.se. Last accessed 24 March 2005.

Integrationsverket (2004), *Rapport Integration 2003,*/Report Integration 2003/, Norrköping, Integrationsverket /The Swedish Integration Board/.

Integrationsverket (2005), Statistics from The Swedish Integration Board, at http://www.integrationsverket.se, Norrköping, Integrationsverket /The Swedish Integration Board/.

Kincheloe, J. and Steinberg, S. (1997), *Changing Multiculturalism*, Buckingham: Open University Press.

Knowles, V. (1997), *Strangers at Our Gates: Canadian Immigration and Immigration Policy, 1540–1997*, Toronto: Dundurn Press.

Krahn, H., Derwing, T., Mulder, M. and Wilkinson, L. (2000), 'Educated and underemployed: Refugee integration into the Canadian labour market', *Journal of International Migration and Integration*, 1(1): 59–84.

LeGrande, C., Szulkin, R. and Ekberg, J. (2004), 'Kan diskriminering förklara skillnader i position på arbetsmarknaden mellan invandrare och infödda?' /Could discrimination explain differences concerning position in the labour market between immigrants and natives?/ in SOU 2004:21, *Egenförsörjning eller bidragsförsörjning? Invandrarna, arbetsmarknaden och välfärdsstaten*, Rapport från Integrationspolitiska maktutredningen (pp. 185–220), Stockholm: Justitiedepartementet.

Li, P.S. (2001), 'The market worth of immigrants' educational credentials', *Canadian Public Policy*, 27(1): 23–38.

Li, P.S. (2003), *Destination Canada: Immigration Debates and Issues*, Don Mills: Oxford University Press.

Mansour, M. (1996), 'Qualifications alone will not get you the job you want: Integrating into the Quebec labour market with foreign credentials', unpublished Master Thesis, Concordia University, Montreal, Quebec.

Mata, F. (1999), *The Non-Accreditation of Immigrant Professionals in Canada: Societal Dimensions of the Problem*, http://canada.metropolis.net/events/conversation/MATRPAPER.html. Last accessed 23 March 2005.

Matas, D. (1996), 'Racism in Canadian immigration policy' in James, C.E. (ed.) *Perspectives on Racism and the Human Services Sector: A Case for Change* (pp. 93–102), Toronto: University of Toronto Press.

McLaren, P. (2003), *Life in Schools: An Introduction to Critical Pedagogy in the Foundations of Education*, Boston: Pearson Education.

Mojab, S. (1999), 'De-skilling immigrant women', *Canadian Woman Studies*, 19(3): 123–8.

Moodley, K.A. (1995), 'Multicultural education in Canada: Historical development and current states' in Banks, J.A. and Banks, C.A. (eds) *Handbook of Research on Multicultural Education* (pp. 801–20), New York: MacMillan.

NE (1991), 'Emigration' in *Nationalencyklopedin*, Femte bandet, /Swedish national encyclopedia,/ volume 5, Höganäs: Bokförlaget Bra Böcker.

Ng, R. (1996), 'Homeworking: Dream realized or freedom constrained? The globalized reality of immigrant garment workers', *Canadian Woman Studies*, 19(3): 110–14.

OECD (2005), *Trends in International Migration*, SOPEMI 2004 Edition, Paris: OECD.

Osman, A. (1999), *The 'Strangers' Among Us. The Social Construction of Identity in Adult Education*, Linköping Studies in Education and Psychology No. 61, Linköping, Linköping University: Department of Education and Psychology.

Reitz, J.G. (2001), 'Immigrant skill utilization in the Canadian labour market: Implications of human capital research', *Journal of International Migration and Integration*, 2(3): 347–78.

Statistics Canada (2003a), *2001 Census: Analysis series*, Ottawa: Statistics Canada.

Statistics Canada (2003b), *Ethnic Diversity Survey*, Ottawa: Statistics Canada.

Statistics Canada (2003c), *Longitudinal Survey of Immigrants to Canada: Process, Progress and Prospects*, Ottawa: Statistics Canada.

Wanner, R.A. (2001), 'Diagnosing and preventing "brain waste" in Canada's immigrant population: a synthesis of comments on Reitz', *Journal of International Migration and Integration*, 2(3): 417–28.

Whitaker, R. (1991), *Canadian Immigration Policy Since Confederation*, Ottawa: Canadian Historical Association.

Young, I.M. (1995), 'Polity and group difference: A critique of the ideal of universal citizenship' in Beiner, R. (ed.) *Theorizing Citizenship* (pp. 175–207), Albany: State University of New York.

Young, T.R. and Arrigo, B.A. (1999), *The Dictionary of Critical Social Sciences*, Boulder, CO: Westview Press.

chapter ten

RPL: an emerging and contested practice in South Africa

Ruksana Osman

Introduction

This chapter is concerned with knowledge, pedagogy and power in RPL. It draws on empirical data from pilot RPL projects in higher education in South Africa to explore candidates' and assessors' experiences of portfolio development. This is done within a broad framework of critical theory and situated learning.

The main findings from my study show that RPL in practice raises personal questions for those who implement it and those who receive it. Individual assessors responded to these personal questions in varied ways showing that the epistemological standpoint of assessors strongly influences the way in which prior knowledge and its recognition is handled in higher education. This finding suggests a need for an 'epistemological audit' that requires assessors to question their own epistemological orientations before recognising the prior learning of others. For candidates in the study, RPL was personally empowering but practically and emotionally demanding. Findings suggest that RPL on its own cannot bring about equity and redress in education. These tensions form the focus of this chapter because they have implications for the development of RPL in South Africa and, hopefully, elsewhere.

Critical theory, situated learning and RPL in South Africa
The field of adult education and adult educators, irrespective of paradigmatic

orientation, has always had learners as the centre of its gaze (Oliver, 1999; Stuart and Thomson, 1995). The broad aims of the field include the personal development of adult learners (in the humanist tradition) and a nurturing of their agency in respect of social change and transformation (in the critical tradition).

Critical education theory is well placed to provide the primary frame for this chapter for four inter-related reasons. First, it facilitates a focus on the learning of individuals and groups who have been excluded from formal education. Secondly, it questions dominant forms of knowledge and the 'status of the definitive, the certain and the proven' (Usher, 1992, p. 210). Thirdly, critical educators focus explicitly on reversing practices, attitudes and beliefs that limit the potential and status of people in society. According to Giroux (1983, p. 242), they are propelled by a passion to create a just society: 'one that [. . .] links struggle to a new set of human possibilities'. Critical adult education has therefore always taken sides with social movements to influence equity and justice in a democratic society. Fourthly, critical adult education connects with the material realities of ordinary peoples' lives (Apple, 1993).

Critical theory is particularly pertinent to South Africa because it provides a resource both to criticise and to change unequal educational practices. Research framed by such theory goes beyond interpretive goals of better understanding educational practices, and instead proposes to change those practices in a way that also transforms the context of the practices. For the majority of South Africans, systematic inequality in education, coupled with a policy of undermining the very fabric of African society, has resulted in psychological damage to a point where learners have a skewed sense of who they are and of the value of what they know (Odora-Hoppers, 2001). Taking account of this history, approaches to education framed by critical theory have the potential to support learners in building the intellectual self-confidence necessary for effective participation in education.

Not surprisingly, therefore, critical theory perspectives have influenced RPL discourses in South Africa. RPL has been strongly linked to equity and redress and to personal and collective empowerment and social change for disadvantaged groups, particularly those whose educational paths have been disrupted. It has also been seen as a space for exploring alternative epistemologies and pedagogies – approaches that are highly relevant if education institutions are to understand and position themselves in a transforming society. The educative value of learning from everyday life, work and community is particularly emphasised. There is an acknowledgement that adults' experience comprises knowledge and skills and also attributes such as focus, self-discipline and self-knowledge – which form the basis for further growth and development.

Yet, RPL policy, designed to open 'doors of opportunity' into higher education for South African adults, is not widely implemented. In the small number of instances where RPL is being implemented it is for access into a learning programme rather than for credit or advanced standing within it. Furthermore, debates around RPL in South African higher education have become polarised. One pole (of a continuum) can be characterised by academics who assert that it is not possible to accredit prior knowledge because it is a different type of knowledge, acquired in a site of practice that is remote from the university. The assumption is that students need to be inducted into academic habits and ways of knowing. Only then do they come to acquire academic knowledge. Such a perspective often positions academic knowledge as the uncontested, politically neutral and universal domain of the pedagogue who, in turn, is also seen in asocial and apolitical terms.

These underpinning belief systems are likely to translate into RPL practices that explore prior learning only in relation to how it differs from academic knowledge. The outcome of such approaches would be to render prior knowledge invisible and under-theorised. Opportunities to find connections between different knowledge forms would be missed. Pedagogues would tend to select approaches to pedagogy and assessment that are deemed to be asocial and apolitical, when in fact their social and political natures have simply been erased and rendered invisible.

Recently, such epistemological assumptions and beliefs have been questioned by social practice and situated learning theories which locate the social actor as crucial in the act of knowledge construction (Lave and Wenger, 1993) and posit that the '. . . knower is an intimate part of the known' (Belenky *et al.*, 1986, p. 137). It is argued that knowing is not an objective procedure and the domain of the pedagogue, but a process that weaves the private and public lives of human beings into integrated and whole realities. These theories call into question dichotomies between academic and non-academic ways of knowing, between universal and situated knowers (and pedagogues) and between 'expert' and 'non-expert' definitions of reality (Collins, 1986). It is an 'inclusive' form of theorising, as evidenced by the following quotation:

> ... mutual engagement involves not only our competence, but also the competence of others. They draw on what we do and what we know, as well as our ability to connect meaningfully to what we don't do and what we don't know – that is, to the contributions and knowledge of others. (Wenger, 1998, p. 76)

In my view, such 'inclusive' theorising has potential in the area of RPL, particularly with regard to capturing the knowledge contributions of the collective as well as the individual. Framing with critical theory facilitates the addition of a political dimension to RPL, suggesting that RPL cannot be driven only by questions about competing epistemologies and the equivalence of practical and academic knowledge. In South Africa, particularly, there is a need for theories and actions that deal with the inequalities that characterise the society. So, whilst recognising prior knowledge is an epistemological question it is also a political question. Looked at in this way, RPL provides opportunities for educators to examine the social constructedness of beliefs about the universality and value of academic knowledge and to develop new theoretical and political relationships between academic knowledge and the prior knowledge of those who have been on the receiving end of entrenched educational inequalities.[1]

Critical theory and situated learning intersect and are compatible with a qualitative research paradigm and these together provide the research framework for this study. My aim in the rest of the chapter is to report on the analysis of participants' experiences of RPL in pilot projects in higher education institutions. In analysing these experiences, my research questions focused on the epistemological and philosophical ideas that propelled the practices. I probed assessors' and candidates' experiences – experiences which were valuable sources of information in a field that is embryonic and 'under-researched' in South Africa (Harris, 2000). My inquiry sought to understand and give particular voice to individuals and practices that are at present marginal in higher education. This is consistent with critical theory, which seeks ways to understand how individuals can transform the contexts in which they find themselves, so that . . . 'possibilities may be sought, reflected upon, transformed and deepened' (Taylor, 1985, p. 139).

Research methodology

In 2003, I developed a qualitative research design and conducted interviews with 35 respondents: 12 academics and 23 students, from five RPL pilot projects in four institutions of higher education. The institutions represented a spectrum of universities in South Africa, from historically advantaged institutions (University of the Witwatersrand [Wits], Johannesburg College of Education [JCE] and University of the Free State [UFS]), to historically disadvantaged institutions (University of the Western Cape [UWC]), and from English-language institutions (Wits, JCE and UWC) to Afrikaans-language institutions (UFS). Assessors in the pilot projects had designed and implemented RPL portfolio-development courses for the admission of students to the university into mainly undergraduate, professionally-oriented programmes such as nursing, teaching and leadership.[2]

While the pilot projects provided ready sources of information at a time when such knowledge was vitally needed (making them in Merton's [1987] terminology, 'strategic' projects), the number of participating students and staff was small. However, they did provide an adequate empirical resource for exploring the research questions I outlined above.

Findings

The over-arching finding of the study is that RPL portfolio-development processes are contested practices. Participants' experiences of these practices suggest that RPL is not an activity that is epistemologically or pedagogically neutral. Rather, it is a practice that is dramatically influenced by the epistemological standpoint of the implementer, facilitator or assessor.

Characteristics of the portfolio-development programmes across the institutions

Generally, across the five projects, there was a trend for assessors to design and implement portfolio courses that were 'developmental' in their orientation. By this I mean that they provided opportunities for candidates to express themselves in modes that were different from conventional academic forms of assessment such as essays or examinations. In this way, the portfolios could be seen as creating spaces for prior knowledge to become visible. Or as Preece (2000, p. 8) puts it, experience was 'given its own sense of certainty, pace and place', even if only for a short time. Some portfolio-development processes utilised autobiographies or learning histories. Others focused on analysing critical learning moments. Others were less developmental in that they attempted to match prior learning with course outcomes. In all the portfolios, students were supported and guided in their compilation. The assessors recognised the importance of academic reading and writing skills and all programmes created spaces for students to develop and/or strengthen these abilities by, for example, working critically with academic texts selected by themselves or by the assessors.

Assessors' experiences of RPL

Some assessors experienced dilemmas and tensions during the RPL processes. They experienced a pedagogical complexity in assessing experiential learning and a role conflict between their function as assessors of prior learning and their conventional role as teachers who socialise students into an academic (dis)course. Such assessors distinguished between two levels of action in an RPL process, that is, the 'retrospective action' and the 'prospective action' (see Shalem and Steinberg, Chapter 5, this volume). The former refers to valuing the past learning of a candidate and the latter is about trying to ensure that candidates present their portfolios in ways that chime with academic and discipline-specific concepts and skills. The assessors experienced these two actions, and the corresponding tasks of assessing and teaching/facilitation, as being in tension. They decided that RPL candidates had to be taught how to present their prior knowledge in a way that was academically structured, organised and therefore recognisable to others in the academy. They achieved this by providing the candidates with a theoretical context against which to think about their prior knowledge. The role conflicts and attempts to ameliorate them are captured below:

> In the RPL course there was a need to bring something of the future, into the present and this gave me a conflicting role as an academic. By this I mean when assessing prior learning, you can't just assess off the top of your head, neither can a student present her [prior] learning off the top of her head. There has to be a context. The context we presented was certain academic texts. We did not want the student to learn the contents of the text but rather the texts provided the context for presenting prior learning. But to enable the student to present this prior learning I had to teach some concepts and skills. So in this way I am bringing future learning on the part of the student, and future teaching on my part, into the present process of assessing and recognising prior learning. This gave me a conflicting role as an academic.

Coupled with role conflict, some assessors were challenged by *interfacing prior knowledge with academic knowledge*. They experienced demands on their beliefs about knowledge when they tried to find broad equivalencies between academic and experiential knowledge. They felt uncomfortable and even compromised by such interfacing or 'boundary crossing' (Giroux, 1992) and appeared to be grounded primarily in their role of socialising students into existing academic knowledge. Consequently, they worked with the tools of the field that they knew best (that is, the critical reading of academic texts and the utilisation of academic forms of communication). These resources were used to make sense of the other field, in this case prior knowledge. Assessors expressed a sense of powerlessness and of being overwhelmed by students' accounts of their prior learning. This was mainly because students' accounts were not tight narratives with a structure that was recognisable to them: 'we felt imprisoned in their stories. I felt I had to control the discourse because I was overwhelmed by it.'

Other assessors experienced a collaborative rather than an oppositional relationship between prior knowledge and academic knowledge. Their perspective was that academic knowledge could be enriched by crossing the divide to prior knowledge, because such knowledge emerged from the practice of peoples' lives and learning. One assessor's experience of crossing epistemological boundaries is captured below:

> In the field of education and with students who are education practitioners, I believe that people need to theorise about their life, about their work experience, rather than to see and really maintain a stark distinction between academic theory and their work. If they experience these as two totally divorced things, then what's the use of the academic world? Academic knowledge is almost like a sort of an adjunct to it [experiential knowledge] . . .

The assessors who valued boundary crossing between knowledges and learning also recognised the necessarily *time consuming* nature of portfolio development and assessment, including the intensive writing support that candidates need.

Candidates' experiences of RPL
How did the RPL candidates experience practices that were so contested philosophically and epistemologically? A consistent finding was that they experienced the portfolio-development courses as opportunities to become aware of themselves as learners and to build their confidence (see also Whittaker *et al.*, Chapter 15, this volume).[3] At the same time, they were challenged by the emotional and practical demands of the portfolio.

Portfolio development as academically and personally valuable

Candidates across the institutions valued portfolio activities for the ways in which the development of academic skills of reading and writing were supported. They found they were able to use these skills effectively to write about their prior knowledge. The development of academic skills combined with writing about their prior knowledge gave them a sense of personal confidence to undertake further studies in higher education. One candidate expressed it thus: 'Through the portfolio I realised my potential. The process made me find the real me and what I have achieved in life'. In addition, some candidates felt that the activities of academic reading and writing during portfolio development provided them with an opportunity to epistemologically access the university because they were able to engage in activities that are valued in higher education. This experience is captured thus:

> The RPL programme assisted us to know the standard of the university. It assisted us with academic writing, on how to approach assignments, on avoiding plagiarising and so on. It contributed to my broader understanding of what is needed [in higher education].

Portfolio development as practically and emotionally demanding

A consistent finding was that RPL is not a soft option. Candidates across the institutions found the volume of work in portfolio development extremely demanding, especially the reorganising and restructuring of learning from experience into a coherent and comprehensive portfolio. This task was experienced as particularly challenging when evidence for learning was difficult to obtain, for example, having to refer to previous employers.[4] In addition, the emotional demands of representation were draining for candidates. Like the assessors who were overwhelmed by the situated nature of prior learning, so too, the candidates were overwhelmed by having to bring order and structure to their prior learning. They expressed difficulty in identifying and selecting which learning to include in their portfolio and which not, and experienced an emotional wrench when they had to cast aside learning that was deemed less useful for academic learning, but which had been valuable to them in everyday life: 'I found it traumatic to classify what was valuable experience and what was not valuable'.[5] Another candidate expressed the selection of learning as becoming aware of differential valuings:

> I needed to say something in my portfolio, but I needed the courage to write down some of the personal things. One has to

debate with oneself whether to write it or not. After all this
debating I came to the conclusion that what people have learnt
in life is important even if it is not certificated.

All of the above demands were aggravated when faculty administrators were
inflexible and insensitive. Candidates felt alienated by administrators who did
not know them as individuals and who were not able to provide them with
general information on matters relating to outstanding fees, registration dates,
university calendars, publication of results and so on. The lack of availability
of procedural information (or the assumption that such information should
already be known) was frustrating for the candidates concerned, and resonates
with experiences of RPL candidates elsewhere (Butterworth and McKelvey,
1997; Merrifield *et al.*, 2000).

Discussion

The experiences of RPL from the perspectives of those who receive it and
those who implement it suggest that in South Africa these practices are
epistemologically, academically and emotionally challenging. The experience
suggests further that while policy intends for RPL to deliver on equity and
redress for learners, such possibilities are remote at the level of implementation.

Portfolios as a contested practice for assessors: connectedness and difference

For assessors across all of the institutions the main areas of contestation and
debate rested on the role conflict and epistemological challenges that RPL
throws up in higher education. Following Harris, it appears that positions
regarding the 'epistemological contours of formal knowledge' (2000, p. 48)
were drawn in varied ways by different assessors in this study, showing
clearly that 'the academy' is not as homogenous and monolithic as it is
sometimes made out to be.

How did assessors who experienced conflicting roles and epistemological
dilemmas extricate themselves from this bind? Those who started out with a
dichotomised view of experiential and academic knowledge were left with
few moves. The boundary they set around knowledge and academic ways of
knowing exalted their own epistemological preferences, that is, the value of
formal disciplinary knowledge and the induction and socialisation of students
into a community of practice that 'discourses through writing' and theorising

(Northedge, 2001, p. 308). This preference (and an absence of reflexivity regarding the social contructedness of the pedagogue role) prevented them from sharing their 'epistemological authority'. Moreover, this authority, strongly influenced by a particular epistemological base, prevented the assessors from recognising the candidates' prior learning. The epistemological standpoint that it is only academic discourse that gives coherence, order and meaning, allowed them to bypass experiential knowledge. One assessor's epistemological preference in this regard is captured below:

> I confirmed to myself through this portfolio process that
> academic discourse gives coherence, gives order, gives sense,
> gives meaning to items that are made into a body of knowledge,
> and in fact if I don't have that I am lost.

The pedagogical conflicts between formal teaching and the assessment of prior knowledge were experienced as so overwhelming that the assessors resorted to doing what they do well on a daily basis, that is, teach. Because of their unfamiliarity with prior learning and their standpoint on academic knowledge, they lost faith in the 'retrospective [pedagogic] action' and were guided by the 'prospective action'.

Starting out with a perspective that highlighted fundamental differences between knowledges and between assessing and teaching, resulted in practices in which the pervasive power of academic knowledge prevailed. The academy, its specialist discourses and the assessment processes in RPL were foregrounded for these assessors. Moreover, the experience of RPL seemed to sharpen the distinction between academic and prior knowledge, rather than bridging or blurring it. These assessors were not able to allow interconnectivity to be part of their disciplinary identity and they were unable to make connections among multiple ways of learning and knowing. Rather, their approach and response to RPL mirrored Apple's view that dichotomies are 'a fiction that we tell to make our lives as educators simpler' (1994, p. x).

How did some of the assessors look beyond particular legitimised forms of knowledge? Why did they not experience such intense struggles as their colleagues? Their strategy seemed to be one that did not dichotomise knowledges. Their starting point was more fluid with a tolerance for ambiguity in teaching, learning and assessing. Their practices were informed by an epistemological standpoint whereby knowledge cannot be separated from experience, and where practice-based knowledge is seen as having a complementary role to play with academic knowledge. A view of knowledge as permeable

(Harris, 2000) did not however lead to a theoretical impasse; rather it offered them more choices for an emancipatory view of knowing. For these assessors, this view of knowing did not compromise the assessment process or the specialist role of the pedagogue. Their epistemological standpoint allowed for prior knowledge to be handled differently.

While there is no single approach or standpoint regarding RPL that can be deemed most appropriate, this study suggests that academics who intend to implement RPL may find it helpful to conduct what I would call an 'epistemological audit'. This implies that academics start by questioning their own epistemological orientations, because these orientations impact on the implementation of RPL in significant ways. Such a review would also help to lead institutions and academics towards more awareness of, and transparency about, the purpose and aims of RPL. For example, they may need to ask and decide whether RPL is about assimilating students into existing programmes in an existing institutional culture where the knowledge boundaries and disciplinary bases are fixed, or whether it is about a space in which new forms of scholarship about knowing through experience and knowing through action are explored. Such new forms would be in keeping with broader epistemological possibilities associated with critical theory and situated learning, where knowledge and learning from different sites of practice are treated in more egalitarian ways (see Michelson, Chapter 7, this volume). These new forms could complement academic ways of knowing and contribute to overcoming epistemological and ideological binary oppositions. Such an audit ultimately raises personal questions about knowledge, pedagogy and power in RPL and beyond.

Portfolios as a contested practice for candidates: 'coming to voice' and losing voice

For the RPL candidates, portfolios provided an opportunity to publicly declare what they knew from experience. This had an effect on their sense of who they were and their ability to learn. Knowledge created in the community and in the organisations where they laboured was given space, paralleling what hooks (1994, p. 148) calls 'coming to voice', albeit for a short period of time (and for access into a learning programme rather than credit). The compilation of a portfolio and its various activities allowed prior knowledge and academic knowledge to connect. Again, paralleling hooks (*ibid.*) this moment of interconnectedness was '. . . not just the act of telling one's experience. It is using that telling strategically – to come to voice so that you can also speak freely about other subjects'.

In this sense, RPL portfolio development holds promise for the personal development of adults entering higher education institutions in South Africa. The process affirmed the candidates as individuals; as they learnt about themselves they became more confident human beings. In South Africa, where education under apartheid was synonymous with skewing children's sense of themselves as human beings and as learners, individual development for adults through RPL holds promise and should, in my view, despite its contestations, continue to be focused on as one thrust for equity and redress in education. At the same time, we need to heed Fraser, who cautions that individual empowerment should not be an end in itself, otherwise we may be guilty of '. . . adhering to individual empowerment at the expense of social change' (1995, p. 190). Some candidates do find it difficult to write about their prior knowledge in learning histories and autobiographies and in some cases such modes could serve to silence rather than give voice. Michelson (1996) cautions that portfolio activities that require continuous reflection result in privileging loftier domains like reason over feeling, and academic over experiential, which reinscribe the very binaries that an interconnected and inclusive approach to RPL seeks to overcome. There is also a need to attend to the potential loss of voice when candidates confront those aspects of their learning that have to be let go of in an RPL process. These tensions are highlighted in a slightly different way by Stuart, who advises RPL assessors and candidates to always 'speculate about what is left out of an account. It is here that we come upon the hidden work of everyday life' (1995, p. 168).

Conclusions

In this chapter I have shared some theoretical and empirical insights from research into the experiences of RPL assessors and candidates in a small number of higher education pilots in South Africa. Their experiences suggest that RPL poses epistemological and pedagogical challenges for some assessors. These are particularly intense when assessors define knowledge in oppositional terms and when prior knowledge is pitted against academic knowledge. For assessors who begin with a less insular gaze, portfolio development offers them a pedagogic resource through which to obtain glimpses of prior knowledge and to theorise such knowledge in relation to academic knowledge. For RPL candidates, portfolio development does not offer an easy passage into higher education. At best, portfolios offer an opportunity to declare prior knowledge, and in this sense hold out promise for affirming students entering higher education. While portfolio activities empower candidates to declare their prior knowledge, whether such knowledge is recognised for credit is strongly influenced by the epistemological position of the assessor. The assessor holds the power for such recognition, reinforcing the view that an epistemological audit or review is desirable when implementing RPL.

In South Africa, entrenched educational inequalities compel academics to explore alternatives to the logic of academic knowledge. Yet, as a tool for equity and redress, RPL cannot be said to be currently delivering. Critical theory and situated theory could provide a theoretical language through which to envision alternative practical strategies for RPL. Granted, creating such alternatives requires a concomitant institutional culture that allows for engaging with knowledge created in other sites of practice. Harris (1999, p. 134–5) rightly argues that such shifts take root most effectively in institutions with 'curriculum flexibility and where knowledge boundaries are weakening [. . .] and in contexts where there is strong pressure for [. . .] change.' In this study, some assessors' experiences and some candidates' experiences point to possibilities for the development of practices capable of contributing more effectively to equity and redress.

References

Aarts, S., Blower, D., Burke, R., Conlin, E., Howell, B., Howorth, C., Lammare, G. and Van Kleef, J. (1999), *A Slice of the Iceberg: Cross-Canada Study on Prior Learning Assessment and Recognition*, Tyendinaga Mohawk Territory: First Nations Technical Institute.

Apple, M.W. (1993), *Official Knowledge: Democratic Education in a Conservative Age*, New York: Routledge.

Apple, M.W. (1994), 'Introduction' in Gitlin, A. (ed.) *Power and Method: Political Activism and Educational Research* (pp. ix–xii), New York: Routledge.

Belenky, M., Clinchy, B., Goldberger, N. and Tarule, J. (1986), *Women's Ways of Knowing. The Development of Self, Voice and Mind*, New York: Basic Books.

Blackman, S.J. and Brown, A. (1992), 'Constraints upon portfolio development in the accreditation of prior learning' in Mulligan, J. and Griffin, C. (ed.) *Empowerment through Experiential Learning. Explorations of Good Practice* (pp. 109–17), London: Kogan Page.

Butterworth, C. and McKelvey, C. (1997), 'A study of APEL at four universities', *Journal of Access Studies*, 12: 153–75.

Chiseri-Strater, E. (1991), *Academic Literacies – The Public and Private Discourse of University Students*, Portsmouth, NH: Boynton/Cook.

Collins, P.H. (1986), 'Learning from the outsider from within: the sociological significance of black feminist thought', *Social Problems*, 33(6): 14–32.

Fraser, W. (1995), *Learning from Experience – Empowerment or Incorporation?*, Leicester: NIACE.

Giroux, H. (1992), *Border Crossing: Cultural Workers and the Politics of Education*, London: Routledge.

Giroux, H. (1983), *Theory and Resistance in Education*, Massachusetts: Bergin and Garvey.

Harris, J. (2000), *Recognition of Prior Learning: Power, Pedagogy and Possibility*, Pretoria: HSRC.

Harris, J. (1999), 'Ways of seeing the recognition of prior learning (RPL): what contributions can such practices make to social inclusion?', *Studies in the Education of Adults*, 31(2): 124–39.

hooks, B. (1994), *Teaching to Transgress*, London: Routledge.

Hull, C. (1992), 'Making experience count: facilitating the APEL process' in Mulligan, J. and Griffin, J. (eds) *Empowerment through Experiential Learning. Explorations of Good Practice* (pp. 118–23), London,:Kogan Page.

Lave, J. and Wenger, E. (1993), *Situated Learning: Legitimate Peripheral Participation*, Cambridge: Cambridge University Press.

Merrifield, J., McIntyre, D. and Osaigbovo, R. (2000), *Mapping APEL: Accreditation of Prior Learning in English Higher Education*, London: Learning from Experience Trust (LET).

Merton, R. (1987), 'Three fragments from a sociologist's notebook: establishing the phenomenon, specified ignorance and strategic research materials', *Annual Review of Sociology*, 13: 1–28.

Michelson, E. (1996), 'Beyond Galileo's telescope: situated knowledge and the assessment of experiential learning', *Adult Education Quarterly*, 46(4): 185–96.

Michelson, E. (1998), *Expanding the Logic of Portfolio-Assisted Assessment: Lessons from South Africa, Research Report*, New York, National Centre on Adult Education.

New London Group (1996), 'A pedagogy of multiliteracies: designing social futures', *Harvard Educational Review*, 66(1): 60–92.

Northedge, A. (2001), *Rethinking Teaching in the Context of Diversity: Tertiary Teaching and Learning Dealing with Diversity*, Darwin: Northern Territory University.

Odora-Hoppers, C. (2001), 'Decolonising the curriculum, indigenous knowledge systems and globalisation, part one', Paper presented at a Philosophy of Education Seminar, Pretoria, UNISA.

Oliver, P. (1999), *Lifelong and Continuing Education what is a Learning Society?*, Aldershot: Ashgate.

Preece, J. (2000), 'Changing the discourse of inclusion and exclusion with off limits curricula: working papers supporting lifelong learning', *The Open University Festival of Lifelong Learning*, UK, University of East London, pp. 1–15, available at http://www.open.ac.uk/lifelong-learning/papers.

Stuart, M. (1995), 'If experience counts then why am I bothering to come here? AP(E)L and learning' in Stuart, M. and Thomson, A. (eds) *Engaging with Difference: The 'Other' in Adult Education* (pp. 158–70), Leicester: NIACE.

Stuart, M. and Thomson, A. (1995), *Engaging with Difference: The 'Other' in Adult Education* (pp. 1–24), Leicester: NIACE.

Taylor, C. (1985), *Philosophy and the Human Sciences: Philosophical Papers 2*, New York: Cambridge University Press.

Usher, R. (1999), 'Identity, risk and lifelong learning' in Oliver, P. (ed.) *Lifelong and Continuing Education. What is a Learning Society?* (pp. 65–82), Aldershot: Ashgate.

Usher, R (1992), 'Experience in adult education: a post-modern critique', *Journal of Philosophy of Education*, 26(2): 201–14.

Usher, R. and Johnston, R. (1996), *Experiential learning – some critical reflections, international case study evaluation*, South Africa: HSRC.

Wenger, E. (1998), *Communities of Practice: Learning, Meaning and Identity*, Cambridge: Cambridge University Press.

West, L. and Fraser, W. (1995), 'APEL and admissions to higher education' in Fraser, W. (ed.) *Learning from Experience – Empowerment or Incorporation?* (pp. 135–58), Leicester: NIACE.

Notes

1 This wider view of relevant knowledge resonates with broader epistemological possibilities associated with critical theory and pedagogies, where knowledge and learning from different sites of practice are treated in more egalitarian ways (Belenky *et al.*, 1986; Collins, 1986; Chiseri-Strater, 1991; Michelson, 1996, 1998; New London Group, 1996; Usher and Johnston, 1996; Usher, 1999).

2 In most of the pilots the same people were involved in the design, facilitation and assessment of the RPL processes. I refer to them as 'assessors'.

3 Student gains in personal and academic confidence are corroborated by similar findings in RPL research conducted in England (Butterworth and McKelvey, 1997; Hull, 1992), and in Canada (Aarts *et al.*, 1999).

4 This experience squares with research from England conducted by Blackman and Brown (1992), who are sceptical and question whether evidence of past achievement is easily collected and collated.

5 There was a level of anxiety in these experiences which is reflected in the RPL literature. For example, students at the University of Kent, in the UK, who, like the

South African RPL candidates, were concerned 'that the academics would sit in judgment on what they, the students had only recently discovered, and valued, in themselves' (West and Fraser, 1995, p. 157).

chapter eleven

'Tools of mediation': an historical-cultural approach to RPL

Linda Cooper

I still praise Cosatu today and I will praise it until my bones are
in the ground because it is an organisation and a half. It
educates the workers from both sides, about the community and
the workplace. (Alfred Qabula, South African Worker Poet)

Introduction

In South Africa, the transformational promises of RPL carry greater
significance than in most other parts of the world. Against the background of
the history of apartheid, RPL is viewed as a central mechanism with which to
address past discrimination and disadvantage, and to bring about greater
equity and redress. It is argued that RPL should not only provide access to
educational opportunities for those previously excluded, but should also act as
a vehicle for the recognition of 'knowledge from below'. For example,
Michelson (1998, p. 11), writing of post-apartheid South Africa, emphasises
the importance of recognising and valuing 'the expertise and wisdom that
sustained communities under the harshest of circumstances; [. . .] and that
finally furnished the organisational framework to defeat a deeply oppressive
regime', while Grossman (1999, p. 4) has drawn attention to the 'vast body of
unused, wasted, suppressed, denied knowledge' that exists amongst ordinary
workers.

By valuing such knowledge, RPL can work not only to facilitate access to higher education, but may also facilitate dialogue across different sites of knowledge and learning, thereby helping to enrich the curricular, pedagogical, and critical practices of the academy. Creating a process of dialogue involves bringing prior experiential knowledge into some kind of 'conversation' with academic knowledge. However, as Harris (2004) has shown, we have little understanding of what this dialogue or conversation involves, indicative of a theoretical and conceptual vagueness regarding the form of pedagogy underpinning RPL. I would argue that this pedagogical vagueness is, in turn, related to an epistemological vagueness regarding how to describe and conceptualise the different kinds of knowledge that are brought into relationship with one another within the RPL process.

Ralphs and Motala (2000) have pointed out that within higher education, there is little consensus as to what constitutes academic knowledge. Even less research has been done on the rich and diverse nature of knowledge and processes of learning in informal or non-formal contexts. A growing body of literature on informal learning has pointed to the need to address major gaps in our empirical knowledge of learning in diverse settings (Colley *et al.*, 2003), to locate knowledge generated in informal and non-formal contexts philosophically and explore its relationship to formal, propositional knowledge (Barnett, 2003, pp. 23, 25), and to develop a theory of learning in social, collective contexts (Kilgore, 2003). A number of these writers have pointed to the need for high-quality case-study research, with detailed analyses of specific social contexts using methods of ethnographic study (see for example Foley, 1999).

This chapter draws on a case study of learning in an informal context, and aims to contribute to our understanding of culturally diverse forms of knowing and learning. It is based on my research into processes of learning and forms of pedagogy and knowledge within the non-formal, collective organisational context of a trade union, but is also informed by my practitioner experience of educational work with trade unions, as well as the training of community educators and development workers.

The chapter will explore the role of culture in the processes of knowledge transmission and learning in informal social contexts, and identify the cultural resources that black South Africans have historically drawn upon in the processes of mediating knowledge. I will argue that in order to value fully the knowledge which reflects the racial, gendered and class experiences of black people in South Africa, we need to recognise the distinctive ways in which that knowledge is acquired and transmitted, and the possibility that such knowledge may find expression in ways different to that of academic knowledge. In other words, history, local context and culture shape not only what we know, but also how we learn, and how we are able to express what we know. Following Starr-Glass (2002), I will argue that we need to identify the 'totemic' logic of this particular knowledge system – the system of properties embedded in it – in order to fully appreciate its meaning and significance. In the final part of the chapter, I will assess the significance of these arguments for the implementation of RPL.

Conceptual background: socio-cultural theories of learning

My analysis draws on Vygotskian and post-Vygotskian perspectives on learning, which emphasise the social nature of learning, the key role of human activity as a major impetus for learning, and the importance of culture and history in shaping knowledge (see also Wheelahan, in this volume). In particular, I draw upon Vygotsky's concept of 'tools of mediation' – 'the means by which the individual acts upon and is acted upon by social, cultural and historical factors' (Daniels, 2001, p. 14). Tools of mediation are always sedimented with history (and with historical intelligence), as well as being culturally embedded. Learners bring with them learning histories which are both individual and unique, but which – through their experiences of particular forms of mediation – also reflect a shared and collective history and culture. Vygotsky distinguished between three kinds of mediators (all socio-cultural in nature): material tools; psychological tools; and other human beings. Post-Vygotskians have tended to emphasise either language (see, for example, Wertsch, 1985, 1991; and Wertsch and Smolka, 1993), or 'activity' (see for example, Scribner, 1997; and Engeström, 1999, 2002) as key psychological tools of mediation.

Wertsch's interest in how speech acts as a cultural tool in mediated action led him to consider the work of Bakhtin on speech acts and utterances. 'Dialogicality', meaning the different ways that voices come into contact, is fundamental to Bakhtin's account of human and social processes (Wertsch and Smolka, in Daniels, 1993, p. 73). My analysis will also draw on Bakhtin's later work, in particular, his writings on carnival and everyday life. Bakhtin theorised the everyday as inextricably intertwined with the carnivalesque, and viewed the body as a key site of resistance. Carnival illustrates the 'boisterous, disruptive and libidinous qualities of popular cultural forms and the collective body' (Gardiner, 2000, p. 63), and is an enactment of 'the world

turned upside down', underscoring the inevitability of change and transformation (*ibid*., p. 68).

This chapter draws on an ethnographic case-study of learning within one,
specific social context – a South African trade union – but it seeks to draw
broader conclusions. My findings suggest that in addition to the people
(educators) who play key mediating roles in the union context, there is also a
rich array of symbolic tools of mediation – often involving a *combination* of
language and activity – that play a distinctive role in union pedagogy.
Although rooted in the history of the trade union movement, these symbolic
tools of mediation are embedded in the wider historical and cultural
experiences of black people in South Africa. Thus, while drawing on case
study material from the trade union context in order to make my arguments, I
intend these arguments to have broader applicability to a wide range of 'social
action' and community contexts in South Africa, as well as possibly in other
countries.

Background to the case study

There is a rich body of literature on social movements as sites of learning and
of new knowledge production (see, for example, Newman, 1994; Welton,
1995; Holford, 1995; Spencer, 1995; Martin, 1999; Kilgore, 1999; and Foley,
1999). Some of these writers tend to dichotomise 'old social movements'
(including the labour movement) and 'new social movements' in ways that are
not fruitful in the South African context. In the struggle against apartheid, the
trade union movement played a leading role, and workers not only challenged
the apartheid system of racial capitalism, but also incorporated a creative and
inventive dimension to their struggle.

My case study involves the Cape Town branch of a national, municipal trade
union. The union is unusual and atypical of the majority of black trade unions
in South Africa. Demographically, the majority of union members in this
branch are Afrikaans-speaking, coloured workers.[1] This branch has a very
long history as an independent union dating back to 1927, and its early history
was characterised by politically conservative and elitist forms of leadership,
and racial exclusivity. It was not until the late 1970s that this union underwent
a process of democratisation, de-racialisation and political radicalisation,
leading to its affiliation to the militant trade union federation – Cosatu[2] –
when the latter was established in 1985. The union subsequently merged with
other, black municipal unions and came to constitute the Cape Town branch

of a national municipal trade union. Since South Africa's first democratic elections in 1994, municipal workers have engaged in ongoing and sometimes bitter battles against government policies of privatisation and moves to cut jobs in the public sector. In this process, they have stood face-to-face against a group of employers (town councillors) who include a large number of their 'ex-comrades' from both the union movement as well as the broader political movement.

My data draws mainly on ethnographic observations[3] of three key settings: the union's structured education programme (workshops); meetings of a range of organisational structures within the branch; and branch members' involvement in a national strike of the union in mid-2002. The research was designed on the assumption that learning takes place not only in the structured education programmes of the union, but that through workers' experiences of organising, meeting, taking collective decisions and engaging in collective action, knowledge is also shared and new understandings are sought and produced. In the sections that follow, I will focus not only on the content and form of such knowledge, but more particularly on how such knowledge is mediated.

Orality and performance as tools of mediation

Perhaps the most striking feature of union pedagogy is its reliance on face-to-face, oral forms of communication. Union activists are quite conscious of this. For example, in a workshop preparing for the national strike in July 2002, unionists argued that in educating members about the strike, no form of written communication is entirely reliable and that not even 'distance' modes of oral communication can effectively substitute for face-to-face oral communication with members: 'A telephone report is inadequate – the hearer can distort it entirely. The proper way is going physically to make a report' (union organiser[4]).

'Orality' as a tool of mediation needs to be viewed complexly. Daniels (1993, pp. 119–20) argues that rather than viewing language as a 'generalised or abstract system that mediates activity, interaction and thought', it should be treated as 'a multitude of distinct speech genres and semiotic devices that are tightly linked with particular social institutions and practices.' In my study of the trade union as a social institution and a community of practice, a number of speech genres and semiotic devices are notable. The continual use of 'code-switching' is the most distinctive speech genre in use, while 'ventriloquism', repetition, story-telling, humour and a variety of forms of oral performativity are in widespread use, particularly in settings involving the grassroots membership of the union.

The continual use of code-switching – changing from English to Afrikaans (or Afrikaans to isiXhosa[5]) and vice versa, sometimes in the middle of a sentence – is striking in union workshops. For example, in one workshop a union organiser (himself an ex-shop steward) was lecturing new shop stewards about the importance of understanding the union's constitution: '. . . 'n Huis sonder 'n bybel is nie 'n huis nie . . . [A house without a bible is not a house . . .] Each and every shop steward must have a Constitution in order to understand how the union functions.' Afrikaans (the home language of the majority of workers here) is often used for the particular, the vivid example, and to mobilise personal and emotional resources, while English is used for the more formal, the more distanced and the more abstract. For example, the organiser-facilitator spoke in English when explaining a more abstract legal point, but switched to Afrikaans when dealing with how the shop steward should fight a particular case.

Elsewhere, particularly in meetings involving rank-and-file workers, I noticed the frequent use of 'ventriloquism' – speaking through another's voice (Wertsch, 1991, p. 59). In one case, workers spoke through the voice of management in order to parody it: 'They [management] treat us like dogs: take your bone and go and lie down!' Meetings involving shop stewards and rank-and-file members of the union were also frequently marked by the use of repetitive language, sometimes in an almost evangelical tone. For example, in a series of workshops aimed at establishing how workers thought their work could be reorganised in order to improve service delivery to poor communities, the facilitator summed up what participants had said:

> So we are saying that we need to re-organise the method of
> service delivery; we are saying that we are short staffed; we are
> saying that there is 'dead wood'[6]; we are saying that we don't
> have protective clothing or proper tools; we are saying that
> there is no proper training: computer training, driver training,
> customer care, ABET[7]; we are saying that we are being bullied,
> we are being forced out of our offices down to the bottom –
> from the White House to the dog's kennel . . . ![8]

Many union events are characterised by the use of story-telling and anecdotes. Meetings frequently involve lengthy reports which are typically conveyed by means of lively anecdotes and a creative mixture of language, suffused with emotion and humour, and embedded in strong body language (gesticulating, pointing, slamming the fist into the hand for emphasis). Humour is embedded in the local, working class language-dialect and culture of this region, and is closely intermeshed in language constructions such as code-switching and ventriloquism, strengthening their function of parodying management, 'the boere'[9] and others in positions of power.

Story-telling is an integral part of a process of comparing of experiences, and its clear mediating role is illustrated by the numerous occasions when control over these stories is exerted in order to stop shop stewards relating experiences which do not seem relevant to the item under discussion. Shop stewards do not only learn *from* stories, but also learn *how* and *when* to tell stories – clearly an important part of the skills repertoire of worker representatives. Stories are often intended to make broad, principled points. For example, as workers gathered together in the midst of their major strike in mid-2002, they presented 'war stories' that were not only interesting – sometimes gripping – narratives, but were also structured in such a way so as to surface and analyse the key problems experienced during the strike such as worker disunity, or running the gauntlet of management.

Performance and modelling play important roles in union pedagogy. For example, in one shop steward training workshop, the facilitator gave a presentation involving the creative use of language and body language, drawing on his own past experience as a shop steward. In my field-notes, I noted:

> He speaks with lots of examples – embedded in their
> experience, and he speaks 'Kaapse taal' [a Western Cape,
> working-class dialect of Afrikaans]. He struts up and down –
> giving life to the 'belligerent shop steward' role.

Although post-Vygotskian theoretical traditions have tended to focus *either* on language or on activity as tools of mediation, in the context of this case study, it seems unhelpful to tackle these two forms of mediation separately, as they come together in the union context in the form of oral performativity. Oral tools of mediation are often 'embodied' (in the sense of being linked closely with the symbolic use of the body) and 'impassioned' (embedded in emotion, often anger and/or humour). This is particularly true in the case of ordinary workers, who are not formally recognised as playing a mediating role, but who do so nevertheless. For example, in one meeting, a heated debate around privatisation was accompanied by calls to 'take to the streets', 'We must do something drastic', 'They're trying to destroy the union', and 'this is a matter of life and death!' Elsewhere, a shop steward heatedly attacked management's plans to reduce the number of shop stewards allowed to represent workers. He saw this as an attack on workers' rights: 'rights accrued through actions! Beatings!', and rights which 'people had died for'. During the strike, there seemed to be an overall shift from the languaged discourse of union workshops and meetings to the symbolic use of the body as a tool of mediation, as seen in the toyi-toying[10], marching, dancing, singing and sloganeering. It was abundantly clear that participation in the union community of practice is not simply a responsibility or task, but an act of passion and commitment.

What role for written text?

Thus far, I have focused on the prevalence of oral-performative tools of mediation within the collective, action-oriented context of the union. This is in strong contrast with the apparently ambiguous role played by written text – a tool of mediation which is so crucial in formal educational contexts such as schools and universities. Hofmeyr (1993) has pointed out that there are complex intersections between oral, performed and printed forms in South African history, and that orality and literacy need to be viewed as interdependent (see also Brown, 1999). However, I have found the role of written text in union pedagogy a puzzling one, and deserving of a discussion on its own.

A very rich range of textual forms are prevalent in union workshops and meet-ings. In workshops which I observed, written education materials included handbooks and manuals, booklets on labour law and the union's constitution, and copies of the union's newsletter. In meetings there were often large piles of documents – all of them in English – waiting to be collected by shop-stewards as they arrived. I was struck not only by this abundance of written text, but also by the fact that many of these texts were long and dense, and by the variety of forms of literacy that shop stewards were expected to deal with. There was also a wide range of visual/text images to be found in all facets of union life: for example, union attaché-bags with the slogan: 'Transform Local Government, Crush Poverty, Advance to Socialism' and T-shirts with pictures of ANC President Mbeki and slogans such as 'Keep Local Government in the Hands of the People'! During the strike, workers carried posters with slogans like:

Phantsi [down with] managers and councillors eating
themselves fat while the workers starve!
Down with Gear[11], Starvation wages!
To Hell! It's War!
Privatisation equals Retrenchments equals Poverty

Data from my observations as well as from individual and focus group
interviews indicate that written text, as well as the act of reading widely, is
highly valued within the union. Union leaders are conscious of the need to
gain mastery over the complex written forms that are so central to the
processes of industrial relations and collective bargaining in which they are
involved. Reading is a prevalent form of self-study. Written texts are also an
important means of fixing meaning and ensuring accountability within a large
organisation such as the union, while slogans on union bags, T-shirts, posters
and placards communicate political messages both to members and to the
outside world.

However, in apparent contradiction to the seriousness with which text is
treated, it also clear that most shop stewards and union members do not read
many of the written texts they receive – an issue that was consistently raised
as a complaint by union leaders. There is a general preference amongst
workers not to engage with written text, but rather to communicate orally.
This is not surprising given that almost all the text distributed in meetings is
in a language other than the home language of most workers, and given the
uneven levels of literacy generally amongst shop stewards and workers.
However, there seems to be a broader culture of antipathy towards written text
within the union which extends to those shop-steward leaders who do not
experience problems of reading in English, and this will be explored further
below.

Pedagogic significance of 'oral performativity'

How should the distinctive forms of language use and performance be
understood pedagogically? And how should we make sense of the ambiguous
role of written text within the processes of education and learning within the
union? I will argue here – following Star-Glass (2000) – that these features of
union pedagogy cannot be understood apart from other key properties
embedded in the epistemology of this collective, social-action oriented site.
These include: the democratic values underpinning union pedagogy; the
dispersal of pedagogy authority in this context; the powerful identity-

construction role of union pedagogy and its ideological directiveness; the analytical and critical orientation of union pedagogy; and its transformative, utopian orientation.

The democratising (dialogical) role of oral performativity

All tools of mediation embody power relations (Daniels, 2001, p. 80), and it follows from this that the forms of mediation used in any pedagogic situation can act as a kind of barometer of the power relations embedded in that situation. I would argue that the way in which these tools of mediation are mobilised across different settings within the union reflect shifting power relations across contexts. Oral performativity is generally indicative of 'grassroots creativity' and 'grassroots energy' (Sitas, 1990), and the richly performative culture in the union signals a space for ordinary workers to draw on familiar, historical cultural resources to mediate knowledge and facilitate learning. It is a means whereby rank-and-file workers give voice to their experience and knowledge, and its use is most prevalent where there are greater democratic participative forms of communication.[12]

It is generally recognised in the literature on learning in social movements that in such contexts, there is a weak social division of labour with regard to who possesses valuable knowledge and who may play the role of educator. Eyerman and Jamison (1991, p. 94) have argued that: 'All activists in social movements are, in a sense, "movement intellectuals" because through their activism they contribute to the movement's collective identity, to making the movement what it is . . .'. I would argue that the culturally-embedded tools of mediation outlined above allow for significant dispersal of pedagogic authority in the union context: almost anyone can step into the role of educator at different times and in different spaces, and ordinary workers are seen as sources of epistemological authority, and as having knowledge of value to other workers.

In addition to those formally designated as union educators, more experienced shop stewards and workers play mentoring roles for those with less experience; participants engage in heated debates where different views and positions are contested, but where ultimately a set of common understandings is constructed; many worker representatives play the role of 'boundary workers', participating as the union's spokesperson in different communities of practice (government committees, civic organisations, other social movements and campaigns) and bringing vital contextual information from these forums back into the union. The drawing on memories of 'old-timers' plays an important role in the construction of knowledge within the organisation. During the strike, as workers engaged in marches and demonstrations, they played a role of collective educator where their combined actions powerfully communicated their experiences, identity, world-view and power to the society at large.

The focus on democratising the role of oral-performativity helps to make greater sense of the puzzling role of written text within union pedagogy. It is possible to see the widespread ambivalence of workers towards written text as linked to the broader history of literacy, orality and text in the South African context. Brown (1999, p. 15) argues that the 'orality-literacy' question in southern Africa echoes the processes of colonial domination, and:

> . . . epitomises the conceptual and historical themes of southern African life: colonial dispossession and resistance; ethnic and national identifications; rural-urban contacts and migrations; indigenous belief and Christianity; tradition and modernity; local and global identities; industrialisation and labour organisation; land ownership; black subjugation and assertion; and so on.

Written text is therefore deeply implicated in the origins of the racialised, class-based, gendered and languaged power relations of modern-day South Africa, and it is possible to see why workers may view text not only with respect, but also with suspicion. It is also possible that workers' reluctance to fully engage with written text signals some resistance to the textualisation of union practice that has taken place over the past few years, as black trade unions have increasingly engaged with formal, industrial relations machinery, and the parallel shift from more multi-voiced, oral forms of communication to more univocal (top-down) forms of communication within many unions (see Cooper, 2000).

Oral-performativity and identity-building
Another answer to the question of how the use of these distinctive forms of language and performance should be understood pedagogically lies in understanding the key purpose of union pedagogy: to enable workers to challenge dominant power relations both on the shopfloor, as well as in society more broadly. In order to do this, union education has to reconstruct the workplace identity of workers into a unionist identity, as well as encourage workers to view themselves as part of a wider working-class identity. It will be argued here that the creative, oral-performative genres described above act powerfully to construct this identity, and to include workers within it.

For example, code-switching can be seen as playing an important role in building cross-cultural unity amongst workers who share common problems. Code-switching is a very widespread phenomenon within the South African urban environment, and its growth has stimulated academic research both nationally and internationally. Slabbert and Finlayson (2002, p. 254) describe the extensive code-switching taking place in South African townships as '. . . complex, irrevocable and as such part of the fibre of South African society', and indicative of large-scale language change.

In South African sociolinguistics, code-switching is seen as originating in attempts to circumvent the restrictive laws and practices of apartheid: '. . . both individuals and groups expressed and identified themselves as being capable of breaking down and transcending the institutionalised ethnic barriers of apartheid' (*ibid.*, p. 237). It is seen as a form of accommodation, symbolising the values of democratisation: equality, coming together, mutual understanding and respect (*ibid.*, p. 254). The role of code-switching in establishing identity is also acknowledged: '. . . a speaker can evoke the multiple identities associated with each code' (*ibid.*, p. 245). McCormick's (2002) research on code-switching amongst certain Cape Town speech communities found that the local dialect of Afrikaans is the language of neighbourhood solidarity and informal interaction; English might be used for technological topics, but it would be regarded as being 'too cold' when intimate relationships are discussed; while English is the accepted language of meetings, people switch to Afrikaans when heated debate arises.

It is therefore possible to see code-switching as playing an important role in acknowledging the multiple, cultural identities of workers in the union, helping to build an inclusive, working-class identity, and emphasising the importance of equality and respect amongst workers. Other language devices serve to reinforce this. Ventriloquism and the use of repetition serve to emphasise working-class identity by reinforcing the boundary between 'us' and 'them'. Many of the oral-performative rituals during the strike – ranging from 'Amandlas'[13] and 'Vivas' to impassioned speeches and story-telling – also involve affirmation of worker identity and the weaving together of solidarities.

Oral performativity and the mediation of ideology

Union pedagogy is always ideologically directive, in the sense that it is underpinned by a strong and explicit set of moral and political values. The distinctive use of language and of oral performance genres facilitates the powerful pedagogic role that ideology plays in the context. Impassioned and embodied forms of pedagogy communicate the union's principles of practice as well as the workers' experiences of their world, and underscore the point that union pedagogy is always interested rather than disinterested, ideologically partisan rather than neutral, and always 'takes the side' of workers in their conflict with management. The directive nature of union pedagogy is one of its most distinctive features, and is tied to the key purpose of trade-union education – to challenge the dominant power relations of capitalist society.

Oral peformativity as analysis and critique

Both orality and performance – acting together – are deeply embedded in the history and culture of black South Africans generally, and in the history and organisational culture of the trade unions specifically. Gunner (1999, p. 50) describes orality, performance, festival, spectacle and image as 'the central resources of African culture'. Southern African societies are 'dominated by the politics of performance', and people are 'accustomed to carnivalesque cultural activities in which the body played a central part' (*ibid.*, p. 51). Singing and storytelling form a crucial part of performance. Hofmeyr (1993, p. 56) shows how the 'performance craft of oral storytelling' – where elements such as gesture, intonation and rhythm are central to creating meaning – is deeply embedded in South African cultural history, and notes the genre's bawdy humour, and the role of memory as the 'fundamental prop of oral culture'.

However, the literature on southern African culture stresses that oral performance should not only be seen simply in terms of its 'carnivalesque' functions. Coullie (1999), referring to the 'performance craft' of *izibongo*[14] or praise poems, stresses their crucial role as a means for disseminating political messages, while Gunner (1999, p. 52) argues that 'perhaps more than any other southern African genre – [they are] knottily analytical.' She cites Kromberg's study of worker *izibongo* or poets in the 1980s which argues that this oral genre 'played a crucial role in engaging its audiences [. . .] in a kind of public, ongoing debate about contemporary political issues, the nature of modern black identity, ethnicity, the causes of current political violence, and so on' (*ibid.*). Oral performativity involves the exchange of not only symbolic but also rational capital: the exchange of information, discussion and debate around how to analyse and interpret the world, and the communication of political messages (Sitas, 1990, p. 6).

The tools of mediation of union pedagagy are embedded in local culture and may sometimes convey tacit, embodied forms of knowledge, but they can also function to impart knowledge of a general and abstract kind. Story-telling may draw on local cultural traditions, but this is often done in order to make broader, general points. I would argue that the symbolic action of workers during the strike served to impart a form of 'embodied knowledge' that is perhaps more analytical and abstract, and more universal in its intention, than any of the knowledge drawn on in other union settings.

It is important not to collapse site of knowledge into form of knowledge: 'everyday' knowledge is not undifferentiated and many forms of knowledge other than experiential knowledge are drawn on as resources in trade union pedagogy. One of the most distinctive features of knowledge in this context is its hybridity: workers draw on different forms of knowledge, ranging from local, practical forms to more analytical and conceptual forms, including elements of highly codified forms of knowledge such as economics and law. These different forms of knowledge articulate together in complex ways, and I have tried to devise new categories which can capture the dual- or multi-faceted nature of knowledge in this context, for example: 'embodied knowledge' (which incorporates both the physical and the cognitive), and 'impassioned knowledge' (which incorporates both the intellect and the emotion).

Also connected to the hybridity of knowledge in union pedagogy is the dialectical movement between different forms of knowledge – what I have called *weaving* – which often characterises knowledge use in this context. It is possible that certain language genres such as story-telling or code-switching – rather than being associated with parochial forms of knowledge – may even act as a bridge to connect more concrete and more abstract forms of knowledge.

It seems important not to conflate tools of mediation with form of knowledge. Learning in the union context is deeply situated (as is all learning), and union pedagogy's tools of mediation are embedded in local culture and context; however, the forms of knowledge drawn on include the abstract, the general and the global. In other words, 'local' and 'particular' describe the tools of mediation, but not necessarily the form or content of knowledge.

Utopian vision of oral-performative modes

A final, distinctive feature of union pedagogy is its forward-looking and transformative orientation. Eyerman and Jamison (1991, p. 68) have argued that social movements by definition have a 'utopian mission', and they discuss how nineteenth century labour movements embodied 'socially experimental activity' which 'specified the contours of the desirable' and 'articulated a vision of a future classless society' (*ibid.*, p. 82). Bakhtin argued that 'the everyday' is a source of subversion, resistance and 'utopian impulse' (Gardiner, 2000, p. 17), and that carnivalesque modes of communication in particular are manifestations of *desire* of what is repressed by the social order (Sitas, 1990, p. 6).

Elements of 'socially experimental activity' and the 'subversive everyday' – often embedded in carnivalesque modes of communication – were clearly visible in my case study of learning and knowledge in the union context. They were perhaps most visible during the strike, in workers' demands for change and transformation, and their vision of a united working-class and a socialist future. However, the 'hidden potentialities of the everyday' were also visible in the ordinary, routine events of the union. For example, in meetings, workers frequently voiced their hopes and visions for a future where there would be greater democracy in their union and where the union would 'belong' to its members; where municipal services would meet the needs of poor communities and workers' children and grandchildren would be assured a 'decent future'; and a world where no longer would 'the rich get richer and the poor poorer'.

I would argue that the rich array of oral performativity in union pedagogy facilitates its forward-looking, utopian orientation. One way in which this is accomplished is that oral-perfomative tools of mediation act to transform the meaning of the spaces in which union pedagogy takes place. Wertsch has argued that 'utterances function to presuppose the context of speech in which they occur, on the one hand, or act in a "performative" capacity to create or entail the context, on the other' (quoted in Daniels, 2001, p. 81). Sitas (1990, p. 1), writing about mass worker gatherings in South Africa in the late 1980s, noted that '[t]hey are events that occur within defined material spaces which presuppose definite socio-historical circumstances.' The oral performativity prevalent in such meetings signals the fact that: 'For example, the soccer field used by workers to trumpet their messages might be the company's property and their [workers'] presence there might also be a result of ferocious conflicts and compromises.' In other words, the deployment of oral-performative forms of mediation on the part of workers enables them to claim 'ownership' of their surroundings, and transform these into a context over which they have some control.

Culturally-embedded tools of mediation and RPL

Taking a historical-cultural approach to RPL means not only acknowledging that there are different kinds of knowledge, and that some of these enjoy greater power than others, but also that some forms of 'subjugated knowledge' (Foucault, in Ball, 1990) may be unrecognisable to the eyes of the academy because it is expressed and shared through cultural forms different to those of the academy. The RPL process needs to find ways to enable those who share such knowledge to draw on familiar, cultural and historical resources to mediate what they know.

Socio-cultural tools of mediation are not unchanging across time and space, but assume particular forms in particular situations. Drawing on my experiences of university-level courses which seek to provide access to those from community-based and working-class organisational backgrounds, I would argue that there is a particular constellation of features that disting-uishes knowledge and learning in collective, action-oriented and social movement-type contexts in South Africa, and that this constructs a particular learning history and orientation to learning amongst such adult learners. This has significant implications for RPL. Unlocking the potential of such knowledge on the part of the RPL facilitator requires an understanding of, and an ability to engage with, the tools of mediation familiar to such learners.

In South Africa, this means that the RPL process needs to take account of the potentially silencing effects of written text, and to privilege face-to-face forms of communication that are participatory and dialogical in character, and which allow for the dispersal of pedagogic authority. It means that we have to look carefully for the cultural markers that signal more conceptual and analytic forms of knowledge that may have been acquired experientially in informal ways. We have to find ways to promote and encourage the rich, performative speech genres that are familiar to such learners, and to be alert to the possibility that a surplus of meaning may be embedded in particular speech genres. For example, we have to be careful of simply dismissing descriptive accounts as anecdotal story-telling, and look for the principled understandings and knowledge that may be embedded in these accounts. We have to accept that the forms of collective action that are an important part of the experience of these learners could embody tacit knowledge which is not easily able to be discoursed or made explicit – but which nevertheless embodies social analysis and social critique.

These principles of RPL practice could provide the starting point for designing the scaffolding necessary to help these RPL candidates to engage with the tools of mediation more common to the academic environment such as particular forms of written text, the use of distinctive academic speech genres, and the making explicit of implicit, shared assumptions and understandings. However, if RPL is to be a 'two-way' process (Harris, 2004), then we might also consider how the rich and creative forms of mediation that evolved historically within black, working-class communities in South Africa might be drawn upon to critically reassess and refigure mainstream curricula.

Some examples of attempts to enrich a mainstream curriculum may be drawn from our university entrance-level courses for trade-union educators. Here, we have sought to take as our starting point the fact that learners' 'thirst' for broader social, philosophical and historical knowledge is born not simply out of a desire for knowledge 'for its own sake' or for the purposes of getting a qualification, but emerges out of real, strategic questions arising from their practice as trade unionists. Our curriculum is embedded in a working-class view of the world and takes workers' experiences and needs as a starting point. As a facilitator, I do not claim a politically neutral position, but I attempt to make my positioning explicit and attempt to keep it open to challenge. Our pedagogy foregrounds verbal dialogue and debate, lays emphasis on collective and non-competitive, project-based forms of assessment, and we try to foster networks of peer mentoring where the sources of knowledge drawn upon are varied and by no means privileging only of those with higher levels of formal education. On the other hand, we also incorporate within the curriculum conventional academic principles where these are felt to be of value. For example, we work to insert a boundary (for these learners, often an unfamiliar one) between 'education' and 'action' – continually reminding learners that 'we are not taking decisions here!' – so that we can create a space for wider contestation of positions than is often allowed in trade-union meetings.

Bringing together and attempting to integrate different knowledge systems is a complex task, and it is questionable whether – in the university context – the 'counter-hegemonic' logic of knowledge born out of informal, collective and action-oriented contexts can reasonably be expected to remain in tact. However, an RPL process that acknowledges and seeks to work creatively with the inevitable tensions that arise between complex forms of 'everyday' knowledge and those of the academy, opens up the possibility of new, richer and better forms of knowledge. As Jean Barr (1999, p. 17) has noted in her book 'Liberating Knowledge', these practices can also increase the possibilities of producing knowledge that is useful to those who generate it.

References

Barnett, R. (2000), 'Working knowledge' in Garrick, J. and Rhodes, C. (eds.) *Research and Knowledge at Work*, London and New York: Routledge.

Ball, S. (1990), *Foucault and Education. Disciplines and Knowledge*, London: Routledge.

Barr, J. (1999), *Liberating Knowledge: Research, Feminism and Adult Education*, Leicester: NIACE.

Brown, D. (1999), 'Introduction' in Brown, D. (ed.) *Oral Literature and Performance in Southern Africa*, Oxford: James Curry.

Colley, H., Hodkinson, P. and Malcom J. (2003), *Informality and Formality in Learning: A Report for the Learning and Skills Research Centre*, Leeds: University of Leeds, Learning and Skills Research Centre.

Cooper, L. (2002), 'Union education in the new South African democracy' in Spencer, B. (ed.) *Unions and Learning in a Global Economy*, Toronto: Thompson Educational Publishing.

Coullie, J.L. (1999), '(Dis)Locating selves: Izibongo and narrative autobiography' in Brown, D. (ed.) *Oral Literature and Performance in Southern Africa*, Oxford: James Curry.

Daniels, H. (1993), 'The individual and the organisation' in Daniels, H. (ed.) *Charting the Agenda: Education Activity after Vygotsky*, London and New York: Routledge.

Daniels, H. (2001), *Vygotsky and Pedagogy*, London and New York: Routledge Falmer.

Engeström, Y. (1999), 'Innovative learning in work teams: Analyzing cycles of knowledge creation in practice' in Engeström, Y., Miettinen, R. and Punamaki, R. (eds) *Perspectives on Activity Theory* (pp. 377–404), Cambridge: Cambridge University Press.

Engeström, Y. (2002), Learning by expanding: An activity-theoretical approach to developmental research, available: http://lchc.ucsd.edu/MCA/Paper/Engestrom/expanding/ (Accessed 27 August 2002).

Eyerman, R. and Jamison, A. (1991), *Social Movements: A Cognitive Approach*, Cambridge: Polity Press.

Foley, G. (1999), *Learning in Social Action: A Contribution to Understanding Informal Education*, London: Zed Books Ltd.

Gardiner, M.E. (2000), *Critiques of Everyday Life*, London and New York: Routledge.

Grossman, J. (1999), 'Workers and knowledge', paper presented to Researching Work and Learning Conference, Leeds, September.

Gunner, L. (1999), 'Remaking the warrior? The role of orality in the liberation struggle and in post-apartheid South Africa' in Brown, D. (ed.) *Oral Literature and Performance in Southern Africa*, Oxford: James Currey.

Harris, J. (2004), 'The hidden curriculum of the Recognition of Prior Learning: a case study', PhD Thesis, Open University.

Hofmeyr, I. (1993), 'We Spend our Years as a Tale that is Told.' *Oral Historical Narrative in a South African Chiefdom*, Johannesburg: Witwatersrand University Press.

Holford, J. (1995), 'Why social movements matter: Adult education theory, cognitive praxis, and the creation of knowledge', *Adult Education Quarterly*, 45(2): 95–111.

McCormick, K. (2002), 'Code-switching, mixing and convergence in Cape Town' in Mesthrie, R. (ed.) *Language in South Africa*, Cambridge: Cambridge University Press.

Martin, I. (1999), 'Introductory essay' in Crowther, J., Martin, I. and Shaw, M. (eds) *Popular Education and Social Movements in Scotland Today*, Leicester: NIACE.

Michelson, E. (1998), 'Expanding the logic of portfolio-assisted assessment: lessons from South Africa', Saratoga Springs, NY: National Center for Adult Learning.

Newman, M. (1994), *Defining the Enemy: Adult Education in Social Action*, Sydney: Stewart Victor Publishing.

Qabula, A.T. (1989), *A Working Life, Cruel Beyond Belief*, Durban: NUMSA.

Ralphs, A. and Motala, E. (2000), 'Towards an RPL strategy for 2000–2005: A work in progress', Working document, Johannesburg, Joint Education Trust.

Scribner, S. (1997), *Mind and Social Practice: Selected Writings of Sylvia Scribner* (E. Tobach, R. Falmagne, M. Parlee, L.M.W. Martin, and A.S. Kapelman, eds), Cambridge: Cambridge University Press.

Sitas, A. (1990), 'The voice and gesture in South Africa's revolution: a study of worker gatherings and performance-genres in Natal', paper presented at Wits History Workshop, University of Witwatersrand, Johannesburg, 6–10 February.

Slabbert, S. and Finlayson, R. (2002), 'Code-switching in South African townships' in Mesthrie, R. (ed.) *Language in South Africa*, Cambridge: Cambridge University Press.

Spencer, B. (1995), 'Old and new social movements as learning sites: Greening labor unions and unionizing the greens', *Adult Education Quarterly*, 46(1): 31–42.

Starr-Glass, P. (2002), 'Metaphor and totem: Exploring and evaluating prior experiential learning', *Assessment and Evaluation in Higher Education*, 27(3): 222–31.

Welton, M. (1993), 'Social revolutionary learning: The new social movements as learning sites', *Adult Education Quarterly*, 43(3): 152–64.

Wertsch, J.V. (1985), 'Introduction' in Wetsch, J.V. (ed.) *Culture, Communication and Cognition: Vygotskian Perspectives* (pp. 1–33), Cambridge: Cambridge University Press.

Wertsch, J.V. (1991), *Voices of the Mind: A Sociocultural Approach to Mediated Action*, Cambridge, MA: Harvard University Press.

Wertsch, J.V. and Smolka, A.L.B. (1993), 'Continuing the dialogue: Vygotsky, Bakhtin, and Lotman' in Daniels, J. (ed.) *Charting the Agenda: Education Activity after Vygotsky*, London and New York: Routledge.

Notes

1　There is debate over the continued use of racial categories in the post-apartheid era, but it is difficult to avoid the fact that the historically-constructed racial categories continue to carry important social meanings and effects.
2　Congress of South African Trade Unions.
3　Observational data was supplemented by individual and focus group interviews.
4　Paid staff of the union.
5　One of the indigenous South African languages most prevalently spoken in the Western Cape.
6　This was a reference to an assertion that some white-collar workers were unproductive and undeserving of their jobs.
7　Adult Basic Education and Training.
8　Reference to the fact that management's offices were in a big, white house located on the high ground of the depot, while workers were forced to share as their 'mess-room' a shabby building at the bottom-end of the depot.
9　Literally meaning 'farmers', this is a popular term used by black South Africans of all language groups to describe the 'Afrikaners' in power under apartheid.
10　A militant dance mimicking that performed by guerrilla soldiers during the struggle against apartheid, which in turn drew on older, pre-colonial forms of military 'performance art'.
11　The government's Growth, Employment and Redistribution strategy, which is widely viewed as being neo-liberal in orientation.
12　According to Bakhtin, 'Genuinely participative thinking and acting requires an engaged and embodied . . . relation to the other, and to the world at large' (Gardiner, 2000, p. 54).
13　Power!
14　Izibongo are forms of oral verse used to praise (as well as subtly critique) prominent African leaders or to pay homage to clan or family. Workers have also used this form of praise poetry to criticise their supervisors or bosses or praise their trade uniion (Brown, 1999, p. 3).

chapter twelve

Vocations, 'graduateness' and the recognition of prior learning

Leesa Wheelahan

Traditionally, RPL can be used in two main ways: as credit towards completion of a qualification, and also as an alternative entry mechanism to a qualification where students have not met the 'normal' entry criteria. This last mechanism is particularly important to achieve greater participation by people from groups traditionally excluded from tertiary education. However, it is the direct link between RPL and credit that makes RPL controversial and as a result, engages the attention of teachers, policy makers, employers and unions. RPL is thus at the centre of the intersection between pedagogy and policy, and brings practitioners of each into the same arena. Debates about RPL go to the heart of debates about the role of educational qualifications in societies experiencing perpetual change in the context of globalisation, because RPL calls into question the nature of qualifications and what they signify. Should qualifications specify what graduates can do or the capacities they have? In what way are notions of 'graduate attributes' and 'generic skills' different to notions of 'graduateness'? Should it be possible for someone to be awarded an entire qualification based on RPL, or should there be limits to the extent of RPL within qualifications?

While 'developmental' and 'credentialist' models of learning do not exhaust all the stances it is possible to take in education and training, they do occupy important positions in RPL debates. In Australia, this debate is exemplified in the distinction made between RPL and 'recognition of current competence' [RCC]. Those from the developmental tradition often make the distinction between RPL and RCC so that they can acknowledge that what they do (RPL) is quite different to RCC. RPL is about learning, they say, whereas RCC is about certification of competence (usually workplace competence). Others argue that the focus on learning or competency outcomes renders any distinctions meaningless as learning takes place in a variety of contexts, including at work (Wheelahan *et al.*, 2002).

In this chapter, I argue in favour of the developmental position, while also critiquing it for not sufficiently considering the importance of qualification outcomes for students. I use John Dewey's notion of a vocation to argue that qualifications are more than the sum of their parts, and that 'graduateness' is quite different to either notions of graduate attributes or generic skills. This leads me to the conclusion that it should not be possible for individuals to be granted an entire qualification on the basis of RPL (as a general though not immutable rule), while also arguing that the reflexive and integrative practices associated with developmental models of RPL play an important role in all qualifications.

The first section focuses on the divorce between processes of learning and qualification outcomes in Anglophone countries. This divorce, enshrined in policy frameworks, has given impetus to credentialist models of RPL because where and how learning occurs is less important than the certification of achieved outcomes. However, this divorce is premised on a view of qualifications as the aggregate of their elements, rather than a model which views qualifications as more than the sum of their parts. The second section considers the way in which qualifications need to evolve to meet the challenges of perpetual change, while the third section discusses the relevance of Dewey's notion of vocations for qualifications today, and uses this to consider the differences between generic skills and graduate attributes on the one hand, and graduateness on the other. The fourth section uses activity theory to develop the concept of graduateness, while the final section explores the way in which experts use theory in their everyday practice, and the implications this has for whether entire qualifications should be granted on the basis of RPL.

The divorce between processes of learning and assessment of outcomes

Michael Young (2001b, 2003a) explains that in Anglophone countries, qualification systems have moved from being a guide to devising assessments and normative criteria to compare learners, to 'claiming to be a precise definition of what a person could do – in other words, evidence of his or her competence' (Young, 2003a, p. 199). The aim of Anglophone reforms to qualifications systems was to create 'a system of qualifications based on agreed <u>national criteria</u> [to] underpin all qualifications within a single framework' (Young, 2001b, p. 11, emphasis in original). This is in contrast to previous systems in which the credibility of a qualification was based less on precise statements of what a person could (putatively) do, and more on the confidence of key stakeholders in the integrity of the qualification and processes of learning, and on the shared practices of teachers, the disciplines, the professions and the trades (*ibid.*).

These particular reforms cannot be considered independently of Anglophone neo-liberal political reform processes more broadly. In the context of less 'public ownership and even less direct forms of state intervention in the economy' (*ibid.*, p. 9), Anglophone governments increasingly turned to education and training as part of a broader programme of micro-economic reform, through tying the outcomes of education and training more directly to the needs of the economy. As well as supporting a deregulated market and privatised social provision, governments have sought to transform education and training systems themselves into markets, as a way of making them more 'responsive' to the needs of industry (Marginson, 1997). The provision of education becomes a 'service' like all other services, in which the 'client' stipulates the outcomes. Anglophone neo-liberal market economies have established qualifications frameworks as a currency and qualifications as the unit of currency (masters, degrees, diplomas etc.). They are the mechanism through which fees, qualifications and jobs can be exchanged. That is, a qualifications framework is needed to structure a qualifications market.

A qualifications market needs to be able to specify the goods to be purchased, and this means that outcomes must be specified in advance, and broken down into marketable units (individual subjects or units in programmes) so that they can be transported and reconstituted to make a full qualification. The commodification of qualifications, and in particular components of qualifications, opens the way to credentialist models of RPL. This is because sections of qualifications (individual subjects or units) can be specified and exchanged. The availability and extent of RPL is part of the market information that prospective 'purchasers' (students or employers) need access to in making decisions about their level of investment and likely returns. This is predicated on a model of qualifications as aggregates of outcomes, in contrast to a relational model in which the connections between different elements of a qualification matter more, because 'graduateness' emerges from the interplay and totality of these components.

The commodification of qualifications envisaged by neo-liberal reforms cannot occur unless the link between learning and assessment is broken, because the qualification outcomes must be reified if they are to be exchanged. The divorce between 'inputs' (teaching and learning processes) and 'outputs' (assessment of outcomes), while driven by policy, also relies on simplistic and reductionist behaviourist theories of learning. Efforts by teachers to reassert the complexity of what they do, and the need for the to be included in determining the outcomes of education and training are regarded as self-interested attempts to regain lost status and prestige at best, and at worst to re-engage in 'producer capture' (Marginson, 1997). Teachers have been devalued and deprofessionalised as a consequence, and the relationship between processes of learning and qualification outcomes poorly understood in the wider community.

The separation of learning from outcomes enshrined in Anglophone qualifi-cations frameworks (in theory) gives impetus to RPL, and does not preclude the award of full qualifications on the basis of RPL, particularly in vocational education and training (VET) sectors which are more likely to emphasise workplace skills. Higher education sectors usually have more constraints on the extent to which RPL can be implemented, in part because of the relative autonomy of universities, their self-accrediting status and arguments about the role of universities in knowledge creation (Wheelahan *et al.*, 2002). However, the increasing vocationalisation of higher education qualifications means that debates about the relevance of qualifications to the economy are increasingly important, with arguments that the outcomes of higher education qualifications need to be specified as signifiers to employers of graduate skills and knowledge.

Debates about RPL compared to RCC are, in part, a proxy for debates about the relative emphasis of the needs of industry (and the marketisation of education) versus the developmental and learning needs of individuals or disenfranchised and excluded social groups. These debates are occurring within all sectors of education, and are not just limited to VET. It is a debate about the role of qualifications and the nature of 'graduateness'.

Advocates of developmental models of RPL argue that 'graduateness' involves more than the capacity to perform workplace skills as specified in qualification outcomes. This approach stems from humanist and radical traditions, and emphasises self-development and self-actualisation in the case of humanist approaches, and in the case of radical traditions, giving voice to the excluded and marginalised through challenging hegemonic control over, and access to, powerful knowledge and qualifications both of which act as gatekeepers to power. Both see RPL primarily as processes of learning and knowledge creation (for individuals, social groups or both). Proponents of credentialist models (RCC) emphasise the role of education and training in the preparation for work, and in contributing to economic innovation and development. Individuals and industry cannot (and should not be expected to) invest in education and training which is not necessary. These arguments are driven by human capital assumptions (Harris, 1997; 1999; 2000). Harris (1997, p. 9) explains that RPL, in this tradition, is part of a 'discourse of efficiency, accreditation, competence, access, transparency, equality of opportunity and mobility.' Consequently, the RPL/RCC debate is about the role of qualifications and the link between processes of learning and learning outcomes.

In asserting the difference between RPL and RCC, proponents of the developmental model often fail to make the link between teaching and learning and *policy*. RPL is not either a teaching and learning issue or a policy issue; rather it is both, and to consider RPL we need to explore the relationship between policy and teaching and learning. The lack of acknowledgement of this relationship stems from the divorce between processes of learning and the certification of outcomes (at least in Anglophone countries) (Eraut, 2001; Young, 2001b). While not suggesting that there is no role or place for credentialist models of RPL, I want to argue that credentialist models must be squarely confronted and resisted as a *paradigm*. In particular, the credentialist premise that it is possible and desirable to separate means and ends must be opposed. However, developmental theorists must acknowledge that outcomes matter, because they influence the process used to achieve them. Moreover, outcomes matter to students because they need qualifications, particularly in liberal market economies. Qualifications represent the intersection between teaching and learning on one hand, and policy on the other, and what must be debated is the nature of qualifications and what they signify. This has implications for how RPL is defined and implemented.

What sort of qualifications do we need?

Young (2001b, p. 9) questions whether Anglophone outcomes-based qualifications frameworks are adequate for meeting the needs of societies experiencing continuous technological, social, cultural and economic change. He argues that political reforms that seek to make qualifications independent of awarding institutions and an over-emphasis on the assessment of predefined outcomes have robbed qualifications of the capacity to incorporate the open-ended learning necessary for societies experiencing perpetual change. Given the pace of change 'new kinds of learning may need to be encouraged that cannot easily be predicted in advance and may not be readily assessable for qualifications' (Young, 2001b, p. 10). Young argues that the balance between control and risk may need to shift, 'with less emphasis on assessing pre-defined outcomes and more on enabling learners to explore new possibilities that cannot be predefined' (*ibid.*). This means we need to place less emphasis on the prior specification of learning outcomes, and more 'on learning processes and the judgements of different stakeholders' (*ibid.*).

The decoupling of qualifications from the communities in which they are based (education and training institutions, as well as professional and trade organisations) has resulted in declining importance attached to the 'communities of trust' that underpin them. Communities of trust include teachers, employers, professional bodies and other stakeholders. These are the stakeholders to whom education and training providers traditionally oriented in developing and implementing qualifications. However, the national specification of learning outcomes, in particular the precise form this takes in VET qualifications, has rendered this process less important, despite the importance of government policy rhetoric about 'industry' leadership. Young (2003, p. 208) explains, that while government policy has resulted in less importance placed on communities of trust, this does not change the fact that:

> . . . the credibility, quality and currency of a qualification is only
> partly based on what it says the person qualified can do or
> knows; far more important is the trust that society in general
> and specific users in particular (those whom select, recruit or
> promote) have in the qualification. [. . .] If one or other of these
> communities does not underpin a qualification, it will have a
> problem of credibility, however well-specified its outcomes.

Young (2003) explains that communities of trust have been (and many still are) elitist or exclusionary. However, the alternative – the apparently democratic criterion-based approach – does not do away with the reality that communities of trust underpin the extent to which qualifications are valued. Consequently, government policies need to be directed at building networks that are inclusive, or helping to establish them in new and emerging areas where they do not yet exist.

Young (1998, p. 116) argues that the relationship between qualifications and occupations is more fluid as a consequence of the pace of change, and that:

> ... qualifications framework[s] will need to shift from a weak
> framework with strong qualifications towards a strong
> framework in which the individual qualifications take on the
> role of guidelines for learning continuity rather than as
> gateways to employment.

This analysis has implications for RPL, because it challenges the basis of the credentialist approach to both RPL and qualifications. If qualifications need to be more open-ended and process-oriented, rather than based on the codification of sanctioned knowledge or pre-defined skills, then it means that RPL must support these outcomes. It means that RPL cannot be based on learning or competency outcomes that are assessable, stackable, countable, and can be pushed this way or that. In other words, the analysis challenges the *reduction* of qualifications to units of competency or learning outcomes, and the *commodification* of qualifications as market signifiers of specific and precise skills – skills which by definition emphasise what individuals have demonstrated they can do in a limited range of contexts, rather than their capacity to respond to challenges in the future.

This changes the nature of RPL from being a process of assessment against specific learning outcomes or units of competency which can be added up to make a qualification (the credentialist model), to more emphasis on processes of learning. A developmental model of RPL would help the student to use their current learning to reflect on what they have learnt in the past (and in some cases to make explicit what they have learnt in the past) (Eraut, 2000), and to integrate past and current learning into a new framework of understanding, to be tested and applied in a range of contexts. This precludes granting whole qualifications, but introduces reflection on learning (including RPL) as an intrinsic part of all qualifications, and thereby increases the role and scope for RPL.

Dewey, vocations and graduateness

Arguing that qualifications need to be more open-ended and focus more on processes of learning is interpreted in different ways by developmental and credentialist approaches. Bernstein (2000, p. 59) explains that the current human capital discourse within the 'official' education and training fields is based on a new concept of work and life in which every area of life is perpetually transformed, and that the concept of trainability (or more generously, learning to learn) is now the key principle governing the construction of curriculum and pedagogy. Rather than specific knowledge and skills, the new paradigm calls for 'generic' competencies (in VET) or 'graduate attributes' (in higher education). He explains that the process of perpetual re-formation: 'Is based on the acquisition of generic modes which it is hoped will realise a flexible transferable potential rather than specific performances' (*ibid.*). He says that in this way knowledge is divorced from knowers, and 'from their commitments, their personal dedications' (*ibid.*).

The credentialist approach sees the quest for 'generic skills' and 'graduate attributes' as necessary, because the skills and knowledges to which they refer are the skills and knowledges sought by the market. Because the *market* is the naturalised regulator of human relations (and not vocations or occupations), education and training seek to produce the market individual, or the economic citizen (Marginson, 1997). These marketable skills and knowledges are thus decontextualised from the vocations in which they were originally embedded. It is not the occupation or vocation that defines what is necessary, it is the market, and it is assumed that because the market transcends most occupations, these marketable skills also can be unproblematically translated from one context to another.

However, Bernstein (2000, p. 59) explains that the generic capacities to be taught and 'trained' cannot be considered independently of the vocation or occupation for which individuals are preparing, because it is this that provides their *identity* and the *context* they need to make sense of these 'meta-thinking' and 'meta-learning' strategies. He explains that:

> . . . the ability to respond to such a future [perpetual 'trainability'] depends upon a capacity, not an ability. The capacity to enable the actor to project him/herself *meaningfully* rather than relevantly, into this future, and recover a coherent past. This capacity is the outcome of a specialised identity and this precedes ability to respond effectively to concurrent and subsequent retraining. [. . .] It is not a purely psychological construction by a solitary worker as he/she undergoes the transitions which he/she is expected to perform on the basis of trainability. This identity arises out of a particular social order, through relations which the identity enters into with other

identities of reciprocal recognition, support, mutual
legitimisation and finally through a negotiated collective
purpose. (*ibid.*)

I think Dewey's notion of *vocation* captures Bernstein's meaning of *identity*, because it is the capacity to relate knowledge and skills to oneself and the broader world that makes knowledge meaningful. A vocation links a person to the broader notion of an occupation which encompasses the role of that occupation in society, the values that underpin it and the knowledge and skills that are needed to engage in problem solving. Paradoxically, the notion of a vocation becomes *more* important in the context of rapid change. A vocation is predicated on change, and on active engagement by practitioners in creating change. Dewey (1966 [1916], p. 308) thought of a vocation as a person's *calling*: 'To find out what one is fitted to do and to secure an opportunity to do it is the key to happiness.' It goes beyond the technical requirements of an occupation and includes:

> ... the development of artistic capacity of any kind, of special
> scientific ability, of effective citizenship, as well as professional
> and business occupations, to say nothing of mechanical labor or
> engagement in gainful pursuits. (Dewey, 1966 [1916], p. 307)

On the face of it, this approach may seem to be directly counter to prevailing views about the nature of education and globalisation, in which individuals need to prepare for several careers, and in which skills must evolve constantly to keep pace with technological change. The 'generic' view holds only if education and training for work is restricted to narrow notions of specific skill acquisition. People will need to learn several skill sets throughout their lives, but this does not make a vocation. Graduateness is associated with a vocation, 'graduate attributes' with genericism. Graduateness, as used here, means the way in which an individual connects knowledge, skills, attributes, dispositions and values with a deep knowledge and understanding of their profession, and uses this 'connectedness' to define themselves (their identity in their vocation), and as implicit (or tacit) and explicit guides to action in their practice. This approach sees graduateness as contextualised by, and expressed through, a vocation.

Generic skills or graduate attributes are *general* characteristics, rather than contextualised by the vocation itself, and the disciplines that underpin it. They imply that discrete components can be identified and added up, or that the total consists of the sum which is reducible to the parts. This inevitably leads to divorcing knowledge and skills from the contexts in which both are to be applied and leads to impoverishing both. Experts are distinguished from novices by their capacity to integrate 'diverse aspects of a concept [to reveal] the interconnected nature of its different aspects' rather than capacities for abstract generalisation (Beach, 1999, p. 112). In contrast to genericism, graduateness is expressed holistically through a vocation, and characterised by the capacity to see the bigger picture and its interconnections across different and new contexts, and to consider and apply ideas and concepts in new and creative ways. The total is more than the sum of its parts. When viewed in this way, graduateness can apply to both higher education and VET graduates working in their professions. Credentialist models based on 'getting a ticket' (a qualification) will not achieve these outcomes, and much RPL based on the credentialist model is premised on getting a ticket (Eraut, 2001).

Learning within an activity system

Young (2001b, p. 9) explains that: 'Whereas qualifications as an instrument of policy tend to treat learning in terms of an input-output model, research evidence suggests that learning is considerably more complex than a simple input-output model assumes.' The growing understanding that qualifications must be based in communities of trust if they are to be socially valued and useful is accompanied by a growing understanding of the socially mediated nature of learning. The link between the two is that between means and ends: both are premised on the *relational* nature of knowledge, skills and expertise, and the importance of the social context in shaping both (Beach, 1999). It is not only that socially valued outcomes need social processes embedded in them (or that processes and outcomes need to be in alignment, Biggs, 1999); from a social realist perspective (Archer, 1995; Sayer, 2000), socially valued outcomes and processes of learning are also predicated on a relational view of the individual to knowledge and their social context, and the interaction between them.

This is not to reduce the individual purely to the social context, by denying the existence of an autonomous individual (or in our case, an autonomous learner). Individuals make active choices, reflect on their own and broader social contexts, and have concerns about what they value as important (and not just instrumental concerns, Archer, 2000b). They construct their own lives accordingly, but always in ways that are mediated by a social context that constrains or enables their choices (particularly depending on whether they belong to a privileged or disadvantaged social group). They are not society's dupes (Archer, 2000a; 2003; Billett, 2003).

However, the *capacity* of individuals to learn is *mediated* through social processes, and through active engagement with the world around them, or in other words, through practice. Individuals require both self-understanding and broader social understanding (including of their workplace) and an understanding of the relationship between themselves and the broader context. Consequently, the process of reflection on an individual's *past* learning and how that relates to their *current* learning is of fundamental importance to achieving 'graduateness'.

Activity theory is helpful for understanding the social contexts of learning, and for the way in which individuals learn to become part of the 'activity system' that defines their occupation (see also Cooper, Chapter 11, in this volume). This is helpful for us in understanding that learning involves, fundamentally, learning how to become a member of an activity system, or to use Wenger's (1998, p. 100) approach, how novices come to be recognised as competent and then expert members of their community of practice, or a student/graduate a fully contributing and effective member of a workplace.

Activity theory embraces the interaction between all the elements that make up the activity system in which a community is situated, and the inherent contradictions that characterise such systems (Engeström, 1999). It is these contradictions that lead to change and innovation. Human activity is directed towards an object (for example, the education of students in a school or the treatment of the sick in a hospital) and is characterised by complex inter-actions between individuals, between individuals and social groups, and between different social groups (or collectivities). The activity system emerges from previous practice, is socially and culturally mediated, including through the use of artefacts, which include tools (for example, hammers and other physical equipment) and signs (such as language, theories and concepts), and which is transformed in the process (Stevenson, 2003b). Figure 12.1 is a visual representation of a model of an activity system. It shows the interaction between the various components of the system and the dynamic complexity of this interaction.

Students need to be able to work skilfully within the activity system that frames their community of practice, and to work with the tools of the activity system (which include theories and concepts) as part of their practice (Engeström, 1999). Learning needs to involve becoming part of, learning

Figure 12.1 Model of an activity system
Source: adapted from Engeström (1999) and Stevenson (2003b)

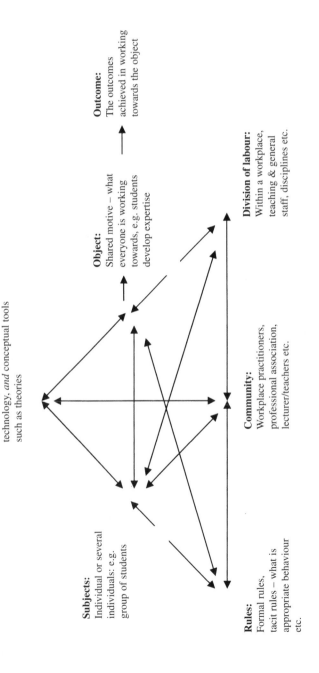

Mediating artefacts:
Tools & signs: e.g. texts, equipment, technology, *and* conceptual tools such as theories

Outcome:
The outcomes achieved in working towards the object

Object:
Shared motive – what everyone is working towards, e.g. students develop expertise

Division of labour:
Within a workplace, teaching & general staff, disciplines etc.

Community:
Workplace practitioners, professional association, lecturer/teachers etc.

Subjects:
Individual or several individuals: e.g. group of students

Rules:
Formal rules, tacit rules – what is appropriate behaviour etc.

about, and making connections between all elements of the activity system. It implies that dividing learning objectives into 'declarative' and 'procedural' objectives is far too narrow a way of conceiving learning, because learning to be part of, to understand, and to use the available tools within the activity system or community of practice involves holistic learning that goes beyond 'knowing that' and 'knowing how' (Stevenson, 2003a). It also implies that dividing learning into 'academic' and 'vocational' objectives or cognitive, psychomotor and affective objectives (or variations along these lines) results in disconnected learning and creates artificial distinctions based on hierarchies between different kinds of knowing (*ibid.*). This is because learning to become a member of a community of practice or activity system must engage students in *all* these dimensions.

Learning (and consequently, RPL) is not just about achieving predefined outcomes that are carved up into distinct parcels of competencies or knowledge, the sum total of which makes a qualification. It is also about developing shared and individual understandings within the community of practice or activity system, and learning how the activity system works, the rules (tacit and codified), the division of labour, the community, and the subjects (including one's self) and how they fit together. It means learning about power relations in the activity system, and developing a critical capacity for exploring good practice. Learning is more complex and multi-faceted than many traditional notions of curriculum suggest. It means that RPL needs to incorporate reflection on all these components within the activity system. Students need to interrogate their past learning and reflect on it in light of their current learning, and consider the implications for their learning histories and their trajectories.

Knowing with, not just knowing how and knowing that

The argument so far is that graduateness is contextualised by the activity system or community of practice within which the individual is placed. This is absent from credentialist approaches to RPL, because they are based on 'ticking off' evidence against abstracted and decontextualised competencies or learning outcomes. This is so even if the RPL candidate uses artefacts and other evidence from their workplace to demonstrate competence, because these are based on the *separateness* of the outcomes, not their *interconnectedness*. Eraut (2001) argues that using qualifications to accredit existing competence results in fragmented outcomes, and is time consuming with little positive gain for either the individual or their workplace. Similarly

Fevre *et al.* (2000), explain the feelings of frustration and pointlessness expressed by those they talked to who were required to become qualified for jobs they had worked in for many years, as part of attempts to credential their industry.

However, if credentialist arguments are to be resisted, we need to explain why someone *should* seek a qualification if they don't have one, and why both they and their workplace (and their community) may be better off if they did. To do so we need to go beyond the activity system and consider the individual holistically in the context of their vocation and their relationship to society. This is also an important antidote to purely situated learning theories which emphasise the situatedness of learning and the importance of 'authentic learning in the workplace', with the corollary that somehow formal learning in education and training institutions is 'inauthentic' and less relevant. For example, in their discussion paper assessing VET qualifications in Australia, Chappell *et al.*, (2003, p. 7), explain that:

> This position proposes that the knowledge required by the contemporary economy is different from the knowledge that has occupied traditional education and training programs. Current thinking emphasises knowledge constructed as practical, interdisciplinary, informal, applied and contextual over knowledge constructed as theoretical, disciplinary, formal, foundational and generalisable.

The danger of this approach is that in promoting the importance of transdisciplinarity and contextual knowledge, the importance of theoretical, codified and disciplinary knowledge will be underestimated, and the relationship between these different ways of knowing not appreciated, not least because transdisciplinary and contextual knowledge are underpinned by codified and disciplinary knowledge. *Both* are necessary (Muller, 2000; Young, 2000; 2003b), and graduateness entails the facility to connect the meanings derived from both. If we include theories, ideas and concepts as part of the tools used within particular activity systems, then practitioners need to be able to use these with the same skill and facility as they do physical tools.

The differences between novices and experts are often depicted as mainly deriving from the tacit knowledge that experts use, which novices have not yet developed. Tacit knowledge is often reduced to skill, whereas Stevenson (2001, p. 657) argues that it is much more complex than this: '. . . it seems inappropriate to dismiss tacitness as a characteristic only of skills. Tacit knowing also seems to have a central place in the situational, conceptual, procedural and strategic knowledge of experts.'

Tacit knowledge or expertise includes the knowledge, concepts, ideas and experiences that we have internalised. Stevenson argues that experts use knowledge in a different way to novices. This stems from their capacity to connect the different types of meaning within the activity system with their experience and knowledge outside the activity system. He explains that: 'An expert derives this facility from many experiences, connecting the various meanings that the experiences offer, as well as meanings that others construct on those experiences' (Stevenson, 2003a, p. 5).

Bransford and Schwartz (1999) also contrast the different ways of knowing of novices and experts. They refer to the differentiated knowledge of the expert as 'knowing with'. This in contrast to 'knowing that' (declarative knowledge), and 'knowing how' (procedural knowledge). People '"know with" their previously acquired concepts and experiences. [. . .] By "knowing with" our cumulative set of knowledge and experiences, we perceive, interpret, and judge situations based on our past experiences' (*ibid*. p. 69–70). For example, in working with a new group of students, the expert and novice teacher both look at the same group of students, but see something different, and under-stand what they must *do* differently. A highly differentiated knowledge structure – knowing with – represents expertise in connecting meanings, and is what separates novices from experts.

Theoretical knowledge derived from formal education and training can consequently become a very important part of expertise or graduateness. In other words, it may be necessary to go beyond the activity system to acquire the theoretical knowledge one needs to work within the activity system, and to make connections between different activity systems and the wider community. Not all knowledge emerges from practice within the activity system, and unequal power relations within workplaces mean that there is differential access to knowledge and learning opportunities (Young, 2001a).

Eraut (2001, p. 93) found in research into mid-career learning that:

> . . . mid-career workers were more successful in making links
> between theory and practice, because they were able to combine
> the sharing of, and reflection upon, practical experience with

the introduction of theoretical knowledge which helped make sense of it. Mid-career students can be encouraged not only to use theory to critique practice but also to use practical experience to critique theory. This raises serious questions about the timing of qualification-based learning, suggesting that it is inefficient to teach too much theory before the relevant practical experience has been acquired. Periodic episodes of qualification-based off-the-job learning may be more effective than large qualifications front-loaded with theory. This is the structural basis of traditional apprenticeships; but it requires closer coordination between classwork at college and workplace experience than is commonly found.

Arguments that someone be awarded a whole qualification on the basis of RPL are often advanced on the basis that the individual is mid-career and has had years of working within their industry. Yet Eraut's argument is that this is precisely the time when people are most able to make connections between theory and practice, but that they may need opportunities to engage in theoretical learning to do so. Eraut argues that the process of qualifying mid-career should be about developing new competence and not certifying past competence. He goes so far as to argue governments should:

> . . . stop providing public funding for the accreditation of pre-existing competence. It is better to design learning pathways which use that competence; and this could be achieved by choosing more challenging and holistic assignments. (*ibid.*, p. 96)

In research in which he participated, Eraut explains that RPL candidates who used their existing competence to develop new competence took about the same amount of time as did those who gathered evidence to certify existing competence. He explains that candidates embarked on ambitious projects, and these projects were valuable to both the candidate and their workplace. In contrast, those candidates who focussed on searching for evidence of past accomplishments (as is the case in most credentialist models) gained relatively little in new knowledge and skills, particularly in integrating that knowledge and skill. He explains that:

> These candidates could equally well have chosen a more developmental pathway but were unaware that this might have been no less burdensome. This is but one illustration of the

unintended effects of designing a qualification with no attention to learning. (*ibid.*)

It also shows the importance of linking policy and learning theory in designing qualifications. Eraut's approach to RPL is a far more positive and developmental one, because it is premised on the existing competence people have, but seeks to support them in developing new competence. This approach precludes the capacity to grant a whole qualification on the basis of RPL, but incorporates RPL as an intrinsic part of all qualifications. One way in which people *could* be awarded a whole qualification through RPL is perhaps through engaging in a project in which they demonstrated their capacity to use and integrate all the tools within their activity system, including the conceptual and theoretical tools. The focus of RPL could be on assisting candidates to develop the skills they need to do that. Eraut (*ibid.*, p. 91) explains that:

> Learning to use prior knowledge is rarely identified as a
> learning need, so learners often fail to appreciate their
> knowledge resources or what is involved in learning to use
> them.

RPL then, should be about helping learners to develop their knowledge, skills and expertise, by explicitly helping them to learn how to use their prior knowledge and experiences and make connections between their different experiences and ways of knowing (which include embodied skills), through integrating these holistically in the context of their vocation. A vocation is more than an occupation; it is where an individual is able to connect the meanings between the different parts of their lives. Dewey (1966 [1916], p. 307) explains:

> . . . each individual has of necessity a variety of callings, in each
> of which he should be intelligently effective; and [. . .] any one
> occupation loses its meaning and becomes a routine keeping
> busy at something in the degree in which it is isolated from
> other interests. [. . .] No one is just an artist and nothing else.
> [. . .] He must, at some period of his life, be a member of a
> family; he must have friends and companions; he must either
> support himself or be supported by others, and thus he has a
> business career. He is a member of some organized political
> unit, and so on. We naturally *name* his vocation from that one
> of the callings which distinguishes him, rather than from those

which he has in common with all others. But we should not
allow ourselves to be so subject to words as to ignore and
virtually deny his other callings when it comes to a
consideration of the vocational phases of education.

Conclusion

A vocation is more than a set of skills. It is a sense of identity and a way of
being in the world that connects different aspects of our lives. If all that were
entailed were the learning of specific sets of skills, accompanied by the
questionable assumption that it were possible (and desirable) to precisely
specify these in advance, then credentialist models of RPL based on 'tick and
flick' would have a place. This is now no longer true, if indeed it ever was.

The notion of a vocation is more important in the context of globalisation.
It is a relational concept, which connects individuals and their occupations
to their community and society. The vocation evolves because society and
individuals change and evolve. Every vocation requires several different
skill sets. Basing RPL *only* on the skill sets, and not the broader knowledge,
skills and attributes intrinsic to the vocation will result in impoverished
outcomes.

In this chapter I have argued that while it should not be possible, as a general
rule, to be awarded a whole qualification through RPL, reflection on prior
learning should be an intrinsic part of all qualifications. This is because
'graduateness' entails the capacity to make connections between different
experiences and different ways of knowing, between theoretical and practical
knowledge, codified and embodied knowledge, and explicit and tacit
understandings. Using prior learning to deepen current learning requires
support, because it is not an automatic process, and this needs to be the focus
of a developmental model of RPL.

References

Archer, M. (1995), *Realist Social Theory: The Morphogenetic Approach*, Cambridge:
  Cambridge University Press.
Archer, M. (2000a), *Being Human: The Problem of Agency*, Cambridge: Cambridge
  University Press.
Archer, M. (2000b), 'Homo economicus, Homo sociologicus and Homo sentiens' in

Archer, M. and Tritter, J.Q. (eds) *Rational Choice Theory Resisting Colonization*, London: Routledge.

Archer, M. (2003), *Structure, Agency and the Internal Conversation*, Cambridge: Cambridge University Press.

Beach, K. (1999), 'Consequential transitions: A sociocultural expedition beyond transfer in education' in Iran-Nejad, A. and Pearson, P.D. (eds) *Review of Research in Education*, 24: 101–39.

Bernstein, B. (2000), *Pedagogy, Symbolic Control and Identity*, 2nd Ed., Oxford: Rowman & Littlefield Publishers.

Biggs, J. (1999), *Teaching for Quality Learning at University*, Buckingham: SRHE and Open University Press.

Billett, S. (2003), *Individualising the Social – Socialising the Individual: Interdependence Between Social and Individual Agency in Vocational Learning*, Enriching Learning Cultures, 11th Annual International Conference on Post-compulsory Education and Training, Gold Coast, Queensland, Australia: Australian Academic Press, Brisbane

Bransford, J.D. and Schwartz, D.L. (1999), 'Rethinking transfer: A simple proposal with multiple implications' in Iran-Nejad, A. and Pearson, P.D. (eds) *Review of Research in Education*, 24: 61–100.

Chappell, C., Hawke, G., Rhodes, C. and Solomon, N. (2003), *High Level Review of Training Packages Phase 1 Report. An Analysis of the Current and Future Context in which Training Packages will need to Operate*, Brisbane: Australian National Training Authority.

Dewey, J. (1966 [1916]), *Democracy and Education: An Introduction to the Philosophy of Education*, New York: The Free Press.

Engeström, Y. (1999), 'Activity theory and individual and social transformation' in Engeström, Y., Miettinen, R. and Punamäki, R.-L. (eds) *Perspectives on Activity Theory* (pp. 19–38), Cambridge: Cambridge University Press.

Eraut, M. (2000), 'Non-formal learning, implicit learning and tacit knowledge in professional work' in Coffield, F. (ed.) *The Necessity of Informal Learning*, Bristol: Policy Press.

Eraut, M. (2001), 'The role and use of vocational qualifications,' *National Institute Economic Review*, 78: 88–98.

Fevre, R., Gorard, S. and Rees, G. (2000), 'Necessary and unnecessarily learning: the acquisition of knowledge and "skills" in and outside employment in South Wales in the 20th century' in Coffield, F. (ed.) *The Necessity of Informal Learning*, Bristol: The Policy Press.

Harris, J. (1997), *The Recognition of Prior Learning (RPL) in South Africa?: Drifts and Shifts in International Practices: Understanding the changing discursive terrain 1*, Cape Town: Department of Adult Education and Extra-Mural Studies, University of Cape Town.

Harris, J. (1999), 'Ways of seeing the Recognition of Prior Learning (RPL): What contribution can such practices make to social inclusion?', *Studies in the Education of Adults*, 31(2): 124–39.

Harris, J. (2000), 'Re-visioning the boundaries of learning theory in the assessment of prior experiential learning (APEL)', *SCUTREA, 30th Annual Conference*, University of Nottingham, 3–5 July 2000.

Marginson, S. (1997), *Markets in Education*, St Leonards: Allen & Unwin.

Muller, J. (2000), *Reclaiming Knowledge. Social Theory, Curriculum and Education Policy*, London: Routledge Falmer.

Sayer, A. (2000), *Realism and Social Science*, London: Sage.

Stevenson, J. (2001), 'Vocational knowledge and its specification', *Journal of Vocational Education and Training*, 53(4): 647–62.

Stevenson, J. (2003a), 'Expertise for the workplace' in Stevenson, J. (ed.) *Developing Vocational Expertise*, Crows Nest: Allen & Unwin.

Stevenson, J. (2003b), 'Vocational teaching and learning in context' in Stevenson, J. (ed.) *Developing Vocational Expertise*, Crows Nest: Allen & Unwin.

Wenger, E. (1998), *Communities of Practice: Learning, Meaning and Identity*, Cambridge: Cambridge University Press.

Wheelahan, L., Dennis, N., Firth, J., Miller, P., Newton, D., Pascoe, S., Veenker, P. and Brightman, R. (2002), *Recognition of Prior Learning: Policy and Practice in Australia*, report commissioned by the Australian Qualifications Framework, October 25, Lismore, Southern Cross University.

Young, M. (1998), *From Curriculum to Learning: Studies in the Sociology of Educational Knowledge*, Florence: Taylor & Francis.

Young, M. (2000), 'Rescuing the sociology of educational knowledge from the extremes of voice discourse: towards a new theoretical basis for the sociology of the curriculum', *British Journal of Sociology of Education*, 21(4): 523–6.

Young, M. (2001a), 'Contextualising a new approach to learning: some comments on Yrjo Engestrom's theory of expansive learning', *Journal of Education and Work*, 14(1): 157–61.

Young, M. (2001b), *The Role of National Qualifications Frameworks in Promoting Lifelong Learning*, Discussion paper, Paris, Organisation of Economic Co-operation and Development.

Young, M. (2003a), 'Comparing approaches to the role of qualifications in the promotion of lifelong learning', *European Journal of Education*, 38(2): 199–211.

Young, M. (2003b), 'Durkheim, Vygotsky and the curriculum of the future', *London Review of Education*, 1(2): 100–17.

chapter thirteen

Recognising prior learning: what do *we* know?

Helen Pokorny

Introduction

In the UK, RPL is known as the Assessment of Prior Experiential Learning [APEL] and has been at the margins of higher education [HE] since its introduction in the late-1970s. This chapter considers the nature of APEL in English HE and asks why it has failed to establish itself as a part of the mainstream. It examines underpinning assumptions and the nature of knowledge that is privileged through APEL. Aspects of actor-network theory [ANT] are discussed and illustrated through a case study to explore the construction of knowledge as distributed through networking practices.

Background

Interest in APEL has re-emerged in recent years in England as part of the debate around lifelong learning and widening participation (Fryer, 1997; Wailey, 2002). For example, the government launched a two-year foundation degree [FD] qualification in 2000 in which specific emphasis is placed on work-based learning and APEL. The latter is expected to be both a means of opening access for mature students without formal qualifications and of accelerating progression through the course for experienced students. Nevertheless, an evaluation of FDs by the Quality Assurance Agency (QAA, 2003, p. 8) found little evidence of the use of APEL within those courses evaluated and reported that:

> arrangements for [APEL] raise concerns in seven reviews.
> Although [APEL] systems are generally in place, there is only
> limited evidence of their use. In some cases, this is because they
> are not clear and students find them difficult to use, for example
> demonstrating that all outcomes for a particular module have
> been achieved. In other cases students are not enthusiastic about
> [APEL] and do not apply for it. [. . .] Generally students' prior
> skills and knowledge developed in the workplace, were not
> accredited at entry and industrial partners were not involved in
> [APEL] procedures.

This finding reflects an earlier survey of APEL practice in the English HE sector that found APEL policies in place in a high proportion of universities, but very little evidence that students were accessing the process. It was noted that 'APEL is widely regarded as time consuming and difficult' (Merrifield *et al.*, 2000, p. 3). The report also concluded that: 'While APEL had its roots in widening participation, the most significant growth has been in continuing professional development and corporate courses' (*ibid.*, p. 2).

One of the claims made for APEL is that it gives value to learning wherever and however acquired, including work-based, community, voluntary, family and informal learning (Forrest, 1977; Buckle, 1988). This recognition of diverse sites of learning stands in contrast to the disciplinary canons of the academy. A key issue raised by APEL is that of reconciling the differences between learning developed through experience or practice and learning developed through formal education. Two barriers to implementation are commonly raised in discussions:

1. It is problematic to find appropriate space for prior experiential learning within the mainstream academic curriculum.
2. The process of reinterpreting learning gained outside of the academy within an academic context is difficult and time consuming for the student.

The aim of this chapter is to explore how it is that these barriers to APEL have been successfully maintained given the promotion of lifelong learning and widening participation policy agenda and the endeavours of APEL advocates over the years. Moreover, there has been a shift in educational practice towards learner-centred approaches to education (Trilling and Hood, 1999) and an increase in the development of work-based and vocational curricula that appear to be 'an acknowledgement that problem-solving in practice is very important to learning, perhaps more so than abstract decontextualised knowledge' (Fox, 2005, p. 101). How is it that so little recognition is accorded to the prior learning that students bring with them into HE institutions? The chapter explores the relevance of actor-network theory to ask the questions: By what means are these barriers kept in place? To what extent do our practices as APEL practitioners collude in this process of exclusion?

Actor-network theory

Actor-network theory is a perspective on the mechanics of power. Originating in social studies of science, it has developed from the early-1980s through the work of Law (1986), Callon (1986), Latour (1985) and others. From an actor-network perspective, knowledge is a social rather than scientific product, arising not 'through the operation of a privileged scientific method [. . .] but as a product or effect of a network of heterogeneous materials' (Law, 1992, p. 2). Knowledge is seen as taking material form as skills, practices, papers, presentations etc., organised and ordered into a patterned network of heterogeneous materials. In addressing the question where does knowledge come from, ANT is concerned with the processes of 'translation' by which any network expands or contracts and through which knowledge becomes patterned in particular ways. The focus of analysis is on '[h]ow it is that some kinds of interactions more or less succeed in stabilising and reproducing themselves: how it is that they seem to generate such effects as power, fame, size, scope or organisation with which we are all familiar' (*ibid.*). A key component of ANT is the process of 'symmetrical analysis' that is, the principle that human and non-human elements of a network should be analysed in the same way, because non-human elements also influence the actions of others. Law argues that:

> What counts as a person is an effect generated by a network of heterogeneous, interacting, materials. [. . .] If you took away my computer, my colleagues, my office, my books, my desk, my telephone I would not be a sociologist writing papers, delivering lectures, and producing 'knowledge'. I'd be something quite other. [. . .] The argument is that thinking, acting, writing, loving, earning – all the attributes that we normally ascribe to human beings, are generated in networks that pass through and ramify both within and beyond the body. Hence the term, actor-network – an actor is also, always, a network (*ibid.*, p. 4).

ANT works with a Foucauldian conception of power and knowledge as co-implicated in each other. Power is not viewed as a possession of dominant individuals or organisations but as an aspect of networked concrete practices, actions and activities: 'Power is not a possession, it is manifest only as it is used.' (Fox, 2000, p. 859). Therefore, in seeking to apply an ANT approach to analysis the focus is upon processes: How it is that any actor comes to be and to function like an actor? Through what nests of relational practices, animate and inanimate, does this occur? ANT asks the question: 'How does one come to represent *many*?' Fox (*ibid.*, p. 862). In the context of APEL the question becomes: How does the traditional model of academic knowledge come to represent the diversity of knowledge students bring with them to higher education? This question can be explored by beginning with two principles which are common to many university APEL processes:

1. Learning must be measurable; credit cannot be awarded for experience itself.
2. Learning must satisfy the syllabus objectives. (Lueddeke, 1997, p. 217)

The assumption appears to be that outcomes of prior learning and university learning processes must be identifiably similar in order to be deemed equivalent. Law suggests that, in analysing the processes of translation by which power is distributed into patterns of knowledge-making, ANT is concerned with the empirical processes of 'exploring and describing local processes of patterning, social orchestration, ordering and resistance . . .' (Law, 1992, p. 5). In the discussion that follows I consider some of the processes of translation at work in and around APEL.

Learning outcomes

One of the significant influences upon processes of patterning and ordering in UK higher education has been the attention given to learning outcomes as an integral part of an audit culture with a focus on the measurement, accountability and monitoring of education and educators. Learning outcomes can therefore be seen as an actant in the higher education network. Colley *et al.* (2003) have criticised the enthusiasm with which advocates of APEL have embraced modularity and learning outcomes to promote a form of APEL that uses outcomes as a framework for the mapping and matching of learning experiences. Such a process reinforces the principle that prior learning must satisfy syllabus objectives. This approach to APEL has been very influential due to associated assurances of validity and reliability and because of the reassurance it offers to members of the academic community concerned about the academic relevance of learning derived from different contexts. However Colley *et al.* (*ibid.*, p. 63) note that: 'the fundamental and rarely addressed problem with audit approaches . . . [is their claim] . . . to provide a neutral, objective and self-evidently useful measure of what already exists. In fact they change its very nature, sometimes significantly . . .' They ask: 'What are the implications of increasing the formalisation of learning previously regarded as largely spontaneous, student-centred and not focused on outcomes specified?' (*ibid.*, p. 58). The implications for APEL are twofold. First, to render invisible a very large proportion of prior learning which is not reflected in existing learning outcomes. Secondly, to require prior learning to be re-shaped to fit within established curricula. Those students excluded from the dominant culture through class, race, gender and disability, for example, are likely to have the most diverse learning experiences. Brah and Hoy (1989) have suggested that the interpretation of lived experience needs to be related to the wider social structure, and argue for deploying well-integrated and coherent frameworks within which to locate and understand individual and group experience. Although many APEL modules and guidance programmes offer innovative frameworks of support to candidates making a claim (see for example Michelson *et al.*, 2004), the requirement often remains that learning is presented in accordance with certain academic conventions. This makes APEL difficult and onerous. It is also misleading. In fact, in many cases, the credit is not awarded for prior learning but for the value added through current learning, often prescribed by particular academic paradigms with distinct values, social and cultural structures and language. Cleary *et al.* (2002) note in their study that despite the rhetoric of valuing learning wherever and however acquired, APEL in the UK has failed to develop as a socially or epistemologically inclusive concept.

The role of reflection

A further practice which supports processes of translation, ordering and patterning of knowledge is the emphasis given to the principles of reflective practice, based on Kolb's (1984) learning cycle which 'popularised the assumption that experience is "concrete" and split from "reflection" as though doing and thinking are separate states.' (Fenwick, 2003, p. 11). APEL candidates are asked to revisit and reflect on their experience and through this mental process to identify learning which can then be presented for assessment: 'What becomes emphasised are the conceptual lessons gained from experience, which are quickly stripped of location and embeddedness . . .' (*ibid.*). Butterworth (1992) defined this reflective approach to APEL as 'developmental'. Trowler (1996, p. 21) has noted that it is likely to gain favour with academics because:

> . . . the developmental approach does not require academic staff
> to accredit a different form of knowledge from that normally
> accredited in higher education . . .

The developmental approach often requires students to place their prior learning within an academic framework, re-packaging that learning to fit the contours and reference points of traditional disciplines. Reflection is seen by some as empowering for APEL candidates – providing them with a transformative learning experience resulting from a critical evaluation of their learning experiences (Cleary *et al.*, 2002; Whittaker *et al.*, Chapter 15, this volume). Whilst many APEL candidates do report positively upon their APEL experience and do subsequently give greater value to themselves and their skills and knowledge, Usher (1989) has argued that the focus on reflection alienates the individual from their context and represents a rejection of the legitimacy of learning acquired outside of the university environment – which is only accredited once transformed. Freedman (2000, p. 9) notes that: 'In essence all varieties of adult learning take experience as the unmediated raw material to be acted upon and transformed [. . .] but somehow insufficient unto itself.' Trowler (1996, p. 28) also observes that:

> . . . going through the process of assisted reflection requires
> personal qualities such as confidence, facility in language use
> and in conceptual thought, all aspects of the cultural capital
> important to educational success as that concept is currently
> defined [. . .] exactly the sort of (socially derived) qualities
> which have ensured that under represented groups remain under
> represented in higher education.

The normalising and potentially disempowering effect on individual experience is clear. From an ANT perspective this process of ordering knowledge through reflective or developmental approaches to APEL signifies one of the processes of translation by which individuals are admitted into the dominant knowledge network.

A distributed perspective of knowledge construction

An alternative approach, which accords with ANT, would be to view learning as a distributed process. Brown and Duguid (2000) argue that knowledge is the product of interacting social, economic, historic, cultural and physical networks encompassing community, tools and activities. From this perspective, learning takes place *within* activities and experiences and not from reflection upon them. There is no separation of person and context, knowledge is distributed within networks and is constantly emerging and shifting into other networks. This suggests that any APEL process which aims to recognise and value learning from different contexts would have to engage with the heterogeneity of the knowledge distribution process rather than seeking familiarity. The focus in ANT is upon complexity and poses a challenge to the simplification of complexity. Law (1999, p. 12) notes that:

> The God eye is alive and well and seemingly incurable in its greed for that which is flat and may easily be brought to the point. But, or so I firmly believe, the real chance to make a difference lives elsewhere. It lies in the irreducible. In the oxymoronic. In the topologically discontinuous. In that which is heterogeneous. It lies in a modest willingness to live, to know, and to practise in the complexities of tension.

To view knowledge as networked, dynamic and distributed locates the value of the prior learning within the experience itself. For example, the learning of a community worker will be embedded and adaptive to interactions with people and with a range of objects (textual and otherwise) and activities. This type of knowledge does not manifest itself as a result of post-hoc reflection and academic repackaging. Rather, it is 'woven into fully embodied nets of ongoing action, invention, social relations and history in complex systems' (Fenwick, 2003, p. 16). This suggests that we need to consider approaches to APEL that focus on exploration of this complex experience, with the assessor learning from candidates' experiences, and considering candidates' learning within an inclusive set of criteria for defining what counts as equivalent. As APEL practitioners, we will not be able to consider the totality of the learning or to make visible all of its tacit and distributed elements via mental processes evidenced through a reflective document. What we can do is recognise its complexity. To achieve that, we need to be willing to recognise the validity of individuals' networked knowledge practices and to articulate 'equivalent' learning by considering the inherent activities, responsibilities, artefacts, technologies, narratives and language of practice (see also Fenwick's treatment of complexity theory, Chapter 14, this volume). Similarly in his critique of higher education's search for a generic vocabulary of capabilities. Holmes (1995, p. 6) suggests that '[r]ather than look for the supposed attributes and "mental tools" which underlay these practices it is the practices themselves which should concern us.'

APEL assessments

Law (1992) argues that in order to understand the mechanics of power, it is important not to take for granted the macro-social system on the one hand and bits and pieces of microsocial detail on the other. He argues for a focus on interactions, asking: 'how some kinds of interactions overcome resistance and seem to become macrosocial [. . .] how it is that networks may come to look like single point actors' (*ibid.*, p. 2). In the context of APEL, we are interested in how it is that the heterogeneous actors and actants in the candidates' knowledge networks are patterned and ordered into the academic knowledge network. The implications of these processes for the recognition of prior learning can be examined through the interactions around assessment, some of which are discussed in the following sections. Law (*ibid.*) has also suggested that 'the character of network ordering' is 'better seen as a verb – a somewhat uncertain process of overcoming resistance – rather than the *fait accompli* of a noun.' Consequently the discussion that follows highlights those interactions which shift the power relationships inherent in APEL interactions or which appear to have the potential to do so.

The dominant APEL assessment tool in the UK is the portfolio (Merrifield *et al.*, 2000) within which candidates collate evidence of learning and supply a reflective narrative relating this to their aims in compiling the claim. Portfolios can become very weighty documents as students try to convince assessors of their learning. Brown and Duguid (2000, p. 202) note: 'where there are problems with information, the solution offered is usually to add more. The history of documents and communities points in the other direction – towards less information, more context'. This suggests that one reason why assessors often advise against portfolios is that the volume of documentation adds little to their understanding of candidates' knowledge. Engagement with the candidates' contexts is likely to be more fruitful. Harris (2000, p. 125) has suggested that in the context of APEL 'interviews are [. . .] particularly good for [. . .] exploring the depth, breadth and richness of knowledge and its application'. They offer a potential means for an assessor to explore candidates' contexts through dialogue.

However the written text remains predominant in APEL assessment. Brown and Duguid (2000, p. 190) note how, in relation to the development of academic communities, 'shared texts as much as anything gave texture to the notion of a discipline . . .'. This is illustrated in the outcome of interviews with six tutors in my own institution who were sympathetic to APEL. When asked what they would look for in an APEL claim:

> [Tutors] mentioned abstracts, contents pages, synopses, resumés and bibliographies, exemplifying a recurring theme of summarizing or distillation of information within the academic context. They used phrases such as 'written appropriately', 'to comply with certain academic requirements' and wanted to see 'examples of good practice in essay writing'. One lecturer remarked, '. . . there's absolutely no literature, there's no reference to the critical literature or what the academic context of this would be.' The expectation was definitely therefore that students would have acquired a set of skills related to the production of texts in an academic context and that they would be able to apply these in the APEL portfolio. The discourse is primarily general academic discourse with little to mark it out as specific to the genre of APEL. (Peters and Pokorny, 2003, p. 343)

These comments illustrate the processes through which knowledge developed outside of the curriculum is ordered and translated into familiar academic knowledge. One of the questions for APEL is how to validate experiential learning without diminishing or changing it. In some instances this could perhaps be a relatively straightforward process as Harris (2000) suggests, with assessors engaging in dialogues that explore candidates' experience and confirm authentication of that experience. On the face of it this does not appear to be a significant departure from existing practices and power relationships. However, an ANT perspective would encourage explicit recognition that knowledge is contained within the experience itself which lies within the territory of the candidate.

The role of the assessor

This shift in perspective means that although the assessor is a key actor in the APEL process, the active engagement of the candidate is also necessary to provide the interpretive context that defines the significance of practices. Such a conceptualisation of prior learning challenges those APEL assessment practices that seek to abstract and transform learning from experience but also demands a re-conceptualisation of the assessor-candidate relationship. Holmes (2002, p. 7) has suggested that:

> Once the candidates are brought into the analysis and
> theorisation of assessment as co-producers of what are taken as
> facts about them, the assessors themselves are transformed from
> judges, separated from the world in which students engage in
> the performance to be judged [. . .] with mysterious powers to
> 'infer' . . . [the student's learning]. They become ordinary
> human beings engaged in fact production.

This is not to suggest that prior learning should be accredited without any form of validation on the grounds that as we cannot know first-hand the discontinuities, tensions and experiences from which it arose, we must accept it unquestioningly. Rather, what is suggested is that learning can only be recognised through an exploration of the individual's experience, with an acceptance of heterogeneity, and through a willingness to engage in a dialogue around what counts as significant without forcing the use of academic discourse.

However Holmes (1995, p. 6) also points out that:

> . . . assessment processes extend beyond the assessor-candidate
> interaction, implicating a range of procedures and regulations
> which require situated interpretative enactment. The assessor as
> 'lone agent' implied by much of the literature on assessment
> ignores the complex web of actants which include
> administrative procedures and associated artefacts . . .

In APEL, these actants would include a variety of assessment documentation, validation panels, assessment boards, second markers, external examiners and external bodies, regulations and curriculum specifications, all of which can result in interpretations of practice that serve largely to exclude prior experiential learning and to support the recognition of familiar constructions of knowledge. However, where there are communities of practice around APEL,

Merrifield *et al.* (2000, p. 46) report that assessors, 'got more familiar with APEL and more practised at making judgements [and were] able to be more flexible.' A deliberate focus upon the development of APEL assessment actor-networks within an institution could potentially lead to more socially and epistemologically inclusive processes.

A case study: Charlotte

The example that follows is an illustration of micro-social interactions in practice. It is based on a case study from Peters (2004) and illustrates the translation processes at work in what appears to be a straightforward APEL claim. Charlotte claimed credit for a second-year undergraduate module 'Principles of Video Production', and produced a video, which was the form of assessment given to students who studied the module in the conventional way. The learning outcomes of the module were to:

- Facilitate skills development to a level where students are sufficiently competent to produce a short 5-7 minute video.
- Expose students to the process of media (video) production by interrogating and documenting the experience.

Her video was a highly professional production, incorporating clips of film and photographs showing her in action, and illustrating her work in different stages of her extensive career in media. The APEL submission focused on learning outcomes but integrated these with descriptions of her experience. She provided written documentation which was predominantly work-related, although she did include academic references and some theoretical background. The demonstration of equivalence appeared to be straightforward. The learning outcomes were recognised as relevant by all parties and the work to be assessed was produced with these in mind. However, the assessor considered the work insufficient for credit to be awarded for the module. As a result Charlotte was asked to write a theoretical essay on the subject of genre in film. She felt that this was 'a complete waste of time'. She also felt that the assessor had not recognised the breadth and depth of the experience she held, but rather, had focused on what students studying the module were required to cover in class. Nevertheless, in order to obtain the credit Charlotte had to conform to this form of assessment. This process resembled Fox's (2000, p. 859) observation (based on the later work of Foucault) of a 'self which acts forcefully upon itself, either conforming to instruction or resisting that instruction.'

The example illustrates what can happen when different actor-networks meet and the power dynamics that operate at these boundaries. In order to cross the boundary Charlotte was expected acquire to new learning that reflected the knowledge production practices of the established curriculum. Law (1992, p. 5) asks the question: 'Why is it that the networks which make up the actor come to be deleted, or concealed from view?' He suggests that this is because it is easier to deal with a single coherent view of an object than to engage with complex networks, and that most of the time we are not in a position to recognise network complexities. Consequently, the way in which experiential learning is generated becomes invisible. In ANT this process of simplification is sometimes called *punctualisation* – when one thing, in this case an essay, stands in for another, thus simplifying complexity and providing familiarity. Charlotte's extensive prior learning became punctualised and had to be represented by new learning of familiar and conventional content and format. Charlotte expressed frustration that her professional expertise went beyond that afforded by a 15-week module for novice video-makers. She was an experienced, highly-regarded television producer. Her case is interesting in the context of current UK education policy which aims to adapt the curriculum in order to enable students to be more employable on graduation. As such, it is concerned with the assessment of anticipated future performance in employment, but does not consider it appropriate to accredit the expertise of those students who are demonstrably employable upon arrival at university. Starr-Glass (2002, p. 223) asks:

> . . . whether validity [of APEL claims] should be seen as
> essentially concurrent or predictive. Concurrent validity looks
> for similarity between [APEL claims] and [. . .] presently
> enrolled students [. . .] which tends to make the practice of
> APEL an exercise in mapping and confirming the familiar.

He goes on to suggest that if APEL was viewed as a process that had predictive validity then, as facilitators, we might wish to examine a: 'much broader correlation between the ways in which knowledge is acquired, processed and utilised by those who prove long term to be successful or well adapted' (*ibid.*). Charlotte reported that although her tutor had been supportive, he perhaps, 'didn't understand what it [APEL] was all about and if he'd understood more he'd say, well, look, actually you have had the experience and it doesn't exactly match but you've done more and I think that would balance it out so maybe it's their lack of understanding makes it difficult for us.' Her comments are insightful in that she sees the process of APEL as about recognising differences in learning experiences whereas the APEL assessor seeks to accredit the familiar.[1]

The ANT translation process

The chapter so far has considered a number of interactions inherent in APEL. These practices contribute to the patterning and ordering of knowledge and result in the *translation* – or expansion of the academic network, often at the expense of recognising prior learning. In pursuing further the actor-network theorists' interest in the processes of network consolidation, Callon (1986) presents a four-stage process which he described as the sociology of translation. I outline this process below, relating each stage to ways in which candidates' prior knowledge is moved into academic networks.

Stage one he called *problematisation*: 'in which one set of actors defines a problem in such a way in which others can recognise it as their problem too, but in the process, the first set of actors indicate that they have the means of resolving the shared problem.' (Fox 2000, p. 862). Obtaining credit through APEL has already been described as a difficult, time-consuming process requiring expert guidance. Johnson (2002, p. 27), in his guide *Models of APEL and Quality Assurance*, warns that: 'one must be careful not to create an erroneous impression whereby APEL is seen to be easier and quicker for the student to acquire than taking the course.' The guide, distilled from the practice of 27 UK higher education institutions, provides detailed information regarding the nature of the workshops, interviews and guidance processes necessary to support APEL. Accordingly, if the candidates accept the problem and solutions offered, then the APEL advisors or academics become the '*obligatory point of passage* in what followed.' (Fox 2000, p. 862, emphasis in original).

The second is a stage of *interessement* in which the first set of actors 'locked their allies into the roles they proposed for them by their gaining commitment to a set of goals and a course of action they also proposed.' (*ibid.*). In APEL, these goals and actions may include mapping learning from experience against pre-determined syllabi or learning outcomes followed by assessment predicated upon competence in a specific form of documenting. Johnson (2002, p. 44) describes the typical APEL assessment: '. . . this would set out each set of learning outcomes. [. . .] The student must be reminded that credit is awarded NOT for the experience per se but rather from the learning derived from that experience. The student will need to reflect on that learning in a manner consistent with the level of credit being sought.' Fox (2005) discusses the role of the teacher in power relations, suggesting that power is not brought to bear by brute force, but by the way in which an individual learns the art of self-surveillance and through which 'we learn to see ourselves from a teacher's or therapist's point of view . . .' (Turkle, cited in Fox, 2005, p. 100).

The third stage is *enrolment*: the phase 'in which the allies were defined and coordinated . . . through many means: persuasion, threat, inducements etc.' (Fox, 2000, p. 862). APEL processes have already been described as networked within a chain of actants including candidates, assessors, guidance tutors, regulations, credit, qualifications and guidance documentation, all of which contribute to the processes of enrolment.

The fourth phase, involving the *mobilisation of allies*, is where the one speaks for the many as progress is made towards shared goals, and communication is made possible with the aid of *immutable mobiles*, for example, a portfolio or other form of assessment. At this stage the candidate's knowledge has been translated into the academic network.

ANT and the challenge of APEL

APEL poses a challenge to the role of the university as the primary site for the construction of knowledge and the development of learner identity. Nespor (1994, p. 10) writing about ANT has noted that within academia:

> Identities are shifting contested stakes of networking practices
> that seek to produce or maintain a certain configuration of
> social space by excluding or restricting some people and things
> from participation while recruiting and reconstructing others to
> fit the network [. . .] and that students enter into disciplinary
> practices when they begin to move along the trajectories that
> keep them within the narrow range of space times and
> distributions that constitute the discipline.

In the light of the above quotation, APEL cannot but present a challenge to the academic identity of a subject, discipline and individual. It presents different sites of knowledge production. Interestingly, it may be precisely those applied/vocational disciplines seeking to establish an academic identity for their knowledge base, where networking practices are most resistant to accepting different forms of knowledge development as relevant in the academic context. As Merrifield *et al.* (2000, p. 33) notes: 'Some disciplines have the professional experience base but are still resistant to accrediting learning from experience.'

However, as Nespor (1994) notes, networking practices are contested and shifting. In France, for example, the *Validation des Acquis de l'Experience* [VAE] ('the validation of prior experiential learning') introduced in 2003, is embedded in legislation which provides a right for individuals who have been in paid, unpaid or voluntary employment for at least three years to claim accreditation for their experience against a whole- or part-qualification. VAE 'emphasises the learner's ability to engage in problem solving and critical thinking' (Cleary, 2002, p. 58). Feutrie (2000, p. 108) explains: 'Therefore, it is not the candidates' stock of formal knowledge which is assessed but rather the ability to prove a level of intellectual development.' VAE is seen as a developmental process and where the award is for a part-qualification, the outcome is linked both to learning demonstrated and to a strategy for achieving the full award. Space is made for learning from different contexts. The process of assessment includes not only the academic assessor and candidate but also representatives of the occupational sector, half of whom are employer representatives and half employee representatives familiar with the candidates' context. Dialogue is encouraged and the totality of a candidate's experience is taken into account, not only their professional and/or work experience (Transfine, 2003). Whilst acknowledging that commitment to and involvement in the process varies, Feutrie (2000, p. 115) emphasises that:

> From the moment the university agrees to recognise the fact that
> an equivalence can be made between knowledge acquired on
> the job or in life [. . .] that university has evolved into
> something different [. . .] the university becomes less of a
> 'distribution centre' for knowledge . . . [and] makes students
> active partners . . .

This approach reinforces the importance of providing a liminal space (Starr-Glass, 2003) where APEL candidates and assessors jointly seek equivalence with a curriculum framed by inclusive criteria rather than tied to predetermined syllabi. An exact match of experiential and curricula learning will not exist; instead we need a willingness to engage in the uniqueness and complexities of candidates' experience. Law (1999, p. 9) is concerned that: 'as we practice our trade as intellectuals, the premium we place on transportability, on naming, on clarity, on formulating and rendering explicit what it is that we know ... [though] often appropriate, also imposes costs.' Developing APEL requires us to live with tension, to recognise learning which is not amenable to precise and easy measurement, and to provide flexibility and space in the curriculum for 'all the voices that would otherwise be silent or muted beyond recognition' (Fuller, 1999, cited in Delanty, 2001, p. 156).

Approaches like ANT can support a challenge to principles such as those set out by Lueddeke above. They can encourage an analysis of how power is enacted through APEL practices in ways that militate against the aims of the practices. They also lend support to the argument that the focus in APEL should indeed be the experience itself, for it is in the experience that the knowledge lies. David Starr-Glass (2002, p. 228) proposes some powerful suggestions for implementing APEL in ways that remain true to the complexities of practice and do not seek to transform experience:

1. *We should learn the candidate's language*: The candidate should not be forced to use academic language [. . .]This new language of experience has to be heard, explored and seen in action . . .
2. *We should explore the territory not the map*: A map is faulty when the logic of its construction belongs exclusively [to the candidate or evaluator]. The evaluation of prior experience is an exploration of the candidate's territory, an exploration that must engage both the candidate and the invited evaluator . . .
3. *We should focus upon the metaphor not metonym*: In exploring prior learning, exact replicas will not be found of the structures and logic that have been created in the academic world. [. . .] The issue that should be of concern is not the likeness but the degree of likeness. . .
4. *We should look for totemic systems*: The fragments and pieces that the candidate brings [. . .] have to be dealt with. Yet in the appreciation of the logic and potential of these pieces there lies the ability to fabricate a new object that resembles the academic construct.
5. *We should accentuate assessing novelty and not accrediting the status quo*: The grounding in notions of concurrent validity should not be allowed to reduce [APEL] to a sterile, norm-related examination of the status quo [. . .] The emphasis might more profitably be placed on using the [APEL] process in a

creative and insightful manner rather than on the recognition, documentation and accreditation of familiarity.

Conclusion

This chapter has drawn on ANT to demonstrate that current APEL practices in the UK have served largely to absorb prior learning into established curricula and pedagogic networks with the result that we recognise only learning that is familiar. In order to cross the boundary into the academic network, candidates have to be prepared to locate themselves in this network. Not surprisingly Merrifield *et al.* (2000, p. 49) found that:

Most higher education institutions expect that APEL students, like students in their taught courses will:

- Provide evidence that they have achieved specific learning outcomes – usually those designed by the [university]
- [. . .] show not just skills and knowledge in practice but that they have mastered the theory as well
- Produce a piece of academic writing – a distinctive form of literacy . . .

The effect has been to marginalise the APEL process and the candidates who undertake it. APEL cannot flourish in a context where the emphasis is on seeing equivalence in terms of homogeneity of learning and on ignoring the embedded nature of learning through experience (see also Michelson, in this volume). ANT can support an analysis of the APEL process through highlighting 'how power is mobilised and subjects and objects constituted [including] the material arrangements [. . .] through which decisions are made possible.' (Dugdale, 1999, p. 116). Whilst the audit approaches common in higher education clearly militate against the facilitation of this type of APEL and represent one of the ways in which power is distributed currently, resistance to the recognition of alternative sites of knowledge production goes deeper than this. APEL is a challenge to the networking practices that define knowledge as academic.

The 'drivers' for APEL in UK higher education do not encourage recognising different sites of knowledge production, but rather seek to accelerate qualification routes in response to market forces. APEL offers the potential to reinforce the credibility of higher education through the direct involvement of a diversity of knowledgeable and experienced individuals:

'after all academia has, arguably, always been concerned with the practical affairs of society, including the occupational' (Holmes, 1995, p. 6). Merrifield *et al.* (2000, p. 5) argue that 'the future for APEL is in flexible learning'. This chapter has proposed some changes to traditional APEL practices which could contribute to that flexibility by supporting a movement away from mapping and matching exercises, towards the development of APEL assessment as genuine dialogue, based on inclusive criteria and the encouragement of critical evaluations of local APEL assessment networking practices. To view knowledge as embedded within complex networks of actors, physical and social, can help us to understand why the focus should turn to what the candidate knows, and not remain on what *we* know: '[A]ctors know what they do and we have to learn from them [. . .] It is us [. . .] who lack knowledge of what they do, and not *they* who are missing the explanation . . .' Latour (1999, p. 19).

References

Brah, A. and Hoy, J. (1989), 'Experiential learning: A new orthodoxy ?' in Weil, S. and McGill, I. (eds) *Making Sense of Experiential Learning: Diversity in Theory and Practice* (pp. 70–81), Milton Keynes: SRHE/Open University Press.

Brown, J.S. and Duguid, P. (2000), *The Social Life of Information*, Boston, MA: Harvard Business School Press.

Buckle, J. (1988), *A Learner's Introduction to Building on your Experience*, London: The Learning from Experience Trust.

Butterworth, C. (1992), 'More than one bite at the APEL', *Journal of Further and Higher Education*, 16(3): 39–51.

Callon, M. (1986), 'Some elements of a sociology of translation: domestication of the scallops and the fishermen of St Brieuc Bay' in Law, J. (ed.) *Power, Action and Belief. A New Sociology of Knowledge?*, London: Routledge and Kegan Paul.

Cleary, P., Whittaker, R., Gallacher, J., Merrill, B., Jokinen, L. and Carette, M. (2002), *Social Inclusion through APEL: the Learners' Perspective*, Glasgow: Glasgow Caledonian University.

Colley, H., Hodkinson, P. and Malcolm, J. (2003), *Informality and Formality in Learning: A report for the Learning and Skills Research Centre*, London: Learning and Skills Research Centre.

Delanty, G. (2001), *Challenging Knowledge: The University in the Knowledge Society*, Milton Keynes: SRHE and Open University Press.

Dugdale, A. (1999), 'Materiality: juggling sameness and difference.' in Law J. and Hassard, J. (eds) *Actor Network Theory and After* (pp. 113–36), Oxford: Blackwell Publishers/The Sociological Review.

Fenwick, T. (2003), 'Inside out of experiential learning: troubling assumptions and expanding questions', keynote paper presented to the *Experiential: Community: Workbased: Researching learning outside the academy Conference*, Glasgow, UK.

Feutrie, M. (2000), 'France: the story of *La Validation des Acquis* (Recognition of Experiential Learning)' in Evans, N. (ed.) *Experiential Learning Around the World: Employability and the Global Economy* (pp. 103–17), London: Jessica Kinglsey.

Forrest, A. (1977), *Assessing Prior Learning – A CAEL Student Guide*, Columbia: Cooperative Assessment of Experiential Learning.

Fox, S. (2000), 'Communities of practice, Foucault and actor-network theory', *Journal of Management Studies*, 37(6): 853–67.

Fox, S. (2005), 'An actor-network critique of community in higher education: implications for networked learning', *Studies in Higher Education*, 30(1): 95–110.

Freedman, P. (2000), 'The patronised self of critical management education', paper presented at the 2nd *Connecting Learning and Critique* International Conference, Lancaster, UK.

Fryer, R.H. (1997), *Learning for the Twenty-First Century: First Report of the National Advisory Group for Continuing Education and Lifelong Learning*, London: HMSO.

Harris, J. (2000), *RPL: Power, Pedagogy and Possibility*, Pretoria: Human Sciences Research Council.

Holmes, L. (1995), 'The capability curriculum, conventions of assessment and the construction of graduate employability', paper presented at *Understanding the Social World Conference*, University of Huddersfield, UK.

Holmes, L. (2002), 'Emergent identity, education and distributed assessment: an ethnomethodological exploration', paper presented at *Ethnomethodology: A Critical Celebration conference*, University of Essex, UK.

Johnson, B. (2002), *Models of APEL and Quality Assurance*, Southern England Consortium for Credit Accumulation and Transfer, SEEC, UK.

Kolb, D.A. (1984), *Experiential Learning: Experience as the Source of Learning*, Englewood Cliffs, NJ: Prentice Hall.

Latour, B. (1985), 'Give me a laboratory and I will raise the world' in Knorr-Cetinaa, K.D. and Mulkay, M.J. (eds) *Science Observed. Perspectives on the Social Study of Science*, London: Sage.

Latour, B. (1999), 'On recalling ANT' in Law, J. and Hassard, J. (eds) *Actor Network Theory and After* (pp. 15–26), Oxford: Blackwell Publishers/The Sociological Review.

Law, J. (1986), ' On the methods of long-distance control: vessels, navigation, and the Portuguese route to India', in Law J. (ed.) *Power, Action and Belief. A New Sociology of Knowledge?*, London: Routledge and Kegan Paul.

Law, J. (1992), 'Notes on the theory of the actor network: Ordering, strategy and heterogeneity' published by the Centre for Science Studies, Lancaster University,

England at http://www.comp.lancs.ac.uk/sociology/papers/Law-Notes-on-ANT.pdf

Law, J. (1999), 'After ANT: complexity, naming and topology' in Law, J. and Hassard, J. (1999) *Actor Network Theory and After* (pp. 1–15), Oxford: Blackwell Publishers/The Sociological Review.

Lueddeke, G. (1997), 'The accreditation of prior experiential learning in higher education: Discourse on rationales and assumptions', *Higher Education Quarterly*, 51(3): 210–44.

Merrifield, J., McIntyre, D. and Osaigbovo, R. (2000), *Changing but not Changed: Mapping APEL in English Higher Education*, London: Learning from Experience Trust.

Michelson, E. and Mandell, A. (2004), *Portfolio Development and the Assessment of Prior Learning: Perspectives, Models and Practices*, USA: Stylus Publishing.

Nespor, J. (1994), *Knowledge in Motion: Time and Curriculum in Undergraduate Physics and Management*, London: Falmer Press.

Peters, H. (2004), 'Cracking the Code', EdD Thesis, Open University.

Peters, H. and Pokorny, H. (2003), 'The runaway horse: attempting to harness prior learning in the academic context' in *Researching Learning outside the Academy, proceedings of the Experiential: Community: Workbased: Researching learning outside the academy Conference* (pp. 342–48), Glasgow, UK.

QAA (2003), *Overview report on Foundation degree reviews: conducted in 2003*, published by The Quality Assurance Agency for Higher Education, http://www.qaa.ac.uk/public/foundation/contents.htm, (accessed 18 July 2004).

Starr-Glass, D. (2002), 'Metaphor and totem: exploring and evaluating prior experiential learning', *Assessment and Evaluation in Higher Education*, 27(3): 222–31.

Starr-Glass, D. and Schwartzbaum, A. (2003), 'A liminal space: challenges and opportunities in accreditation of prior learning in Judaic studies', *Assessment and Evaluation*, 28(2): 179–92.

Transfine Seminar (2003), http://www.transfine.net/Results/Seminar2/French%20Summary.doc. Last accessed 6 May 2003.

Trilling, B. and Hood, P. (1999), 'Learning technology and education reform in the Knowledge Age or we're wired, webbed and windowed, now what?', *Educational Technology*, 39(3): 5–17.

Trowler, P. (1996), 'Angels in marble? Accrediting prior experiential learning in higher education', *Studies in Higher Education*, 21(1): 17–29.

Usher, R. (1989), 'Qualifications, paradigms and experiential learning in higher education' in Fulton, O. (ed.) *Access and Institutional Change* (pp. 63–79), Buckingham: SRHE and Open University Press.

Wailey, T. (2002), *How to do AP(E)L*, London: Southern England Consortium for Credit Accumulation and Transfer.

Notes

[1] Compare this to the divergent and convergent assessment approaches, discussed by Andersson (Chapter 2, this volume).

chapter fourteen

Reconfiguring RPL and its assumptions: a complexified view

Tara Fenwick

Introduction

Many have argued critically that RPL is based on a view of knowledge that creates a disjuncture between private experience and public discourse, producing a fundamental paradox when the private journey of discovery and learning is brought under public scrutiny and adjudication. This mentalist or representational view of knowledge separates mind from world, subject from object, and observer from observed. In this chapter I show these and other problematic conceptions underpinning RPL practices. I argue that a view of knowledge inspired by complexity science challenges our conventional notions of 'prior learning', and opens possibilities for rethinking ways to 'recognise' it.

A personal interlude

I am staring at Janie Anderson's file. Janie has applied to our certificate programme in adult education, and has dutifully prepared a little dossier that purports to demonstrate her 'prior learning'. Like many post-secondary certificate programmes, ours accepts applicants without Bachelor's degrees. Many go on to Bachelor's programmes and receive substantial credit for the certificate. As an enticement to attract applicants, we offer advanced credit for learning acquired through life experience. Most apply for it, and this is the process through which they get it.

'Well, what do you think?' Sharon is the committee chair, and she looks around the table.

Darlene shrugs. 'I don't see much here,' she offers. 'So she's led some communications workshops for ABC bank and done a little mentoring on the job for the government, but it's not like five years of college teaching, like some of the other applicants are showing.'

'But', Gary interrupts, 'it looks like she also developed the workshops. And, they were all different. See – she's listed her learnings in negotiating with different clients, developing initiative, flexibility, and self-directed learning, creating innovative instructional activities – I mean, some college teachers are just handed a curriculum which they repeat year after year. Just because someone shows up to work for five years doesn't mean they've learned anything.'

'That's your assumption. But I'm willing to give her half credit.' Darlene has already flipped to the next file. 'Besides, lots of teachers don't think to write down all their specific knowledge because it's so ingrained and complex they don't have words for it. And – you are automatically penalising someone because they stay in one job.'

Sharon sighs. 'Tara, are you with us? Anything to contribute?'

I am still staring at Janie's file. So much work has gone into preparing it. Janie seems smart. Her lists of skills fit the minimal descriptors for the advance credit. She has imitated the language of the prior learning assessment directions, and has borrowed some phrases from our own course objectives. I think she ought to get credit for learning expert manipulation of institutional strategy. But then, this just rewards those who slide unthinkingly into dominant discourses. I think back to an earlier file that we rejected today: Frank Bird. Frank is Aboriginal and has lived on reserve in the northern forests of British Columbia much of his young adult life. He described his learning in the sweat lodge, and as the tea fetcher, and as the drum lead for his community. His dossier contained many drawings and symbols, but few words. Of course it was rejected. Frank had had *the wrong sort of experience*, so his learning did not count.

The whole process seemed absurd. And I believed everyone around the committee table knew this in their stomachs. But we also knew that some system of advance credit avoided sending adult students back to years of undergraduate course-taking. What we did not take time to talk about were the problematic assumptions about learning and experience that we were making. Nor did we talk about who we were as 'recognisers' of experiential learning, both individually in our roles as judges and collectively as an institution shaping people's sense of self and knowledge. We always pretended these individual applications could be treated as isolated knowledge islands. We never once talked about the larger systems in which these people, and we ourselves, were participating.

When I discovered the literature on RPL, I found many authors had criticised practices for separating learning from doing and people from environments, and for shaping human experience and selves to fit institutional categories (Fraser, 1995; Harris, 2000). But I also still believe that 'recognising' experiential learning is important. This is partly to help people fit our straitjacketing institutional requirements and slide more easily into the cult of credentialing. We would, I think, be negligent in not accepting this responsibility given the slim likelihood that such 'disciplinary' technologies, however repellent, will change anytime soon. But more important, recognition of knowledge created in contexts other than formal curricula and academic disciplines is critical to challenge institutional power, champion local and personal knowledge, and remind us that we actually know very little about the fluid and contradictory rhythms of knowledge-making amidst everyday human turmoil. The puzzle for me is, how can recognition and representation be rethought as ways to engage with, rather than to fix and measure, other's knowledge? How do we avoid the trap of commodifying and objectifying learning as a *product* to be acquired, rather than recognising its continuously expanding *processes*, in which all of us, including our intentions, perceptions, relationships and activities, are caught up?

In my reading and research of experience-based learning over the years, I have come to believe that a view of knowledge inspired by complexity science can open possibilities for rethinking ways to 'recognise' learning. A complexity-based view of knowledge helps expand, rather than suppress and colonise, our understandings of people's learning. So later in this chapter, I describe 'complexified' processes of learning: learning as participation in nested systems, as relations among parts rather than the sum of parts, as emergent, and as continuously slipping out of reach of the observable present and representable. At the end I suggest possible ways forward for our practices of recognising learning.

'Prior learning' and its representation

People like our applicants for advance credit are asked to assume that the knowledge-creating experience is historical, prior to the present moment of mentally remembering and reconstituting it. The learning produced through this rational reconstitution is treated as an object or product of the experience, something previously acquired and representable. In appealing to us to acknowledge this learning, they divide it into categories and represent it in forms and language recognisable to generalised academic knowledge.

False separations of mind and body

Feminists have long disparaged this Cartesian bifurcation of mind and body in a Western epistemological tradition that privileges mental detachment, the observation and calculation of the world from a disembodied and abstract rationality. This is what Donna Haraway (1991, p. 188) calls 'the god trick of seeing everything from nowhere'. Hesoon Bai (2001) argues that it is precisely this problematic illusion of a floating rationality rooted in a fundamental western split of subject and object that produces 'the predominance of the conceptual mind sustained by preoccupations with symbolic manipulation and a corresponding eclipse of the nonconceptual, that is, unmediated sensory, consciousness' (*ibid.*, p. 86). In conventional practices of recognising experiential learning such as those based on Kolb's (1984) model representing experience as 'concrete' and split from 'reflection', the observing person is distanced from her own experience – including the learning experience unfolding as she remembers and represents the 'prior learning'. Janie might have told many different stories of her work as a training developer, perhaps contradictory, or apparently illogical. But our prior learning exercise asked her to gaze on everything from nowhere, stripping her 'learning' of her subjectivity, location and embeddedness in material and social conditions. Elana Michelson (1996) asks: 'Where, precisely, are we standing when we "reflect", and what kind of self is constructed in the process?' (*ibid.*, p. 449) (see also Michelson, Chapter 7, in this volume). I wonder, when Janie shaped her experiences to reflect the properly flexible, innovative, enterprising self evoked by our institutional template, to what extent her own desires and identity become disciplined accordingly?

'Fixing' experience

In such practices of representing 'prior' learning, individual mental conceptions of events become prominent, static and separated from the interdependent commotion of people together in action with objects and language. Experience is cast as a fixed thing, separated from knowledge-making processes. Yet reflection itself is an experience, of recalling, recreating, and ruminating to make meaning of the thousands of contradictory details, to 'get grounded': finding some sense of personal control, even identity. But experience as event cannot be separated from these imaginative interpretations and re-interpretations that rely upon socially available meanings. What we imagine to be 'experience' is rooted in social discourses that influence how we perceive and name problems, which experiences become visible to us, and what knowledge we consider them to yield.

Postmodern theorists of adult education (Usher *et al.*, 1997) write that: 'to see experience as originary in relation to learning fails to recognise that any approach to using experience will generate its own representations of experience and will itself be influenced by the way experience is conceived or represented, by the framework or interpretive grid which will influence how experience is theorised' (*ibid.*, p. 100). So language, audience, purpose, and identity make the reflective act itself a performance of remembered experience, rather than a realist representation of it. Patti Lather (2000) concludes that lived experience is undecidable. What we think we see, when we reflect, 'is always already distorted':

> [Remembrance is] less a repository for what has happened than
> a production of it: language, writing, a spectacle of replication
> in an excess of intention. Remembrance is not about taking hold
> but a medium of experience, a theatre for gathering information.
> (*ibid.*, p. 154)

Emphasis on rational ordering

Critics such as these, caution against the sort of valorising of reflection that occurs in recognising and assessing experiential learning. In such renderings, reflection is treated as an unproblematic conduit from event to knowledge to representation, as Dennis Sawada (1991) has shown, transforming 'raw' experience into worthwhile learning. This centres learning in a rational knowledge-making mind, somehow rising above messy bodily dynamics to fix both experience and a singular experiencing self. The continuing emphasis on rational mind despite persuasive work on embodied knowledge (such as Varela *et al.*, 1991) is disturbing. Reflection orders, clarifies, manages and disciplines experience – which internalises relations of ruling. Those whose knowing is not so easily ordered and rationalised, like Frank Bird's, must change or suffer invisibility.

Further, in this ordering act of representation, learning is depicted as an object possessed by an individual. The webs of relationships and joint activity which caused a person to have participated in particular ways and which drew forth certain capabilities at particular times are ignored. For example, Janie's list of skills developed through giving corporate workshops are not viewed within the trajectories of her department's history, demands and supports; participants' and colleagues' histories and intentions, and so on. These environments dissolve into an invisible background, or are treated as useful resources from which the learning subject excavates learning experiences. The individual is assumed to be a stable fixed identity, an autonomous self having learning experiences. The question of how notions of prior learning contribute to this self-making are rarely asked in practice.

RPL/APEL practices: Critical concerns

Recognition and assessment of prior experiential learning [RPL/APEL] are by now highly contested practices. Critics claim that shaping and judging the worth of adults' experience through prior learning assessment processes to fit institutional standards and understandings of knowledge ensures their conformity and upholds existing dominant categories of knowledge. In North America, assessment of experiential learning is typically used to help adults gain credits in post-secondary education, theoretically saving them time and money while honouring their experiential knowledge. However Michelson (1996) claims that in the process, peoples' experiences are subjected to the interests, authority, and understandings of knowledge pervading higher education institutions. RPL practices, she argues, distort everyday experience in the process of tearing it from the changing social contexts that give it meaning, assessing and dividing it into visible/invisible knowledge categories. Human learning is thus colonised by the recogniser's gaze, which is rarely identified. Further, the ways in which processes of recognition mobilise and evoke certain identities are rarely acknowledged in practice.

Vocational accreditation

In the United Kingdom, APEL is often used for vocational accreditation. Wilma Fraser (1995) laments how the objectives of programmes such as Making Experience Count [MEC] have become linked to legitimising prior learning, within vocational and non-vocational certificating bodies, towards awarding National Vocational Qualifications [NVQ] as well as granting standing in higher education. MEC also intended to facilitate understanding and thence ownership of the learning process, to enhance self-esteem and confidence in a process designed to be andragogical in the humanistic tradition of Malcolm Knowles. The original MEC walked a careful line between the demands for accredited outcomes related to courses and a philosophy of empowering students, upholding their own life experience, and making it count.

Disjunctures between public discourse and private experience

However, Fraser argues that although originally designed to value diverse individual experience, formal and informal, RPL has restricted what counts as experience. Much potential for valuing individual experience and finding creative outlets for its expression is being eroded as market forces hold sway over issues of vocational and educational relevance. Fraser describes this as a disjuncture between public discourse and private experience, producing a fundamental paradox when the private journey of discovery and learning is brought under public scrutiny and adjudication. The underlying assumption is of a coherent unified self who excavates, narrates, and manipulates raw experience into learning. The process compels adults to construct a self to fit the APEL dimensions, and celebrates individualistic achievement: adults are what they have done.

'Different' experience

This orientation does not address social inequities, or the issue of different and often painful lessons learned from experiences related to our subjectivity as members of different cultural, economic, gendered environments. The so-called disadvantaged, claims Fraser, often experience great barriers to opportunity and fulfilment; it is unfair to measure what they have done according to institutional categories of valued and recognisable knowledge. One important area of inequity relates to the gendered nature of standards for assessing adult experience. She describes how, in one example, student autobiographies were adjudicated. Fewer than 60% of women's auto-biographies passed compared to 80% of men's. Fraser claims this was due to men's life patterns – self-chosen events pursuing rational goals - being more aligned to institutional ideas. Women's life stories were parts of others' lives, with diffuse voices and shifting identities.

These critical arguments underscore the potential for pedagogy to colonise and control adults' experiential learning, ultimately creating further social problems despite its best intentions to help people. Judy Harris (2000) suggests a complete re-theorisation of RPL, scrutinising its own boundaries defining knowledge and selves through power relations, to truly realise its potential to restore equity to credentialing practices. But Harris also is insistent that RPL practices offer hope for reclaiming individuals' knowledge and life experiences in their education. One way forward, I believe, is through a different understanding of experiential learning. For me, hopeful directions are opened through complexity science, particularly the early theorising of learning informed by complexity science[1] that are now emerging.

A complexified view of learning

Discussions of learning informed by complexity science (Doll, 1993; Sumara and Davis, 1997; Varela *et al.*, 1991) highlight the phenomenon of co-emergence in complex adaptive systems. From this perspective learning is defined as expanded possibilities for action, or becoming 'capable of more sophisticated, more flexible, more creative action' (Davis *et al.*, 2000). The first premise is that the systems represented by person, learning and context are inseparable, and the second that change occurs from emerging systems affected by the intentional tinkering of one with the other. Humans are completely interconnected with the systems in which they act through a series of 'structural couplings' (Maturana and Varela, 1987). That is, when two systems coincide, the 'perturbations' of one system excites responses in the structural dynamics of the other. The resultant 'coupling' creates a new transcendent unity of action and identities that could not have been achieved independently by participants.

Embodied action and co-emergence
Francisco Varela (1999) explains that:

> Perception does not consist in the recovery of a pre-given
> world, but rather in the *perceptual guidance* of action in the
> world that is inseparable from our sensorimotor capacities [. . .]
> cognition consists not of representations but of embodied
> action. (*ibid.*, p 17, emphasis mine)

A workplace project, for example, is a collective activity in which interaction both enfolds and renders visible the participants, the objects mediating their actions and dialogue, the problem space that they define together, and the emerging plan or solution they devise. As each person contributes, she changes the interactions and the emerging object of focus; other participants are changed, the relational space among them all changes, and the looping-back changes the contributor's actions and subject position within the collective activity. This is 'mutual specification' (Varela *et al.*, 1991), the fundamental dynamic of systems constantly engaging in joint action and interaction. Environment and learner emerge together in the process of cognition, although this is a false dichotomy: *context* is not a separate background for any particular system such as an individual actor. Brent Davis *et al.* (2000) describe co-emergence as 'a new understanding of cognition':

> Rather than being cast as a locatable process or phenomenon, cognition has been reinterpreted as a joint participation, a choreography. An agent's knowing, in this sense, are those patterns of acting that afford it a coherence – that is, that make it discernible as a unity, a wholeness, identity. The question, 'Where does cognition happen?' is thus equivalent to, 'Who or what is perceived to be acting?' In this way, a rain forest is cognitive – and humanity is necessarily participating in its cogitations/evolutions. That is, our habits of thought are entwined and implicated in unfolding global conditions. (*ibid.*, p. 74)

Our individual reconstructions of events too often focus on the learning figure (most usually, ourselves) and ignore the complex interactions constituting 'background'. Complexity theory interrupts the natural tendency to seek clear boundaries between figures and grounds, and focuses on the relationships binding humans and non-humans (e.g. desks, cell phones, bacteria, buildings, language, smells, memories) together in multiple fluctuations in complex systems. Thus, argue complexity theorists, the boundaries between self and non-self (nature as well as society) are actually more permeable and the flow between them more continuous than we might be prepared to accept.

Complex adaptive systems

For a brief overview of some principles underlying this work, a good starting place is the complex adaptive system. A person is a whole system, made up of many biological (digestive, neuromuscular, etc.), sensory, mental, and emotional systems. These systems in turn are made up of parts, like organs, which are complete systems in themselves. But a person is also a part of other systems: family systems and social systems, which in turn are nested in national systems, which are part of even larger forces like global market systems. A system is *self-modifying* – sensitive and responding to changes within it and around it - in constant dialogue with its environment. Its many components are always alive, always interacting creatively with parts directly around them. These interactions form patterns all by themselves – they do not organise according to some sort of externally imposed blueprint – so we say that such systems are *self-organising*.

The outcome of these dynamic interactions of a system's parts is *unpredictable*. So many things are going on all at once that the system is quite literally impossible to understand by breaking it down and studying these parts or by trying to reduce it to a series of causes and effects. Thus everything from a weather system to an economic system to a human being is described as a *complex* system, rather than simply a complicated one with a mechanical, predictable system of parts, such as a car or a coffee-maker. A complex system is never stable or fixed, but always *adapting* in unpredictable ways. The key to a healthy system – able to adapt creatively to changing conditions – is *diversity* among its parts. A human body, for example, relies on highly specialised subsystems that not only each respond to different circumstances and different needs, but also have learned to cohabit and communicate with one another. One final interesting characteristic of many complex adaptive systems is *self-similarity* in their patterns. A large fern, for example, closely resembles the structures of one branch of the fern, and one single leaf of the branch. Thus, a system can be studied by looking closely at one part as well as at the whole body of relationships among parts.

Disturbance and disequilibrium

All complex adaptive systems learn – where learning is defined as transformation that expands a learner's potential range of action. Research on HIV-AIDs systems, for example, demonstrates that the immune system remembers, forgets, recognises, hypothesises, errors, adapts, and thus learns (Davis *et al.*, 2000). Forests and other ecosystems, weather systems, corporations, schools, and market systems all learn. Part of this learning is the continuous creation of alternate actions and responses to changing situations, undertaken by the system's parts. More sudden transformation can occur in response to a major shock to the system, a *disturbance* that throws it into *disequilibrium*. Computer-generated images of systems undergoing disequilibrium show that they go through a phase of swinging between extremes, before self-organising gradually into a new pattern or identity that can continue co-habiting with and adapting to the other systems in its environment. After the episode the system resumes its continuous improvisation, although more resilient and more flexible to learn its way through further anomalies it encounters.

Learning, then, does not simply occur within the worlds of isolated individuals, although human beings do function as whole systems that learn, adapt, organise, and transform themselves as distinct identities. But human beings are also part of larger systems that learn, adapt, organise and transform themselves as distinct identities. As parts of these continuously learning larger systems, humans themselves bear characteristics of larger patterns, larger identities – a little like the single fern leaf resembling the whole fern plant. But individuals also participate, contributing through multiple interactions at micro-levels. The outcome of all these dynamic interactions of a system's parts is unpredictable and inventive.

Continuous emergence

Learning is thus understood as continuous invention and exploration, pro- duced through relations among consciousness, identity, action and inter- action, objects and structural dynamics. New possibilities for action are constantly emerging among these interactions of complex systems, and cognition occurs in the possibility for unpredictable shared action. Know- ledge cannot be contained in any one element or dimension of a system, for knowledge is constantly emerging and spilling into other systems. For exam- ple, studies of safety knowledge in the workplace (Gherardi and Nicolini, 2000) show that experiential learning emerges and circulates through exchanges among both human and non-human elements in a net of action. The foreman negotiates the language of the assessment report with the industrial inspector, the equipment embeds a history of use possibilities and constraints, deadlines and weather conditions pressure a particular job, and workers adapt a tool or safety procedure for particular problems – depending on who is watching.[2] No actor has an essential self or knowledge outside a given network: nothing is given in the order of things, but rather performs itself into existence.

Such studies of objects, people and learning as co-emerging systems are helping to challenge our conceptual subject/object splits, refusing the notion that learning is a product of experience, and revealing a complexified view of learning as woven into fully embodied nets of ongoing action, invention, social relations and history in complex systems (see also Pokorny, Chapter 13, this volume).

Limitations of complexity theory

Like all theories of learning, those informed by complexity science bear certain limitations. The first is that complexity scientists do not tend to discuss social power as a key dimension of systems' evolution. Nor do they emphasise the practices and discourses of human culture in explaining how communities emerge. Some reject the structural view of a dominant elite subordinating other groups as too deterministic or simplistic (rarely, outside of despotic regimes, can a group of intentional oppressors be clearly delineated). They also reject the separation of individual from the sociocultural history and dynamics of the collective. Sumara and Davis (1997) suggest that traditional frameworks of domination/oppression perpetuate negative views of power. Systems theories of learning place much greater emphasis on mutual affect, collectivity, and co-emergence of human action, objects, and environment.

However, the question of actors' positionality within a system remains. Power flows through the system according to how, in everyday interactions, people take up positions and understand others' positions in relation to themselves. The positions are in constant flux, for they change each time someone turns to a new activity or subject. The consequent directions of power and changing locations influence different individuals' ability to participate meaningfully in the systems. Individuals potentially become vulnerable to a few who manipulate the system's discourses to sustain their own power, ensuring that their experiences become the most valued knowledge in the collective. There appears not to be, among complexity theory perspectives, satisfactory responses to important questions for RPL: Whose knowledge, among the various participants in the system, is afforded the greatest influence over the movements and directions of the system? And who gains the power to grant recognition to others' learning?

Finally, although Sumara and Davis (1997) claim that personal subjectivities are by no means abandoned in complexity theory, but rather understood as 'mutually specifying' one another, it is unclear how individual agency and integrity are maintained in the 'commingling of consciousness' (*ibid.*, p. 110) that supposedly links community and cognition seamlessly through interaction. Those who emphasise subjectivity might wonder how, without educational assistance, connections are made between one particular context of an individual's personal history and his or her dynamic processes of change within other systems.

For those whose view of learning is informed by constructivist, psychological, feminist or critical theories, these issues may be seen as limitations. In fact learning theory and research using complexity science continues to address them, and to explore dialogue with perspectives rooted in fundamentally different ontologies (see for example, Davis, 2003). For the present discussion, these issues serve to remind us that no one narrative of learning, including that offered by complexity theory, is sufficient in and of itself to transcend and collapse within it all other conceptions. Nonetheless, as shown in the next section, insights drawn from complexity theory can be fruitfully applied to practice in efforts to address concerns raised earlier about RPL practices.

Conclusion: implications of complexity theory for RPL practices

When learning is viewed through the lens of complexity science, important questions are raised about the process of its recognition. What and who participated in a situation recognised as significant in changing behaviour and individual understandings? What emerged that yielded 'expanded possibilities for action'? How did participating elements (people, actions, objects, cultural patterns) interact in ways that effected mutual expansion? One person's story of this complexity of course cannot capture, nor even pretend awareness, of all the interactions or even the patterns that emerged. Further, that person's story is told from a changed perspective – the consciousness that emerged through lived participation in the situation and the experience of imaginative re-interpretation of it.

New questions open in considering the audience who draws forth this recognition of learning. Who is doing the recognising, and how is this actor (whether a goal, institutional checklist, language, knowledge discipline, or individual assessor) now implicated in the emergence of learning and action connected with the situation being examined? What perturbations are caused by the introduction of this actor to the system, and what new structural couplings, alignments and learning co-emerge?

While addressing these sorts of questions may be difficult in an institutional context where those championing RPL are motivated by sincere commitment to champion adult students' experiential knowledge, they are not impossible. Three suggestions are described below, including: emphasising learning as a process in complex systems distinguishing representation from learning as a constructed (distortive) act, and foregrounding the participation of the recogniser in the learning system.

From product to process
The first task is to shift emphasis from thinking of learning as a *product* that has been acquired by an individual, to understanding learning as a *process* involving complex systems that unfold continuously, even (especially) during

practices of representation such as RPL. As process, learning invites questions about the rhythms of joint activity in a situation, the nature of the interactions among people/objects/ideas, small changes that occurred over time, puzzlements, emotions, and desires. Adults can still be invited to recall and 'story' situations they consider important to their personal understandings. However, a process orientation might ask for more descriptive details about their everyday participation, probing their recollections of who/what they engaged with and how, rather than requiring them to codify these stories as abstract lists of acquired knowledge and skill. Questions might encourage people to reflect beyond their own participation as if they were central actors in systems, and ask about the larger dynamics at work in the situation, the expectations and shared behavioural patterns, the histories mobilising the situation, the participation of others and its effect on their own behaviours.

Highlight the constructed representation

The second task is to treat the representation of the co-emergent learning process as a fixed artefact that excludes, even distorts, much of the complex system being considered: a simplistic sketch rather than the process itself. Different forms of representation drawing on visual art, poetry, found objects as well as story telling may help interrupt formal standardised written representations. But in the final analysis, as Osberg and Biesta (2003) point out, all representation *misrepresents* a knowledge system by always excluding the change in consciousness that moved a living experience to its own representation. And, all representations reflect individuals' partial, limited perspectives – that are not often aware of the received meanings and social discourses constituting them. Nonetheless individuals' stories of participation in situations are valuable, provided their limitations as representations of learning are acknowledged. When people are encouraged to return to these texts, expanding, playing with and inverting them, restorying and adding additional insights as new versions emerge, they engage recursively with the representation as an undecidable object in their unfolding learning. People might even be encouraged to consider ways this object participates in their learning practices.

Highlight the 'recognisers'

The third task in RPL is to make explicit the problem of who and what is doing the 'recognising', and the politics of this recognition. Adult learners who request formal acknowledgement or accreditation of their learning histories may not see the limited partiality of the recogniser, and the assumptions guiding the gaze that only perceives and values the knowledge created by selected forms of their participation but ignores the rest. At the very least,

RPL processes should make these assumptions clear. Greater institutional reflexivity is required to name assumptions about epistemic claims and forms of representation, and even to examine these critically to identify and expand overly narrow knowledge categories. Clearly this involves flexible conceptions of knowledge as well as political negotiations, for in many institutions the unit handling the RPL procedures must translate its terms and criteria to articulate with the abstract codified disciplines of academic knowledge in the broader institution which are not going to change anytime soon.

In practical terms, these tasks suggest RPL processes guided more by conversations and portfolios than written checklists. They also suggest a longer-term process involving multiple meetings with learners. Many pedagogical resources offer suggestions that might be applied to develop creative, feasible ways to occasion such conversations. Pierre Dominicé (1992), for example, describes approaches to construct what he calls 'educational biographies' in groups, where the learning stories are situated in systems (both the learner's and the environments' histories), and continually expanded in analytic conversation that reflexively foregrounds the very effects of learning's representation on the group and the individual story-teller.

Educators' possible roles

An educator might be helpful in these processes as an interpreter. The activity is assisting participants to name what has been and continues to unfold around them and inside them, to continually rename these changing nuances, and to unlock the tenacious grasp of old categories, restrictive or destructive language that strangles emerging possibilities. Further, particularly in RPL processes consisting of group dialogues held over a period of time, an educator might function as a story-maker, tracing and meaningfully recording the interactions of the actors and objects in the expanding spaces. An educator might help participants to make community sense of the patterns emerging within the group's complex system, and understand their own involvements in these patterns. Educators can introduce or draw attention to the system's disturbances that create learning potential, and help amplify these disturbances by focusing, naming, and highlighting their significance. Educators can also provide feedback loops to a system as participants experiment with different patterns leading out from disequilibrium. Naturally, educators must be clear about their own entanglement and interests in the emerging systems of thought and action. Questions for facilitators are offered by Sumara and Davis (1997): How does one trace the various tangled involvements of a particular activity in a complex system, while attending carefully to one's own involvement as participant? How can actors' and objects' trajectories of movement be recorded in a meaningful way?

These practices and questions mean that Janie's and Frank Bird's and our other stack of 'prior learning experience' files would not be dealt with in one afternoon's committee meeting. In fact our first act might have been a com-mittee gathering to talk about what knowledge we valued in our programme and what different ways we might recognise it. Perhaps we would have tried representing our own 'prior learning' to experiment with different ways of expressing it and to identify what vital dynamics were excluded in our representations. We might have gathered prospective students in a series of group dialogues, in-person or technologically-mediated, to explore their learning stories. And certainly, rather than shutting Janie and Frank away from our rather perfunctory assessments of their stories, we would have enlisted their assistance in making sense of these. At the very least we can make transparent to them the constructed and imprecise nature of the whole process.

So while not particularly new and certainly not easy, these suggestions informed by complexity theory may help to reconfigure RPL practices to avoid separating individual and environment, mind and body, prior and present, learning and doing. When learning is understood to be continuously co-emergent with persons and environment, part of complex adaptive systems occurring at micro and macro levels, it simply makes no sense to treat knowledge as a product that is carried around like a handbag, able to spill its contents upon request by RPL assessors. The notion of co-emergence directs our gaze to the relationships among things and people rather than the things themselves. When we consider these relationships, we focus on the currents of participation that are apparent, the limits of language blinding us to what is not, and the indelible traces we each have on the other.

References

Bai, H. (2001), 'Beyond the educated mind: towards a pedagogy of mindfulness, body and mind' in Hocking, B., Haskell, A. and Linds, W. (eds) *Body and Mind: Exploring Possibility Through Education* (pp. 86–99), Vermont, NH: Foundation for Educational Renewal.

Davis, B. (2003), *Inventions of Teaching: A Genealogy*, Mahwah, NJ: Erlbaum.

Davis, B., Sumara, D.J. and Luce-Kapler, R. (2000), *Engaging Minds: Learning and Teaching in a Complex World*, Mahwah, NJ: Erlbaum.

Doll, Jr., W. (1993), *A Post-Modern Perspective on Curriculum*, New York: Teachers College Press.

Dominicé, P. (2000), *Learning from our Lives: Using Educational Biographies with Adults*, San Francisco: Wiley/Jossey-Bass.

Fraser, W. (1995), *Learning from Experience: Empowerment or Incorporation?*, Leicester: NIACE.

Gherardi, S. and Nicolini, D. (2000), 'To transfer is to transform: The circulation of safety knowledge', *Organization*, 7(2): 329–48.

Haraway, D. (1991), 'Situated knowledges' in *Simians, Cyborgs and Women: The Reinvention of Nature*, London, New York: Routledge.

Harris, J. (2000), *RPL: Power, Pedagogy and Possibility*, Pretoria: Human Sciences Research Council.

Karpiak, I. (2000), 'Evolutionary theory and the new sciences', *Studies in Continuing Education*, 22(1): 29–44.

Kolb, D.A. (1984), *Experiential Learning*, Englewood Cliffs, NJ: Prentice-Hall.

Lather, P. (2000), 'Reading the image of Rigoberto Menchú: Undecidability and language lessons', *Qualitative Studies in Education*, 13(2): 153–62.

Law, J. and Hassard, J. (1999), *Actor Network Theory and After*, Oxford: Blackwell Publishing.

Maturana, H. and Varela, F. (1987), *The Tree of Knowledge: The Biological Roots of Human Understanding*, Boston: Shambhala.

Michelson, E. (1996), 'Usual suspects: Experience, reflection, and the (en)gendering of knowledge', *International Journal of Lifelong Education*, 15(6): 438–54.

Osberg, D. and Biesta, G. (2003), 'Complexity, representation and the epistemology of schooling' in Conference Proceedings of the First Conference of Complexity Science and Educational Research, www.complexityandeducation.ualberta/ca/pub03proceedings.htm

Sawada, D. (1991), 'Deconstructing reflection', *The Alberta Journal of Educational Research*, 37(4): 349–66.

Sumara, D. and Davis, B. (1997), 'Enlarging the space of the possible: complexity, complicity, and action research practices' in Sumara, D. and Carson, T. (eds) *Action Research as a Living Practice* (pp. 299–312), London and New York: Peter Lang.

Usher, R., Bryant, I. and Johnston, R. (1997), *Adult Education and the Postmodern Challenge: Learning Beyond the Limits*, London and New York: Routledge.

Varela, F.J., Thompson, E. and Rosch, E. (1991), *The Embodied Mind: Cognitive Science and Human Experience*, Cambridge, MA: MIT Press.

Varela, F.J. (1999), *Ethical Know-How: Action, Wisdom and Cognition*, Stanford, CA: Stanford University Press.

Notes

[1] William Doll (1993) suggests a new, more fluid and emergent way to develop curriculum and classroom practice. Irene Karpiak (2000) develops a model for higher education teaching based on complexity theory. And in Canada, Brent Davis, Dennis Sumara and Rebecca Luce-Kapler (2000) have created teaching ideas, research approaches, and curriculum theory applying complexity theory to what they now call ecological learning.

[2] This explanation draws upon 'actor-network theory', a particular formation of sociology of technology articulated by writers such as Law and Hassard (1999). It has been included here for two reasons: (1) actor-network theory shares with complexity science the notion of co-emergence of actants, cognition and environment, and the erasure of distinctions between subject/object, particular/universal, and human/nonhuman; and (2) educational research and studies of work-based learning are increasingly taking up actor-network theory to examine experiential learning.

chapter fifteen

Understanding the transformative dimension of RPL

Susan Whittaker, Ruth Whittaker and Paula Cleary

Introduction

The impact of participation in RPL can be transformative for the individuals involved. This transformation can occur in the form of changes in identity. This was reflected in the findings of an EU-funded Socrates project which explored learners' experiences of the RPL process in five European countries (Cleary *et al.*, 2002). Evidence for this transformative aspect of participation in RPL is suggested by participants to be increased self-awareness as a learner, increased self-confidence, and increased self-esteem (see also, Osman, Chapter 10, this volume). In most cases these outcomes are neither explicit, nor anticipated, but are in fact regarded by learners as the most valuable aspect of the RPL experience.

This chapter will explore the extent to which participants who engage in RPL undertake four levels of redefinition: a redefinition of what learning is, or can be; a redefinition of what a learner is; as a result of this, a redefinition of their own experiences as learning experiences; and finally a redefinition of themselves as a learner. The processes through which RPL acts as a transformative mechanism will be theorised by drawing on the principles of symbolic interactionism (Blumer, 1969; Mead, 1934; Meltzer *et al.*, 1975); social identity theory (Tajfel, 1978; Turner, 1985; Ellemers *et al.*, 1999) and situated learning (McLellan, 1996; Wenger, 1998).

These theoretical approaches all place the development of identities in a changeable social context. (When we use the word 'social' in this chapter, we are referring to the aspects of the environment, including other people, in relation to which an individual acts, interacts or reacts). The theories suggest that this context is the location for activities and relationships through which one can learn norms and situate oneself in relation to others, which can, in turn, lead to a changed identity or identities. They also suggest that the key to this process is the way one learns to attribute meaning to experiences, which then leads one to attribute new meaning to oneself in relation to these experiences.

In this chapter, the ideas underpinning these three theories will be summarised and applied to RPL, in particular to the reflective process. It will explore the extent to which the proposed theories can contribute to an understanding of participation in RPL as transformative, particularly in terms of developing an identity as a learner, and will consider the implications of such an understanding for practice.

Understanding experiential learning

In recognising prior informal, non-formal or experiential learning, a common approach has been to engage learners in a process of critical reflection through which they first describe their experiences using everyday language, and then actively reflect upon these experiences in order to identify the learning, in terms of the skills and knowledge they feel they have gained (Boud, Keogh and Walker, 1985, 1996; Brockbank and McGill, 1998; Mezirow *et al.*, 1990; Mezirow, 1998; Moon, 1999; Schön, 1991). As part of this process, a tutor or facilitator normally provides guidance and support, and validates the learning.

In general, attempts to understand how people learn have been dominated by concerns about individuals' psychological and cognitive processes and have been less concerned with the social, political and cultural dimensions of learning. Fenwick (2000, 2003) provides a useful analysis of the theoretical underpinnings of experiential learning. She argues that such theories are dominated by a psychological-constructivist perspective which stresses the individualistic nature of experiential learning and the concept of '(critical) reflection'. The constructivist perspective derives from the belief that learning is best understood in terms of the individual's cognitive processes. Individuals receive information or knowledge, either passively or more actively, and engage with that information to form constructs and understandings which provide them with meaning.

Much of the existing literature on RPL focuses on particular examples of implementation. Theoretical understandings and underpinnings are less well developed. Theories in use revolve principally around the notion of experiential learning cycles as the key to understanding processes of learning. There are a variety of models of these cycles with different suggestions about the nature and number of stages involved in the learning process. As many as seventeen different four-stage learning cycle models have been identified (Juch, 1983).

Perhaps the best-known model is that of Kolb (1984, 1993). His experiential learning cycle has provided a basis for much of the understanding of RPL in the UK today. His particular four-stage process derives from John Dewey, Kurt Lewin and Jean Piaget, all of whom stressed the importance of experience as a basis for education. Kolb (1984) argues that learning is: best understood as a continuous process grounded in experience; involves a resolution of conflicts between different ways of viewing the world; is an holistic human activity, not specific just to notions of perception or cognition; involves interaction between the learner and their environment; and is the process of creating knowledge. Learning is presented as involving a process of interaction between the individual and the environment in a broad sense.

Building on this notion, we were interested in exploring the extent to which theories that propose ideas about the importance of context and the significance of social interaction in identity development can add to our understanding of RPL processes. More recently, for example, researchers have begun to address the issue of learning as a social act through theories of situated learning, symbolic interactionism and in terms of social identity (for example, Bloomer and Hodkinson, 2000; Claxton, 2002; Clegg and McNulty, 2002; Fowler and Mayes, 1999; Gallacher *et al.*, 2000; Whittaker and Mayes, 2001). In these theories the focus is on the interaction between learners and their social contexts, and about how identities are influenced by these contexts.

Situated learning

One of the early theorists to challenge the dichotomy between cognitive processes and social interaction was Vygotsky (1962, 1978). He argues that consciousness is inextricably linked to processes of socialisation, and that social interaction is crucial to full cognitive development.

A clear impact of Vygotsky's ideas on learning theory can be seen in the situated learning model (McLellan, 1996). The model aims to make the learning activities that occur in the classroom more meaningful and effective. Lave and Wenger's (1991) development of the model took the ideas into contexts that were less clearly learning-oriented; into the realms of informal, everyday learning. Proponents of the situated learning model define meaningful learning as the understanding and skill development that results from participation in 'authentic' activities – that is, activities that are contextualised rather than abstract and require the use of techniques such as problem-solving, reasoning, critical thinking, collaboration, story-telling, reflection, scaffolding and cognitive apprenticeship (Brown *et al.*, 1989), but used in the way that 'experts' in the field of study would use them.

One of the most widely adopted notions to have emerged from the situated learning perspective is that of 'communities of practice' (Lave and Wenger, 1991; Wenger, 1998), described by its authors as a 'social theory of learning'. Lave and Wenger developed the concept from ethnographic studies of workplace practices, defining them as social networks that exist around the sustained pursuit of a shared practice. According to the theory, practice at the heart of a community occurs in a social and historical context, and relies on sustained generational encounters between new and more experienced members of the community.

The process of becoming a member of a community of practice has been termed legitimate peripheral participation. This involves moving from the edge of a community to its centre through increased engagement with the practice. Learning is seen as not just the learning of facts, ideas and skills, but is about learning to be – about becoming. That is, there is an identification process within this learning: moving from being a novice to an expert is not just about learning in terms of gaining knowledge and ability; it is about taking on a new identity through that learning. Within the constraints of a social milieu, one comes to understand the possibilities and limits of what one can be.

Situated learning is an idea that emphasises interaction between people with different degrees of context-specific experience and knowledge, and the role of this interaction in learning to be more like those with greater experience and knowledge. This emphasis on context-specific interaction in identification processes is also seen in symbolic interactionism, though this latter perspective has a wider focus than interaction between 'experts' and 'novices'.

Symbolic interactionism

Meltzer *et al.* (1975, p. 1) describe three premises of symbolic interactionism:

> First, human beings act towards things on the basis of the
> meanings that the things have for them. Secondly, these
> meanings are a product of social interaction in society. Thirdly,
> these meanings are modified and handled through an
> interpretive process that is used by each individual in dealing
> with the signs he/she encounters.

Mead (1934), whose ideas were highly influential in the development of symbolic interactionism, argued that the self cannot develop outside of social context, which he defined as social experiences and relationships. He proposed that the ability to treat the self as an object in its own right is vital to the process of the development of the self, 'by taking the attitudes of other individuals toward himself within a social environment or context of experience and behaviour in which both he and they are involved' (*ibid.*, p. 146). Awareness of, and incorporating the attitudes of the other are therefore purported to play a crucial role in the nature of interaction and the development of the self. Mead refers to the 'generalised other', a concept representing the attitudes of the whole community, which exercises control over the individual's conduct. He also believed that all behaviour is cumulative and takes place with reference to both future and past events in people's lives.

The concepts of 'role' and 'reference groups' are also important in symbolic interactionism. Depending on the perspective of the interactionist, role-making or role-taking take place in the interaction between the individual and society. Role-making emphasises individual agency and creativity; role-taking emphasises the internalisation of prescribed roles. For Sherif (1953, p. 285), reference groups can be defined as 'those groups to which the individual relates himself as a part or to which he aspires to relate himself psychologically'. In relation to this latter point, Merton and Kitt (1969, p. 289) describe the process of anticipatory socialisation:

> For the individual who adopts the values of a group to which he
> aspires but does not belong, this orientation may serve the twin
> functions of aiding his rise into that group and of easing his
> adjustment after he has become part of it.

In lifelong learning research, symbolic interactionism has been used in the development of the concept of learning careers (for example, Bloomer and

Hodkinson, 1997; Gallacher *et al.*, 2000). The theory is used to try and understand how an individual's experiences of learning over a period of time positively or negatively impact on the development of learner identity. The influence of the theory on the concept of learning careers can be seen in this by the importance placed on the emphasis given to interaction with aspects of the social context.

Symbolic interactionism therefore emphasises the role of the other in identification processes, including individuals taking on a social identity to enhance the view others have of them; having attitudes or displaying behaviours that fit with the values of a group; and being perceived by others as having an identity which can lead individuals to act in ways appropriate to that identity. As well as these, identity change is proposed to potentially result from situational change, and could occur to fit with a past or future image of the self. To add to this sociological view of social influence on identification processes, we would like to add a psychological view.

Social identity theory

Social identity theory (Ellemers *et al.*, 1999; Tajfel, 1978, 1982; Turner, 1985, 1999) has as its focus the process of becoming a member of a group or category and of becoming committed to that membership. It asserts that a social identity is a distinct social category, but may only be recognised as such by people who have reason to compare themselves to this category of person. The existence of such a social category and of its distinctiveness would be determined by a set of norms being attributed to the category or label. It is proposed that people develop their own understanding of themselves and of others as belonging to the social category by comparing their own behaviours, attitudes, values, beliefs, and so on, with those that fit with the norms of the category.

Ellemers, Kortekaas and Ouwerwerk (1999) describe three components to social identity: the cognitive component, the evaluative component and the affective component. The cognitive component is considered to be present in an individual when the processes of self-categorisation (Turner, 1985) and depersonalisation have occurred. Self-categorisation indicates a willingness to define oneself by membership of the category. The level of an individual's self-categorisation corresponds with the degree to which they feel they fit within their view of a 'typical' person with that social identity. They are, however, likely to be aware of differences between themselves and this typical other. The extent to which these differences negatively affect the individual's sense of identity depends on the importance they attribute to the differences. The proposition is that not all norms have to be adhered to in order to have a social identity. Individuals themselves can, at least at times, exercise selectivity over which norms are the most necessary. Depersonalisation would indicate that individuals see themselves more as members of the group than as unique persons when in relevant situations.

The perception of the evaluative component in a social identity depends on the extent to which similarities with others who have the identity, and differences to those perceived as not having the identity, allow a person to evaluate their group membership as favourably as possible. A positive self-perception, often referred to as high self-esteem, attached to an identity would appear to be based on an individual's subjective evaluation of the societal position of that category of people, rather than on an objective evaluation of the group's status (Stets and Burke, 2000).

On the subject of status, the activation of learner identity would depend in part on the permeability of this social identity. Groups that are of a higher status to one's present status are likely to be perceived as less permeable than those of a lower status. Relative status could be determined either by the individual or by wider society.

The evaluation of the group, and any positive self-perception derived from membership of it, can have an impact on the extent to which social identification is felt. This is the level of commitment to the identity, which is the affective component of social identity. There are several ways in which commitment to an identity may be understood or evaluated. First, the relationships to which an identity can be tied can influence degree of commitment. Secondly, level of commitment might be exhibited by the desire to maintain the identity. Thirdly, commitment may be shown in the extent to which the identity is played out in situations that would not be described as relevant contexts. Fourthly, the identity, or at least the situations to which the identity is attached, may help fulfil needs and meet goals. Finally, commitment to the identity may be influenced by having achieved that identity or having voluntarily become a member of the group, rather than being attributed membership.

One can hold an identity to which one feels little commitment, and one can be committed to an identity that one does not hold. Along these lines, Cinnirella (1998) describes 'anticipatory identification' as present when individuals or subgroups of larger social categories attempt to gain a new desired social identity, and perhaps abandon an old social identity at the same time. This can elicit information-seeking and advance the preparation for identity change. For anticipatory identification to take place, an individual must perceive that group boundaries are permeable, and that desired possible social identities are available and attainable to that individual. We can see in this notion of anticipatory identification a clear relationship with the earlier notion of anticipatory socialisation *vis-à-vis* reference groups, and also links with the concept of legitimate peripheral participation.

Comparison with others underlies social identity theory's view of identity development and maintenance. In this, we can see again the predominant role of 'others' in the theorisation of the influence of social factors on social identification.

Summarising the theories

These have necessarily been short summaries of three perspectives on identity development and maintenance. It is important to acknowledge that all these theories are subject to criticism and challenge. 'Identity' and 'learning' are both contested concepts, and views differ widely on what constitutes the 'social context' and which aspects of that context have a significant impact on both identity and learning. This summary of some key assertions made by these three theories simply demonstrates common threads in the conception of learning as a social act or process, which supply the basis of a conceptual-isation of the RPL process in these terms.

There are, as can be seen from these outlines, significant points of overlap between the ideas of social identification presented in these three theories, if not in exact terminology. They all place social identification in a social context. Key to their definitions of the social context is the concept of the other. We can also see the importance given to notions of norms and practices. Essentially, they propose the importance of what we do and with whom we interact, and the meanings attached to these behaviours and interactions in relevant social contexts.

There are, in these theories, a whole set of ideas around interaction with others. One suggestion is that influence on identification can come from interaction with those more knowledgeable or expert in an area in which an individual is involved or aspires to be involved, or those with a more developed social identity in relation to that area. These others can serve as a point of comparison, allowing the individuals to position their own identity, and possibly provide a model to which they aspire or wish to avoid. Another suggestion is that these types of others can be seen to have a view of the individual which is valid, and whose view should therefore be taken on board in that individual's self-perception.

An alternative type of other is someone who does not have the social identity, or has the same level of identity as the individual, whose views are considered important enough by the individual to take on in their self-perception. For example, the individual may feel that taking on or maintaining an identity will enhance how significant others see them.

These points also link closely to the idea that comparison with others can play an important role in social identification. 'Others' might be perceived to have a more developed version of the social identity in question. However, these others equally may not serve as a model of a desired social identity. They may be others who are similar to the individual, in ways relevant to that identity. Comparing themselves to these others might serve to locate the individual in relation to that identity. There may equally be others who the individual does not wish to be like, and this may encourage the development or maintenance of an identity that allows them to perceive themselves as different to these people.

There is an important suggestion in all of this that one can aspire to a social identity or can be committed to a future social identity. Such an identity may be desired or expected, and depends on being able to have a view of oneself in the future. It also depends on the perceived availability or permeability of the identity. The latter point could be influenced by others – by comparison with others – or by being taught directly or indirectly the norms of that identity by others, an individual can develop a view of whether they are ever likely to hold that identity.

An understanding and/or adherence to norms of the identity are in all cases considered to be a necessary part of having a social identity. Norms can be defined as how one acts, communicates and understands, and the values and beliefs one holds. Having a particular identity does not necessarily mean adherence to all the norms associated with it. Others (or the self) may indicate which norms are considered most necessary, or desirable, for that identity.

Identity-specific practices, activities or behaviours are proposed to be an important set of norms. Practices are not only a question of engaging with others, responding to situations and social contexts, having shared goals, needs or values, all of which can form part of 'shared practices', but they are a question of the meanings attributed to all these aspects. It is principally in how these aspects are interpreted that the connection with identification processes can be found. And it is principally through interacting with others that the interpretation comes.

All of these ideas about the influence of relationships with others on the development of social identity suggest that they will lead to some change in the person – either in terms of how they define themselves, how they define others, the value they place on different aspects of themselves, their vision of their future, the practices in which they engage, or the meanings which they attribute to physical, social and symbolic objects.

Development of learner identity through participation in RPL

Our suggestion is that participation in an RPL process has the potential to alter social identities, specifically by providing a context for the development of an identity as a learner. If the RPL process is the social context for this, the questions we need to consider are: who are the others and how can they influence this identity development; and what would the norms of that identity be?

The RPL process generally involves the redefinition of the candidate's experiences as learning experiences. Attention has been paid by various authors to the importance of critical reflection in the process (for example, Boud *et al.*, 1985, 1996; Brockbank and McGill, 1998; Mezirow *et al.*, 1990; Mezirow, 1998; Moon, 1999; Schön, 1991). Boreham (1987, p. 89) for example, notes that it holds the key to interpreting and understanding the learner's experiences.

RPL is a process that requires candidates to broaden their understanding of what can be viewed as learning. By redefining previous experiences as learning, they may be able to gain a better understanding of what it means to be a learner, assuming an acceptance of the notion that to be a learner requires participation in learning activities. In relation to the theories above, to accept this notion is to accept that learning is an 'authentic activity' of learners, the common practice in a community of practice, or an expected behaviour or norm associated with learner identity. This recognition of fitting in with a key aspect of being a learner could therefore help the development of a learner identity, or reinforce an existing view of themselves as a learner.

The role of others

A form of social influence on the redefinition of activities, that can in turn influence the redefinition of participants' identities, is through the recognition they can get from others. This applies not only to the reflective process but also to the act of validation that follows it. The tutor, and any other involved in the reflective process, can help the participant see what they have done in terms of the learning it involved. The tutor, on the basis of being seen as an 'expert', has views which may be perceived as particularly valuable by the participant in this regard. Someone with greater knowledge can encourage participants to regard their experiences as learning experiences; reinforce the participant's understanding of the norms or practices of learning and being a learner; and also reinforce their willingness to apply these norms to themselves. This external recognition is one way the influence of others can play a role in the redefinition of an individual's identity.

Another way would be through other participants in the process. This can include those with whom the participant may be in direct contact. It could equally include those whose existence is more abstract than concrete (for example, others that the participant is aware of who are going through, or have gone through, this process, but with whom they have not actually met or communicated). Other participants, as well as the tutor, can supply a point of comparison. Participants may recognise similarities with other participants that encourage them all to see themselves as learners; or they may consider themselves different to others in ways that strengthen their learner identity (that is, 'I am a learner because I am different from those people who are not learners').

Cognitive, evaluative and affective components

The strength of the learner identity that develops through participation in RPL may be evidenced, according to social identity theory, by the degree to which the three components (cognitive, evaluative and affective) exist in that candidate's learner identity. What has principally been suggested up to this point is that participation in RPL can lead to the development of the cognitive, and to some extent, the evaluative component.

The cognitive component refers to the participant developing a concept of what a learner is, and coming to define themselves as a learner, in that context at least. The evaluative component refers to the participants comparing themselves favourably with other learners, or with people who are not learners.

The presence of the evaluative component also indicates that a learner identity is valued because it is important that others see them that way, and indicates that there are positive connotations, or a high-status value, attached to the identity. It suggests that if being a learner is seen as desirable by others, then acquiring or enhancing this identity will lead to an improved self-evaluation.

This leads on to a third, affective, component. A learner identity could be seen as a desirable identity to have (though this may not be explicitly connected to how others see them). There would be a sense of loss if that identity were no longer held. Consequently, efforts would be made, where social conditions allow, to develop or maintain the identity. Such a commitment could potentially be either the outcome of participation in RPL, or could be a factor in making the decision to participate in the first place.

Whilst participants may already see themselves as a learner, making RPL seem accessible, it has also been suggested above, in terms of legitimate peripheral participation, anticipatory socialisation and anticipatory identification, that one can choose to undertake RPL without already having a strong sense of being a learner. Clearly this supports our proposal that RPL can provide the context for the development of learner identity, but suggests particularly that it can provide a context in which the participant has access to information on what this means, and access to expert others who can pass on knowledge directly or provide a learner model. It also suggests that this preparation for becoming a learner may necessitate the loss of another contradictory identity. This underlines the potentially disruptive nature of participation in RPL where this results in transformation of identity.

Future view of oneself as a learner

Notions of legitimate peripheral participation, anticipatory socialisation or anticipatory identification all point to the idea that one can have a future view of oneself, which in the example we are discussing would include a future view of oneself as a learner. There is an interesting question here about where a wish to develop an identity as a learner would come from, but again possible answers are suggested by the ideas contained in the three theories. For example, the wish may come from wanting to be like others; wanting to be different from others; a sense that being a learner is considered desirable; or because an individual believes it will help them meet a need or achieve a goal.

This last point suggests that developing a learner identity can be a means to an end rather than an end in itself. The wish to become a learner may depend on a future view of oneself that is projected beyond participation in the RPL process.

Context and norms

It is also important to bear in mind though that by emphasising the social context in which identities develop, we are accepting the notion of the situation-dependency of identities. This signifies that identities are salient to different degrees in different contexts. Learner identity may only be predominant in a limited number of contexts, including during activities related to RPL. Its degree of disruptiveness would depend not just on whether it contradicted other identities that were either important to the participant or the participant's significant others, but on the degree to which the learner identity is predominant in contexts not so directly related to learning as the RPL process.

As for the norms of the particular social identity 'RPL participant as learner', these may consist of some or all of the following: the ability to recognise learning from experiences; a willingness to recognise learning that has taken place; a wish to be perceived (by self, others or both) as a learner; a wish to make the most of experiences in order to use them to get somewhere/achieve a future goal; valuing learning; and wishing to engage in future learning.

Possibility of negative, rather than positive, outcomes

The danger inherent in this theoretical approach is the potential development of a negative self-perception on the part of the participant rather than a positive one. The outcome of RPL and the reflective process may be a decrease, rather than an increase, in self-esteem. The participant may not emerge from the RPL process feeling like a learner. As a result, negative views of learning could be created or reinforced. This potentially negative aspect of RPL could perhaps be the result of participants finding it difficult to convert experiences into learning experiences; of not regarding tutors, or other learners involved in the process, as positive role models or legitimate judges of their learning; of feeling a failure and a non-learner if for some reason they have been unable to complete the process. The RPL process might not be as transformative as theorised, or at least not for all people.

Evidence of transformation

In our earlier study (Cleary *et al.*, 2002), we found three principal types of transformative effect of participation in RPL. First, it was found that informal experiential learning became more formalised through the process, involving a redefinition of experiences through the transformation of discourse from everyday language to more academic forms of discourse. Secondly, there was a perceived change in status amongst the participants by way of a change from 'non-learner' to 'learner'; and thirdly, there was a personal element of transformation in which individuals who lacked self-esteem and confidence in themselves and in the learning process gained in both of these.

These transformative elements of the process were unforeseen, but were perceived by learners themselves as an important part of the RPL experience. In the midst of educational emphasis on the achievement of credits and gaining access to programmes of study, these transformative effects of RPL often go unnoticed and unrecorded.

New approaches to RPL

New approaches to RPL could focus on making this transformative dimension of RPL more explicit. Learners undertaking RPL as a route into further learning should be encouraged to think about their involvement in the process more directly in terms of the way it can transform their sense of self. They should be encouraged to perceive themselves as taking control of their own learning, which is both empowering and motivating, rather than as simply responding to the demands of academic validation, which, though necessary, can be highly de-motivating.

Models of RPL based on group work rather than one-to-one interactions might allow for greater flexibility in approaches and broaden the interactions between tutor and learners. The main aim of working in groups would be to generate discourse that involves an exchange of ideas and perspectives aiming to help individuals in the group identify their learning from these experiences. In terms of the discussion on learner identity, group work also offers more opportunity to position one's identity in relation to others. These others may be considered more knowledgeable or expert, from whom participants can receive validation or learn how to become a learner. There may be other learners to whom one can relate to help enhance a sense of belonging. Transformation of the participant's sense of identity in relation to learning can also be aided by a biographical approach. This has the dual function of ensuring that the participant is central and that an historical approach is built into the process. This has the potential to allow the participant's self-perception to be the focus of the process, and for that perception to be placed in the context of past and future views of the self.

Such an approach could operate both within a context of guidance and counselling – similar to the operation of RPL systems in France (*validation des acquis de l'experience [VAE]* meaning 'the validation of prior experiential learning') – or within systems such as those that exist in higher education in the UK. For the purposes of the latter, the approach could be developed into a personal development module that could fit into programmes of study.

It is an approach that makes no claims to be a radical departure from earlier models of RPL. However, there are some differences. In particular, the emphasis on social interaction in the learning process – based on working in groups – is an approach that is not widely used at present. Clearly, this approach raises new issues – for example, issues of sensitivity and confidentiality when information is shared within a group situation. However, such issues are not new to most tutors/educators, who should be able to set out guidelines for learners to observe. Traditionally, training for tutors working in the area of RPL has been neglected. In order for this to change, processes of RPL need to be perceived in new ways – as simply a variation in mainstream learning approaches, rather than as a completely different type of activity.

More pertinently to our discussion, the approach has the potential to provide more opportunities for identity development, and so to perhaps aid the development of a learner identity, which could be seen as a key, though rarely explicit, objective of participation in the process.

Conclusion

In this analysis we have summarised three theoretical perspectives and explored ways in which ideas of social identity development in learning contexts might offer an explanation for the capacity of RPL to have a transformative effect on at least some participants in the process. Those who experience RPL in this way and engage in critical reflection, framed through both group discussion and individual contemplation, may emerge, to some extent, as changed people. They are likely to be able to better recognise their own skills, knowledge and abilities. Engagement in the process may involve a change in their conception of learning. Engaging with their own prior learning and experiences illustrates the point that learning is not simply about studying academic and vocational subjects as defined by and within educational institutions. By the same token, engaging in this type of learning shows that an understanding of what constitutes a learner can be broader than traditional understandings would suggest. Through the processes of discussion and critical reflection that characterise RPL, participants are able to re-evaluate their experiences. The experience of RPL may involve a transition in identity from 'non-learner' to 'learner', from 'unable to learn' to 'able to learn'. These transitions are not simple ones – they involve processes of negotiation and legitimisation through time and through interaction with others.

If we believe that participation in RPL has the potential to change identities that are likely to have some impact even outside of this immediate social context, this means it is a potentially disruptive process for the participant. If it indeed leads to the development or strengthening of learner identity, then it could lead to a more positive self-perception. However, such an identity may be incompatible with a former identity, that is to say, the transformation requires giving something else up. If what is given up is important in relationships with others or in other contexts more broadly, then this disruption can potentially have negative consequences for the participant, as well as positive ones. Equally, involvement in the process may create or reinforce a negative self-perception as a learner if the experience of undertaking RPL is problematic and unsatisfactory.

As participation in RPL does not require any prior qualifications, it is in principle accessible to all. The types of demands that are made of the participant are a willingness to participate actively in the process, a willingness to engage with and accept help from others, and a willingness to accept change. Despite this, the potential of RPL to contribute to widening access strategies to under-represented groups in post-compulsory education remains unfulfilled. A model of RPL that explicitly supports the development of a learner identity with individuals who lack confidence as learners could be an essential component of lifelong learning strategies at national and international levels.

References

Bloomer, M. and Hodkinson, P. (1997), *Moving into FE: the voice of the learner*, London: FEDA.

Blumer, H. (1969), *Symbolic Interactionism: Perspective and Method*, New Jersey: Prentice Hall.

Boreham, N.C. (1987), 'Learning from experience in diagnostic problem-solving' in Richardson, J.T.E., Eysenck, M.W. and Warren Piper, D. (eds) *Student Learning: Research in Education and Cognitive Psychology* (pp. 89–97), Milton Keynes: SRHE and the Open University.

Boud, D., Keogh, R. and Walker, D. (eds) (1985), *Reflection: Turning Experience into Learning*, London: Kogan Page.

Boud, D., Keogh, R. and Walker, D. (1996), 'Promoting reflection in learning: A model' in Edwards, R., Hanson, A. and Raggatt, P. (eds) *Boundaries of Adult Learning*, New York: Routledge.

Brockbank, A. and McGill, I. (1998), *Facilitating Reflective Learning in Higher Education*, Buckingham: SRHE and Open University Press.

Brown, J.S., Collins, A. and Duguid. P. (1989), 'Situated cognition and the culture of learning', *Educational Researcher*, 18(1): 32–42.

Cinnirella, M. (1998), 'Exploring temporal aspects of social identity: the concept of possible social identities', *European Journal of Social Psychology*, 28: 227–48.

Claxton, G. (2002), 'Education for the learning age: a sociocultural approach to learning to learn' in Wells, G. and Claxton, G. (eds) *Learning for life in the 21st century*, Oxford: Blackwell Publishing.

Cleary, P., Whittaker, R., Gallacher, J., Merrill, B., Jokinen, L., Carette, M. and Members of CREA (2002), *Social Inclusion Through APEL: the Learners' Perspective - Comparative Report*, Glasgow: Glasgow Caledonian University.

Clegg, S. and McNulty, K. (2002), 'The creation of learner identities as part of social inclusion: gender, ethnicity and social space', *International Journal of Lifelong Education*, 21(6): 572–85.

Ellemers, N., Kortekaas, P. and Ouwerwerk, J.W. (1999), 'Self-categorisation, commitment to the group and group self-esteem as related but distinct aspects of social identity', *European Journal of Social Psychology*, 29: 371–89.

Ellemers, N., Spears, R. and Doosje, B. (eds) (1999) *Social Identity*, Oxford: Blackwell Publishing.

Fenwick, T.J. (2000), *Experiential Learning: A Theoretical Critique Explored Through Five Perspectives*, Monograph for ERIC, Alberta: Department of Educational Policy Studies.

Fenwick, T.J. (2003), *Learning Through Experience: Troubling Orthodoxies and Intersecting Questions*, Florida: Krieger Publishing Company.

Fowler, C.J.H. and Mayes, J.T. (1999), 'Learning relationships: from theory to design', *Association for Learning Technology Journal* (ALT-J), 7(3): 6–16.

Gallacher, J., Crossan, B., Leahy, J., Merrill, B. and Field, J. (2000), *Education for All? Further Education, Social Inclusion and Widening Access*, Glasgow: Centre for Research in Lifelong Learning.

Greenaway, R. (2002), 'Experiential learning cycles', http://reviewing.co.uk/research/learning.cycles.htm. Last accessed 28/5/04.

Juch, A.H. (1983), *Personal Development Theory and Practice in Management Training*, Chichester: John Wiley & Sons.

Kolb, D.A. (1984), *Experiential Learning – Experience as the Source of Learning*, Englewood Cliffs, NJ: Prentice Hall.

Kolb, D.A. (1993), 'The process of experiential learning' in Thorpe, M., Edwards, R. and Hanson, A. (eds) *Culture and Processes of Adult Learning*, London: Routledge.

Konrad, J. (2001), 'Accreditation of prior experiential learning in the United Kingdom', Working Paper, Education-Line, http://www.leeds.ac.uk/educol/documents/00001831.htm (Accessed 15/5/04).

Lave, J. and Wenger, E. (1991), *Situated Learning – Legitimate Peripheral Participation*, Cambridge: Cambridge University Press.

McLellan, H. (1995), *Situated Learning Perspectives*, New Jersey: Educational Technology Publications.

Mead, H. (1934), *Mind, Self and Society*, Chicago: University of Chicago Press.

Meltzer, B.N., Petras, J.W. and Reynolds, L.T. (1975), *Symbolic Interactionism – Genesis, Varieties and Criticism*, London: Routledge Keegan Paul.

Merton, R.K. and Kitt, A.S. (1969), reprinted in Coser, L.A. and Rosenberg, B. (eds) *Sociological Theory: A Book of Readings*, Third edition, New York: The Macmillan Company.

Mezirow, J. and Associates (eds) (1990), *Fostering Critical Reflection in Adulthood*, San Francisco: Jossey-Bass.

Mezirow, J. (1998), 'On critical reflection', *Adult Education Quarterly*, 48: 185–98.

Moon, J.A. (1999), *Reflection in Learning and Professional Development – Theory and Practice*, London: Kogan Page.

Schön, D. (1991), *The Reflective Practitioner – How Professionals Think in Action*, Aldershot: Ashgate Publishing Limited.

Sherif, M. (1953), 'Reference groups in human relations', reprinted in Coser, L.A. and Rosenberg, B. (eds) (1969), *Sociological Theory: A Book of Readings*, Third edition, New York: The Macmillan Company.

Stets, J.E. and Burke, P.J. (2000), 'Identity theory and social identity theory', *Social Psychology Quarterly*, 63(3): 224–37.

Tajfel, H. (1978), 'Social categorization, social identity and social comparison' in Tajfel, H. (ed.) *Differentiation Between Social Groups: Studies in the Social Psychology of Intergroup Relations*, London: Academic Press.

Tajfel, H. (1982), *Social identity and intergroup relations*, Cambridge/Paris :

Cambridge University Press/Editions de la Maison des Science de l'Homme.

Turner, J.C. (1985), 'Social categorization and the self-concept: a social-cognitive theory of group behaviour' in Lawler, E.J. (ed.) *Advances in Group Processes: Theory and Research*, Vol. 2 pp. (77–122), Greenwich, CT: JAI Press.

Turner, J.C. (1999), 'Some current issues in research on social identity and self-categorization theories' in Ellemers, N., Spears, R. and Doosje, B. (eds) (1999), *Social Identity*, Oxford: Blackwell Publishing.

Vygotsky, L.S. (1962), *Thought and Language*, Massachusetts: MIT Press.

Vygotsky, L.S. (1978), *Mind in Society*, Massachusetts: Harvard University Press.

Wenger, E. (1998), *Communities of Practice – Learning, Meaning and Identity*, Cambridge: Cambridge University Press.

Whittaker, S. and Mayes, J.T. (2001), *Learner Identity, Motivation and Relationships: A Theoretical Framework for the Design of Effective Learning Environments*, Paper presented at Researching Widening Access: International Perspectives Conference, Glasgow Caledonian University, 29 June – 1 July 2001.

chapter sixteen

Endword

Michael Young

As a sociologist who has not worked in the field of adult education and has only been somewhat tangentially involved in RPL itself, I found this collection of papers refreshing and provocative even when I disagreed with some of the arguments. Not only do many of the papers give insights into the dilemmas and difficulties faced by RPL practitioners in different contexts, but they provide a concrete way of raising much broader educational issues concerned with learning, knowledge and pedagogic authority.

The book stands in stark contrast to most other publications both on RPL and adult education more generally. This contrast is exemplified in a number of ways. First, by locating its discussion of RPL in a critique of the widely pervasive educational philosophies of experientialism, constructivism and progressivism, the book reminds readers of the closed intellectual world that many adult educators tend to take for granted. Secondly, it demonstrates that RPL, like most apparently bounded educational practices, is also a lens for examining the most fundamental questions about the purposes and practices of education. Thirdly, the book reminds us that like progressivism, RPL did not become popular with policy makers just because it was a 'good thing'. Notwithstanding the association of RPL with arguments for social justice, redistribution and redress, most noticeably in the USA and in South Africa, it is economic forces that have led to the need to recognise and accredit informal learning and to the search for fast-track routes for adults into higher education. Fourthly, the book does not treat RPL or the wider provision of adult education as some kind of moral and political good that is almost beyond criticism except within very limited parameters. RPL is presented here as a complex and often contradictory set of practices, which at best offer new possibilities to disadvantaged learners. A useful distinction in this context is between *RPL for access* and *RPL for credit or qualifications*. Where there is evidence from a number of countries that access courses based on broad RPL principles have provided important new routes for adults into higher education, it is far from certain that RPL-based qualifications on their own bring similar benefits. In challenging existing educational hierarchies, RPL is unequivocally a 'standpoint theory'. In other words it is a claim to knowledge based on the position of the claimant, rather than on the knowledge itself. It is an understandable position to take for those who have been excluded from access to academic knowledge. It is less clear that such debunking of academic knowledge by RPL practitioners, themselves often based in universities, is in the interests of those who have been excluded.

Fifthly, several of the papers explore the contradictions that lie at the heart of the RPL project. If *recognition* of learning from experience is the emancipatory goal of RPL, is this goal not undermined by techniques which seek to show that experiential learning is of equal value to formal academic learning, and thus validate the latter as a criterion for recognising the former? Furthermore, if this 'parity of esteem' between formal and experiential learning is the basic assumption of the RPL project, why would RPL practitioners want to expand access to formal education and not just celebrate experience?

Sixthly, there is another point that is noted by Judy Harris in her introduction in Chapter 1. Not only does the book as a whole problematise the purposes and practices of RPL, the authors themselves are at odds with each other on the most fundamental issues of knowledge, pedagogy and learning. Whereas all the contributors share a common critique of past work on RPL – that its assumptions have been 'under-theorised' – they have little in common in the theoretical resources that they draw on in mapping out alternatives.

This tension between shared critical assumptions and sharp theoretical differences is not unique to this book nor is it specific to RPL practice. It is a feature of much educational research, especially that associated with some form of Left politics. Such issues concerning the politics of educational research are often raised in highly abstract ways that are very difficult to relate to any specific educational practice. This is as true of most of the debates around postmodernism as it is of the many commentaries on the work of the Italian Marxist and educational theorist, Antonio Gramsci. As Harold Entwistle put it many years ago, 'in order to be a political revolutionary, do you, like Gramsci, have to be an educational conservative?' Whether or not one accepts Entwistle's interpretation of Gramsci as an educational conservative, it is a strength of this book that it locates such dilemmas in the very concrete case of RPL where adult experience confronts specialist or academic knowledge.

Is RPL a way of opening access to academic knowledge, or of undermining it? Is it a way of providing a new 'experiential' basis for higher education (in which case in what sense can we claim it to be higher?)? Or, more radically, is it the beginning of a new 'transformative' pedagogy and curriculum that integrates theory (or specialist knowledge) and experience? In the remaining part of this short paper, I want, albeit indirectly, to answer these questions by considering a number of issues that lie at the centre (although not always explicitly so) of many contemporary educational debates and which a 're-theorised' RPL forces us to address. These issues concern the role of knowledge, specialisation, politics, authority and qualifications.

RPL and knowledge

One of the strengths of this book is that it makes public a core dilemma for RPL practitioners, which has up to now gone largely unexamined. Recognising prior experiential learning is not an end in itself (or is it?). It can only be a strategy for providing access to knowledge that takes learners beyond their experience. The relationship between knowledge and experience is as old as education itself. It is both an epistemological issue (where does 'true' knowledge come from?) and a pedagogic issue (how can learners be enabled to acquire knowledge that takes them beyond their experience?). RPL merely dramatises these issues; it is not a short cut to resolving them. Current approaches which reject the relativism of postmodernism are located in debates between varieties of social or critical realism, as articulated by Roy Bhashkar and others, and what I will here call forms of relationism. Realist approaches stress the importance of the objectivity of knowledge that is separate from the processes of knowing and acquisition. However, they inherit from Durkheim a tendency both to equate knowledge with natural science, and to adopt an unresolved dualism in separating knowledge from the world and, it follows, theory from practice. Therefore, while realist theories can provide a basis for a curriculum which separates theoretical and everyday knowledge, they cannot be a basis for a pedagogy which seeks to overcome such a separation. One consequence is that realist-based curriculum policies can appear to differ little from those derived from conservative political philosophies. Relational approaches seek to avoid the problem of dualism between mind and world by recognising the pre-conceptual nature of the external world and, following Vygotsky, the embeddedness of everyday and scientific concepts in each other. However by not addressing the *disembeddedness* as well as the *embeddedness* of the two types of concepts, they can easily slip into a sophisticated form of relativism. Further research on the different meanings of 'recognition' in RPL practice could make a valuable contribution to the broader debate between theories of knowledge as well as to the viability of RPL itself.

RPL and specialisation

Most RPL practitioners, as well as the majority of authors in this book, seek to challenge what they see as the 'hegemony' of specialist (or academic) knowledge and, by implication, the hegemony of specialist educational institutions. They appear ambivalent about whether RPL provides a route to greater access to specialist institutions or an opportunity to undermine them. From the point of view adopted here, the issue for RPL practitioners is clear. Specialisation in education as in other fields has been a crucial factor in the improvement of people's quality of life; one has only to look to South-East Asian and Nordic countries for examples. This process has however also created barriers and boundaries, which in some countries preserve inequality and privilege. One of the positive outcomes of RPL strategies is that they can force educational gatekeepers to be more explicit about the grounds of their practice and the purposes of the boundaries that they seek to defend. It may be a shortage of places or resources which raises political questions about inequalities; it may be a form of occupational conservatism which needs to be challenged. However, it may be that certain students are excluded on the grounds that they will not be able to cope with the way that access to specialist knowledge is sequenced; in such cases the barriers to access for some students are genuine opportunities for others and as such may need to be defended.

RPL and politics

As noted in Chapter 1, most RPL programmes have arisen from concerns about social justice and the lack of educational opportunities experienced by many adults. The dilemma for all teachers, but starker for RPL practitioners, is where broader issues of social justice end and where issues that are specific to education begin. Not so long ago the phrase 'the personal is the political' was popular. It had important political implications, especially for gender relations. However the only societies where the personal and the political have actually been fused have been highly authoritarian and left very little space for the personal at all. Learning is a social process but not necessarily a political process; it is policy on learning that is political. RPL practitioners have to guard against the over-politicisation of learning and the potential of the language of democratic politics to undermine the real conditions for teaching and learning.

RPL and authority

This point is linked to the previous one and confronts the RPL tradition of opposing hierarchies. Many hierarchies are indeed oppressive and need to be challenged. However there is a good case for arguing that a key difference between informal and formal learning, which is central to RPL, is that whereas informal learning may be located in authoritative relationships – as in the case of children and parents or employer and employees – much informal learning is not so located. Formal learning, on the other hand, explicitly involves an authority relationship even when the teacher is defined as facilitator. The transition between the two types of relationship is inescapable if RPL is to lead to progression. However it may not be straightforward and it may be an issue that RPL researchers with their understandable scepticism towards any authority have not given sufficient attention to.

RPL and qualifications

As Judy Harris points out in Chapter 1, RPL developed in parallel with the growing interest on the part of governments in expanding the numbers of people gaining qualifications. RPL appeared to offer the potential for adults with considerable life and work experience to gain qualifications without attending school or college. The idea that some people may be 'qualified', in the sense of being capable even though they lack any formal qualifications is important. However, it does not necessarily follow that they should be persuaded to get their experience formally accredited. As several of the contributors to this book note, the assumption that adults always stand to benefit if their experiential learning is accredited as a qualification neglects what happens to learning and experience when it is transformed into a qualification by an RPL process. It may be that the strengths it had in being not accredited (and by definition not formalised) may be lost in the RPL process. It is here that the distinction between recognition and accreditation as different forms of valuing experience are important.

A concluding note

The general point I have tried to make in this short Endword is that RPL is not only a practice that needs *re-theorising*, but one which offers the possibility of *new theorising*. Questions about knowledge, authority, qualifications and different types of learning will always be with us. Once RPL is freed from its largely rhetorical role as the great radical strategy or the great solution to inequality, it offers a unique and very concrete set of contexts for debating the fundamental educational issues that such questions give rise to and for finding new ways of approaching them.

Index